INCENTIVES

A successful organization must coordinate the activities of its constituent parts. Effective coordination is problematic when the components of the organization are managed by individuals whose primary concern is personal gain, not the success of the institution. However, if everyone is motivated by narrow self-interest, the pursuit of self-interest will be self-defeating unless individual decisions are made under incentives that foster the organization's goals. This book studies incentive environments, and evaluates the resulting performance of a wide range of institutions. It also investigates the extent to which performance can be improved by modifying the incentives.

Professor Campbell's treatment of the economics of information, mechanism design, and game theory from the standpoint of incentives can be followed by anyone with a basic knowledge of single-variable calculus and intermediate microeconomic theory. Readers learn the principles by working through examples, and not by digesting proofs of general theorems. Upper-level undergraduates and masters-level students will find the material particularly useful, as will Ph.D. students seeking a better grasp of theoretical principles through worked examples.

INCENTIVES

Motivation and the Economics of Information

DONALD E. CAMPBELL

The College of William and Mary

CAMBRIDGE
UNIVERSITY PRESS

Published by the Press Syndicate of the University of Cambridge
The Pitt Building, Trumpington Street, Cambridge CB2 1RP
40 West 20th Street, New York, NY 10011-4211, USA
10 Stamford Road, Oakleigh, Melbourne 3166, Australia

First Published 1995

Printed in the United States of America

Library of Congress Cataloging-in-Publication Data
Campbell, Donald E. (Donald Edward), 1943–
Incentives : motivation and the economics of information / Donald E. Campbell.
p.   cm.
Includes bibliographical references and index.
ISBN 0-521-47264-4. – ISBN 0-521-47857-X (pbk.)
1. Social choice – Mathematical models.   I. Title.
HB846.8.C365   1995
302'.13 – dc20   94-41816
CIP

A catalog record for this book is available from the British Library.

ISBN 0-521-47264-4 Hardback
ISBN 0-521-47857-X Paperback

Contents

Preface

There is a wide variety of topics covered in this book, and all have to do with asymmetric information and the dispersion of knowledge. Rarely does the book teach by presenting a general theorem. Sometimes a principle is presented by means of a numerical example, and sometimes by means of a more general examination of a family of functional forms. The tendency is to begin with a general treatment and then switch to a numerical example when the analysis gets deeper and harder. In each application I try to use the approach that works best in providing insight *and* the ability to continue on one's own.

The prerequisite economics background is intermediate microeconomics. Single-variable calculus provides sufficient mathematics background. Once the economic model has been set up, the point of departure for the use of mathematics is often the maximization of an objective function f of two variables x and y, subject to a linear equality constraint. I use the constraint to solve for y in terms of x and then substitute that expression for y in $f(x, y)$. If the constraint is not linear then I employ a quasi-linear objective function: $f(x, y) = B(x) + y$. This usually allows efficient outcomes (etc.) to be identified as a function of x. It won't be the mathematics that slows students down; it will be the subtle notions of equilibrium and interaction that economists employ.

Each section of each chapter can be read independently (with the possible exception of some of the introductory material in Chapter 1). This calls for some redundancy, and for that I apologize; the benefit seemed to justify the cost.

Don Campbell
Williamsburg, VA

For Edna

Acknowledgments

This book is the offspring of my lectures to an advanced undergraduate class and to the first-year group in the Masters in Public Policy program, both at The College of William and Mary. I am grateful for the vigilance of my students in catching mistakes, particularly to Susan Bagley, Seth Carpenter, Yuan Chou, Nandini Gupta, Heather Loehr, Donald McGuire, Margit Vanberg, and Georg Vanberg. They not only brought routine 'typos' to my attention; they spotted serious anomalies that forced a reconsideration of some of the principles and thus enhanced my own understanding. My colleagues in the economics department at William and Mary were also quite helpful, as was a correspondence with Mancur Olson that influenced my presentation of agency theory. Finally, I owe a special debt to Dan Arce, Jon Hamilton, Jerry Kelly, and Andy Schotter for their great care in reading the book manuscript. Their suggestions led to significant improvements, and their generous evaluation encouraged me to put more effort into the work than I might otherwise have. I thank them on behalf of my readers. I hope that they are pleased with the final result, and will accept my apology for allowing space limitations to thwart a few of their suggestions.

The diagrams were superbly drawn by Tanya Utt, and I'm pleased to have the opportunity to acknowledge her talent and dedication. Tanya did the graphs, with software that was new to her, at a time when she was extremely busy with her dissertation. I found it ironic – and instructive – to conclude my work on a book dealing with the importance of material incentives in principal–agent relationships with a single encounter with an agent who did her job perfectly because that's the way she likes to do things.

I am grateful to Fung Chia University in Taiwan and the National Science Council of Taiwan for financing my visit to Fung Chia University, where I presented a first draft of Chapter 8 to graduate students in economics. I received support from the U.S. National Science Foundation for my work on social choice (grants SES-9007953 and SES-9209039). The NSF grants contributed to Chapter

8, which contains some original material, and they contributed indirectly by enhancing my other work.

I would like to thank Janis Bolster, Robert Graham, Scott Parris, and Susan Thornton of Cambridge University Press for their expert editorial help at various stages.

I dedicate this book to my wife's mom, Edna Philpotts, for her lifelong devotion to her family – which now includes me – and for her example of grace under pressure.

1

Introduction

This book examines institutions in which coordination of the activities of the individuals involved is essential to the success of the institution. The institutions may be large or small. We will look at an entire economy, as well as a single firm in that economy. Even two-person institutions will receive attention: a car owner and a mechanic hired to repair the car, for instance. In all cases, a satisfactory outcome requires coordination among the participants, and coordination requires *information transmission and motivation:*

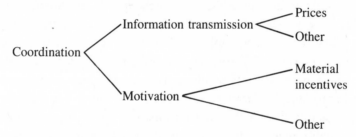

The individual members of the institution cannot do their part in the production of a successful outcome unless they receive information telling them what their roles are. In the case of a private ownership market economy, information is frequently transmitted via prices. Even when the information has been received by an individual member of a team, there may be little direct incentive to use that information in a way that contributes to the success of the institution. In some cases there *is* perfect alignment of the incentives of the agent and the group. For instance, the pilot of an aircraft is just as determined as the passengers to arrive safely at the destination. But a natural alignment of interests is rare. For example, the welfare of the mechanic on the ground is not *directly* linked with the interests of the airline passengers. The passengers need to be reassured that the mechanic has a strong incentive to act *as though* her chief concern is the passengers' well-being. With *in*appropriate incentives, mechanics may succumb to the temptation to avoid hard work by doing a superficial job of inspection and repair. This incentive issue is obviously of vital concern to air travellers, and is worth studying for that reason alone. But it is also vital to society as a whole. Given the decisions made by others, a worker – whether a mechanic or professor or company president – may find it in her interest to expend little effort on the job while drawing a full salary. If a large fraction of the labor force can get away with shirking, the economy's output of goods and services will be greatly diminished, and per capita consumption will be very low. In that case, each worker will wish that *everyone* had been prevented from shirking, to enable each to consume less leisure but more produced goods and services. A more appropriate system of incentives could have accomplished this – giving everyone a higher standard of living, even though each individual is maximizing his own welfare *given the decision of others* when everyone shirks because of poor incentives.[1] Appropriate incentives are vital to the success of any institution, whether large or small. This book examines incentive environments and evaluates each in terms of its ability to promote individual welfare generally. In a wide range of cases this requires that each person incur a cost equal to the cost that her action imposes on the rest of society. We refer to this as social cost pricing. It is not always easy to identify social cost – even for economists on occasion, but especially for newcomers to the field. In some cases, social cost pricing is not quite the right prescription: In situations where the decision maker seeks shelter from risk, incentives have to be less than fully efficient to allow for insurance. We will look at incentive schemes currently in use, and we also consider the prospects for designing superior schemes. The key is that the decision taker's actions affect the welfare of a wider group, but the decision maker usually has far more information than the others. For example, the manager of a factory has much better information about the production process and product quality than the firm's consumers or the residents of the neighborhood in which the factory is located. If the government attempts to regulate the firm – to affect product quality or the emission of toxic waste – it can do a much better job if it taps the manager's expertise instead of issuing a list of commands. Incentives must be provided to harness the factory manager's self-interest and inside information. Incentive based regulation is coming into widespread use, at least in the U.S. (See Sappington, 1993, and Laffont, 1994.)

Transmission of information goes hand in hand with incentives. Although market prices have their limitations as conduits of information, they do serve us well. For example, wages are important determinants of individual career choices, and wages contain information about the value to consumers of various skills. An occupation will command a high wage if it contributes significantly to the production of highly valued goods and services. That is because the high demand by consumers for a commodity translates into high revenue for the producer. There will be high demand for workers who are crucial to the production process because they generate large revenues for their employers. The high demand for these workers leads to high wages. Competitive bidding in the labor market raises the wage of the most productive workers above that of other workers. The wage signals information about the value of the skill to the economy as a whole. We not only acquire the information that a particular activity – career choice – is valuable to consumers as a whole; at the same time, individuals have a strong incentive to take this information into consideration in their decision making, because higher wages provide more income.

In the case of a private ownership market economy, prices often do a good job of solving the information transmission problem, and the way prices enter our budget constraints gives us the incentive to use that information in a socially optimal way. However, it is important to make a distinction between information transmission and motivation. Most commuters know that large scale carbon dioxide emission is suspected of causing a greenhouse effect, leading to gradual and dangerous warming of the planet. A chief culprit is the combustion of fossil fuel. Commuters also know that car pools have a beneficial effect on the quality of the air and the environment. But they do not have a strong incentive to act on that information. For many, the inconvenience of using a car pool more than offsets the benefit *to the individual commuter* from reduced CO_2 emission, so the selfish strategy of opting for convenience is adopted. However, if car pools were widely used, we would all benefit from the inconvenience *of others* and the overall gain to each individual could well be great enough to make each better off, net of the personal inconvenience, than under existing incentives.

Obviously, information transmission can be more or less costly. It is important for an institution to have a low-cost method of transmission. This is problematic. If the institution is the entire economy, the delivery of information throughout the economy can be exceedingly costly.[2] Prices typically transmit information at low cost but, as the diagram at the beginning of this chapter indicates, other devices are used. Warranties are a good illustration. An extensive warranty on a manufactured good is a signal that the manufacturer believes that the likelihood of a defect is small. If an entrepreneur set out to deceive customers by manufacturing low-quality television sets and passing them off as high-quality sets, he could not offer a good warranty without losing the profits that his deception was designed to yield. He would know that a very high number of sets would be returned for replacement or repair under the warranty.[3]

Even when the information transmission problem is solved, the motivation problem cannot be assumed away. As we have seen with the pollution example, there must also be an incentive for the individual to use the information in a way that promotes the goals of the institution. If the institution under study is an entire economy, the goal is the achievement of a high level of welfare by individuals generally. The incentive issue is problematic, because the individual's paramount concern is her own welfare, and not the institution's welfare. This book is primarily devoted to the study of material incentives: How can they be designed to harness self-interest, and prevent the pursuit of self-interest from being self-defeating? Nonmaterial incentives play a role in any institution. In one of the first influential articles on the modern economics of information, Kenneth J. Arrow (1963) noted that the information advantage possessed by physicians (the agents) in treating their patients (the principals) has led to the emergence of institutions based on trust and delegation, to offset partly the adverse effects of market incentives. Hence, the code of medical ethics.[4] However, this book is concerned almost exclusively with material incentives – that is, incentives that have their impact on the decision maker's welfare through their impact on her consumption opportunities. An automobile repair shop illustrates nicely how incentives will come into play in this book. The car owner who takes his car to the shop for repair wants a reliable job done at low cost. He has neither the expertise nor the time required to monitor the mechanic. If the car owner suspects that the mechanic cut corners he is likely to broadcast his suspicions to acquaintances. This implicit threat, along with the existence of other repair shops competing for business, gives the owner of a garage some incentive to ensure that the repairs are well done and that customers are not overcharged. But how does the garage owner motivate the mechanic that she employs? Competition and reputation effects may give the right incentives to the owners of firms, but they are just part of the solution. The owner – in general, the *principal* – now has the problem of providing appropriate incentives to the *agents* that she hires. We will consider the extent to which appropriate material incentives can be found. We will see that the private ownership market economy is very sophisticated when it comes to generating devices for solving these principal–agent problems. We will also see, however, that there are serious limits to the ability of *any* institution to overcome incentive difficulties in many situations. The difficulties are compounded by the presence of random effects. If the car breaks down a week after it was repaired, should that be attributed to shirking on the part of the mechanic or to bad luck?

One advantage of focussing on material incentives in a model with selfish individuals is that we are alerted to potential difficulties when the pursuit of narrow self-interest is shown to undermine general individual welfare. Moreover, we are much less likely to recommend policies that are naively utopian when we work within this framework. As one measure of the importance for public policy of a formal study of incentives, McAfee and McMillan (1988, p. 149) estimate that switching to appropriate contract design could reduce government costs by at least 8%, and sometimes by as much as 30%. Consider another example. The switch to the "responsibility system" in Chinese agriculture under Deng resulted in a remarkable increase in productivity over a short period of time (McMillan, 1992, pp. 96–98). The responsibility system requires each farm to deliver a fixed amount of output to the state, but the farm keeps the proceeds of all output above this quota. This is an example of social cost pricing: The social cost of the farmer's leisure consumption is the output that society loses when the farmer consumes an hour of leisure. But that is also equal to the cost imposed on the farmer because the farmer would have been allowed to keep the harvest from that hour of labor.

We will examine incentives at work to see whether we can expect efficient outcomes to result when individuals are motivated by selfish considerations. The study of incentives can also explain apparent anomalies in pricing schedules, etc. In each case study we will assume that an individual takes whatever course of action leads to the highest possible personal benefit for himself or herself given the limitations inherent in the choices made by others. Of course, in real life there are situations in which some or all individuals behave altruistically, at least up to a point. But self-seeking behavior is pervasive enough to warrant independent study, particularly when the economy as a whole is our concern. Therefore, our goal is to work out the implications of self-motivated behavior, by means of examples and theorems, and we will try to learn from them without being distracted by the many real world features that are left out of the models. To encourage you to accept abstract models as useful laboratory devices for analyzing complex real world phenomena I offer two metaphors.

A road map is an abstract representation of a particular region. It abstracts from almost everything about the region that is important – scenery, the location of shops, and so on. Because it is so abstract it is very easy to use to work out a route from one part of the region to another; it can even be used to compute a short route. Similarly, an economic model can be exceedingly abstract and still allow us to determine the effect of an excise tax on a commodity's price, or the nature of a salary contract that will be offered when the employer can observe the quality of the employee's work but cannot validate that observation with evidence that would be credible to a third party, such as a judge. Such conclusions are drawn from abstract, formal economic models via theorems. The second metaphor illustrates how a theorem can support valuable inferences about the real world even if it comes from a very abstract model that uses assumptions that are obviously violated in the real world.

You are setting out on a two hundred mile trip with your family, and to pass the time you play a simple game of 'count the trucks' with your five year old sister. You take one lane of traffic and your sister takes the other, and whichever of you spots more trucks wins. (It is a two lane highway.) You want your sister to win. Should you give her the oncoming lane or the lane that your car is travelling in?

Here is a 'proof' that more trucks will be observed in the oncoming lane: Assume that all vehicles travel at exactly the same speed and that once you enter the throughway no vehicles will enter or exit either lane until you reach your destination. Also assume that in both lanes the trucks are evenly spaced, precisely one mile apart. It follows that exactly two hundred trucks will be observed coming towards your car, but only the number of trucks that can be seen in your own lane at the instant you enter the highway will be spotted in your lane. Therefore, the person who takes the oncoming lane will win the game. The three assumptions that we employed are quite silly as a description of reality, but the simple model allows us to see quite clearly why your sister has an extremely *high probability* of winning the game if she takes the oncoming lane. We could construct a more realistic model in which speed, entry, and exit were random variables drawn from probability distributions, but that would block insight into the reason why it's smart to take the oncoming lane if you want to win the game. Of course, if this were an important problem, it would be comforting to know that someone had taken the trouble to construct a sophisticated model that confirmed our intuition by means of a rigorous proof. This would require some nontrivial technical skills, but the proof would not be constructed without the right conjecture, and valuable conjectures are usually based on the insight that comes from a sketchy model, whether or not it is given a formal structure.

Many students are impatient with economists for abstracting – and, worse, employing assumptions that are at odds with reality. It may comfort you to know that this is standard practice in physics. It can even be useful for a physicist to assume that a cow is a sphere! (See Krauss, 1993, pp. 1–7.) "The set of tools physicists have to describe nature is limited. Most of the modern theories you read about began life as simple models by physicists who didn't know how else to start to solve a problem. . . . *Before doing anything else, abstract out all irrelevant details!* . . . Overcoming the natural desire *not* to throw out unnecessary information is probably the hardest and most important part of learning physics" (Krauss , 1993, p. 4). Substitute "economics" for "physics" and you have a statement that academic economists would applaud heartily.

Let's agree, then, that we will work with simple models; part of the streamlining comes from our assumption that each individual evaluates outcomes exclusively in terms of their effect on his or her own well-being. This will allow us to work out an individual's response to a change in the 'incentive environment'. The assumption of selfish utility maximization implies that there *will* be a response. Not everyone is able to grasp this point. For example, a lot of people argue against long prison sentences for someone responsible for killing or maiming others while driving under the influence of alcohol: "It could happen to anyone." Well, wouldn't you make sure that it couldn't happen to you if a long prison sentence were the penalty for drunk driving? To adapt a phrase of Dr. Johnson's, the prospect of a long jail sentence focusses the mind wonderfully. (Japan is a country in which public drunkenness is not uncommon, but drunk driving is very rare because of the severe penalties. A professional person can even be disqualified from practicing if convicted of drunk driving.) Although a simple, abstract model can be very useful, it is essential to determine whether the application of a principle learned from the model is appropriate to a specific situation. It may be that real world forces, not present in the model, would result in an outcome that is quite different from what was anticipated.

Exercises

1   The services of garbage collectors have far more total value to the community than the services of heart surgeons: Compare a world without garbage collection – plagues, low life expectancy, only 50% of children surviving to the age of five – to a world without heart surgeons – no appreciable difference in life expectancy. But heart surgeons are paid far more per hour than garbage collectors. What information is being signalled by this wage rate differential?

2   "More than 2000 television sets a year exploded in Moscow alone" (Milgrom and Roberts, 1992, p. 13). What is it about private ownership market economies that results in the production of appliances that are evidently far more reliable than Russian ones used to be?

1 Asymmetric information

When you hire a taxi you are employing an *agent* to carry out an assignment. You, the *principal,* want to get to your destination quickly and at low cost, but the taxi driver wants to maximize his revenue. The driver appears to have an incentive to overcharge, and your ability to monitor this is very limited because you know very little about traffic patterns and expedient routes, especially if you are a visitor to the city. This is an instance of a *hidden action* problem. The passenger cannot directly determine if the driver has acted in a way that minimizes the travel time. In section 2 we will see that it is easy to design an incentive scheme – a mechanism – that induces the driver (the agent) to behave as though the passenger (the principal) possessed the hidden information that the principal does not in fact have. In general, this book investigates the possibility of providing appropriate incentives to agents to induce them to behave in the way the principals would direct them to act if the principals themselves possessed the relevant information. In section 3 the principal is a state government that wants to monitor cars to get unsafe ones off the highway. This is a *hidden characteristic* problem, and the hidden characteristic is the quality of the car, safe or dangerous. The agent is the automobile owner, who may not wish to put money into repair work. In other settings the hidden characteristic could be an individual's preference scheme, or some statistic based on that preference scheme; the marginal rate of substitution at a point (elicited by some resource allocation mechanisms); the elasticity of demand (elicited by a price-discriminating monopolist); the probability that an automobile driver will have an accident (sought by an insurance company – the probability affects the driver's preference scheme via the expected utility function); a voter's most-preferred candidate (required by the plurality rule voting mechanism). In many cases a production characteristic is sought: a firm's production function for example. Here is an interesting example with a global perspective. Worldwide reduction of carbon dioxide emission is advocated by many as a way of slowing global warming. One widely supported policy would require each country to pay a tax on CO_2 emissions above a specified quota. A country's quota would be a fraction of its current CO_2 emission rate, with the fraction determined by an international committee. The current emission rate is the country's hidden characteristic. It is naive to assume that each country would report its true emission rate if it could be assigned a higher quota by reporting a higher emission rate. On a lighter note, the owners of baseball franchises have become adept at hiding the team's profit. (See Scully, 1989, chapter 7.)

All of the models and examples discussed in this book can be placed in either the hidden action or the hidden characteristic category, and some have elements of both. These two categories constitute the family of *principal–agent* models. The principal is the individual whose welfare is to be served and this welfare is affected by an agent who makes decisions on behalf of the principal. The principal knows that the agent will choose a course of action that maximizes her, the agent's, welfare. But the principal may be able to provide the agent with incentives that cause the agent's welfare to reach its maximum when she takes the action that leads to the maximization of the principal's welfare. What makes this problematic is that the principal cannot observe the agent's action or cannot determine if the agent has acted appropriately. In other situations that we will examine, the principal's welfare depends on the agent's characteristic, which cannot be observed or even verified by the principal. There are two ways in which the principal's utility can depend on agent characteristics: In general equilibrium resource allocation models the principal is an abstract planner whose utility is identified with social welfare. Social welfare in turn is a function of the characteristics (preferences and technology) of the economy's agents (consumers and firms). We examine a special case of this in section 4; Chapters 5 and 6 investigate this subject thoroughly. In more narrowly focussed models the principal may be an insurance company, for instance, and the company's profit depends on the number of claims submitted, and that in turn is a function of the probability that a policyholder has an accident. The potential policyholders are the agents in this case. The agent cannot be relied on to act in the principal's best interest – either to take the appropriate action or to disclose her characteristic – because the agent wants to maximize her own utility. We will see whether and to what extent the agent's self-interest can be harnessed by a judicious deployment of incentives that induce the agent to act in a way that promotes the principal's welfare. In hidden characteristic models, the incentive structure will be deemed a success when the agent's action reveals her characteristic.

Consider a simple example. A customs official on the Canada–U.S. border is required to inspect the cars of motorists crossing the border to determine if duty should be charged on imported goods. The principal is the national government representing its citizens and the agent is the customs officer. It would be too costly to both motorists and the government to conduct a thorough inspection of each car. Motorists are screened by means of some simple questions and a fraction of the travellers are inspected on the basis of their responses. Inspections are arduous, and stressful as well, if the motorist is hostile. It would be much easier (utility enhancing) for the customs officer to let some of the suspicious cases enter without inspections. Can the principal design an incentive scheme that induces the inspector to act in the government's interest in spite of the cost to the customs official of intensive inspections? If you think I am singling out civil servants unfairly, consider instead the case of a professor. What guarantee do you have that your instructor devotes a reasonable amount of time to preparing lectures and designing the course? Surely there is a temptation to increase leisure time and reduce preparation time, or to substitute consulting activity – or research activity, in general – for lecture preparation. In this case the student is the principal and the instructor is the agent. This is an example of a hidden action problem. The committee that *hires* a new faculty member has a hidden characteristic problem, and the characteristic in this case is the prospective employee's quality. (Section 6 of Chapter 3 discusses this issue.) Here are two more examples: Business travellers sometimes choose unnecessarily expensive flights (paid for by their employers) in order to get higher 'frequent flyer' bonus points which are then applied to personal travel. (Can you identify the *social* waste in this case?) The United States federal student loans program involves billions of dollars. Private contractors are hired to collect student debts, and some of the collecting companies are financially tied to firms in the profitable secondary loan market, giving the collectors an incentive to allow students to default on the original loans. (See *The Washington Post*, June 19, 1993, page 2).

The theory of principal and agent is now central to economic theory. K. J.

Arrow (1984) proposed the terms "hidden action" and "hidden information" as substitutes for the terms "moral hazard" and "adverse selection" in widespread use.[5] Arrow (1963 & 1971) was the first to draw attention to the economic significance of moral hazard, called hidden action throughout this book. Stiglitz (1974) is an important early contribution. The hidden characteristic phenomenon is often identified as *adverse selection*, a term employed by Akerlof (1970) in his pioneering article on the used car market. Spence (1973), in his treatment of education as a signal of worker quality, is also credited for turning the attention of the profession to hidden characteristic problems. The terms "moral hazard" and "adverse selection" were borrowed from insurance terminology, and we prefer the terms "hidden action" and "hidden characteristic," respectively, which are more appropriate for the wide variety of applications of these notions in economics. We prefer to apply moral hazard to situations in which there is a hidden action problem that is not handled successfully. Similarly, we use adverse selection to refer to inefficiency due to a hidden characteristic problem.

The adverse selection problem can be so severe that the market can disappear completely. Consider the viability of unemployment insurance if it were to be provided by the private ownership market economy. It would be costly to purchase, so individuals who know that the likelihood of their becoming unemployed is low would not buy it. This would result in a higher number of claims per insured worker, leading to an increase in premiums to enable the insurance companies to offer unemployment insurance without taking a loss. This would lead to more individuals opting out – those who were willing to buy when the premium was lower, but who feel that the probability of their being unemployed is not high enough to justify paying the slightly higher premium. As the premium increases, it is always the low-probability individuals within the group of previously insured workers who discover that it is now rational for them to cancel their insurance coverage because of the increase in the premium. This means that the number of claims per insured person will rise after an increase in premiums, resulting in another round of premium increases. The whole market can unravel in this way. And if that's the case, and protection against the risk is socially desirable – i.e., provides net benefit to consumers generally – there is a case for provision by the public sector.

Here is a better example: A market economy, by its very nature, exposes participants to risk, some of which can be pooled as individuals exposed to a similar risk coordinate, usually with the aid of an insurance company, so that everyone contributes a small amount (the premium) to finance the recovery of the few who have suffered serious losses. In return, the individual paying the premium is assured that he will be recompensed if he suffers a loss. A democratic political system also exposes its participants to risk. I might be formally charged with a crime that someone else committed. Part of the benefit of a democracy has to do with competition for political office, and the consequent realization of incumbents that they will be punished by defeat at the polls (or worse) if too many constituents are falsely accused of crimes. However, it is in our interest as law abiding citizens to have arrests made *before* the authorities are perfectly certain that they have identified the culprit. If they waited until they were certain there would be too few arrests and too much crime, and the arrests that were made would be obtained at too high a cost in resources. (What does "too high a cost" mean? How do we know the cost would be too high?) So, there remains some risk that a law abiding citizen will be arrested and forced to defend himself in court. Why don't private markets insure against that risk by offering policies that pay legal costs? Legal services don't come cheap.[6] The premium would not be trivial and hence not everyone would purchase insurance. But why isn't *some* legal defense insurance provided by the market?[7] The adverse selection problem is quite evident here. The individuals who are most willing to buy this policy would be those who know themselves to be most likely to be in hot water. This means that the premium would be higher than if everyone in the community purchased a legal defense policy. But, the higher the premium the higher the percentage of law breakers among the policyholders. There is no premium at which the claims paid out could be covered by the premiums paid in, and the market breaks down.

Can a case be made for public provision of legal defense insurance as with unemployment insurance? Probably not. Whether the insurance is provided by the public or private sector there is a severe moral hazard problem. A lot of people would increase the scope of their criminal activities if they knew that any necessary legal defense would be funded by taxpayers or holders of private insurance policies. There would be such an increase in the demand for the top, spellbinding courtroom orators that their fees would increase and then so would the flow of students into law schools. This waste of resources[8] is the least of the antisocial effects of the provision of legal defense insurance, a commodity that would substantially increase individual utility were it not for the moral hazard and adverse selection problems.

The market for insurance for chronic health care provides another example of adverse selection. The average cost of a year's stay in a nursing home is $30,000 in the United States. Young people seldom buy insurance to cover nursing home costs, in spite of the fact that the premium for someone in his thirties is very low. The pool of individuals who do buy insurance policies have a high probability of submitting claims, so the premiums are correspondingly high. Consequently, most older people opt out as well. Very few policies are sold.

2 Taxi!

You have just landed at the airport in a city that you are visiting for the first time.
You hail a cab to take you to your hotel. How can you be sure that the driver
chooses the quickest and cheapest route to your destination? You can't, unless you
make an investment beforehand: an investment of money to purchase a map, and
of time to compute the shortest route between your departure point and your
destination. Even then, you will not know which streets are normally congested,
so it would be very costly to discover the cheapest route. Assuming that you are
not prepared to incur that cost is there any way of ensuring that the taxi driver will
not take you out of your way to enhance his or her income at your expense? We
need to find a way of providing the driver with an incentive to choose the least-
cost route, so that even though you don't know what that route is you will be sure
that the driver has chosen it because that choice maximizes the *driver's* return
from operating the cab. This is the purpose of the fixed part of the nonlinear
pricing schedule for taxi rides. The fare is $F + cD$ where D is the distance to your
destination in miles, c is the charge per mile, and F is the fixed initial fee, which
is independent of the length of the ride. (In fact, you will be charged for time
spent idling in traffic, but let's keep things simple.)

If the fixed fee is relatively large – say \$2 when the average variable cost per
ride is \$5 – then the driver has a strong incentive to maximize the number of trips
per day, *given* the total distance covered during the day. This implies that the cab
driver will choose the shortest route to your destination. In other words, the driver
has a strong incentive to choose the route that is optimal from your standpoint.

Of course, any particular trip of distance D would cost less if the charge were
merely cD instead of $F + cD$, but the fee schedule "$F + cD$" results in a lower
actual cost to the passenger because it induces the driver to choose a route with the
smallest value of D. The best way to drive this point home (excuse the pun) is to
make some simplifying assumptions. Assume that the passenger is completely
gullible, so that he doesn't complain even when the ride takes all day. Assume
that only one minute is lost in searching for a new customer when the passenger
leaves the cab. Both assumptions are unrealistic but, as with a road map, they
clear away distractions that allow us to get to the point quickly. We also assume
that the cab driver cares only about her own welfare. Then when F is zero the
income maximizing strategy for the cab driver is to take all day to get her first
passenger to his destination. Why waste even a minute's income searching for a
new passenger? When F is positive but greater than c the income maximizing
strategy is for the driver to get to the passenger's destination as quickly as
possible: The driver will lose c dollars, if we assume that an average of c dollars
of income is lost while waiting for another passenger, but the next passenger will

pay F dollars in addition to the variable fee of c dollars per minute. This yields a net gain of $F - c$, compared to the strategy of driving twice as far as necessary on each trip.

Now, consider a simple numerical example with assumptions that are more realistic. The fixed fee, F, is \$2 and the charge per mile (c) is \$1. Assume that a driver would make 30 trips per day of ten miles each if he chose to take each rider far out of his way in order to pad the fare. To simplify we suppose that it takes only five miles by the shortest route but the taxi driver chooses a route that requires a ten mile drive. The fare for each ride would be $2 + (1 \times 10)$, or \$12. The day's revenue from operating the cab will be \$360 $=$ \$12 $\times$ 30. Now, consider the result when the driver uses the shortest route in each case. A ride will last half as long but we cannot assume that the taxi will serve twice as many customers because time is often lost searching for a new passenger after the previous one has been deposited at his destination. Suppose that there will be 55 passengers per day when each ride covers only five miles. The fare per rider is $2 + (1 \times 5)$, or \$7. The total revenue for the day is \$385 $=$ \$7 $\times$ 55. This is 7% more revenue than when the driver deliberately wastes time. Assuming the use of a "two-part tariff," consisting of the fixed fee F and the charge per mile c, the rates can be set so that passengers are better off (\$7 per ride, versus \$12) and the suppliers are better off (daily revenue of \$385 instead of \$360). When $F = 0$ the driver makes $30 \times 10c$ when she takes the long, inefficient route, and she makes $55 \times 5c$ when she takes the socially optimal route. Because $300c > 275c$, the one-part fee structure, with $F = 0$, is inefficient.

It would be interesting to look into the emergence of the nonlinear taxi fare schedule as a response to market forces. It may have been a device introduced by owners (or managers) of taxi fleets to enhance the performance of their drivers and hence the market share of the company. If it was introduced as a crude device for extracting more money from customers – with the effect on driver performance unanticipated – the company that introduced the nonlinear fare would acquire a reputation for speedy service. This would result in a larger market share and the other companies would likely imitate in an effort to catch up.

Exercises

1   Employ the assumptions of the second last paragraph, except that k passengers per day are served when there is no shirking. Calculate the value of k for which shirking and minimizing the length of a trip are equally profitable. Now show that shirking is unprofitable for any higher value of k.

2   Each trip lasts m miles when there is no shirking and $2m$ miles when the driver shirks. A taxi does n trips per day when the driver does not shirk and

s trips per day otherwise. Of course, $s < n$. The fixed fee is F and the charge per mile is c. Characterize the values of F, c, s, and n for which shirking will not take place.

3 Safety inspections

It is clearly in society's interest to have dangerous automobiles banished from the highways. But how do we identify the dangerous cars? How do we *define* dangerous? Or, as an economist would put it, how do we determine the point at which diverting additional resources to highway safety would not generate enough benefit to justify the sacrifice of other goods and services that could be produced with the inputs devoted to safety? It is clear that there is such a point. Our individual choices in the market place reveal our willingness to sacrifice safety improvements for the sake of other commodities. I do not own a Mercedes Benz even though it is safer than the car I drive. A Mercedes Benz is also much more expensive than my present car; my family prefers our chosen basket of goods and services to one that contains a Mercedes Benz but, say, shorter vacations to enable us to keep up with the payments on a car loan.

We see that there is an optimal deployment of resources for highway safety. We want to focus on incentives, so we examine a simple model that allows us to dodge the question "How much is optimal?" We assume that there are only two kinds of cars on the highway: safe and dangerous. Preferences are such that it is optimal to have each dangerous car made safe. There are three families of schemes for identifying the dangerous cars:

1 Leave it to car owners to take their cars to private repair shops for periodic safety checks. That is, let resource allocation be determined by the market system.
2 Have annual safety inspections mandated by the state and carried out at state operated inspection sites. The owner of a car found to be dangerous would have to take it off the road, or take it to a private shop for repairs and then pass inspection before putting it back on the road.
3 Have annual safety inspections mandated by the state and carried out at private garages. The owner of a car certified as dangerous could have it repaired by the firm that did the inspection, or at another private shop.

With both the second and third approaches, the state still has to decide what incentives inspectors are to be given. If the safety inspections are carried out by the state for a flat fee – inspectors get an annual salary – there might not be a strong enough incentive to make the effort required for a proper diagnosis. If the safety inspectors get a bounty for each car found to be dangerous there is a strong incentive to certify a safe car as dangerous. Things are even more complicated if private garages do the annual state mandated safety inspections. Consider the system used by the state of Virginia. Law requires the private inspectors to charge a flat fee of $10 for each inspection. That is not enough to cover the cost of a thorough examination. An unscrupulous garage has two choices. It can do a superficial job – say, spend $5 worth of labor for its $10 fee. Or, it can find defects where none exists, and recoup expenses by charging for needless repair work. Where does this leave us? Suppose that decisions are left entirely to the private market, and car owners decide when to have their cars inspected and they themselves pay all inspection and repair costs (scheme 1). Then the individual will weigh private costs against private benefits and there will be less than the optimal number of inspections and less than the optimal amount of resources devoted to car repair. That is a consequence of the fact that a dangerous car affects the welfare of individuals other than the owner. With schemes 2 and 3 each car will undergo an annual inspection but unless the incentives are carefully designed, resources will still not be optimally deployed. The following is a scheme that has private garages doing the inspecting and repair work and gives the garage owner the incentive to do exactly what the state wants, even though the state is unable to verify whether inspectors are truthful. The incentives are such that it is in *the garage owner's interest* to certify a car as safe if and only if it is safe, and to certify a car as dangerous if and only if it is dangerous.

For the sake of expositional clarity we further simplify the model before setting up the scheme. A dangerous car requires $1000 worth of repair work if it is to be made safe. The repairs generate $40 of profit for the garage, net of all expenses, including the cost of the original examination. If an unscrupulous private garage declares that a *safe* car is dangerous then it can bill the owner for $500 worth of needless repairs. (We assume that the car owner knows enough about his car to make it impossible for a mechanic to convince the owner that his car requires as much repair work as a car that is truly dangerous.) The $500 repair bill generates a net profit of $20. The cost to the repair shop of examining a car is assumed to be $15, whatever the car's condition. Here is the incentive scheme: If a car is certified safe, and no repair work is needed, then the state pays the garage a flat fee of $45 for the inspection. The garage's profit is then $30. (Alternatively, the car owner can pay the $45 fee to the garage. The garage owner doesn't care where the money comes from, so the two arrangements have the same incentive effects.) If a garage says a car requires mechanical work before it can pass inspection then the state doesn't pay the garage owner anything, but the car owner pays the repair expenses, of course. To make the example as simple as possible, we arbitrarily assume that the garage can't get away with issuing a verdict without examining the car. Here is the garage owner's payoff table, from which we can calculate her decision:

		Car quality	
		Safe	Dangerous
Decision	Pass	$30	$30
	Fail	$20	$40

Suppose that a car is safe. If the garage declares it to be safe it gets $30 = $45 − $15: the flat fee minus the examination cost. If a safe car is pronounced dangerous, the garage will be able to do $500 of needless repairs, from which it earns a profit of $20, which is less than the garage makes when it certifies the car as safe. In short, a mechanic has an incentive to report a safe care as safe. If the car is dangerous, the garage owner will get a (net) fee of $30 by declaring it to be safe, but that is less than the $40 profit it gets when the car is reported as dangerous and the garage does $1000 of repair work. The garage will want to certify the dangerous car as dangerous. In either case the garage owner has an incentive to report truthfully.

Now, let's bring our model more in line with the real world by acknowledging that the amount of repair work required before a car can be certified safe varies from automobile to automobile. For some cars the required expense is zero – those that we have been referring to as 'safe'. For a given automobile, let R represent the number of dollars of repair work that it would take to pass the safety inspection. We assume that mechanics have equal abilities, so that every mechanic would give the same estimate of R dollars *if she reported truthfully*. The only issue is whether the mechanic is giving the car owner a truthful estimate when she states the cost of making the car eligible for a safety certificate.[9] The mechanic knows R but the car owner doesn't. This is a classic situation: You hire an expert to make a diagnosis and provide a remedy – doctor, lawyer, mechanic, tutor, etc. Can you be sure that it is in the expert's interest to apply his skill to your problem in the way that you would yourself if you had the expertise? Or is it likely that the expert's own interest will intervene? The answer depends in large part on the incentives facing the expert. Can we design a successful incentive scheme for the automobile safety inspection problem?

R varies from car to car, so our first scheme doesn't apply to this model. Here is an incentive scheme that works, in the sense that it is always in the garage owner's interest to report R truthfully, whatever the value of R: The car owner chooses a garage – garage A – from which to get an estimate of R. Then the owner gets a second opinion from garage B. (Getting two estimates is very costly; it takes up the car owner's time and 'wastes' the labor of one mechanic. We'll come back to this difficulty.) The owner gets the car repaired by the garage giving the lower estimate, but that garage receives a payment from the car owner equal to the *higher* estimate. Suppose the two estimates are R_A and R_B for garages A and B, respectively. If $R_A > R_B$ then the owner has the repair work and certification done by garage B at a cost to the car owner of R_A. (We allow the estimates to include a normal profit for the garage.) We now prove that it can never benefit a garage to report something different from a car's true R, and it can sometimes hurt. *This is true whatever estimates of* R *are given by rival garages.* In that case we say that reporting the truth is a *dominant strategy* for the garage owner.

Let's examine the case of an arbitrary car with a true R of $200, and an arbitrary garage A. First, we show that it can never benefit A to report an R value above $200. Suppose it does report R_A above $200. If $R_B > R_A > 200$ then A does the repairs and receives R_B, whether it reports R_A or $200. If R_B is less than R_A, then B will be chosen to do the repair work and the price tag will be R_A. Could this ever be a better outcome for A than what would result from a truthful report by A? If $R_A > R_B$ and $200 > R_B$ then a report of R_A and a report of $200 have the same impact on A's profit: The job goes to B and A is paid nothing. But if $R_A > R_B > 200$ then A is better off by reporting $200 instead of R_A: With $R_A > R_B > 200 garage A does not get the job and does not receive a payment. With $R_B > 200$, a report of $200 by A results in A's getting the job, for which it is paid R_B. Even if it received $200 for the job, a garage could cover the expenses incurred in making the vehicle roadworthy and it would have a normal profit as well. When it receives more than $200 for a $200 job the garage makes an above average profit. Therefore, when a garage gives an estimate that is above the true R it will hurt itself some of the time – by missing out on a handsome profit – and at best it will enjoy the same outcome that truthful revelation would have produced. Can it ever benefit a garage to report less than the true R? Again, we investigate the question from the standpoint of garage A. Suppose $R_A < 200$. If $R_B < R_A < 200$, then garage B gets the job. This is the same outcome for A as when A reports $200; in either case A does not get the job and does not receive a payment. If $R_A < 200 < R_B$ then A gets the job and is paid R_B, which is exactly what would have happened if A had reported $200. If $R_A < R_B < 200$ then A gets the job and is paid less than $200, which means that the payment received by A does not cover A's expenses (which include the opportunity cost of capital). In other words, A takes an economic loss when $R_A < R_B < 200$. By submitting a true report of $200, garage A would not be assigned the job, because $R_B < 200$. So, reporting less than the true R can only bring harm to the garage making the report; it can never be beneficial. In summary, whenever a report has a different effect on a garage's profits than truthful reporting it results in less profit than yielded by a truthful report. And this is the case whatever the other garages decide to do – whether *they* are truthful or not. In the economist's jargon, truthful revelation is a dominant strategy.[10]

The scheme that we have outlined is a success in that it gives garages a strong incentive to provide a truthful diagnosis, because there is no incentive to give an incorrect diagnosis. Let's look at some of the problems that arise with this scheme. What incentive does a car owner have to seek a second opinion? It could lead to a higher estimate of R, and that would require the car owner to pay a higher fee for the repair work. To eliminate this problem we could have the state government pay the difference between the high and the low estimates. Does this mean that the state treasury will suffer? No! Truthful reporting is a dominant strategy, so all the estimates will be the same for a particular car – the car's true R. This also implies that relatively few owners will have to obtain more than one estimate. The implied threat that a car owner can get a second opinion will keep the estimates close to the true R. Why is a second opinion a threat? The answer is entailed in the calculations of the previous paragraph.[11] But there is another difficulty with our scheme, and this one is far more serious. Collusion between a car owner and two garages could be very profitable for all three. Say that the true R is \$200. *A, B,* and *C* strike the following agreement. (*C* is the car owner.) *A* gives an estimate of \$1000 and *B* gives an estimate of \$100. *C* has the repair work done at garage *B* and pays \$100 for the job, and the state treasury gives *B* a payment of \$900 = \$1000 − \$100. *A, B,* and *C* split the difference between the true cost of repairs, which is \$200, and the subsidy of \$900 provided by the state. Whether our scheme has practical value depends on whether this type of collusion could be prevented at low cost. At least we have seen how it is possible to design incentive schemes so that *independent* pursuit of self-interest will be socially beneficial. The difficulties mount when we have to worry about coalition formation – i.e., collusion.

Exercises

1   This question pertains to the simple model in which a car is either danger-ous or safe. A dangerous car always requires exactly \$1000 worth of mechanical work before it can be declared safe. Now, suppose that there are some owners of safe cars who could be persuaded that their car needs more than \$500 dollars of work before it can be certified as safe. How high can that number – the dollar value of needless repairs that the owner of a safe car can be persuaded to finance – go before a garage owner has the incen-tive to report a safe car as dangerous?

2   Using the second scheme, with a variable R, provide a numerical example

showing how two garage owners could profit from nontruthful reporting if they colluded without the cooperation of the car owner.

4 Resource allocation

In this section we look at the coordination problem in a simple resource allocation model. A (possibly fictitious) planner wants to identify a best outcome and so needs to elicit information from consumers and producers about their respective preferences and production functions.[12] This issue is thoroughly examined in Chapters 5 and 6, so in this section we will make things easy on ourselves and the planner by assuming only one consumer and one firm. This also makes it easy to define a "best" configuration of production and consumption activities: It is one that maximizes the single individual's utility, given the limitations inherent in technology and available resources. (Section 5 of this chapter tackles the difficult problem of determining a performance criterion when there are many individuals.) We have an extremely simple model, but it exhibits the information transmission phenomenon very nicely, and it brings out some essential incentive features of the market system. We are going to be very specific. Let's examine the equilibrium of a private ownership market economy to see how prices transmit information about the relevant characteristics to identify the utility maximizing outcome.

4.1 The model

There are two goods, named X and Y, with x and y denoting the respective amounts of the two goods. There is one consumer whose utility function is $u(x, y)$ $= B(x) + y$, where B is a real-valued function such that $B'(x) > 0$ (i.e., positive marginal utility for X) and $B''(x) < 0$ (diminishing marginal utility) for all x. The consumer is endowed with Ω units of X and zero units of Y. In other words, before production begins the individual has Ω units of commodity X, and this can be disposed of as he wishes. He can consume all or part of it, or transfer his ownership of it to the firm. Therefore, if nothing is produced the individual's utility will be $u(\Omega, 0) = B(\Omega) + 0$. Think of X as leisure and Y as food, which is produced by employing labor. Commodity X cannot be produced but it can be used as an input to produce Y. Suppose that the employment of L units of X results in $f(L)$ units of Y as output, where f is a twice-differentiable production function with $f(0) = 0, f'(L) > 0$ (i.e., positive marginal product) and $f''(L) \leq 0$ (diminishing, or at least nonincreasing, marginal product) for all L.

With only one consumer we determine the best outcome by maximizing $u(x, y)$ subject to the constraints $0 \leq x \leq \Omega$, $0 \leq y$, and $y = f(\Omega - x)$. (If $0 \leq x \leq \Omega - L$

then x is feasible, but utility maximization obviously requires $x = \Omega - L$.) This is equivalent to maximizing $V(x) \equiv B(x) + f(\Omega - x)$ subject to $0 \le x \le \Omega$. Suppose that the maximum of $B(x) + f(\Omega - x)$ occurs at a point x^* such that $0 < x^* < \Omega$. For some specifications of B and f we will have $x^* = \Omega$ (the individual consumes zero units of food because none is produced) or, at the other extreme, $L = \Omega$ and $x^* = 0$ which means that the individual converts all of his time into labor supply with nothing left as leisure. But such economies are completely unrealistic. If $0 < x^* < \Omega$ at the maximum of V then $V'(x^*) = 0$. Now, $V'(x) = B'(x) - f'(\Omega - x)$. (We have applied the chain rule here: f is a function of L, but $L = \Omega - x$ so $dL/dx = -1$. Therefore, $df/dx = df/dL \times dL/dx = -f'$.) $V''(x) = B''(x) + f''(\Omega - x)$, which is negative for all x. Therefore a (unique) maximum does indeed occur at a point where the first derivative is zero. (See section 9 of this chapter.) Clearly, the best outcome is attained by producing x^* units of X. The individual consumes x^* units of X and $y^* = f(\Omega - x^*)$ units of Y.

4.2 Market equilibrium

Let's see how the best allocation of resources arises as the equilibrium of the decentralized price system. Let the prices of X and Y be denoted W and P, respectively. The consumer will choose x and y to maximize u subject to the budget constraint, which is $Py = W(\Omega - x) + R$, where R is the profit realized by the firm – i.e., the firm's revenue minus its costs. There is only one consumer, who must be the firm's sole owner, so all profit is turned over to the consumer as income. The consumer also gets income by supplying $\Omega - x$ units of X to the firm. We suppose that the individual chooses the most-preferred consumption plan subject to the budget constraint, and that he doesn't take into consideration the effect of his decision on prices and profit. This is an unrealistic assumption in a society with only one member, but we adopt it in order to model real-world markets with many traders. Setting

$$y = (W\Omega - Wx)/P + R/P$$

and substituting this value of y into the utility function, we can state our problem as one of maximizing $B(x) + (W\Omega - Wx)/P + R/P$, a function of one variable, x. The first order condition is $B'(x) - W/P = 0$ and because the second derivative is $B'' < 0$ the first order condition identifies a unique maximum. Let x^D satisfy $B'(x^D) = W/P$. Then the consumer chooses $x = x^D$ and $y = y^D = (W\Omega - Wx^D)/P + R/P$.

The firm is required to produce the amount of Y that maximizes profit *given* the prices. If L units of labor are employed then the firm's total cost is WL and the level of output is $f(L)$. The firm's revenue is $PF(L)$. Thus the firm will maximize

$Pf(L) - WL$. (In Chapter 5 we will consider whether there is a strong incentive for the firm to take the prices as given and for the consumer to choose a package that maximizes utility given the budget constraint.) Given the prices, profit is maximized by setting the first derivative, $Pf'(L) - W$, of the profit function equal to zero. Then $Pf'(L) = W$. Equivalently, $f'(L) = W/P$. Let L^D satisfy this equality. Set $y^S = f(L^D)$, the supply of commodity Y. Set $L^S = \Omega - x^D$. At equilibrium we will have $L^D = L^S$ and $y^S = y^D$. The first equality says that demand for labor equals its supply. The second equates demand and supply for Y. The consumer demands x^D units of X for his own consumption, thereby supplying $L^S = \Omega - x^D$ units to the firm to be used as input. The firm demands L^D units of X to produce $y^S = f(L^D)$ units of output.

We have $B'(x^D) = W/P = f'(L^D)$ as a consequence of budget constrained utility maximization and profit maximization, respectively. Then $B'(x^D) = f'(L^D)$. At equilibrium, $L^D = L^S$ and thus $L^D = \Omega - x^D$ because $L^S = \Omega - x^D$. Then $B'(x^D) = f'(\Omega - x^D)$. But x^* is the unique value of x satisfying $B'(x) = f'(\Omega - x)$. Therefore, $x^D = x^*$, and thus $L^D = L^S = \Omega - x^*$. Thus $y^D = y^S = y^*$. Therefore, we have *proved* that the market equilibrium is the unique best outcome.

Because x^* is the unique optimal level of X it would be contrary to the consumer's interest to have a higher wage and lower output price than the ones that clear both markets. A different price ratio would lead to a different level of x, but x^* is the only one that maximizes consumer utility subject to limitations inherent in the resource constraint and production recipes. Note that $W/P = f'(L)$ can be written $P = W/f'(L)$, which states that price equals marginal cost. This follows from the fact that $f'(L) = dy/dL$ and thus $1/f'(L) = dL/dy$, the amount of extra labor required per unit of additional Y produced. Therefore, W times $1/f'(L)$ is the *cost* of employing the extra labor needed to produce one additional unit of Y.

Note that the consumer has exactly enough income to purchase y^*. Money for the purchase of Y comes from the sale of X and from profit. Income from the sale of X is $W(\Omega - x^*)$ and profit is $Pf(\Omega - x^*) - W(\Omega - x^*)$. The total is $Pf(\Omega - x^*)$, which equals Py^* which equals Py^D.

4.3 Planning

Let's pretend for a minute that we want to abandon the market system as a device for making production decisions, so that a central authority can explicitly plan for the maximization of the welfare of the households in its jurisdiction. We'll call the central authority *the planner,* and assume, naively, that the planner is able to set aside self-interest and arrange production activities so as to maximize consumer welfare. To keep things simple we continue to assume two goods. Labor/leisure (commodity X) and food (commodity Y). There are many agents in the model now, and each household h has the utility function $u_h = B_h(x_h) + y_h$, where x_h denotes the amount of leisure consumed by h and y_h is h's food consumption. Different individuals will have different tastes, so the B_h functions can be different for different households, hence the h subscript. Again for expositional simplicity, we have assumed that each individual h's marginal utility of food is constant. (Verify: whatever the current level of y_h, if this value increases by 1 then h's utility will increase by 1.)

The planner instructs firms to maximize the net value of their activities to consumers.[13] But this is rather vague, so the planner will need to give the firm more explicit instructions. How do the firm's activities affect individual welfare? The firm's output will have *some* value to consumers, so that will be given positive weight in computing the net value of the firm's activities. But pencils and automobiles should not receive the same weight, because they make different contributions to utility. A good start would be to weight the output by the marginal utility of the good to consumers. That is, if a firm produces Q units of output the firm should get credit for creating

$$MU_Y \times Q$$

units of value. In our simple model the marginal utility of good Y is always 1, so that value of output to consumers will be just Q.

Because production requires the input of resources that could have been used to produce a different array of goods and services, the firm's activities impose costs on society. In our simple model, the cost of producing food (Y) is the amount of leisure that has to be removed from consumers' 'baskets' so that the necessary amount of labor is available. Once goods and services have been produced, an efficient allocation of these goods to consumers requires equality of MB_h across all consumers.[14] (MB_h is the marginal utility of h's leisure, or the first derivative of B_h.) Suppose to the contrary that we had $MB_1 > MB_2$ [and person 1 is currently consuming a positive amount of Y, and 2 is currently consuming a positive amount of X]. Let ϵ, the exchange rate, equal $\frac{1}{2}MB_1 + \frac{1}{2}MB_2$. Now have person 2 deliver $\delta > 0$ units of X to person 1 in exchange for $\epsilon\delta$ units of Y. The changes in utility, Δu_1 and Δu_2, for 1 and 2, respectively, will be arbitrarily close to the following numbers for δ sufficiently small.

$$\Delta u_1 = +\delta MB_1 - \epsilon\delta = \delta \times [MB_1 - \epsilon]$$
$$\Delta u_2 = -\delta MB_2 + \epsilon\delta = \delta \times [\epsilon - MB_2].$$

(Note that each unit of Y added to consumption adds exactly one unit to utility.) Now, $MB_1 > \epsilon$ because ϵ is the average of MB_1 and MB_2, and $MB_1 > MB_2$. For the same reason, $\epsilon > MB_2$. But $\delta > 0$ and thus Δu_1 and Δu_2 are both positive. We have made individuals 1 and 2 better off without changing the consumption of anyone else. Therefore, the original outcome was inefficient. We have discovered that if a system is efficient it must equate individual marginal utilities.[15]

Because efficiency implies equality of individual marginal utilities, we can refer to a single number, MB_X, as the cost to society of the employment of an additional unit of labor. Therefore, if the firm uses L units of labor then the cost to society of its activities is

$$MB_X \times L.$$

Therefore, the *net* value to society of the firm's activities is

$$Q - MB_X \times L.$$

The planner instructs the firm to maximize this quantity. But how is the firm to estimate MB_X? If the economy uses competitive markets to allocate consumer goods and households supply labor so as to maximize their utility subject to a budget constraint, then MB_X will equal W/P as we saw in 4.2. For convenience, the planner can tell the firm to maximize.

$$Q - [W/P] \times L. \tag{1}$$

But that is equivalent to maximizing profit given the prices W and P! To see this, multiply the expression through by P to get

$$P \times Q - W \times L, \tag{2}$$

which is revenue minus cost. Any decision that maximizes [1] will maximize [2] because they differ only via multiplication by a constant P. (If you're having trouble with this, draw two diagrams, one for each expression, with profit on the vertical axis as a function of L, which will be measured along the horizontal axis. An even easier way out is to measure Y in units so that its price is one dollar.)

Here is another way to show that profit maximization is implicit in the solution to the maximization of consumer welfare problem. The line ℓ in Figure 1 is the consumer's budget line at equilibrium. ($Wx + Py$ = Income.) Because $C^* \equiv (x^*, y^*)$ is the chosen basket, the indifference curve through C^* is tangent to ℓ at C^*. We can think of ℓ as an approximation to the indifference curve. It is a good approximation near C^*, and it is a bad approximation far away from C^*. What the consumer really wants is for the firm to produce a basket of goods and services that puts her in the shaded region. But this would require the firm to obtain and process an enormous amount of information about consumer preferences. If the firm used the approximation ℓ instead, it would have to employ only two numbers, W and P. Moreover, if the firm treats

$$Wx + Py = \text{constant}$$

as the equation of an indifference curve and it chooses a production plan such that there is no other feasible production plan that will put the consumer above ℓ –

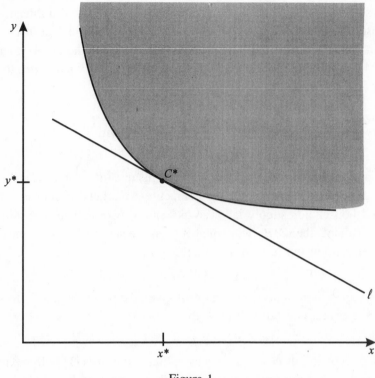

Figure 1

i.e., no other feasible production plan puts the consumer on a higher *approximate* indifference curve than the one through C^* – then there is certainly no feasible production plan that will put the consumer in the shaded region. Therefore, the approximate indifference curves would lead the firm to the socially optimal deci- sion. It is in the consumer's interest to have the firm maximize $Wx + Py$. Recall that x, the consumption of leisure, is equal to $\Omega - L$, the endowment of time less the amount of labor supplied. Therefore, it is in the consumer's interest to have the firm maximize $W(\Omega - L) + Py = Py - WL + W\Omega$. Because Ω is a constant and a *competitive* firm will treat prices (P and W) as constant *at equilibrium*, maximization of $Py - WL + W\Omega$ is equivalent to maximization of $Py - WL$, in the sense that the same values of y and L achieve the maximum value. Therefore, it is in the consumer's interest to have the firm maximize $Py - WL$, which we call profit: revenue ($P \times y$) minus cost of production ($W \times L$).

Using a linear approximation to the individual's indifference curve works: It solves the information transmission problem. There is no need for anyone to encode and transmit information for an entire utility function. The linear ap- proximation can be conveyed with two numbers – the two coefficients, W and P, of the linear approximation. Also, we have gone a long way toward solving the incentive problem, but there is more work to be done. Once we have decided that it is in society's interest to maximize profit *given* the prices, we have to find a way to get the manager of the firm to do that. Sections 1 and 7 of Chapter 2 consider this problem.

Suggestions for further reading: Koopmans (1957), especially pages 1–126.

Exercises

1   Consider a simple economy with one household, one firm, and two private goods, X and Y. The household has an endowment of good X, but there is no endowment of good Y which has to be produced using X as the input. Let L represent the amount of good X used as input in the production of Y. Good X itself cannot be produced. (Think of X as labor/leisure.) For each of the following cases determine the outcome that maximizes utility subject to the resource and production constraints, being mindful of second order conditions and the possibility of a corner solution. (For both b and c the base of the logarithm is e. Recall that ln z is the name we give to the function of z that has as its first derivative $1/z$.)

a The utility function is $u(x, y) = \sqrt{x} + y$. The endowment of X is 276. And each unit of Y requires 12 units of X as input.

b The utility function is $u(x, y) = \ln(x + 1) + y$. The endowment of X is 5. The production of y units of commodity Y requires $\frac{1}{4}y^2$ units of commodity X as input.

c The utility function is $u(x, y) = \ln(x + 1) + y$. The endowment of X is 100. Employment of L units of commodity X leads to the output of $\ln(L + 1)$ units of commodity Y.

2   Find the private ownership competitive equilibrium for each of the economies of question 1. To say that the equilibrium is competitive means that each agent, including the producer, takes the prices as given at equilibrium.

3   There are two goods, X and Y. Y is a composite commodity and its price is always unity. Let P denote the price of X and let m represent income. The consumer's utility function is

$$U = 10x - \tfrac{1}{2}x^2 + y \qquad \text{if } x \le 10 \quad \text{and}$$
$$U = 50 + y \qquad\qquad \text{if } x \ge 10.$$

a Explain why the following is the individual's demand function for X.

$$x = 10 - P \qquad \text{if } 0 \le P \le 10 \quad \text{and}$$
$$x = 0 \qquad\qquad \text{if } P \ge 10.$$

b State the demand function for Y.

c Use the utility function to derive the consumer's surplus that is realized when $P = 4$. That is, compute the utility when x is equal to the amount demanded when $P = 4$ and y is equal to $m - 4x$, and then subtract from that the utility of the basket with $x = 0$ and $y = m$. Show that it is equal to the area under the demand curve minus expenditure on X.

5 Efficiency

A *minimal* test of the ability of a system, or institution, to promote individual welfare generally is *efficiency.* An outcome x is efficient if, with respect to the group of individuals under study, there is no available outcome that would leave everyone at least as well off as x and would make at least one person better off than x. This is a standard definition of efficiency. Sometimes efficiency is referred to as Pareto optimality, but we will use the latter term only when the group of individuals whose welfare is at issue is the entire society. When we focus on some subset, such as the group of owners of a particular firm or the residents of a specific neighborhood, the term "efficiency" will be applied to an outcome that cannot be improved upon to the extent of increasing the welfare of someone in the given group without reducing the welfare of anyone else in the group. Whether it *is* possible to make one or more individuals better off in this way depends critically on the nature of the alternative outcomes that are available. These have to be specified before it can be determined whether any outcome is efficient. In testing an outcome for efficiency, the set of available alternatives must be constructed according to the rules imposed by society at large governing the relationship between the behavior of the group members and the payoffs that they receive. Because the various outcomes are evaluated in terms of the preferences of the members of the group it is also vital to know these preferences.

Suppose, for example, that the group in question is a family which must decide whether to spend a total of $30 to attend a movie or stay home and watch television. If everyone in the family prefers the first option to the second, then staying at home is not efficient (we say that it is inefficient), and attending the movie is efficient. Of course, everyone *would* be made better off if the family stayed home and each member received a check for $100,000. These payments could be financed by collecting relatively small amounts from others in the larger community – the nation, say. Because these transfers are feasible for the country as a whole there is a sense in which this contrived outcome can be said to be an available option. But if we are going to take others into consideration we should also take their welfare into consideration, in which case the transfers certainly would harm some people. On the other hand, if the society is the family, then the $100,000 payments are not feasible, so staying home to watch television would make each person worse off, not better off. Consider the same problem with different preferences: Suppose that one of the family members preferred to stay home and everyone else preferred to attend the movie. Then *both* options are efficient. Attending the movie will make all but one person better off relative to staying at home, but attending the movie adversely affects one person. Therefore, remaining at home is efficient with the new specification of individual preferences.

Because efficiency depends on the list of available outcomes, as well as on individual preferences, the set of available outcomes must be clearly defined before the set of efficient outcomes can be determined, as we have said. We could modify the example of this paragraph by allowing some family members to stay home while others attend the movie. This increases the number of options and could result in the ejection of some alternatives from the set of efficient outcomes, depending on the individual preferences. If we further modify the rules to allow someone who stays home to help pay for the movie tickets then there is another expansion of the set of alternatives, and the set of efficient outcomes could change again.

An outcome is efficient, then, if it is not possible to make someone better off without leaving someone else worse off. A little more formally, we can say that outcome x is efficient if it is feasible and there is no other feasible outcome y that gives everyone at least as much utility as x while giving someone strictly more utility than x. Consider the problem of dividing a cake among n individuals. Assume that each person's preference scheme is independent of the amount of cake received by anyone else and that each person always prefers more to less. An allocation x (or division) of the cake assigns the fraction x_i to individual i. Of course, $x_i \geq 0$ for all i and $\Sigma\, x_i = x_1 + x_2 + \ldots + x_n \leq 1$. This is the feasibility condition. Our assumptions on preferences imply that individual i will prefer allocation x to allocation y if and only if $x_i > y_i$.

If $\Sigma\, x_i < 1$ then x is not efficient because we can set $y_i = x_i + (1 - x_1 - x_2 - \ldots - x_n)/n$ for each i, resulting in an allocation y such that $y_i > x_i$ for all i. On the other hand, if $\Sigma\, x_i = 1$ then x is efficient because

$$y_i \geq x_i \quad \text{for all } i \quad \text{and} \quad y_h > x_h \quad \text{for some } h$$

implies $y_1 + y_2 + \ldots + y_n > x_1 + x_2 + \ldots + x_n = 1$ and thus y is not feasible. In short, an allocation $x \geq 0$ is efficient for the division of a cake problem if and only if $\Sigma\, x_i = 1$. This means that there are many efficient allocations, and that is typical of almost all economic models. Efficiency rules out every conceivable kind of waste; if there is waste somewhere in the system it should be possible to eliminate the waste and raise someone's utility without diminishing anyone else's utility. In fact, inefficiency is the perfect all-inclusive definition of waste. If all waste has been eliminated, it is still possible to increase someone's utility, but only by transferring some commodity or benefit – "cake" – from someone else. If the transfer is made in a nonwasteful fashion we will have a new efficient outcome. This can be done in many ways, accounting for the large number of efficient outcomes.

Assume that $n = 3$. Then $x = (x_1, x_2, x_3)$ assigns the fraction x_1 to person 1, x_2 to person 2, and x_3 to person 3. The allocation $(\frac{1}{3}, \frac{1}{3}, \frac{1}{3})$ is efficient and $(0.4, 0.4, 0.1)$ is not. However, both persons 1 and 2 prefer $(0.4, 0.4, 0.1)$ to $(\frac{1}{3}, \frac{1}{3}, \frac{1}{3})$. Therefore, it is false to say that everyone prefers any efficient allocation to any inefficient allocation. Of course, there is *some* allocation that everyone prefers to $(0.4, 0.4, 0.1)$. For example, everyone prefers the feasible allocation $(0.42, 0.42, 0.16)$ to $(0.4, 0.4, 0.1)$. Note that $(0.2, 0.2, 0.2)$ is not efficient; the allocation $(\frac{1}{4}, \frac{1}{4}, \frac{1}{4})$ gives everyone more utility. But $(\frac{1}{4}, \frac{1}{4}, \frac{1}{4})$ is not efficient either. (Why?) So, it's false to say that if y gives everyone more utility than x then y is efficient. Now, compare allocations $(\frac{1}{3}, \frac{1}{3}, \frac{1}{3})$ and $(1, 0, 0)$. Both are efficient. Therefore, a move from $(1, 0, 0)$ to $(\frac{1}{3}, \frac{1}{3}, \frac{1}{3})$ will make at least one person worse off. But it is false to say that the efficiency criterion stands in the way of such a change. All that we are entitled to say is that there is no *efficiency* argument justifying a move to allocation $(\frac{1}{3}, \frac{1}{3}, \frac{1}{3})$ from allocation $(1, 0, 0)$. There may be a strong *equity* argument for the change, however.

We will say that an outcome is *weakly* efficient if it is feasible and there is no feasible outcome that would make *everyone* strictly better off. In the division of a cake model an allocation is efficient if and only if it is weakly efficient. If, say, y is feasible, $y_1 > x_1$, and $y_i \geq x_i$ for all i set $\xi = y_1 - x_1$. Define z by setting $z_i = y_i + \xi/2n$ for $i > 1$ and $z_1 = y_1 - \xi/2$. Then everyone is better off under z than under x, and z is feasible because $\Sigma z_i < \Sigma y_i$. Therefore, an allocation is not weakly efficient if it is not efficient. In other words, a weakly efficient allocation is efficient.

Obviously, an efficient allocation is weakly efficient in general. If everyone can be made strictly better off then it is certainly possible to make one person better off without harming anyone. But in noneconomic contexts it is possible to have weakly efficient allocations that are not efficient. Consider, for example, the following situation. A house party is to take place involving n persons. A guest may dress casually or formally. Consequently, there are then 2^n outcomes. Assume that no one cares how anyone else dresses so each person is one of two types: C (someone who prefers to dress casually) or F (someone who prefers to dress formally). There is only one efficient outcome, the one that assigns to each person his or her most-preferred mode of dress. Any other outcome assigns to at least one person his least-preferred attire. This person can be made strictly better off without affecting anyone else and thus the original outcome is not efficient. On the other hand, every outcome but one is weakly efficient. Unless everyone is assigned his least-preferred mode of dress the outcome is weakly efficient. If at least one person is assigned his most-preferred attire then that person cannot be made better off so it is impossible to make everyone better off.

We have remarked that an efficient allocation is weakly efficient in any model. We conclude this section by proving that a weakly efficient allocation is efficient in any standard *economic* model. To show that weak efficiency implies efficiency suppose that feasible outcome z makes person 1 strictly better off than x and leaves no one else worse off. Construct outcome y from z by having 1 giving up a small amount of some commodity, money perhaps. Make this amount small enough so that 1 prefers y to x. Now divide this amount evenly among the remaining individuals to complete the specification of y. Each person likes z at least as well as x. Thus, with the extra money each person $j \neq 1$ will be strictly better off (at y) than under x. We already know that 1 prefers y to x. Therefore, everyone strictly prefers y to x. Hence, if it is possible to make one person better off without leaving anyone worse off then it is possible to make everyone strictly better off. The proof requires the assumption of a commodity such as money that could be divided into arbitrarily small amounts, and that everyone wants more of, and such that each person cares only about his own assignment of that good. We take it as axiomatic that this is possible in any *economic* context.

Exercises

1   This question concerns a husband (H) and wife (W) who must decide how to spend their evening. Each prefers being with the other to any outcome in which they attend different events but H likes opera better than baseball and W like baseball better than opera. The following table of payoffs can be used to recover their preferences. The first number in each cell is H's payoff (level of utility) and the second number is W's.

	W to opera	W to game
H to opera	(10, 4)	(2, 1)
H to game	(0, 2)	(3, 9)

List the weakly efficient outcomes. Now list the efficient outcomes.

2   Explain why any outcome that maximizes the sum of individual utility functions (subject to feasibility constraints) is efficient.

3   This question concerns a situation in which three roommates, A, B, and C, have to choose among the following three alternatives:

   x: studying together
   y: going to the basketball game together
   z: going their independent ways

These three alternatives, and only these alternatives, are feasible. The utility derived by each individual from each alternative is revealed by the following table.

	U_A	U_B	U_C
x:	1	2	3
y:	2	4	1
z:	3	1	0

"Alternative x is efficient yet it does not maximize the sum of individual utilities." Is this statement correct? Explain.

4   This question asks you to identify the efficient outcomes in a simple model with two individuals, A and B, and six outcomes, F, G, H, J, K, M. The table below gives the level of utility obtained by each individual under each outcome. All six outcomes are feasible and there are no further feasible outcomes. Which of the outcomes are efficient?

Outcome	A's utility	B's utility
F	0	170
G	60	60
H	200	65
J	100	40
K	40	110
M	205	95

Suppose that a seventh option becomes available and it provides utility levels of 206 for person A and 172 for person B. How would the set of efficient outcomes be affected?

5   There are three individuals (1, 2, and 3) and five feasible outcomes (A, B, X, Y, Z). The table below specifies the utility function for each person.

	U_1	U_2	U_3
A	1	50	10
B	2	0	20
X	5	100	15
Y	4	100	5
Z	3	0	25

List the efficient outcomes.

6   Consider a simple economy with *ten* households, one private good Y, and one public good X. Each household is endowed with some amount of commodity Y and zero unit of X which has to be produced using Y as input. Let y_i denote the consumption of commodity Y by household i. Commodity Y itself cannot be produced. (Think of Y as land.) For the following two situations determine the efficient level of output of X. (Question 2 provides

the key.) Why are there many efficient *outcomes* even though there is only one efficient level of *output* of X?

a Each household i has the utility function
$$u_i(x, y_i) = 2\sqrt{x} + y_i.$$
Each unit of X requires one unit of Y as input. The total endowment of Y in the community is 300.

b Each household i has the utility function
$$u_i(x, y_i) = 2\ln(x + 3) + y_i.$$
The production of x units of commodity X requires x^2 units of Y as input. The total endowment of Y in the community is 20.

6 Joint ventures

Two companies, located in different countries, embark on a joint project in a third country. If one of the parties wants to be released from its commitment at some stage, how should the break-up of the partners be adjudicated? Before addressing this question, we briefly reconsider the problem of dividing a cake among n persons. A particular outcome (or division, or allocation) is specified by a vector $x = (x_1, x_2, \ldots, x_n)$ of nonnegative fractions summing to unity. We let x_i denote the fraction of the cake assigned to individual i so, formally, we have $x_i \geq 0$ for each i with $x_1 + x_2 + \ldots + x_n \leq 1$. The set E of feasible allocations is the set of vectors (lists) x satisfying these two conditions. Assume that each individual's preference scheme is self-regarding and monotonic. By definition, i's preference scheme is self-regarding if i cares only about the amount of cake that he himself receives – his utility is never affected, positively or negatively, by a change in anyone else's consumption. Monotonicity means that i's utility increases if his consumption increases. *In this setting,* to say that i's preference scheme is self-regarding and monotonic is equivalent to saying that i prefers allocation x to allocation y if and only if $x_i > y_i$.

Which allocations in the feasible set E are efficient? Each individual's preference scheme is uniquely determined by the two axioms – i.e., by the assumption that preferences are self-regarding and monotonic. Therefore, feasible allocation x is efficient if and only if there is no allocation y in E such that $y_i > x_i$ holds for all i. Therefore, x is efficient if and only if $x \geq 0$ and $x_1 + x_2 + \ldots + x_n = 1$. In particular, the allocation that assigns all of the cake to individual i is efficient. In symbols, $(0, 0, \ldots, 0, 1, 0, \ldots, 0, 0)$ is efficient. Which allocations are fair? If we define fairness to be the absence of envy then *in this setting* the only efficient allocation that is fair is the one that assigns equal shares, namely $x^* = (1/n, 1/n,$

$1/n$, ..., $1/n$, $1/n$). Within the family of efficient outcomes, only x^* has the property that no individual is envious of someone else's share.

Suppose that our aim is to implement this unique fair and efficient allocation in a decentralized way so that the cake is distributed evenly as the result of selfish utility maximizing behavior on the part of the n individuals. This cannot be done without specifying the rules of the game. These rules will detail the strategies or choices available to each of the n players and will also specify the allocation as a function of the n-tuple of individual strategies. An appropriate mechanism is not hard to find for the case $n = 2$. Let person 1 cut the cake into two pieces, with the sizes of the two pieces determined by individual 1, and then let person 2 choose one of the two pieces for his own consumption. Person 1 then consumes the remaining piece. The only equilibrium allocation generated by this game is the fair allocation $x^* = (\frac{1}{2}, \frac{1}{2})$. Here is the proof: Person 1 knows that person 2 will choose the larger piece if 1 cuts the pieces unequally. Therefore, 1 is sure to receive less than half the cake if he cuts the pieces unequally at stage 1. He can prevent this by cutting the cake precisely in half and this, therefore, is the strategy that ensures him the largest payoff.

This simple institution has an important application in the business world. It often happens that two companies from different countries find themselves involved in a joint business venture in a third country. If at some point one of the parties is presented with a more profitable opportunity elsewhere and wants to abandon the project there will be considerable uncertainty about the legal resolution that will be handed down by the courts. This prospect can inhibit the firms from undertaking the project in the first place, and some socially desirable investments may not be adopted. Some joint ventures have been undertaken after the two participants have agreed to settle disputes over withdrawal by the following straightforward variant of the division of the cake mechanism: The partner that wishes to withdraw from the project names a price P at which he is willing to sell his share of the venture to the second partner. If that were all there were to it, the withdrawing partner would have a strong incentive to name an exorbitantly high price (and there would be a strong incentive to withdraw) just as person 1 would have a strong incentive to cut a cake unequally if he were the one to decide who gets the larger piece. But there is a second stage to the game: The second partner now chooses whether to buy the other out at the named price P *or* to *sell out* to the partner that set the price P. This forces the withdrawing partner to set a price equal to one-half of the present value of the project. Proof: Suppose that the present value of the project is $\$V$ and the contracting parties have equal ownership shares. If the project is completed then each gets a payoff of $\frac{1}{2}V$. If partner 1 (the company wishing to withdraw) names a price $P > \frac{1}{2}V$ then partner 2 is better off selling to 1 at that price than insisting on completion. If 1 sets P below $\frac{1}{2}V$ then 2 will want to buy out 1 at that price and complete the project at its own expense for a net gain of $V - P > \frac{1}{2}V$. In either case, by choosing a value of P different from $\frac{1}{2}V$ company 1 will wind up with less than $\frac{1}{2}V$ and it can always ensure a payoff of exactly $\frac{1}{2}V$ by setting $P = \frac{1}{2}V$.

Because the only equilibrium solution has the withdrawing partner setting $P = \frac{1}{2}V$, why don't they simply agree in advance that $\frac{1}{2}V$ will be the price at which a company can be bought out should it decide to withdraw before the project is completed? Because there will be disagreement about V. The remaining partner will claim that the project has little likelihood of generating substantial profit and will offer to buy out the other at a very low price, claiming that it is offering $\frac{1}{2}V$ but that V is very small. The company selling its share in the enterprise will have a strong incentive to claim that V is very large, whatever its owners really believe, and that $\frac{1}{2}V$ is relatively large. However, if company 1 names a price and then company 2 has the right to buy out the other at that price *or* to sell its share to company 1 at that price, then company 1 could lose heavily by naming a price that was much above $\frac{1}{2}V_1$, where V_1 is 1's estimate of the present value of the project. If 2's estimate of the present value were no higher than 1's, then 2 would opt to sell to 1 at any price P above $\frac{1}{2}V_1$ and the net value to 1 of the project would then be $V_1 - P$, which is less than $\frac{1}{2}V_1$, the payoff that company 1 could be sure of obtaining just by setting $P = \frac{1}{2}V_1$.

Exercises

1   This question concerns a simple economic problem of distribution involving three persons, A, B, and C. Specifically, there is a six pound cake to be divided among the three. Five specific assignments, or divisions, are given below.

$$v:\ 6 \text{ lb to } A,\ 0 \text{ lb to } B,\ 0 \text{ lb to } C$$
$$w:\ 2 \text{ lb to } A,\ 2 \text{ lb to } B,\ 2 \text{ lb to } C$$
$$x:\ 2 \text{ lb to } A,\ 1 \text{ lb to } B,\ 2 \text{ lb to } C$$
$$y:\ 1 \text{ lb to } A,\ 2 \text{ lb to } B,\ 3 \text{ lb to } C$$
$$z:\ 2 \text{ lb to } A,\ 0 \text{ lb to } B,\ 4 \text{ lb to } C$$

(That is, proposal v assigns six pounds of cake to A and nothing to B or C. The other proposals are interpreted analogously.) Each individual cares only about his own consumption of cake and prefers more to less. Any assignment of cake that does not exceed six pounds in total is feasible. Of the five specified assignments list the ones that are efficient (or Pareto optimal).

2   How does the division of the cake game generalize to $n > 2$ players?

7 The prisoner's dilemma

This section discusses a simple situation in which the interplay of incentives leads to an outcome that the participants deeply regret, even though the outcome is the consequence of the pursuit of self-interest: Self-interest drives individual behavior but self-interest is self-defeating in this setting. The phenomenon under discussion, "the prisoner's dilemma paradox," has a wide range of applications; it explains many organizational failures. It is a model of a situation in which individual incentives are *not* well aligned.

The prisoner's dilemma refers to a simple game involving two players, each of whom must choose one of two options independently of the other. It was contrived by Dresher and Flood at Rand in the 1950s. Professor Albert Tucker of Princeton University immediately recognized its great significance for social studies. The game can be described abstractly but we will introduce it in its original guise.

Two individuals A and B have been arrested and charged with bank robbery. The police are convinced of their guilt but there is no admissible evidence on which they can be convicted of robbery, although they were carrying revolvers when caught and for this each can be sentenced to one year in jail. In order to obtain confessions to the crime of robbery the authorities decide to interrogate them separately and to offer each his complete freedom if he confesses to the robbery and his partner does not. The partner who does not confess will receive ten years in jail, but if *both* confess, then both will receive a sentence of five years. The situation confronting each prisoner is summarized by Table 1. The first number in parentheses in each cell is A's sentence and the second number is B's sentence. A and B cannot communicate with each other – or if they can communicate, they can't make binding agreements. Suppose that A believes that B will not confess. Then A will receive a sentence of one year if he does not confess, but he will not have to serve any time if he confesses. A receives a lighter sentence by confessing. On the other hand, suppose that A believes that B *will* confess. Then A will receive five years if he confesses but ten years if he doesn't. Again, A's self-interest is served by confessing. Whichever decision the partner in crime is expected to make, an individual does better by confessing than not confessing. They both confess and each receives a sentence of five years. If neither had confessed then each would have been free after only one year.

In this situation self-interest drives each person to take a course of action that leaves each worse off than if they had coordinated their strategies. (But notice how strong the incentive is to get one's partner to agree not to confess and then, having also solemnly sworn not to confess, to confess and go free.)

Consider the general formulation of this game, with the outcomes translated to

Table 1

A's decision		B's decision	
		Don't confess	Confess
A's decision	Don't confess	(1, 1)	(10, 0)
	Confess	(0, 10)	(5, 5)

Table 2

A's decision		B's decision	
		Cooperate	Defect
A's decision	Cooperate	(20, 20)	(1, 30)
	Defect	(30, 1)	(5, 5)

money payoffs, which an individual wants to *maximize*. Each person must decide whether to cooperate or to defect without knowing what choice the other will make. The payoff for each of the four possible combinations of strategies is given in Table 2. The first number of each pair is A's payoff and the second number is B's payoff (in money). If B is expected to cooperate then A can get \$20 by cooperating but \$30 by defecting. If B is expected to defect then A can get \$1 by cooperating and \$5 by defecting. In either case the higher payoff for A is obtained by defecting. Defecting is a *dominant strategy*. A dominant strategy is one that is the best course of action for a decision maker regardless of the actions that others are expected to take. (The payoff actually received by the decision maker in question usually depends on the decisions of others. For Table 2, by defecting person A gets \$30 when B cooperates but only \$5 when B defects, but in either case defecting gives A a higher payoff than cooperating and thus defecting is a dominant strategy for A.) B is in exactly the same position; both will defect and each receives a payoff of 5. If each had chosen to cooperate then each would have received a payoff of 20. The equilibrium outcome is not efficient. The equilibrium, which is the outcome when each plays his dominant strategy, gives each a lower payoff than when both cooperate. The incentive to defect is irresistible, however, assuming that the game is played under three conditions. First, the two players cannot undertake a binding commitment to cooperate. Second, the game is played only once. And third, each player cares only about the money payoff, and only *his* money payoff at that. If the players can make commitments then the incentives can be quite different. Suppose, for example, that before playing the game the two players anticipated that each would succumb to the temptation to defect and each signed a document that required one person to pay the other

$1000 if he defected. This contract could also state that it was binding on a signatory only if the other person signed. This results in a new game in which both can be expected to sign the document and cooperate. Now, suppose that binding agreements are not possible but the same game is repeated a number of times by the same two players. Then we have a different game with different incentives, although the tension that we have uncovered in the 'one shot' game still plays a role in the repeated game. We can still have an equilibrium in which each person defects at each stage, but the justification of this as an equilibrium is feeble compared to the story for the one shot game. For one thing, there are no dominant strategies in the repeated version of the prisoner's dilemma game. The repeated game is discussed in more detail in 7.9 and in section 5 of Chapter 4. Finally, if the players care about more than just their own monetary reward then things can be very different. For example, suppose that both individuals get utility from the act of cooperation itself, or suppose that each person cares about the welfare of the other. It is easy to see how the cooperative outcome – both persons cooperating – can emerge if the players get utility directly from cooperating. But this explains too much. It *could* turn out to be the best explanation of why cooperation is sometimes observed in prisoner's dilemma type situations. (During one week in 1994 many residents of Williamsburg, Virginia, sacrificed their leisure time to help construct a children's playground. In most cases the volunteer was unacquainted with the other helpers, and their children would have been able to use the facility even if their parents had not contributed.) But we should turn to the "utility from cooperating" explanation only as a last resort: We can explain *all* behavior by saying that the participants are acting the way they do because they get utility from so acting. Obviously, if one player is adversely affected by the other's misfortune the incentives are different. To illustrate, suppose that each person i's utility function is $u_i = x_i - \frac{1}{2} \max\{0, x_i - x_j\}$ for $j \neq i$. This means that i's utility is less than x_i, the amount of money that i receives, if individual j gets less. This leads to a revision of Table 2, which displays the utility levels of each person for each pair of strategies because it was assumed that i's utility is equal to the amount of money received by i. With the utility functions just defined for $i = A$ and $i = B$ (and $j \neq i$) the payoffs in utility terms are given in Table 3. The cooperative outcome is now a plausible candidate for equilibrium. If B cooperates then A gets more utility by cooperating than by defecting. And if A cooperates then B gets more utility by cooperating than by defecting.

If the game is to be repeated, or if players attach some value to cooperation for its own sake, or if players are somewhat altruistic then the forces driving each to defect are weaker, but the model still has considerable applicability and explanatory power. We now turn to a consideration of eight situations where the prisoner's dilemma game is applicable. The first six illustrate how the prisoner's dilem-

Table 3

		B's decision	
		Cooperate	Defect
A's decision	Cooperate	(20, 20)	(1, 15.5)
	Defect	(15.5, 1)	(5, 5)

ma incentive structure can work to the disadvantage of society. In the case of the last two, the individuals playing the game regret their choice of the dominant strategy "defect," but this works to the advantage of society as a whole. In each of the eight cases there are more than two persons "playing the game," but the extension to the several person case is straightforward.

7.1 Economic sanctions

Shortly after Iraq invaded Kuwait in August of 1990 the United Nations Security Council imposed sanctions against Iraq. Most countries endorsed the sanctions and publicly stated a commitment not to allow imports from Iraq or to permit exports to Iraq. By December, observers in the Middle East were reporting serious leakages in the blockade against trade with Iraq. Let's look at sanctions from the standpoint of the incentives facing a typical country. Oil is the chief export of Iraq. A ban on the purchase of goods from Iraq is costly to an importing country because it reduces its options for acquiring energy. The restriction on exports is costly because trade is mutually advantageous, and to the extent that a country restricts trade it obviously limits the benefits that it receives from trade. The ban on exports would be seen in the legislature and in the press of the banning country as a threat to income and employment in that country. In addition, compliance with the sanctions would have to be monitored by the central government and that involves direct costs. If a large number of countries joined in the imposition of sanctions then country A would be tempted to relax its grip in order to recapture some of the benefits of trade, hoping that others would maintain the sanctions with sufficient determination to allow A to reap the benefit of sanctions without having to pay the cost. On the other hand, if quite a few countries allow trade to continue then country A will benefit little from any embargo that it imposes, because sanctions have little effect if they are not widely enforced. In short, the dominant strategy for each country is to allow its firms to disregard the sanctions. This is not an argument against multilateral sanctions. However, the prisoner's dilemma problem teaches that sanctions must be implemented with a clear understanding of the incentives facing individual countries and with the determination to use diplomacy and ongoing consultation to keep everyone on side.

7.2 Public opinion

It is quite costly for an individual to stay well informed on most issues that are before national legislatures. On the one hand, the cost of investing the time required to develop an intelligent opinion on each critical public event is considerable, and on the other hand, the personal benefit from the resulting improvement in the quality of public opinion is negligible because a single individual's viewpoint, whether sound or silly, has a negligible effect on public opinion. Whether others are well informed or not, an individual's own utility is maximized by his investing in knowledge up to the point where the benefit *to him* from any additional investment would be more than offset by the cost that he would bear. This results in citizens' generally not being well enough informed from the standpoint of their own welfare. If everyone were to invest additional time in studying current events then public opinion would induce better public decisions and that would benefit everyone. See Downs (1957), pages 207–219, for a thorough discussion of this problem.

7.3 Pollution

Suppose that consumers have a free choice between automobiles produced without emission control devices and automobiles costing $3000 more that have equipment that eliminates most harmful exhaust. (The emission control equipment costs $3000 per car to manufacture and install.) Consider the typical consumer's decision problem. Given the choices made by others, whatever they are, the purchase of a pollution-free car would cost the individual $3000 extra but would not appreciably improve the quality of the air. Clearly, purchasing the cheaper, polluting automobile is a dominant strategy. Everyone makes this choice and thus automobile traffic generates substantial pollution. Everyone would be better off if each paid a $3000 charge to eliminate pollution caused by automobile exhaust, but the individual incentives push the society away from this outcome.

The Environmental Protection Agency was formed in the U.S. in 1970. Before that time pollution was regulated in part by private lawsuits. The prisoner's dilemma phenomenon was involved here as well. An individual gets the benefit of any pollution reduction strategy financed by his neighbors, whether or not he makes a contribution himself. Declining to help pay the legal costs of a lawsuit is a dominant strategy for each individual. Hence, there is less than the socially optimal amount of pollution abatement when we rely exclusively on private lawsuits to regulate behavior.

7.4 Beggar-thy-neighbor policies

The great depression of the 1930s had most industrial countries in its grip, and individual nations were unable to resist the temptation to devalue their currencies. Given the exchange rates of other countries, if one country devalued its currency then its goods would be cheaper to the rest of the world and its own citizens would import less as other countries' goods rose in price in terms of the domestic currency. The result is a stimulus to the devaluing country's industries at the expense of other countries. (It was called a beggar-thy-neighbor policy.) But the same temptation confronts each nation. Devaluation is a dominant strategy. Each country attempts to lower the price of its currency relative to others and adopts additional measures to restrict imports. As all countries restrict imports all countries' exports dwindle and the worldwide depression deepens.

7.5 "Fire!"

If fire is detected in a movie theater almost no one will escape alive if there is panic and all attempt to get through the exit door at once. But if the crowd is orderly it is advantageous to me to run past everyone to get to the exit first. Panic will prevail if everyone comes to the same conclusion. On the other hand, if everyone runs to the exit I will gain nothing by walking slowly.

7.6 Disarmament

In this example the players are countries. Defecting in this case is a decision to arm heavily. Cooperation is the decision to maintain only a defensive posture. If a country expects others to cooperate there is a strong incentive to obtain an extra measure of security by arming heavily. If the same country expects others to arm heavily then national security demands that the country arm heavily. Arming heavily is a dominant strategy for each country. Alternatively, imagine that war has broken out between *A* and *B* and that defecting corresponds to the use of chemical weapons in combat. Without introducing any other considerations, our analysis predicts that the use of chemical weapons would be commonplace. But that's not what we observe. *Because* defecting is a dominant strategy in this situation, nations generally have a responsibility to convince belligerents that the employment of particularly heinous methods of warfare (or violations of the

Geneva conventions on the treatment of prisoners of war, etc.) will be counterproductive. In other words, it has to be brought to bear on *A* and *B* that they are playing a larger game than the immediate 'one-shot' prisoner's dilemma game.

7.7 Cartels

A producers' cartel has formed in order to keep industry supply low and price high. This provides each member of the cartel with more profit than when they compete vigorously against each other. When the firms actively compete then the industry output will be high, and price low, because each firm's output will be relatively high. Cooperating corresponds to a firm sticking to the cartel agreement by restricting its own supply. But if each firm does this the market price will be high, and if the market price is high then an individual firm has a strong incentive to increase its profit by producing more output. If every firm does this the market output will be high and the price low. This is one case where the incentive structure, which leads to an inefficient outcome from the standpoint of the *group of producers,* works to the benefit of society as a whole: Individual incentives promote competition in spite of the substantial profits awaiting the shareholders in firms that can get their competitors to agree to cooperate in restricting output. The original prisoner's dilemma is another instance in which society is served although the individuals playing the game deeply regret the outcome.

7.8 Hostile takeovers[16]

Doncam corporation has two owners, *A* and *B*, each of whom owns two shares in the firm. The current market value of a share is $10. Max wants to acquire all four shares in the firm and then replace the current manager with a more efficient one. This will raise Doncam's profit and hence the market value of a share from $10 per share to $18. Therefore, Max offers to buy the outstanding shares at $15 each. This would give *A* and *B* a nice profit. But, why would they sell if the shares will be worth even more after the takeover? Max can get around this difficulty by means of a *two-tier offer.* He offers to pay $20 per share for the first two shares tendered and buy the next two at $10 each, but if *A* and *B* simultaneously tender two shares each then Max will pay each owner $20 + $10 for two shares. *A* and *B* now face a prisoner's dilemma problem represented by Table 4. If *A* holds on to her shares, waiting for the takeover to drive their value up to $18, then *B* will get $18 per share if she also holds out,[17] but $20 for each of her two shares if she tenders them to Max. On the other hand, if *A* tenders her two shares immediately then *B* gets $10 for each of her two shares if she holds out,[18] but a total of $20 + $10 if she also sells right away. Whatever *A* elects to do, *B* does better by selling

Table 4

		B's decision	
		Hold	Sell 2 Shares
A's decision	Hold	(36, 36)	(20, 40)
	Sell 2 shares	(40, 20)	(30, 30)

her shares immediately. Similarly with *A*. Because selling is a dominant strategy, the takeover will be consummated. (From an economywide perspective, takeovers may improve the performance of managers and so work to the advantage of shareholders in the long run. See the discussion in section 1 of Chapter 2.)

The preceding discussion assumes that the prisoner's dilemma game is to be played only once. Intuition suggests that if the game were to be played by the same two individuals several times in succession they would appreciate that narrowly selfish play – i.e., defecting – would provoke future punishment by one's opponent and consequently, the cooperative outcome would be sustained. Let's see if a formal analysis supports this conjecture.

7.9 Repeated play

Repeated play is discussed in depth in Chapter 4, but a brief look at this situation is warranted here. If the same two individuals play the original prisoner's dilemma game many times will they be induced to cooperate sooner or later? It would be comforting to think that continued interaction induces cooperation. Sometimes this happens when forces other than narrow self-interest are at work. (See Rapoport, 1989.) If, however, we stick to the assumption of selfishness at every turn the only equilibrium when the game is played a fixed *finite* number of times has each person defecting at each stage. (Assume that both players know when play will end.) At each stage the players simultaneously and independently choose between defecting and cooperating and payoffs are then awarded according to Table 2. This is repeated, say n times. What will happen? At the nth and last stage there is only one possible outcome: both defect because there is no further play, and thus no opportunity for their choices to affect future payoffs. Knowing that both will inevitably defect at the last stage, independently of what has happened previously, there can be no advantage to anyone who cooperates at the second last stage; it will not induce one's opponent to cooperate in the last round. Therefore, both will defect in round $n - 1$. Knowing that both will inevitably defect in the last two rounds, independently of what has happened previously, there can be no advantage to anyone who cooperates in stage $n - 2$. Therefore, both will defect in round $n - 2$, and so on. The only equilibrium has each person defecting at each stage.

Even though the only *equilibrium* in the finitely repeated prisoner's dilemma game has each person defecting each period it is not true to say that defecting each period is a *dominant strategy*. This is not even true for two repetitions. Suppose that A announces his intention to cooperate in the first period and then to cooperate again in the second period *if B* has also cooperated in the first period and to defect in the second period if B defected in the first period. (I don't mean to imply that this is a smart decision on A's part; it may or may not be.) This is called the *tit-for-tat* strategy. If B defects in both periods his payoff will be $30 + 5$ but if B cooperates in the first period and then defects in the second period his payoff will be $20 + 30$. *Given A*'s 'tit-for-tat' strategy the 'cooperate then defeat' strategy gives B a higher total payoff than the 'defect then defect' strategy, and therefore the latter is not a dominant strategy. Defecting both periods is, however, a payoff maximizing response of B to the announcement by A that he will defect both periods. (Will that give A second thoughts about playing tit for tat?) Therefore, we have not contradicted the assertion that A and B each defecting each period is an equilibrium. (To prove that it is the *only* equilibrium you need to do more, hence the argument of the preceding paragraph.)

We often observe individuals playing cooperatively in the real world. How can this be reconciled with the apparent inevitability of the dismal outcome 'everyone defects all the time'? This phenomenon is not well understood, but one approach is to accept an *approximate* equilibrium as a solution concept. The pair of strategies (S_A, S_B) is an approximate equilibrium if S_A gives A a payoff that is extremely close to the maximum payoff available to A given that B plays S_B, and similarly S_B gives B a payoff that is extremely close to the maximum payoff available to B given that A plays S_A. Now, suppose that the game in question consists of n repetitions of the prisoner's dilemma game and B announces that he will play 'tit for tat'. The payoff maximizing response for A is to cooperate in each of the first $n - 1$ periods and then defect in the last round. The resulting payoff is $20 + 20 + 20 + \ldots + 20 + 30$, which yields an average payoff per period of $20 + 10/n$. If instead A responds to the announcement that B will play 'tit for tat' by playing 'tit for tat' then both will cooperate every period and A's payoff will be 20 every period, which obviously yields A an average payoff of 20. If n is very large then the difference between $20 + 10/n$ and 20 is very small,[19] so there is a sense in which playing 'tit for tat' is approximately a best response to 'tit for tat' and thus when both play that strategy we have an approximate equilibrium. But this is not a very satisfactory explanation if we can't provide a foundation for the employment of approximately best strategies.

Consider another approach: Suppose that neither player knows how large n is.

In other words, neither knows when the game is going to end. We can model this by investigating the equilibria of a supergame in which the one-shot prisoner's dilemma game is played period after period without end. When the game is played an infinite number of times there is an abundance of equilibria. At each stage there are two choices, defect or cooperate. As in any repeated game, a strategy specifies one's choice at each stage as a function of the previous choices of both players, so there is a vast number of strategies and many of these are equilibria. We stop at this point merely to point out that if each player announces his intention to cooperate until the opponent is observed defecting, whereupon the former will defect forever after, then we have an equilibrium in which each actually cooperates at each stage. But there are many other equilibria as well. For example, if each person announces that he will defect at every stage regardless of his opponent's behavior then there is nothing that a player can do that will lead to a higher average payoff over the first t periods (no matter how large t is) than is realized when he defects every period. About the only restriction we can place on the equilibrium is that each person can guarantee himself a payoff of at least 5 per period by defecting each period, and therefore any equilibrium would have to be at least as desirable to a player as the outcome in which he receives 5 per period. If an outcome assures each player of at least the amount that he can guarantee for himself independently of what others do it is said to be *individual rationally*. The celebrated 'folk theorem' of game theory asserts that any pattern of payoffs with the individual rationality property is an equilibrium if it is feasible. (This is proved in section 6 of Chapter 4. Feasibility here means that the payoff stream can be realized by repeated play of the prisoner's dilemma game for some pair of sequences of actions for the players.)

An important contribution to the study of the repeated prisoner's dilemma game, and hence to the understanding of the conditions under which cooperation will be induced by rational self-motivated behavior, is the competition devised by Robert Axelrod in which opponents formulated strategies for playing prisoner's dilemma. (Reported in Axelrod, 1984.) The strategies competed against each other in a round robin tournament in which each match consisted of repeated play of the prisoner's dilemma game. The "Tit for Tat" strategy, submitted by Anatol Rapoport, was the winner. Although it did not beat any other strategy it scored highest because it was a survivor: other strategies reduced each other's scores when pitted against each other. Tit for Tat requires a player to begin by cooperating and at every subsequent stage chooses the action selected by the opponent at the previous stage. (At each stage the players simultaneously choose between defecting and cooperating. Can you explain why Tit for Tat can *never* beat another strategy?)

Suggestions for further reading: Poundstone (1992) and Binmore (1992).

Exercises

1   Analyze the outcome of a prisoner's dilemma game that is played three
     times, one game after the other, by the same two persons, who know in
     advance that the game will be repeated but who are unable to make binding
     agreements. Before beginning your analysis describe a typical individual
     strategy. Comment on the efficiency of the equilibrium that you derive.

2   Is there a dominant strategy for the game described in question 1?

3   Consider a market served by two firms with identical cost functions $C_i =
     Q_i$, where Q_i is firm i's output and C_i is the firm's total cost. The market
     demand curve is $Q = 82 - 2P$.

   a Determine the market output and price when the two firms form a cartel
     which restricts output in order to maximize industry profit.
   b Assuming that the cartel imposes a quota on each firm equal to half the
     industry profit maximizing level of output, what is the firm's profit under
     the cartel arrangement?
   c Now assume that consumers will buy exclusively from firm i if it breaks
     the cartel agreement and charges a price of $15 if the other firm contin-
     ues to charge the cartel price. What profit will each firm receive if firm i
     maximizes profit given a price of $15 and given the market demand
     curve above?
   d If a firm has a choice of only two strategies – charge $15 or charge the
     cartel price – show that they are playing a prisoner's dilemma game.

4   Determine which of the five two-person games below are examples of the
     prisoner's dilemma game. In each case each individual must choose one of
     two strategies: A controls the rows and B controls the columns. In other
     words, A must choose between 'Up' or 'Down' and B must choose between
     'Left' or 'Right'. Each combination of strategies determines a money pay-
     off to each person as indicated in the tables: the first number in a cell is A's
     payoff and the second number is B's. Each player wants to maximize his or
     her payoff and the players cannot make binding contracts. (All of which
     says that we have the standard setting).

	Game one			Game two	
	B			*B*	
A	(15, 15)	(8, 2)	*A*	(12, 12)	(20, 2)
	(2, 8)	(10, 10)		(2, 20)	(5, 5)

	Game three			Game four	
	B			*B*	
A	(5, 50)	(50, 0)	*A*	(7, 7)	(4, 10)
	(0, 500)	(10, 100)		(4, 10)	(5, 5)

Game five
B

A | (100, 100) | (4, 102) |
|---|---|
| (102, 4) | (5, 5) |

5   Consider the following prisoner's dilemma game:

		Max	
		Coop	Defect
Liz	Coop	(10, 10)	(2, 15)
	Defect	(15, 2)	(5, 5)

Suppose that Max and Liz play the game three times in succession and each
knows that the game will end after three periods. Show that defecting every
period is *not* a dominant strategy even though the unique (Nash) equilibrium results in each person's defecting each period. (You don't have to prove
that a Nash equilibrium results in each person's defecting at each stage; you
just have to show that the player who always defects is not employing a
dominant strategy.)

8 Equilibrium

The discussion of the prisoner's dilemma game in the previous section rested on
the notion of equilibrium but we did not take time to define it. If each individual
has a dominant strategy then we can say with confidence that the outcome that has
each individual playing his dominant strategy is an equilibrium. There exists a
dominant strategy for the one-shot prisoner's dilemma, but dominant strategies do
not usually exist. For example, the game resulting from replication of the prisoner's dilemma does not have dominant strategies. Let us see what we can say about
equilibrium in general.

There are two players, Samantha and Jordan. Samantha has to choose an action
from those specified by the rules of the game, say T, B, C, etc. Jordan has to
choose from the list L, R, D, etc., which may or may not be different from the
actions available to Samantha. If Samantha chooses C and Jordan chooses D then
Samantha's utility is $U_S(C, D)$ and Jordan's utility is $U_J(C, D)$. We require an
equilibrium to be *self-enforcing*. This means that each individual maximizes his
utility given the constraint on his payoff implicit in the strategy or action assigned
to the other player. In other words, the strategy pair (C^*, D^*) is self-enforcing if
C^* is Samantha's best response to D^* and D^* is Jordan's best response to C^*. In
symbols, a self-enforcing outcome must satisfy

$U_S(C^*, D^*) \geq U_S(C, D^*)$ for every strategy C available to Samantha,   and
$U_J(C^*, D^*) \geq U_J(C^*, D)$ for every strategy D available to Jordan.

A pair of strategies (C^*, D^*) with this property is said to be a *Nash equilibrium*.
We may want an equilibrium to have additional properties but it should at least be

Table 5

| | | Jordan's decision | |
		L	R
Samantha's decision	T	(12, 10)	(15, 5)
	B	(10, 20)	(5, 25)

self-enforcing. It might be useful to compare the best response property to a dominant strategy. If C^* is a dominant strategy for Samantha then for every strategy D available to Jordan we must have $U_S(C^*, D) \geq U_S(C, D)$ for every strategy C available to Samantha. Consider the game described by Table 5. (The first number in a cell is Samantha's payoff, and the second is Jordan's.) Verify that (T, L) is the only Nash equilibrium. Samantha's best response to L is T, and Samantha's best response to R is also T. Therefore, T is a dominant strategy for Samantha. But L is not a dominant strategy for Jordan. *If* Samantha were to select B then Jordan's best response would be R, not L.

In spite of the plausibility of Nash equilibrium, there are games that have a single Nash equilibrium that is not a reasonable forecast of the game's outcome. One of the niftiest examples is the so-called centipede game characterized by the game tree of Figure 2a. The two players are Jordan and Samantha. As time passes we move from left to right along the diagram. They take turns moving, and when it's a player's turn to move he has to choose between grabbing the money (g) and passing (p). If he passes then the total amount of money available doubles. When one of the players grabs then the game is over and Jordan's payoff is the first number in parentheses and Samantha's is the second number. If each player passes at each turn then the game ends at the extreme right of the diagram with Jordan receiving \$256 and Samantha receiving \$64. (Note that the only efficient outcomes are this one and the second last outcome, in which Jordan receives \$32 and Samantha receives \$128.) What makes the outcome problematic is that, although the total payoff doubles every time a player passes, the amount that he will receive if the other person responds by choosing g is cut in half. Suppose that each player passes every time it is his turn to move. Then Samantha will receive \$64. But she can get twice as much money by 'grabbing' on her last move instead of passing. Passing at the last stage is not a best response by Samantha to Jordan's strategy of passing at every opportunity. Therefore, the outcome that results when each player passes at each opportunity is not self-enforcing and hence not part of a Nash equilibrium. Therefore, both players can predict that the game will not end with a player passing. Suppose both players anticipate that the game will end after move t with Samantha 'grabbing' at that stage. Then Jordan will not let the game

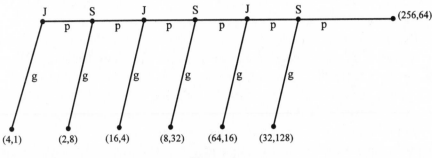

Figure 2a

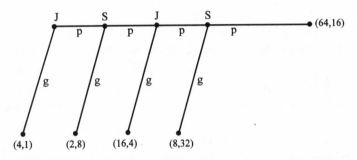

Figure 2b

survive to that stage because he can get twice as much money by grabbing on the previous move instead of passing and letting the game continue. Therefore, the only self-enforcing outcome has Jordan 'grabbing' at the first opportunity and this results in a payoff of $4 for Jordan and $1 for Samantha. This is obviously far from efficient. (The game is called the centipede game because the associated diagram looks like a centipede. Moreover, one could extend the game by adding 94 more moves, with the pot continuing to double each time. The starting point would remain the only equilibrium but it offers minuscule payoffs relative to those available later on.) Our intuition tells us that if the game were actually played the two players would not end up at the Nash equilibrium. In fact, McKelvey and Palfrey (1992) conducted experiments and found that the players typically wound up somewhere near the middle of the centipede, not at either extreme of grabbing at the first opportunity or passing until the last move or two. Therefore, Nash equilibrium is an inappropriate solution concept in this case. What's wrong with this notion of equilibrium as a solution concept for this game? In order to identify the difficulty, we will truncate the game so that each player potentially has only two moves, as illustrated in Figure 2b. We refer to the later move as the player's second move.

Here is a difficulty: We have implicitly assumed that both players are 'rational'. Rationality means that an agent cares only about the impact of an outcome on his own welfare, and he always acts so as to enhance his welfare in any situation where that has an unambiguous meaning. If Samantha is rational and she has the opportunity to make the last move – her second move – she will grab rather than pass because she gets $32 by grabbing and only $16 by passing. Nothing remarkable about the background assumptions so far. Now, suppose that Jordan is rational *and* that Jordan knows that Samantha is rational. Then Jordan will anticipate that Samantha will grab if she has a second move. This means that Jordan deduces that he will get $8 if Samantha is given an opportunity to make a second move. Therefore, if Jordan has the chance to make a second move, he knows that he is really choosing between $8 – if he passes – and $16 – if he grabs. He is rational, so he will grab if he has a second move. Now, suppose that Samantha is rational *and* Samantha knows that Jordan is rational and Samantha knows that Jordan knows that Samantha is rational. Then Samantha can anticipate that Jordan will grab if Jordan has an opportunity for a second move. Then Samantha will wind up with $4 if Jordan has a second move. Therefore, on Samantha's first move – if she has one – she can obtain $8 by grabbing or $4 by passing. She is rational, so she will grab on the first move if Jordan hasn't grabbed first. And so on. The conclusion that Jordan will grab at the first opportunity is based on the following suppositions:

1 *Jordan and Samantha are each rational.*
2 *Jordan knows that Samantha is rational.*
3 *Samantha knows that Jordan is rational and that Jordan knows that Samantha is rational.*
4 *Jordan knows that Samantha knows that Jordan is rational and that Jordan knows that Samantha is rational.*

Statement 1 implies that Samantha will grab if she is given a second move. Statements 1–2 imply that Jordan will grab if he is given a second move. Statements 1–3 imply that Samantha will grab on her first move if Jordan passes on his first move. Statements 1–4 imply that Jordan will grab on the first move. Therefore, assumptions 1–4 collectively imply that the unique Nash equilibrium has each person grabbing whenever he is given an opportunity to move. But these assumptions are extremely problematic. If Jordan actually passes on the first move then Samantha knows that one of the four statements is false – perhaps Jordan is not rational, or perhaps he is unsure that Samantha knows that he knows that Samantha is rational – and the logical chain directing Samantha to grab at the first opportunity is broken. *Anything* can happen now. The longer the game, the larger is the spread between the payoff a player gets by grabbing early and the payoff that awaits both players if the game ends much later. Moreover, the longer the game, the longer is the chain "I know that he knows that I know that he knows . . ." that is required to support the backward induction derivation that the game will end on the first move. For long games of this nature – or short ones, for that matter – we don't have a good model for predicting behavior, but at least we can see why results in which the game ends after seven or eight rounds of passing are not inconsistent with our basic rational choice model. It's just that the results are inconsistent with the implicit assumption about what individuals know about what others know. We will avoid models in which we do not have confidence in our definition of equilibrium.

Exercises

1 Generalize the definition of Nash equilibrium to the case of n persons. Let S_i denote the typical strategy of player i and let $U_i(S_1, S_2, S_3, ..., S_n)$ specify the payoff to i when each player j selects strategy S_j. Let $(S_1^*, S_2^*, S_3^*, ..., S_n^*)$ denote a Nash equilibrium.

2 One hundred and one individuals choose between two options x and y by voting in the conventional way. Suppose that everyone prefers x to y. Explain why the outcome in which everyone votes for y is a Nash equilibrium. (There is no mistake here; I mean to write y.) Would you expect the outcome to be y? Explain. Are there any other Nash equilibria?

9 Introduction to calculus

Consider the standard consumer choice problem:

Maximize $U(x, y)$ subject to $P_1 x + P_2 y = \Omega$.

Of course, U is the utility function, and utility depends on the amounts x and y consumed of the two goods. P_1 is the price of good X and P_2 is the price of Y, with Ω representing income. The constraint is the budget line, which we can solve for y as a function of x.

$$y = \Omega/P_2 - P_1 x/P_2.$$

Now, substitute this value of y into the utility function. We want to maximize

$$V = U(x, \Omega/P_2 - P_1 x/P_2),$$

and V is a function of only one variable, x, because Ω, P_1, and P_2 are constants – they are outside the control of the consumer, at least in the short run, at the time a consumption decision must be made. This means that we can apply elementary calculus to the problem and maximize $V(x)$. We no longer have to worry about the budget constraint because that is built into V. With one stroke we have eliminated one variable and the budget constraint as well. If this were all there were to the problem we could say at this point that $V'(x^*) = 0$ is a necessary condition[20] for x^* to be the optimal consumption level for x. And once we have obtained x^* we simply use the budget constraint to solve for y. But there are some implicit constraints that we have to respect. We cannot have $x < 0$, but the calculus does not guarantee that $x < 0$ will be ruled out. Also, we cannot have $x > \Omega/P_1$. If we did then the cost of purchasing x would exceed Ω, the individual's income. Therefore, our problem really is:

$$\text{Maximize } V \qquad \text{subject to } 0 \le x \le \Omega/P_1.$$

This is a lot easier than the original problem, but we still have to determine when the solution value x^* will satisfy $V'(x^*) = 0$, and also what we can say about x^* when $V'(x^*) \ne 0$ at the maximum. If you think that this is bizarre or unnecessary then solve the following:

$$\text{Maximize } V(x) = 2x \qquad \text{subject to } 0 \le x \le 100.$$

(Set $\Omega = 100$ and $P_1 = 1$.) The maximum is clearly achieved by $x^* = 100$; we can determine this by inspection, without using calculus. Clearly, $V'(100) = 2 \ne 0$.

So, we turn to the problem of characterizing the maximum of a function of x subject to the constraint $a \le x \le b$, where a and b are constants. Let $f(x)$ represent the function in question, with x a real variable. This means that x can be any real number; and for any choice of x the function f specifies another real number $f(x)$. Initially, *we assume that there is no constraint of any kind on the range of values that* x *can assume*. Now let x^* represent any real number that maximizes the function f. Formally, this means that $f(x^*) \ge f(x)$ holds for every real number x. Another way of saying this is $f(x^*) \ge f(x^* + \epsilon)$ for every real number ϵ. (Just replace x by $x^* + \epsilon$, defining ϵ as the quantity $x - x^*$.) We can think of ϵ as an increment, positive or negative, taking us away from x^*. Because f is maximized at x^*, this increment, or step, cannot increase the value of f. More formally, we write:

$$f(x^* + \epsilon) - f(x^*) \le 0 \qquad \text{for } all \ \epsilon. \tag{1}$$

Condition [1] is just another way of saying that f is maximized at x^*. This is pretty obvious, but we only need to pursue this a little further to get a striking and useful result.

If ϵ is positive (strictly greater than zero) then $f(x^* + \epsilon) - f(x^*)$ will still be less than or equal to zero after we divide that expression by ϵ. We state this formally as condition [2]:

$$\frac{f(x^* + \epsilon) - f(x^*)}{\epsilon} \le 0 \qquad \text{for all } \epsilon > 0. \tag{2}$$

As ϵ approaches zero through positive values, the limit must also be less than or equal to zero as a consequence of condition [2]. For future reference, we state this as condition [3]:

$$\text{The limit of } \frac{f(x^* + \epsilon) - f(x^*)}{\epsilon} \leq 0 \qquad \text{as } \epsilon > 0 \text{ approaches } 0. \qquad [3]$$

Similarly, if we divide $f(x^* + \epsilon) - f(x^*)$ by any $\epsilon < 0$ the inequality sign will change direction from $\leq$ to $\geq$, so we have condition [4].

$$\frac{f(x^* + \epsilon) - f(x^*)}{\epsilon} \geq 0 \qquad \text{for all } \epsilon < 0. \qquad [4]$$

As ϵ approaches zero through *negative* numbers the limit must be nonnegative because each term is nonnegative by condition [4]. This is represented as condition [5].

$$\text{The limit of } \frac{f(x^* + \epsilon) - f(x^*)}{\epsilon} \geq 0 \qquad \text{as } \epsilon < 0 \text{ approaches } 0. \qquad [5]$$

If f has a derivative at x then, by definition, the limit of $[f(x^* + \epsilon) - f(x^*)]/\epsilon$ is the same when ϵ approaches 0 through positive values as it is when ϵ approaches zero through negative values. But then [3] and [5] can both be satisfied only if the limit is zero in both cases. In short, $f'(x^*) = 0$ is a necessary condition for f to have a maximum at x^*.

Here is an alternative derivation of the fact that $f'(x^*) = 0$ if f is maximized at x^*. (You don't need to master both treatments; just adopt the one that you are more comfortable with.) Suppose that $f'(x) > 0$. We show that f cannot have a maximum at x. Let δ represent $f'(x)$. Then we know that $\delta > 0$. Intuitively, we know that a small move to the right will increase the value of f. It may have to be a very small move, as in Figure 3 below, if x is close to the top of the hill. A move to z will lower the value of f, but a sufficiently small move to the right, such as the one taking us to x', will increase f. Here is the formal argument: The limit of

$$\frac{f(x + \epsilon) - f(x)}{\epsilon}$$

is δ. For $\epsilon > 0$ sufficiently close to 0 we can get

$$\frac{f(x + \epsilon) - f(x)}{\epsilon}$$

close enough to δ to guarantee that the ratio is greater than $\frac{1}{2}\delta$. But then

$$f(x + \epsilon) - f(x) > \epsilon \times \tfrac{1}{2}\delta > 0.$$

This means that $f(x + \epsilon) - f(x) > 0$, or $f(x + \epsilon) > f(x)$. Then x does not yield the maximum value of f, because $f(x + \epsilon)$ is larger than $f(x)$.

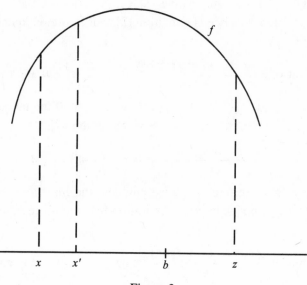

Figure 3

Now we want to show that f cannot have a maximum at x if $f'(x) < 0$. Let δ again represent $f'(x)$, with $\delta < 0$ this time. Intuitively we know that a small move to the *left* increases the value of f. It may have to be a very small move, as in Figure 4, if x is close to the top of the hill. A move to z will lower the value of f, but a sufficiently small move to the left, such as the one taking us to x', will increase f. Consider:

$$\text{The limit of } \frac{f(x + \epsilon) - f(x)}{\epsilon} = \delta.$$

For $\epsilon < 0$ sufficiently close to 0 we can get

$$\frac{f(x + \epsilon) - f(x)}{\epsilon}$$

close enough to δ to guarantee that the absolute value of the ratio is greater than $-\frac{1}{2}\delta$. Therefore,

$$\frac{f(x + \epsilon) - f(x)}{\epsilon} < \tfrac{1}{2}\delta$$

for ϵ sufficiently close to zero and negative. Now if we multiply this last inequality on both sides by $\epsilon < 0$ we change the sign, yielding

$$f(x + \epsilon) - f(x) > \epsilon \times \tfrac{1}{2}\delta > 0.$$

We have $\epsilon \times \tfrac{1}{2}\delta > 0$ because both ϵ and δ are negative. But then $f(x + \epsilon) - f(x) > 0$, or $f(x + \epsilon) > f(x)$. Then x does not yield the maximum value of f, because $f(x + \epsilon)$ is larger than $f(x)$. Therefore, if f is maximized at x we can rule out both $f'(x) > 0$ and $f'(x) < 0$.

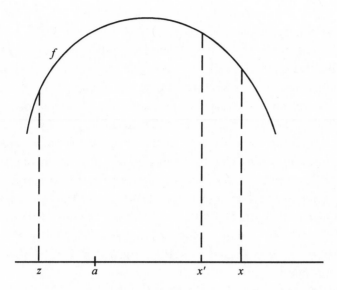

Figure 4

Let's look at an example: $f(x) = 10x - x^2 - 25$. We want to find the point at which f is maximized. Note that $f(x) = -(x - 5)^2$, which can never be positive. When $x = 5$ the value of the function is zero, so that is the point at which f reaches a maximum. Every other value of x will yield $f(x) < 0$. So we don't need calculus in this case. But let's see how calculus brings us to the same conclusion. We need to calculate the first derivative of f.

$$f(x + \epsilon) = 10(x + \epsilon) - (x + \epsilon)^2 - 25.$$
$$= 10x + 10\epsilon - x^2 - 2\epsilon x - \epsilon^2 - 25.$$

Therefore,

$$f(x + \epsilon) - f(x) = 10\epsilon - 2\epsilon x - \epsilon^2$$

and hence

$$\frac{f(x + \epsilon) - f(x)}{\epsilon} = \frac{10\epsilon - 2\epsilon x - \epsilon^2}{\epsilon}$$

and the right hand side of the last equation equals $10 - 2x - \epsilon$. Clearly, as ϵ approaches zero this approaches $10 - 2x$. Therefore, $10 - 2x$ is the first derivative of f. Formally, $f'(x) = 10 - 2x$. Now, we said that $f'(x) = 0$ is necessary for a maximum. Set $f'(x) = 0$ and solve for x: $10 - 2x = 0$, which yields $x = 5$.

Return to the general case. Suppose that we want to maximize f subject to the restriction $a \leq x \leq b$. Our first observation is that if we actually have $a < x^* < b$ at the point x^* where the constrained maximum is achieved, then $f'(x^*) = 0$ is still a necessary condition.[21] The proof of that fact is actually embedded in the discussion of the unconstrained case. If $f'(x) > 0$ then for $\epsilon > 0$ sufficiently close to zero we will have $[f(x + \epsilon) - f(x)]/\epsilon > 0$ and hence $f(x + \epsilon) > f(x)$. Check the above argument to confirm that we will have $[f(x + \epsilon) - f(x)]/\epsilon > 0$ if we make $\epsilon > 0$ smaller still. Therefore, if $f'(x) > 0$ and $x < b$ then we can find $\epsilon > 0$ small enough so that we get *both* $x + \epsilon < b$ and $f(x + \epsilon) > f(x)$. And we will certainly have $x + \epsilon \geq a$ if $x \geq a$. Therefore, if $a \leq x < b$ and $f'(x) > 0$ the function x cannot be maximized at x even if we are not allowed to consider values of the independent variable larger than b or smaller than a. Similarly, we can show that f cannot be maximized at x if $f'(x) < 0$ and $a < x \leq b$, even if we are not allowed to go below a or above b. (Figures 3 and 4 above illustrate this nicely.) We have proved the following: If x^* maximizes f subject to the constraint $a \leq x \leq b$ and $a < x^* < b$ actually holds, then we can't have $f'(x^*) > 0$ and we can't have $f'(x^*) < 0$. This means that $f'(x^*) = 0$ must hold. Be careful! There is nothing to guarantee that $a < x^* < b$ will actually hold at the solution value x^*, as we saw in the case $f(x) = 2x$, $a = 0$, and $b = 100$. But *if* $a < x^* < b$ *does* hold at the solution point then we must have $f'(x^*) = 0$.

Now, what if we do have $x^* = a$ or $x^* = b$ at the point x^* where f is maximized, subject to the constraint $a \leq x \leq b$? Calculus is still a big help here, but you have to know how to use it. In general, calculus is not a formula for cranking out an answer to a problem, but rather a useful device for finding the solution quickly.

We are going to confine attention to a special class of functions, but it is a family that arises most of the time in economics. We consider only functions for which the *second derivative* $f''(x)$ is negative at all values of x. By definition, f'' is the derivative of the derivative. For $f(x) = 10x - x^2 - 25$ we have $f'(x) = 10 - 2x$ and hence $f''(x) = -2$, which is negative. The second derivative tells us how the first derivative changes as x changes. If we always have $f''(x) < 0$ then $f'(x)$ gets smaller (algebraically) as x increases. This has two important implications. First, if $f'(x^*) = 0$ then there is no other value of x for which f' is zero: To the right of x^* the first derivative is negative. Why? Because $f'(x)$ falls as x increases and it is zero at x^*, so $f'(x) < 0$ for all $x > x^*$. Therefore, we cannot find any $x > x^*$ for which $f'(x) = 0$. Now, consider $x < x^*$. The first derivative decreases as we move to the right, so it increases as we move to the left. If f' is zero at x^* and it increases as we move to the left then $f'(x)$ is positive for all $x < x^*$. Therefore, we cannot have $f'(x) = 0$ for any $x < x^*$. In short, if f'' is negative at all points then there is at most one value of x for which f' is zero.

Here is the second important consequence of the fact that $f'' < 0$ at all points: If $f'(x^*) = 0$ we know that f' is positive to the left of x^* and f' is negative to the right of x^*. When f' is positive the value of the function f itself is increasing. We know that because $f'(x) > 0$ is just another way of saying that f is increasing at x. To the right of x^* we have $f'(x) < 0$ and hence the value of the f itself falls as x increases beyond x^*. This is a consequence of the fact that f' is negative to the right of x^* and $f'(x) < 0$ is just another way of saying that f is falling at x.

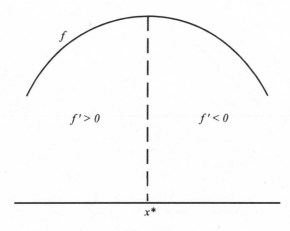

Figure 5

Now, let's summarize all this: Suppose f'' is negative everywhere and $f'(x^*) = 0$. Then f' is not equal to zero for any other value of x. Moreover, f falls as we move to the right of x^* and f rises as we move *toward* x^* from the left. This means that the graph of f is a hill with the peak at x^*, as in Figure 5. In other words, f has a unique maximum at x^*. Therefore, if we seek the value of x that maximizes f and $f'(x^*) = 0$ then $f(x^*) > f(x)$ for all $x \neq x^*$. Suppose, however, that we are restricted to the region $a \leq x \leq b$. If we find some x^* in that interval such that $f'(x^*) = 0$ then we are sure that is the unique solution to our problem. Why? Because $f'(x^*) = 0$ implies that $f(x^*) > f(x)$ for *all* other x and therefore we certainly have $f(x^*) > f(x)$ for all $x \neq x^*$ satisfying $a \leq x \leq b$. (*Caveat:* This all depends on $f'' < 0$ holding everywhere.) Suppose, however, that the value of x for which f' is zero is outside the interval $a \leq x \leq b$. Consider first the case $f'(x^*) = 0$ and $x^* > b$. We know that f is rising to the left of x^*. Therefore f is increasing at all x in the constraint region, because $a \leq x \leq b$ implies that x is to the left of x^*. Therefore, $f'(x^*) = 0$ and $x^* > b$ implies that $x = b$ is our solution: $f(b) > f(x)$ for all x satisfying $a \leq x < b$, as illustrated in Figure 6. Now suppose that $f'(x^*) = 0$ and $x^* < a$. Because $f'' < 0$ at every point, f is falling to the right of x^*. Therefore f is decreasing at all x in the constraint region, because $a \leq x \leq b$ implies that x is to the right of x^*. Therefore, $f'(x^*) = 0$ and $x^* < a$ implies that $x = a$ is our solution: $f(a) > f(x)$ for all x satisfying $a \leq x < b$, as illustrated in Figure 7.

Here is a simple consumer choice example to make all of this concrete.

$$\text{Maximize } U(x, y) = xy \qquad \text{subject to } 5x + 2y = 1000.$$

The utility of a basket with x units of commodity X and y units of commodity Y is the product of the two numbers x and y. (It may help at this point to draw a typical indifference curve; say, the set of baskets that yield a utility of 12.) The price of

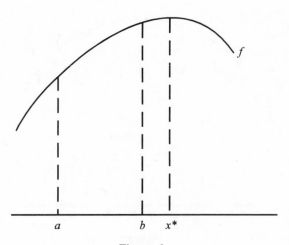

Figure 6

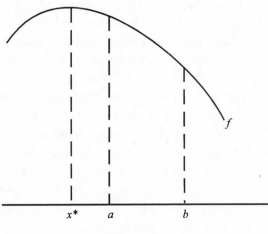

Figure 7

good X is 5 and the price of good Y is 2. Income is 1000. Solving the budget constraint for y yields

$$y = 1000/2 - 5x/2 = 500 - 2.5x.$$

Now, substitute this value of y into the utility function. We want to maximize

$$V = (x)(500 - 2.5x) \qquad \text{subject to } 0 \le x \le 200.$$

(Verify that all income will be spent on X if $x = 200$.) Now, utility is zero when x or y is zero. That is, $U = xy = 0$ if $x = 0$ or $y = 0$. Even a tiny amount of money spent on each good will yield a positive product xy, so we know that the consumer can do better than zero utility. Therefore, the utility maximizing basket will have $x > 0$ and $y > 0$. But if y is positive we can't have $x = 200$; we must have $x < 200$. Therefore, the solution value x^* will have to satisfy $0 < x^* < 200$. We know that in this case we must have $V'(x^*) = 0$.

$$V(x) = 500x - 2.5x^2, \quad \text{hence} \quad V'(x) = 500 - 5x.$$

Then $V'(x) = 0$ yields $500 - 5x = 0$ and thus $x^* = 100$. There is only one value of x that gives $V' = 0$. The solution to the consumer choice problem *must* have $V' = 0$. Therefore, there can be only one utility maximizing value of x, namely $x = 100$. Now we can use the budget constraint to solve for y.

$$y = 500 - 2.5x = 500 - 2.5(100) = 500 - 250 = 250.$$

Therefore, the chosen basket has $x = 100$ and $y = 250$.

We can use the same technique to solve for the *demand functions*. We have the same consumer in mind, so $U(x, y) = xy$, which we maximize, subject to the budget constraint

$$P_1 x + P_2 y = \Omega,$$

where prices and income are parameters. We will solve for the demands x and y as a function of prices and income. Then $y = \Omega/P_2 - P_1 x/P_2$, and we substitute this into the utility function.

$$V = (x)(\Omega/P_2 - P_1 x/P_2).$$

Again, utility is zero if x or y is zero, so we will have $x > 0$ and $y > 0$ if (x, y) is the utility maximizing basket. Therefore, the solution value x^* will have to satisfy $0 < x^* < \Omega/P_1$, and hence $V'(x^*) = 0$. $V = \Omega x/P_2 - P_1 x^2/P_2$ so $V'(x) = \Omega/P_2 - 2P_1 x/P_2$. If $V'(x) = 0$ then

$$\Omega/P_2 - 2P_1 x/P_2 = 0, \quad \text{so} \quad x = \Omega/2P_1.$$

This is the only value of x that gives $V' = 0$, so the consumer choice problem has a unique solution $x = \Omega/2P_1$. From the budget constraint, $y = \Omega/P_2 - P_1 x/P_2$, or

$$y = \Omega/P_2 - P_1 [\Omega/2P_1]/P_2 = \Omega/2P_2.$$

Therefore, $x = \Omega/2P_1$ and $y = \Omega/2P_2$ at the chosen basket. These are the demand functions. If we are given particular values for prices and income we can plug them into the demand functions to get the *amounts* demanded at that price and income regime. (Verify that $x = 100$ and $y = 250$ when $P_1 = 5$, $P_2 = 2$, and $\Omega = 1000$.) Note that we have $V''(x) < 0$ for all x when V is derived from the utility function $U = xy$ by solving the budget constraint for y and substituting. But we don't really need to use that information because $U(x, y) = xy = 0$ if x or y is zero. This tells us that $0 < x < \Omega/P_1$ will hold at the value of x that maximizes V subject to $0 \le x \le \Omega/P_1$. Therefore, the solution to the consumer decision problem must satisfy $V'(x) = 0$ and there is only one such value of x for the example that we have been working with. The next example is one for which $x >$ 0 and $y > 0$ cannot be deduced at the outset.

This time $U(x, y) = (x + 5)(y + 2)$, which we maximize subject to $Px + y = \Omega$, $x \geq 0$, and $y \geq 0$. We fix P_2 at 1 and set $P = P_1$ to streamline the computations. $y = \Omega - Px$, and substituting this into the utility function yields

$$V(x) = (x + 5)(\Omega - Px + 2) = (\Omega + 2 - 5P)x - Px^2 + 5\Omega + 10.$$

$V'(x) = \Omega + 2 - 5P - 2Px$. Then $V''(x) = -2P$, which is always negative. Therefore, if $V'(x) = 0$ yields a unique value of x satisfying $0 \leq x \leq \Omega/P$ this will be the demand for x. $\Omega + 2 - 5P - 2Px = 0$ implies $x = \frac{1}{2}(\Omega + 2 - 5P)/P$. If $P = 1$ and $\Omega = 100$ then $x = 97/2 = 48.5$, which certainly satisfies $0 \leq x \leq 100$. (How much Y will be demanded in that case?) If $P = 25$ and $\Omega = 100$ then $V'(x) = 0$ implies $x = -0.46$, which is inadmissible. The consumer will demand $x = 0$ units of X and 100 units of Y when $P_1 = 25$, $P_2 = 1$, and $\Omega = 100$. (Can you prove this?)

Finally, we consider an example for which $V''(x) < 0$ does not hold for all x. Calculus will still give us enough information to locate the solution, but we have to be creative in using it. We can't be creative if we merely think of calculus as a collection of rules and formulas. This very powerful tool is much more efficacious if we have a good intuitive understanding of the information conveyed by derivatives.

Here is our new consumer choice problem:

$$\text{Maximize } U(x, y) = x^2y \qquad \text{subject to } 5x + 2y = 60.$$

From the budget equation we have $y = 30 - 5x/2$. Substitute this for y in the utility function to obtain

$$V = x^2[30 - 5x/2] = 30x^2 - 2.5x^3.$$

We want to maximize this function of x subject to $0 \leq x \leq 60/5$. $V'(x) = 60x - 7.5x^2$ and $V''(x) = 60 - 15x$. Setting the first derivative equal to zero yields $x = 0$ or

$$60 - 7.5x = 0 \quad \text{which implies} \quad x = 8.$$

Because the second derivative is not negative for all values of x we'd better confirm that $x = 8$ does identify a maximum. The only other point where a maximum could be achieved is at a boundary point. There are two of these: $x = 0$ and $x = 12$. (In the first case all income is spent on Y, and in the second case all income is spent on X.) But $30x^2 - 5x^3/2$ is zero when $x = 0$ or $x = 12$. Therefore, $x = 8$ is the optimal value of x, and the budget constraint yields $y = 10$.

You will probably have encountered other techniques for generating the demands. For your peace of mind, we will apply each of them to the problem "maximize $U(x, y) = x^2y$ subject to $5x + 2y = 60$" to confirm that they yield the same solutions.

9.1 The tangency approach

Notice that utility is zero if either $x = 0$ or $y = 0$. Because utility is positive if x and y are both positive, however small, we have an interior solution. The economic argument based on indifference curves reveals that the marginal rate of substitution (MRS) equals the price ratio at an interior solution. The partial derivative of U with respect to x is $2xy$ (treat y as a constant and take the derivative of U with respect to x), and the partial derivative of U with respect to y is x^2 (treat x as a constant and take the derivative of U with respect to y). Therefore, the MRS, which is the ratio of partial derivatives,[22] or marginal utilities, is $2xy/x^2$, which equals $2y/x$. The price ratio is $5/2$. Therefore, the solution will satisfy $2y/x = 5/2$ or $4y = 5x$. This equation does not have a unique solution, nor should we expect one. We can't pin down the choice without the budget equation. Substituting $4y$ for $5x$ in the budget equation yields $4y + 2y = 60$, which yields $y = 10$. Then $4y = 40 = 5x$ and hence $x = 8$. (Verify that $x = 8$ and $y = 10$ satisfies the budget equation and equates MRS and the price ratio.)

9.2 The total derivative and the chain rule

We have $y = 30 - 5x/2$ from the budget constraint. In general, $U(x, y)$ depends on x and y. Let U_x denote the partial derivative of U with respect to x and let U_y denote the partial derivative of U with respect to y. If we think of y as a function of x, then the total derivative of U with respect to x is

$$\frac{dU}{dx} = U_x \frac{dx}{dx} + U_y \frac{dy}{dx}.$$

We have $U_x = 2xy$, $U_y = x^2$, $dx/dx = 1$, and, from the budget constraint, $dy/dx = -2.5$. Therefore, $dU/dx = 2xy - 2.5x^2$. Now, set this equal to zero to find a maximum:

$$2xy - 2.5x^2 = 0.$$

Dividing through by x (do we have to worry about dividing by zero?) yields

$$2y - 2.5x = 0 \quad \text{or} \quad 4y = 5x.$$

Substituting $4y$ for $5x$ in the budget equation yields $y = 10$, and thus $x = 8$.

9.3 The Lagrangian multiplier

With $Z = x^2y - \alpha[5x + 2y - 60]$ let Z_x denote the partial derivative of Z with respect to x and let Z_y denote the partial derivative of Z with respect to y. Setting the first partials equal to zero yields

$$Z_x = 2xy - 5\alpha = 0 \quad \text{and}$$
$$Z_y = x^2 - 2\alpha = 0.$$

The first equation yields $\alpha = 2xy/5$ and substituting this value of α into the second equation leads to

$$x^2 - 2[2xy/5] = 0, \quad \text{or} \quad 5x = 4y$$

after dividing both sides by x, assuming an interior solution. Of course the last equation along with the budget equation yields $x = 8$ and $y = 10$.

Now, substitute the solution values of x and y into the equation $Z_x = 0$ to solve for α. We get $2(8)(10) - 5\alpha = 0$ and hence $\alpha = 32$. To interpret α write the budget equation with income, Ω, as a variable:

$$5x + 2y = \Omega.$$

Solve once more for the consumer's chosen basket. We still get $5x = 4y$ whatever solution technique is employed. Substituting into the budget equation yields $4y + 2y = \Omega$, or $y = \Omega/6$. Because $4y = 5x$ we have $5x = 4\Omega/6$, or $x = 4\Omega/30$. This gives us the demands as a function of income: $x = 4\Omega/30$ and $y = \Omega/6$, given $P_1 = 5$ and $P_2 = 2$. Now, substitute these demands into the utility function. We get a utility level of

$$F = [4\Omega/30]^2[\Omega/6] = 16\Omega^3/5400.$$

Then $dF/d\Omega = 3(16)\Omega^2/5400 = 8\Omega^2/900$. When $\Omega = 60$ this yields $dF/d\Omega = 32 = \alpha$. This is a general phenomenon. The Lagrangian multiplier always gives the increase in utility per unit increase in income.

9.4 Remark on planning and Lagrangians

Suppose that U is a social planner's utility function, representing the social value of output in the economy, and the equation $5x + 2y = 60$ represents a resource constraint on the capacity of the economy to produce x and y. In practice, there would be many variables and many production constraints. This means that the Lagrangian technique would be by far the best route to a solution. But, as section 9.3 demonstrated, once the social planner starts using Lagrangians she is using prices. The Lagrangian is the marginal value of an additional unit of the scarce resource that gives rise to the constraint. (This is explained more thoroughly in section 2 of Chapter 8.) How are prices used in a market system? Their role is to signal marginal values to the agents in the economy.

Exercises

1   Solve for the demand functions of a consumer whose preferences can be represented by the utility function $U(x, y) = x^\lambda y^\beta$, where λ and β are positive constants.

2   Solve for the demand functions of a consumer whose preferences can be represented by the utility function $U(x, y) = (x + 1)y$.

3   Solve for the demand functions of a consumer whose preferences can be represented by the utility function $U(x, y) = \sqrt{x} + y$.

4   We are going to investigate Lagrangians, but to keep things simple we'll consider a problem with only one constraint. Consider the standard consumer choice problem:

   Maximize $U(x, y) \equiv xy$ subject to $x + 4y = 24$.

Of course, U is the utility function. Utility depends on the amounts x and y consumed of the two goods. The price of X is $1 and the price of Y is $4. Income is $24. The constraint is the budget line.

a Draw the indifference curves – reasonably accurately – through the baskets (4, 3) and (4, 5). (*Note:* (4, 3) is the basket with $x = 4$ and $y = 3$.)

b Use calculus to find the basket that maximizes utility subject to the budget constraint. To turn this into a one-variable problem, first solve the budget constraint for y as a function of x, and then substitute this expression for y into the utility function.

c Let $g(x, y) = x + 4y$ represent the left hand side of the budget constraint. Compute the following four partial derivatives:

$$\frac{\partial U(x, y)}{\partial x} \qquad \frac{\partial U(x, y)}{\partial y} \qquad \frac{\partial g(x, y)}{\partial x} \qquad \frac{\partial g(x, y)}{\partial y}.$$

Remember: The partial derivative of f with respect to x, denoted by $\partial f/\partial x$, is obtained by treating y as a constant. Therefore, if $f(x, y) = x^2 + yx + y^2$ then $\partial f/\partial x = 2x + y$. Similarly, the partial derivative of f with respect to y, denoted by $\partial f/\partial y$, is obtained by treating x as a constant.

   Now, evaluate these partial derivatives at the chosen basket. (If $f(x, y) = x^2 + yx + y^2$ then $\partial f/\partial x$ evaluated at (4, 3) is $2 \times 4 + 3 = 11$.) Find a positive number α such that

$$\frac{\partial U(x^\circ, y^\circ)}{\partial x} = \alpha \times \frac{\partial g(x^\circ, y^\circ)}{\partial x} \quad \text{and} \quad \frac{\partial U(x^\circ, y^\circ)}{\partial y} = \alpha \times \frac{\partial g(x^\circ, y^\circ)}{\partial y}$$

   where (x°, y°) represents the chosen basket from (b).

d Now solve this problem:

   Maximize $U(x, y) \equiv xy$ subject to $x + 4y = \Omega$.

Note that we have just replaced income in the budget constraint with the variable Ω. The chosen basket (x°, y°) will now be a function of Ω. Now substitute x° and y° into the utility function $U = xy$ to get utility as a function of Ω. Now, take the derivative of this function (with respect to

Ω) and evaluate it at $\Omega = 24$. The number that you get will equal the value of α from part c.

10 The composite commodity theorem

This section explains why a two-commodity model can be quite useful. X is a conventional commodity, which we also refer to as the $0th$ good, and good Y is the total amount of money spent on the n goods other than X. Y is called a composite commodity. The composite commodity theorem was discovered independently by Hicks (1939) and Leontief (1936). We begin with an informal exposition.

10.1 Sketch of the proof

To justify a model with only two goods we must *begin* with a complete model with $n + 1$ commodities. Let x denote the amount of commodity X. Assuming for a moment that all prices are constant, let y denote an amount of money allotted to expenditure on all goods other than X. Given x, the consumer can determine the basket A of other goods that maximizes his utility subject to the constraint that expenditure on these other goods must not exceed y dollars and the consumption of X must equal x. This basket A along with x defines a specific overall basket which yields a specific level of utility which represents the level of utility derived from consuming the two 'goods' x and y.

What we have done is split the consumer's decision problem into two stages. Stage 1 involves an arbitrary determination of the level x of good X consumed and this determines the amount of money y available for expenditure on other goods: The number y is just the consumer's income less expenditure on X. And expenditure on X is just the price of X multiplied by the quantity x. If it helps, you can think of x as the consumer's first round guess at the utility maximizing level of consumption of X. The real decision problem in stage 1 is the determination of the basket A of goods other than X that maximizes utility subject to the constraint that expenditure on these other goods must not exceed y dollars and the consumption of X must equal x. This defines a comprehensive basket that comprises x and A and provides a specific utility level U. Now, stage 2 requires the individual to choose x and y so as to maximize U subject to the budget constraint $px + y =$ income, where p is the price of x. (The price of the *composite commodity* y is \$1 because a dollar's worth of expenditure costs \$1.) The solution values of x and y have the property that for some basket A costing exactly y dollars, the comprehensive basket (x, A) is the consumer's chosen basket for the true $n + 1$−commodity decision problem. Knowledge of x and y doesn't permit us to recover A, so we lose some information. But we are able to derive the optimal value of x, and very often that is our only goal. And it is a great advantage to be able to do so in a simple two-commodity model.

I do not claim to have described how households actually determine their consumption plans. The argument does provide a foundation of highlighting a single good X without having to deal with a large number of other goods, even though many of these other goods play an important role – through prices as well as preferences – in the determination of the utility maximizing amount of X. The other goods are collapsed into a single composite commodity. The role of individual preferences (over all goods) has been fully captured because the level of expenditure y on other goods implies a utility maximizing assortment A of these other goods, given x and the expenditure y on other goods. And A depends critically on the individual's preferences.

The two-stage problem yields the same utility maximizing value of X that we would get from a direct computation of the individual's optimal consumption plan, given prices and income. To help you grasp this point let's be explicit about the composition of the basket A. A is a basket of n goods, commodities 1, 2, 3, ..., n. Let z_c be the amount of commodity c in basket A. Of course, z_c may be zero for many of the c. Let u be the utility derived from the overall basket containing x units of X, which is commodity 0, and the z_c units of commodity c, for $c = 1, 2, 3, ..., n$. The diagram

$$x, z_1, z_2, z_3, ..., z_n \rightarrow u$$

expresses this relationship. If the price of X is P_x then the cost of A is the individual's income minus $P_x \times x$, which we can call y. Notice that y does not depend on the values of the z_c, but only on income, the price of X, and the amount of X consumed. If x is held constant and the consumer adjusts the values of the z_c so as to maximize u subject to the restriction that expenditure on goods 1 through n cannot exceed y dollars then, as the diagram indicates, this will result in the realization of specific values of the z_c and a particular utility level u. Let U represent that utility level. This suggests a new diagram:

$$x, y \rightarrow U.$$

That is, x units of commodity X and y dollars spent on the n other goods yields a utility of U, if it is implicit that the y dollars are allocated to goods 1 through n in a way that maximizes u subject to the restriction that expenditure on goods 1 through n cannot exceed y dollars, and that exactly x units of commodity X are consumed. Now, if the consumer chooses the values of x and y so as to maximize U subject to the stage 2 budget constraint

$$[P_x \times x] + y = \text{income}$$

the solution will provide the same level of x as the basic consumer choice problem of maximizing the function u of the $n + 1$ commodities subject to the restriction that expenditure on these goods cannot exceed income. Of course, we lose information when we represent the consumer's decision in this way: We only keep track of the utility maximizing amount of good X. We will have determined the *expenditure* on the n other goods but not the amount consumed of goods 1 through n. But this model will be very useful if we only want the value of x because we only have to work with two variables x and y, and not $n + 1$ variables. (In any real-world economy $n + 1$ will be a very large number.)

Is there a simpler justification of the two-commodity model? How about putting the spotlight on two conventional goods x and y and then holding the consumption levels of all other goods Z constant? Then $U(x, y) = u(x, y, z_1^\circ, z_2^\circ, z_3^\circ, ...)$ with the $z_1^\circ, z_2^\circ, z_3^\circ, ...$ treated as constants. And $U(x, y)$ will allow us to derive indifference curves for the goods X and Y. However, if the price of X or Y changes, or if income changes, the values of one or more of the $z_1^\circ, z_2^\circ, z_3^\circ$ will change. But when that happens we have to use a different utility function, $U^1(x, y) = u(x, y, z_1^1, z_2^1, z_3^1, ...)$. So, assuming constant consumption levels for all but two commodities will not work for most purposes. Now, we turn to a rigorous derivation of the two-commodity model.

10.2 Formal proof

Here is a rigorous proof that the two-stage problem yields the same utility-maximizing value of X that we would get from a direct computation of the individual's optimal consumption plan, given prices and income.

There are $n + 1$ goods. Let x_c denote the amount of commodity c consumed, for $c = 0, 1, 2, ..., n$. It is not necessary to consider more than one consumer at this point, so there is no need for a subscript identifying the individual. Let $u(x_0, x_1, ..., x_n)$ represent the individual's utility function and let p_c represent the price of commodity c. The *basic problem* (Problem B) is the following:

Problem B Find the values $x_0, x_1, x_2, ..., x_n$ that maximize $u(x_0, x_1, x_2, ..., x_n)$ subject to $p_0 x_0 + p_1 x_1 + p_2 x_2 + ... + p_n x_n \leq \Omega$.

Of course, Ω is the consumer's income. As we have seen, this problem is closely related to the *contrived problem* (Problem C), which we set up as follows. Assume that all prices are constant and let y denote an amount of money allotted to expenditure on goods 1 through n. Given (for a moment) z_0, the level of consumption of good zero, the maximum utility available from y can be denoted $U(z_0, y)$. Specifically:

> $U(z_0, y)$ is the maximum value of $u(x_0, x_1, x_2, ..., x_n)$ as the $x_0, x_1, x_2, ..., x_n$ vary, subject only to the restrictions $x_0 = z_0$ and $p_1 x_1 + p_2 x_2 + ... + p_n x_n \leq y$.

This defines the function U. Now, given an income level Ω and the price p_0 of x_0 we can specify the contrived problem:

Problem C Choose α and β to maximize $U(\alpha, \beta)$ subject to $p_0\alpha + \beta \leq \Omega$.

The solutions to Problems B and C are related the following way:

> If $(z_0, z_1, z_2, ..., z_n)$ is a solution to Problem B then $\alpha = z_0$ and $\beta = p_1z_1 + p_2z_2 + ... = p_nz_n$ comprise a solution to Problem C. And if (α, β) is a solution to Problem C there is some solution $(z_0, z_1, z_2, ..., z_n)$ to Problem B such that $z_0 = \alpha$ and $p_1z_1 + p_2z_2 + ... + p_nz_n = \beta$. Moreover, for any solutions $(z_0, z_1, z_2, ..., z_n)$ and (α, β) to the respective Problems B and C we have $u(z_0, z_1, z_2, ..., z_n) = U(\alpha, \beta)$.

Proof First, suppose that $(z_0, z_1, z_2, ..., z_n)$ is any solution to Problem B. Set $\alpha^* = z_0$ and $\beta^* = p_1z_1 + p_2z_2 + ... + p_nz_n$. We have $U(\alpha^*, \beta^*) \geq u(z_0, z_1, z_2, ..., z_n)$ by definition of U, because $\alpha^* = z_0$ and $p_1z_1 + p_2z_2 + ... p_nz_n \leq \beta^*$ certainly hold. Clearly, $p_0z_0 + \beta^* \leq \Omega$ holds. Therefore, (α^*, β^*) satisfies the constraints of Problem C. Then $U(\alpha, \beta) \geq U(\alpha^*, \beta^*)$ if (α, β) maximizes U subject to the constraint of Problem C. By definition of U, there is some $(x_0, x_1, x_2, ..., x_n)$ such that

$$U(\alpha, \beta) = u(x_0, x_1, x_2, ..., x_n), \text{ with } x_0 = \alpha \quad \text{and}$$
$$p_1x_1 + p_2x_2 + ... p_nx_n \leq \beta.$$

But $p_0x_0 + p_1x_1 + p_2x_2 + ... p_nx_n \leq p_0\alpha + \beta \leq \Omega$. This means that $(x_0, x_1, x_2, ..., x_n)$ is feasible for Problem B. Therefore,

$$u(z_0, z_1, z_2, ..., z_n) \geq u(x_0, x_1, x_2, ... x_n)$$

because $(z_0, z_1, z_2, ..., z_n)$ gives the maximum value of u subject to the feasibility constraints. We have proved the following:

$$u(z_0, z_1, z_2, ..., z_n) \geq u(x_0, x_1, x_2, ..., x_n) =$$
$$U(\alpha, \beta) \geq U(\alpha^*, \beta^*) \geq u(z_0, z_1, z_2, ..., z_n).$$

This can only hold if all of the inequalities are satisfied as *equalities*. Then $U(\alpha^*, \beta^*) = U(\alpha, \beta)$. Note that (α, β) is the name we have given to an arbitrary solution to Problem C, and (α^*, β^*) satisfies the constraint of Problem C. Therefore, (α^*, β^*) is also a solution to problem C. We have thus proved the first part of our claim. We have also proved the last part, because we have shown that $u(z_0, z_1, z_2, ..., z_n) = U(\alpha, \beta)$ holds for any two solutions $(z_0, z_1, z_2, ..., z_n)$ and (α, β) of the respective problems. It remains to show that if (α, β) is a solution to Problem C then there is some solution $(z_0, z_1, z_2, ..., z_n)$ to Problem B such that $z_0 = \alpha$ and $p_1z_1 + p_2z_2 + ... + p_nz_n = \beta$.

Suppose that (α, β) is a solution to Problem C. By definition of U there is some $(z_0, z_1, z_2, ..., z_n)$ such that $\alpha = z_0$, $\beta \geq p_1z_1 + p_2z_2 + ... + p_nz_n$, and

$$u(z_0, z_1, z_2, \ldots, z_n) \geq u(x_0, x_1, x_2, \ldots, x_n)$$

for all $(x_0, x_1, x_2, \ldots, x_n)$ such that $x_0 = \alpha$ and $p_1 x_1 + p_2 x_2 + \ldots p_n x_n \leq \beta$. Because (α, β) satisfies the constraint of Problem C we have

$$p_0 z_0 + p_1 z_1 + p_2 z_2 + \ldots p_n z_n \leq p_0 \alpha + \beta \leq \Omega$$

and hence $(z_0, z_1, z_2, \ldots, z_n)$ satisfies the constraint of Problem B. Now show that $(z_0, z_1, z_2, \ldots, z_n)$ is a solution to Problem B. Let $(x_0, x_1, x_2, \ldots, x_n)$ be any plan satisfying the constraints of Problem B. Set $\alpha^* = x_0$ and $\beta^* = p_1 x_1 + p_2 x_2 + \ldots + p_n x_n$. Then

$$p_0 \alpha^* + \beta^* = p_0 x_0 + p_1 x_1 + p_2 x_2 + \ldots + p_n x_n \leq \Omega.$$

Therefore,

$$u(x_0, x_1, x_2, \ldots, x_n) \leq U(\alpha^*, \beta^*)$$

by definition of U. We have $p_0 \alpha^* + \beta^* \leq \Omega$, and therefore $U(\alpha^*, \beta^*) \leq U(\alpha, \beta)$, because (α, β) solves Problem C and (α^*, β^*) is feasible for C. Therefore, we have proved the following:

$$u(x_0, x_1, x_2, \ldots, x_n) \leq U(\alpha^*, \beta^*) \leq U(\alpha, \beta) \leq u(z_0, z_1, z_2, \ldots, z_n).$$

Therefore, $u(x_0, x_1, x_2, \ldots, x_n) \leq u(z_0, z_1, z_2, \ldots, z_n)$ for any values $x_0, x_1, x_2, \ldots,$ x_n that satisfy the constraint for Problem B. This proves that $(z_0, z_1, z_2, \ldots, z_n)$ is a solution to Problem B.

11 Quasi-linear preferences

Having simplified things by reducing the number of commodities to two, we now show how a simple family of utility functions can be used to bring additional clarity. Suppose the individual has utility function $U(x, y)$ with the special form

$$B(x) + y$$

with $B'(x) > 0$ and $B''(x) < 0$ for all $x \geq 0$. This function is linear in y but not necessarily in x. Quasi-linear preferences are very nice to work with, and we will use them to uncover basic principles at relatively low cost. One of the advantages is that efficiency is equivalent to maximization of the sum of individual utilities (subject to the limitations inherent in resource constraints, etc.). We begin by proving this.

11.1 Efficiency with quasi-linear preferences

There is a set N of n individuals indexed by $i = 1, 2, \ldots, n$. There are two goods X and Y; an allocation (x, y) determines the amount x_i and y_i of the respective goods consumed by each i in N. Each individual i has the quasi-linear utility function

$$U_i(x_1, x_2, \ldots, x_n, y_i) = B_i(x_1, x_2, \ldots, x_n) + y_i.$$

Note that an individual's utility depends only on his own consumption of Y, but may depend on the amount of X assigned to other consumers. If it is the case that B_i depends only on x_i, then we have the pure private goods model. The pure public goods model corresponds to the special case for which B_i depends on $\Sigma_{h \in N} x_h$, with $B_i(x_1, x_2, \ldots, x_n) = B_i(a_1, a_2, \ldots, a_n)$ whenever $\Sigma_{h \in N} x_h = \Sigma_{h \in N} a_h$.

For the rest of this section we will let x represent the assignment $(x_1, x_2, \ldots, x_n)$. Let $(\tilde{x}, \tilde{y})$ be a feasible allocation. Suppose that there is another feasible allocation (x, y) such that

$$\sum_{i \in N} [B_i(x) + y_i] > \sum_{i \in N} [B_i(\tilde{x}) + \tilde{y}_i]. \qquad [1]$$

That is, $(\tilde{x}, \tilde{y})$ does not maximize the sum of individual utilities. Define a new allocation $(x°, y°)$ such that $x_i° = x_i$ for all i in N, and

$$y_i° = B_i(\tilde{x}) + \tilde{y}_i - B_i(x) + (1/n) \sum_{h \in N} [B_h(x) + y_h - B_h(\tilde{x}) - \tilde{y}_h].$$

Verify that $\Sigma_{i \in N} y_i° = \Sigma_{i \in N} y_i$. This means that $(x°, y°)$ is feasible, because $(x°, y°)$ assigns the same X consumption to individuals as (x, y), while the total amount of good Y is the same under $(x°, y°)$ and (x, y) – it is just redistributed. But for each i in N

$$B_i(x°) + y_i° = B_i(\tilde{x}) + \tilde{y}_i + \text{a positive number.}$$

The positive number is $(1/n) \Sigma_{h \in N} [B_h(x) + y_h - B_h(\tilde{x}) - \tilde{y}_h]$, which is positive by inequality [1]. Therefore, there is a feasible allocation that gives everyone more utility than $(\tilde{x}, \tilde{y})$. Therefore, $(\tilde{x}, \tilde{y})$ is not efficient. This argument depends on the divisibility of Y – think of Y as money – but X could be available only in discrete units, although the argument applies equally well when X is divisible. The argument above is valid as long as the redistribution does not require anyone to consume a negative amount of good Y.

Now, suppose that outcome σ maximizes the sum of individual utilities. Therefore, $\Sigma_{i \in N} U_i(\sigma') \leq \Sigma_{i \in N} U_i(\sigma)$ for every feasible outcome σ'. This rules out the possibility that σ' gives one person more utility than σ without giving someone else less utility. Therefore, σ is efficient. We can claim the following: *Assuming that everyone's utility function is quasi-linear,* a feasible outcome is efficient if and only if it maximizes the sum of individual utilities over the set of feasible outcomes.[23] Now we turn to individual choice and quasi-linear preference.

11.2 Quasi-linear preference and demand

We now focus on a single individual, so we can drop the subscript i. We prove the following two statements: (1) Beyond a minimum income level, all additional income will be allocated to consumption of Y. In other words, there is no income effect on the demand for X beyond a certain point. (2) The function B, and hence true consumer's surplus, can be obtained directly from the demand function for X. Before presenting a general proof we illustrate these points with a simple example.

Set $U(x, y) = \ln(x + 1) + y$. Now maximize utility subject to $P_1 x + P_2 y = \Omega$. (If y is a composite commodity set $P_2 = 1$.) Because the budget constraint implies $y = (\Omega - P_1 x)/P_2$ we can maximize $V(x) = \ln(x + 1) + (\Omega - P_1 x)/P_2$ subject to $0 \le x \le \Omega/P_1$. The first derivative is $(x + 1)^{-1} - P_1/P_2$ and the second derivative is $-(x + 1)^{-2}$, which is always negative. Therefore, if x^* maximizes V when the constraint on x is ignored and we get $0 < x^* < \Omega/P_1$ then we will have $(x^* + 1)^{-1} - P_1/P_2 = 0$, which implies $x^* = P_2/P_1 - 1$. If $P_2/P_1 - 1 < 0$ or $P_2/P_1 - 1 > \Omega/P_1$ we know that $P_2/P_1 - 1$ cannot be the demand for X: the consumer will demand either zero or Ω/P_1 units. (If $0 < x < \Omega/P_1$ at the solution value of x then the first derivative $(x + 1)^{-1} - P_1/P_2$ must equal zero. See section 9.) That is, there will be a corner solution, with either $x = 0$ and $y = \Omega/P_2$ or $x = \Omega/P_1$ and $y = 0$. But which corner will provide the solution? Let $B(x) = \ln(x + 1)$. Suppose that $P_2/P_1 - 1 > \Omega/P_1$, or equivalently, $\Omega < P_2 - P_1$. Then P_1 must be less than P_2. But $B'(0) = 1$ so for a small increase in the consumption of X, from 0 to dx, the increase in B is approximately dx while the reduction in Y is $P_1 \, dx /P_2$. The change in utility is very close to $dU = dx - P_1 \, dx /P_2$ which is positive for $P_1/P_2 < 1$. Therefore, $x = 0$ cannot maximize utility subject to the budget constraint if $\Omega < P_2 - P_1$. The maximum must occur at $x = \Omega/P_1$ because the first order condition implies $x > \Omega/P_1$. (If a maximum does not satisfy the first order condition then the maximum must occur at a boundary point and we have just ruled out the boundary $x = 0$.) Of course, the tip-off that $x = \Omega/P_1$ is the solution is that $V'(x) = 0$ implies $x > \Omega/P_1$. If the mathematics tells us to set x above Ω/P_1, the maximum amount of the good our consumer could buy, then it's a good bet that setting $x = \Omega/P_1$ solves the consumer decision problem. We don't have to gamble, however; we can *prove* that $x = \Omega/P_1$ is the solution.

Now, consider the case where the first order condition implies $x < 0$. That is, $P_2/P_1 - 1 < 0$, or $P_1/P_2 > 1$. Again $B'(0) = 1$ and $B'' < 0$ so $B'(\Omega/P_1) < 1$. This time take $dx < 0$ and reduce x from Ω/P_1 to $\Omega/P_1 + dx$. This will release $-P_1 \, dx$ dollars for expenditure on Y and the change in utility will be approximately $dU = B'(\Omega/P_1)dx - P_1 \, dx /P_2$ which is greater than $dx - P_1 dx/P_2$ because $dx < 0$ and $B'(\Omega/P_1) < 1$. But $dx - P_1 dx/P_2 > 0$ so utility will increase: we cannot have $x = \Omega/P_1$. Then the solution must satisfy either the first order condition (which is impossible if $P_2/P_1 - 1 < 0$) or $x = 0$. Then we can now display the demand curve for x:

$$x(P_1, P_2, \Omega) = 0 \qquad\qquad \text{if } P_2/P_1 - 1 < 0.$$
$$x(P_1, P_2, \Omega) = P_2/P_1 - 1 \qquad \text{if } 1 \leq P_2/P_1 \leq 1 + \Omega/P_1.$$
$$x(P_1, P_2, \Omega) = \Omega/P_1 \qquad\quad \text{if } P_2/P_1 - 1 > \Omega/P_1.$$

By solving the budget constraint $P_1 x + P_2 y = \Omega$ for y we can obtain directly the demand function for y:

$$y(P_1, P_2, \Omega) = \Omega/P_2 \qquad\qquad\qquad \text{if } P_2/P_1 - 1 < 0.$$
$$y(P_1, P_2, \Omega) = (\Omega + P_1 - P_2)/P_2 \qquad \text{if } 1 \leq P_2/P_1 \leq 1 + \Omega/P_1.$$
$$y(P_1, P_2, \Omega) = 0 \qquad\qquad\qquad\qquad \text{if } P_2/P_1 - 1 > \Omega/P_1.$$

Fix P_1 and P_2 and allow Ω to vary. If P_1 is larger than P_2 then we have $x(P_1, P_2, \Omega)$ $= 0$ for all values of Ω. The income effect on the demand for X is zero. If $P_2/P_1 > 1 + \Omega/P_1$ then all income is spent on X and this continues to be the case as Ω rises until it reaches $P_2 - P_1$. At this point we have $x = \Omega/P_1 = (P_2 - P_1)/P_1 = P_2/P_1 - 1$. As Ω rises beyond $P_2 - P_1$ all additional income is spent on Y. Note that if $1 \leq P_2/P_1 \leq 1 + \Omega/P_1$ holds then it continues to hold as Ω rises. In summary, for $\Omega \geq P_2 - P_1$ or $P_1 > P_2$ we have $\partial x/\partial \Omega = 0$. There is an income effect on the demand for X only when $P_1 < P_2$ and even then only in the extreme case of incomes below $P_2 - P_1$ (or below $1 - P_1$ if Y is a composite commodity and $P_2 = 1$).

11.3 Consumer surplus

The demand curve can be used to recover the benefit derived from x. This time fix Ω and P_2. Assume that $B(0) = 0$ and that we are only interested in the range of prices of good X for which $x = P_2/P_1 - 1$. Solving for P_1 gives us the demand function, $P_1 = P_2/(x + 1)$, which is the algebraic version of the demand curve with the independent variable, price, on the vertical axis. Given $P_1 = P_2/(x + 1)$, the area under the demand curve between 0 and x is

$$\int_0^x P_2/(t + 1)\, dt,$$

which is $P_2 \ln(x + 1) - P_2 \ln 1 = P_2\ln(x + 1)$. ($\ln 1 = 0$.) Therefore, the area under the demand curve from 0 to x is $P_2 B(x)$, where x is the amount demanded at P_1. Let A denote this area: $A = P_2 B(x)$. Assume that Y is a composite commodity, so $P_2 = 1$ and $A = B(x)$. The individual spends $P_1 x$ dollars on the good when the price is P_1. The consumer's surplus at price P_1 is $B(x) - P_1 x$ because

$$U(x, \Omega - P_1 x) = U(0, \Omega - P_1 x + B(x)) \qquad\qquad [2]$$

for the quasi-linear utility function $U = B(x) + y$. Equation [2] holds for any value of the original income level Ω (as long as we stay on the demand curve where $x = 1/P_1 - 1$). In words, the consumer is indifferent between being able to purchase X at a price P_1 on the one hand, and receiving $B(x) - P_1 x$ units of additional income but consuming no X on the other hand. Therefore, $A - P_1 x$ is the true consumer's surplus.

Now consider the general case. Maximize $B(x) + y$ subject to $P_1 x + P_2 y = \Omega$ and $x \geq 0$, $y \geq 0$. Equivalently, maximize $B(x) + \Omega/P_2 - P_1 x/P_2$ subject to $0 \leq x \leq \Omega/P_1$. (Note that $y = \Omega/P_2 - P_1 x/P_2$ from the budget constraint.) The first order condition is $B'(x) - P_1/P_2 = 0$. There will be a unique x^* solving this equation (because $B'' < 0$). If $B'(0) < P_1/P_2$ the solution to the constrained utility maximization problem will be $x = 0$ and the inequality $B'(0) < P_1/P_2$ is unaffected by Ω: There is no income effect on the demand for X in this case. If $0 < x^* < \Omega/P_1$ then x^* must be the solution, because $B'(x) < B'(x^*) = P_1/P_2$ for $x > x^*$ and $B'(x) > B'(x^*) = P_1/P_2$ for $x < x^*$. There can be an income effect on the demand for X only if $B'(\Omega/P_1) > P_1/P_2$ and this inequality will fail for Ω large enough, because B' falls as x increases. Let Ω^* satisfy $B'(\Omega^*/P_1) = P_1/P_2$. For $\Omega > \Omega^*$ there is no income effect on the demand for X, and even when $\Omega \leq \Omega^*$ there is no income effect if $B'(0) < P_1/P_2$. But beyond a minimum income level Ω^* there is no income effect for sure.

Note that the marginal rate of substitution (MRS) is

$$\frac{(\partial U/\partial x)}{(\partial U/\partial y)} = B'(x)/1 = B'(x).$$

The MRS is independent of y so, with x on the horizontal axis, the MRS is constant along any vertical line in the plane. If we have a consumer optimum (x^*, y^*) that does not occur at a corner point of the budget region we will have MRS $= P_1/P_2$, and that can occur at only one point on the budget line. As income increases and the budget line shifts out parallel to itself the new optimum will also occur at a point where MRS $= P_1/P_2$, the same MRS. This can only happen on the vertical line through x^*: there is no change in the demand for X.

Let's compute the consumer's surplus. Taking the case $P_2 = 1$, $\Omega > \Omega^*$, and $B'(0) > P_1$ we fix the income level Ω. The first order condition is $B'(x) = P_1$ and this is also the demand function $P(x)$ for X with x on the horizontal axis and P_1 on the vertical axis. Assuming $B(0) = 0$ and using the fundamental theorem of calculus we have

$$B(x) = \int_0^x B'(t)dt = \int_0^x P(t)dt.$$

Again we see that the area under the demand curve is the utility derived from
X. The consumer pays $P_1 x$ for this, so $A - P_1 x$ is precisely the consumer's
surplus.[24]

We conclude this section by showing that the area under the *market* (or total)
demand curve is equal to the aggregate consumer surplus, and hence is equal to
the total utility realized by the community when each individual is able to purchase X at a price of P_1. But we cannot prove this unless we assume that each
individual i has a quasi-linear utility function $U_i = B_i(x_i) + y_i$, where x_i is
the amount of X consumed by household i and y_i is the amount of Y consumed by
i. The function B_i can be different for different individuals, hence the i subscript.

Before looking at the general result, consider a simple example. Suppose $B_i(x)$
$= \ln(x + 1)$ for each i. (The consumers are identical, so they will make identical
choices, and we don't need a subscript on x.) Y is a composite commodity whose
price is 1. Therefore, we can drop the subscript on price and just let P denote the
price of X. We know that the consumer surplus is equal to utility. Therefore, the
individual consumer surplus is

$$\ln(x + 1) - Px$$

when the price is P, which is the area below the demand curve and above the
horizontal line through P. There are n identical consumers. The total utility
derived from X when the price is P is the sum of the individual utilities. Because
each individual's change in utility is equal to individual consumer surplus, the
total change in utility (aggregate consumer surplus) is

$$n \ln(x + 1) - nPx. \qquad [3]$$

Now, let's look at the market functions. $x = P^{-1} - 1$ is individual demand, so
market demand is n times that. Let q denote the market (total) demand:

$$q = nP^{-1} - n \quad \text{and thus} \quad P = n(q + n)^{-1}.$$

The second equation is the inverse market demand function, which we want to
integrate to determine the area under the market 'demand curve' above the line
$\rho = P$: The area minus aggregate expenditure on X is

$$n \ln(q + n) - n \ln n - Pq \qquad [4]$$

But $n \ln(q + n) - n \ln n = n \ln(nx + n) - n \ln n = n \ln[nx + n)/n] = n \ln(x + 1)$.
Therefore, the aggregate consumer surplus equals the area under the demand
curve. ([3] and [4] yield the same numbers.)

Now, consider the general case. Individual consumer surplus is

$$\int_0^x P(t)\,dt, \qquad [5]$$

the area below demand curve and above the horizontal line through P. But we can also integrate along the vertical axis: The area under the individual demand curve is

$$\int_P^\infty x_i(\rho)d\rho, \qquad\qquad [6]$$

where x_i is consumer i's quantity demanded as a function of the price ρ. Total market demand q is the sum of the individual demands, so we can write $q(\rho) = \Sigma_i\, x_i(\rho)$. Therefore, the area under the market demand curve is the sum of the areas under the individual demand curves. And because the sum of the areas under the individual demand curves is equal to the total utility, we can say that total utility is exactly equal to the area under the market demand curve when each individual's utility function is quasi-linear.

12 Decision making under risk

Most of the models in this book either employ a framework in which there is no uncertainty or assume that there are only two possible random outcomes, 'bad' and 'good', and that the probabilities of the two outcomes are known. Therefore, we begin with a study of choice when an action leads to one event with probability π and a complementary event with probability $1 - \pi$. Of course, $0 \leq \pi \leq 1$.

12.1 Discrete events

An individual with a current wealth of Ω is confronted with a choice between a safe asset (money) that preserves her wealth at Ω with certainty and a risky asset (an investment) that reduces her wealth to x with probability π but will cause her wealth to increase to y with probability $1 - \pi$. Of course, $x < \Omega < y$. We can think of this as an experiment that has a bad outcome with probability π and a good outcome Ω with probability $1 - \pi$. If this experiment were repeated over a large number of periods, then the average wealth per period would be very close to the *expected monetary value,* which is $\pi x + (1 - \pi)y$. (This fact is known as the law of large numbers.) In that case it would be in her interest to choose the investment every time if $\pi x + (1 - \pi)y$ is greater than Ω but to reject the investment every time if $\pi x + (1 - \pi)y$ is smaller than Ω. But what if the experiment is not repeated?

For most of us there is a value of π sufficiently close to 0 (perhaps *extremely* close) that would induce us to choose the risky asset. And there would be a value of π sufficiently close to 1 that would prompt us to take the safe asset. But what about realistic, intermediate values of π? Clearly, the decision would depend on the magnitudes Ω, x, y, on the probability π, and on the individual's preferences regarding uncertainty. Under a wide range of circumstances it is possible to model an individual's preferences by a utility-of-wealth function $U(m)$, where m is the market value of the individual's current wealth. The utility function represents the individual's preferences in the sense that she would prefer the risky asset if and only if

$$\pi U(x) + (1 - \pi)U(y) > U(\Omega).$$

This means that the individual can be represented as an *expected utility* maximizer. The quantity $\pi U(x) + (1 - \pi)U(y)$ is called the expected utility of an investment that results in a wealth level of x with probability π and a wealth level of y with probability $1 - \pi$. In general, given a choice between an investment I that yields x with probability π and yields y with probability $1 - \pi$ and an investment J that yields a with probability ρ and b with probability $1 - \rho$ the individual will choose I if

$$\pi U(x) + (1 - \pi)U(y) > \rho U(a) + (1 - \rho)U(b)$$

and will choose J if

$$\rho U(a) + (1 - \rho)U(b) > \pi U(x) + (1 - \pi)U(y).$$

We say that an individual is *risk averse* if she chooses the safe asset whenever the risky asset has an expected monetary value $\pi x + (1 - \pi)y$ that does not exceed the wealth level Ω guaranteed by the safe asset. The risk averse individual would prefer Ω for sure if the opportunity of obtaining a higher level of wealth brought with it the chance of winding up with a lower level of wealth *and* Ω is at least as high as the average (expected) wealth associated with the gamble. We generalize this as follows: If $y \geq x$ then a risk averse individual is one who would prefer an asset A that yielded y with probability $\frac{1}{2}$ and x with probability $\frac{1}{2}$ to an asset B that yielded $y + \delta$ with probability $\frac{1}{2}$ and $x - \delta$ with probability $\frac{1}{2}$ as long as δ is positive. Notice that A and B have the same expected monetary value, $\frac{1}{2}x + \frac{1}{2}y$. For a risk averse individual asset B will have a lower expected *utility* because there is a greater spread between the bad outcome and the good outcome. This definition of risk aversion leads directly to a proof that risk averse individuals have utility functions with negative second derivatives: Set $\pi = \frac{1}{2}$ and $\delta > 0$. Suppose that $y > x$. By definition of risk aversion

$$\tfrac{1}{2}U(y) + \tfrac{1}{2}U(x) > \tfrac{1}{2}U(y + \delta) + \tfrac{1}{2}U(x - \delta)$$

and therefore

$$U(x) - U(x - \delta) > U(y + \delta) - U(y)$$

which implies

$$\frac{U(x) - U(x - \delta)}{\delta} > \frac{U(y + \delta) - U(y)}{\delta} \qquad [1]$$

because δ is positive. As δ approaches zero the left hand side of [1] approaches $U'(x)$ and the right hand side approaches $U'(y)$. Therefore, we have proved that $U'(y) \leq U'(x)$ holds whenever $y > x$. But we can do better than this. Suppose that $U'(x) = U'(y)$ and $x < y$. Then $U'(x) = U'(z) = U'(y)$ for $x \leq z \leq y$ because we have just proved that U' cannot increase as wealth increases. That is, $U'(x) \geq U'(z) \geq U'(y) = U'(x)$ implies $U'(x) = U'(z) = U'(y)$.

Consider the asset that yields $x^\circ = x + \frac{1}{4}(y - x)$ with probability $\frac{1}{2}$ and $y^\circ = y - \frac{1}{4}(y - x)$ with probability $\frac{1}{2}$. For a risk averse individual this must have a higher expected utility than the asset that pays x and y each with probability $\frac{1}{2}$ because the latter has the same expected monetary value as the former but a lower bad outcome and a higher good outcome. Therefore, we have

$$\tfrac{1}{2}U(x) + \tfrac{1}{2}U(y) < \tfrac{1}{2}U(x + \delta) + \tfrac{1}{2}U(y - \delta)$$

for $\delta = \frac{1}{4}(y - x)$. That is,

$$U(y) - U(y - \delta) < U(x + \delta) - U(x)$$

which is inconsistent with U' being constant on the range of values between x and y. The inconsistency arises from the fact that constant U' implies $U(y) - U(y - \delta) = \delta U'(x) = U(x + \delta) - U(x)$. We must conclude that $U'(x) > U'(y)$ actually holds for a risk averse person whenever $x < y$.

If asset A yields a good outcome y with probability $\frac{1}{2}$ and a bad outcome x with probability $\frac{1}{2}$, and asset B yields $y + \delta$ with probability $\frac{1}{2}$ and $x - \delta$ with probability $\frac{1}{2}$ and $\delta > 0$, then B is unambiguously the riskier asset. The two have the same mean, but B's payoffs have a wider spread than A's. Because A yields a higher level of utility to the risk averse individual, it is clear that a risk averse individual will pay a premium – large or small, depending on preference – to avoid risk. This is one of the foundations of the insurance industry. (The other is the law of large numbers.) In fact, the prominence of insurance in almost all aspects of our economy is strong evidence for the prevalence of risk aversion. Individuals have even been known to buy insurance against the possibility that an existing insurance opportunity will disappear. (See Sheffrin, 1993, p. 51.)

A *risk neutral* individual is one who always chooses the asset with the higher expected monetary value and will be indifferent between two assets with the same expected monetary value, even if one has a much bigger spread between the two payoffs. This means that

$$\tfrac{1}{2}U(x) + \tfrac{1}{2}U(y) = \tfrac{1}{2}U(x + \delta) + \tfrac{1}{2}U(y - \delta)$$

for all values of x, y, and δ. Therefore,

$$\frac{U(y) - U(y - \delta)}{\delta} = \frac{U(x + \delta) - U(x)}{\delta}$$

for all $\delta \neq 0$ and thus $U'(x) = U'(y)$ for all x and y. If the first derivative is constant the function U must be of the form $U(x) = \alpha x + \beta$. If utility is increasing in wealth we must have $\alpha > 0$. Therefore, maximizing expected utility is equivalent to maximizing expected monetary value in the case of a risk neutral individual.

Now, suppose a risk averse individual chooses x and y to maximize $\pi U(x) + (1 - \pi)U(y)$ subject to $px + qy = \Omega$, where π, $1 - \pi$, p, q, and Ω are all positive constants. If $p/q = \pi/(1 - \pi)$ we say that the individual faces *fair odds*, and in that case she will choose $x = y$. Here is the proof (assuming $U' > 0$ and $U'' < 0$ at all points): The individual maximizes $V(x) \equiv \pi U(x) + (1 - \pi)U(y)$ with $y = \Omega/q - px/q$ treated as a function of x. Then $dy/dx = -p/q$ and $V'(x) = \pi U'(x) + (1 - \pi)U'(y) \times (-p/q)$. Because $V'' < 0$ we want $V'(x) = 0$, which yields $U'(x) = U'(y)$ when $p/q = \pi/(1 - \pi)$. If $U'' < 0$ at all points then $U'(x) = U'(y)$ implies $x = y$.

12.2 The continuum case

Suppose that the random variable x could turn out to be any of the real numbers between zero and one inclusive. We often want to know the probability that a value of x between, say α and β, will be realized. (Assume that $0 \leq \alpha < \beta \leq 1$.) In the case of the *uniform probability distribution,* that probability depends only on the length of the interval (α, β). Formally,

$$\begin{aligned} \text{Prob}[\alpha < x < \beta] &= \beta - \alpha \\ &= \text{Prob}[\alpha < x \leq \beta] \\ &= \text{Prob}[\alpha \leq x < \beta] \\ &= \text{Prob}[\alpha \leq x \leq \beta]. \end{aligned}$$

The expected utility of the random variable x over the interval (α, β) with respect to the utility function U is defined by

$$\int_{\alpha}^{\beta} U(x)dx.$$

In general, if there is an integrable function f of x such that for all α and β satisfying $0 \leq \alpha < \beta \leq 1$

$$\text{Prob}[\alpha < x < \beta] = \int_{\alpha}^{\beta} f(x)dx$$

$$\begin{aligned} &= \text{Prob}[\alpha < x \leq \beta] \\ &= \text{Prob}[\alpha \leq x < \beta] \\ &= \text{Prob}[\alpha \leq x \leq \beta] \end{aligned}$$

then the expected utility of the random variable x over the interval (α, β) is defined by

$$\int_{\alpha}^{\beta} U(x)f(x)dx.$$

Exercises

1   An individual has the utility-of-wealth function $U(w) = \sqrt{w}$ and her current wealth is \$10,000. Is this individual risk averse? What is the maximum premium that she would pay to avoid a loss of \$1900 that occurs with probability 0.5? Why is this maximum premium not equal to half of the loss?

2   An individual has a utility-of-wealth function $U(w) = \ln(w + 1)$ and a current wealth of Ω. Is this individual risk averse? How much of this wealth will she use to purchase an asset that yields zero with probability 0.5, and with probability 0.5 returns \$4 for every \$1 invested? (When the asset pays off, a \$1 investment returns \$3 net of the original outlay.)

3   The utility-of-wealth function is $U(w) = \ln(w + 1)$ and the individual's current wealth is \$$\Omega$. How much of this wealth will the individual invest in a project that yields zero with probability π, and with probability $1 - \pi$ pays rC dollars to an investor who has sunk C dollars into the project?

4   For $U(w) = \sqrt{w}$ prove that $U(\tfrac{1}{2}x + \tfrac{1}{2}y) > \tfrac{1}{2}U(x) + \tfrac{1}{2}U(y)$ for $x \ne y$.

5   For $U(w) = \sqrt{w}$ prove that $U(\pi x + (1 - \pi)y) > \pi U(x) + (1 - \pi)U(y)$ for $0 < \pi < 1$ and $x \ne y$.

6   Max has a utility-of-wealth function $U(w) = \sqrt{w}$ and a current wealth of \$2000.

   a Will Max invest in a scheme that requires an initial capital outlay of \$2000 and returns nothing with probability of 0.5 (i.e., the initial outlay is lost and there is no revenue) and returns \$6000 with probability of 0.5?

   b Sam is identical to Max in every respect. If Max and Sam can share the investment (this is called risk *spreading*) will they do so? In this case sharing means that each puts up \$1000 and they split the proceeds of the investment.

7   An individual with utility-of-wealth function $U(w) = \ln(w + 100)$ would have an *after tax* income of 100 *if* she reported all her income. She is taxed at a rate of 50% of earned income (just to keep the calculations simple). If she is caught underreporting her income she will have to pay the taxes due, of course, but in addition she will pay a fine of F dollars for every dollar of income she failed to report.

   a How much income will she conceal (i.e., fail to report) if $F = 2$ and the probability of being caught is 0.10? Let C denote the amount of income concealed.

   b Determine C as a function of the fine F and the probability of being caught ρ. Show that C falls when either F or ρ increase.

8   An individual with utility-of-wealth function $U(w) = \ln(w + 20)$ has \$100

of income before tax and is taxed at a rate of 40% of earned income. If he is caught underreporting his income he will have to pay the taxes due and in addition will pay a fine of $1 for every $1 of income he failed to report. How much income will he conceal (i.e., fail to report) if the probability of being caught is 0.2? (Let C denote the amount of income concealed.)

9   An individual with utility-of-wealth function $U(w) = \sqrt{w}$ has initial wealth of $52. He has an opportunity to invest in a project that will cause him to lose his capital with probability 0.75, but with probability 0.25 will provide a net return of $4 for every $1 of capital he puts up. How much will he invest? (Let A denote the amount invested – i.e., the amount of capital he puts up. He loses A if the project fails, but if it succeeds it will pay him $5 gross for every $1 invested.)

2

Hidden action

This chapter investigates the extent to which an agent can be motivated to act in the principal's interest when the principal cannot accurately determine whether the agent has in fact taken the appropriate action. The agent's behavior is problematic because her goal is to maximize her own utility. As we will see in section 3 on mandatory retirement, difficulties arise even when the principal can determine the appropriateness of the agent's actions but cannot enforce a contract that specifies the agent's payoff as a function of all aspects of her performance because outsiders (e.g., judges) would be unable to verify the principal's claims about the agent's performance. Except for section 2 on the savings and loan crisis and section 4 on insurance, we investigate the principal–agent relationship by looking at the performance of firms and their workers in a market economy.

Hidden action problems are complicated by the presence of uncertainty. If your car breaks down a week after you take it home from the repair shop you do not know whether you are the victim of bad luck or of shirking by the mechanic. This makes it hard to design efficient, incentive compatible contracts. Consider the manager of Supertech Corporation as the agent, and the set of shareholders as the principal. Each owner holds a fraction of the outstanding shares of Supertech, as well as ownership shares in other firms. That is, each Supertech owner has a diversified portfolio. Thus, we assume that "the" principal is risk neutral and simply wants the manager to maximize expected profit. On the other hand, the manager's consumption and utility depend almost exclusively on the pay received for managing the firm. Hence, the manager is risk averse. The manager's effort has a strong influence on the firm's profit, but so do random forces. If the manager's pay went up by a dollar every time profit went up by a dollar, and went down by a dollar every time profit fell by a dollar, then the manager would have the strongest possible incentive to maximize expected profit – the manager has *maximum incentive*. But when the manager's pay moves perfectly in step with the firm's profit her pay is strongly influenced by random variables. Because she is risk averse, the expected payment by the firm's owners to the manager can be lower when the salary schedule shelters the manager from risk to some extent. With maximum incentive the gross expected profit is highest, but the manager's share of that profit would have to be higher on average because of her exposure to risk. The owner's *net* expected profit – net of the manager's emolument – is not maximized under maximum incentives. Shareholders – and society – face a trade-off between incentives and risk spreading. Compared to a contract in which variations in profit have their full effect on the manager's pay, reducing the manager's exposure to risk by providing an insurance element in the pay package allows the shareholders to do better. This weakens the manager's incentive, of course. An extreme example is played out in insurance markets. The consumer who purchases health insurance can influence the size of claims submitted by practicing preventive medicine and by eschewing frills when illness does strike. But the random forces that select one person as a victim of ill health rather than another play a huge role in determining individual medical expenses. Insurance contracts give relatively little scope for incentives and go a long way toward protecting the individual from random events. (This is discussed in more detail in section 4.) At the other extreme, fast food chains commonly employ franchises in which the manager of the local outlet absorbs most of the risk, to enable incentives to have a big impact. (See sections 1 and 7.)

When we model all of this, we will assume that effort is one-dimensional. The agent can supply an additional unit of effort by reducing leisure consumption by one unit. This is the only way that the manager can enhance the firm's profit in our models. In the real world, managers put in long hours, but their activities can still deviate substantially from maximizing the owner's return. At one extreme, a manager can put considerable effort into concealing data about the firm's performance from the shareholders. In such cases, the manager knowingly sets aside the principal's welfare. More subtle is the case of a manager's taking risks that are not in line with the owner's preferences under uncertainty.[1] Happily, we can draw a great deal of insight from the simple, one-dimensional version of the manager's contribution. In our formal models the manager has a simple trade-off between effort and leisure. We begin with nontechnical discussions of the relationship of the owners of a firm to its manager (section 1) and monitoring of the savings and loan industry in the U.S. (section 2).

1 Shareholders and managers

Corporations have many shareholders. (Why?) The owners appoint a manager to run the company on their behalf. The shareholders want the manager to make decisions that lead to the maximum profit, but they will not know when the highest possible profit is attained. If it were obvious how to maximize profit then the shareholders could issue the appropriate orders directly to the workers. As it is, the shareholders need to hire a manager. This creates a new problem. The shareholders wish to design a contract that provides every incentive for the manager to maximize the shareholders' profit, even though the manager's real concern is his or her own material well-being, which will depend on factors such as the manager's future prospects, which are not perfectly correlated with the firm's profit. Even if a substantial portion of the manager's wealth is held in the form of shares in the firm that she manages, the other shareholders cannot be sure that she will do all she can to maximize profits. The firm's long-run profitability will not be the only aspect of the manager's stewardship that affects her welfare. For example, the manager's prospects for future employment and income may be enhanced if she increases the size of her present enterprise, and this may induce her to increase the firm's output beyond the point at which profit is maximized. Or, the manager may expose the firm to more risk than is in the best interest of the owners. She may even negotiate a merger that provides her with tens of millions of dollars of severance benefits but does nothing (or less than nothing) for those who owned the firm before the merger.

The manager will lose her job if the firm suffers losses year after year, and this gives her incentive to avoid losses. This is a long way from claiming that the manager will make every effort to maximize profit. The manager's direct concern is, as we have said, her long-run well-being, and her performance will be designed to enhance her present income, her nonmonetary rewards and future monetary rewards on the job (involving the use of a company airplane, etc.), her perceived value to other companies (to enhance her job prospects elsewhere), and her retirement package. McConnell and Muscarella (1986) have uncovered cases of managers undertaking billion dollar oil explorations that diminish the profitability of the firm.[2] Managers have been known to restrict the flow of information to the firm's board of directors, to make it harder to determine when the manager is acting in the interest of the shareholders. Here is a particularly subtle example: Modigliani and Miller (1958) argue that managers who boast of their company's low debt may be advertising their own incompetence. When they raise money by issuing new stock rather than selling bonds they force existing shareholders to share their profits with a larger group; when bonds are issued, the annual interest payments are an expense to the firm, but a *tax-deductible expense*. Managers may even reduce present value of the annual profit stream by tapping a source of profit slowly, so that it provides a steady flow of comfortable returns over the long haul. This can yield an annual profit that is high enough to survive owner scrutiny, but not so high as to raise expectations for a repeat of the previous year's record return.[3] And a manager can be considered to be shirking if she does not put much effort into solving the problem of shirking by the firm's other employees.[4]

And then there is venality. McMillan (1992, p. 121) presents some interesting examples, including the type that you would expect to see – such as the use of a company jet to fly executives to a trendy resort – and some particularly egregious ones. Examples abound of departures from profit maximizing behavior, and it is usually easy to rationalize these in terms of the *manager's* welfare. Venality is not confined to privately owned enterprises, of course. In 1990 the minister responsible for the transition of state-owned Polish firms to private ownership said that the amount of pilfering by managers of state-owned enterprises under communist rule was "probably under ten per cent."[5] Let's look at some devices that are used in capitalist economies to align managers' incentives and shareholder interests to a degree.

What kind of performance bonus would induce a manager to maximize profit? A substantial bonus that is paid only if the manager realizes maximum profit would provide the appropriate incentive. However, if the shareholders know how much profit the firm is capable of generating they can simply write a contract so the manager's continued employment is conditional on the firm's reaching its potential. How can the owners induce profit maximization when they don't know what the maximum profit is? *Stock options* are a partial answer. A stock option is a commitment by the shareholders to the manager, allowing the latter to purchase a specified number of shares in the company in a specified time interval and at a fixed price, usually the price of the stock at the time the option is presented to the manager. This gives the manager a strong incentive to take actions that lead to the largest increase in the value of the stock over that time interval, and this is usually accomplished by generating the maximum profit for the firm. But too often bonuses and stock options are given to reward service in the past. But it is future performance that the shareholders want to inspire; it is too late to affect past performance. In fact, poor performance may be the result of unfavorable random events – changes in exchange rates, etc. – that are beyond the control of the manager. The manager may have been exceptionally industrious and creative. The aim is to reward effort and effort is imperfectly correlated with performance and profit. (This is studied formally in section 7.) Paradoxically, it may be smart to give a stock option to a manager after a period of *low* profits, giving the manager a strong incentive to work more effectively in the future. This doesn't apply to cash bonuses, of course. In fact, bonuses are usually tied to the *office* – with a chairman receiving more than a vice president. Although executive salaries account for less than 50% of total executive pay in the U.S.,[6] Jensen and Murphy (1990) estimate that a chief executive's pay increases by only $3.25 for every

$1000 increase in the value of the company's shares on the stock market. So, performance bonuses are a potentially useful tool in the shareholders' attempt to induce the manager to maximize profit but they are not often used in the right way. Moreover, shareholders often view these sorts of financial devices as bribes to get the manager to do something that she is paid a salary to do in the first place. Accordingly, shareholders often oppose the use of stock options on ethical grounds and will sometimes sue the manager if the firm's board of directors agree to this type of compensation. Nevertheless, performance bonuses account for over 50% of U.S. executives' pay. Shleifer and Vishny (1988) suggest that the members of the *board of directors* be paid in the form of stock in the company rather than salary. This would align the interests of the board and the shareholders. Although the board of directors represents the shareholders, and shareholders sit on the board, it is often dominated by the manager. (In fact, managers often control the selection of the board members. And they can arrange to have their firms award lavish consulting contracts to board members. Brickley, Coles, and Terry (1994) marshall evidence suggesting that shareholders do better when the board contains a large number of directors who have no significant business ties with the company.)

Performance bonuses have *some* effect on pay and hence on performance. In the U.S., however, the effect on performance is too narrowly focussed on the short run. From the standpoint of consumer welfare it is long-run profit that should be maximized. If the U.S. stock market reflects short-run more than long-run profit maximization, then to the extent that changes in the value of a company's stock affect its manager's performance, it is short-run profit maximization that is encouraged.[7] Why might the U.S. stock market be too insensitive to the long run? Over 50% of the common stock is held by pension funds, mutual funds, educational endowments, and charitable foundations, and these institutions account for 80% of the trading.[8] A mutual fund seldom holds more than 1% of the outstanding stock of a company, and it is illegal for a company pension fund to hold more than 10% of the stock of its sponsoring company. The significance of this is easily seen with a simple example: Doncam corporation is owned by 100 individuals, each with a 1% share. Doncam's annual profit is $50,000, or $500 per shareholder. A one-time investigation of management practices would cost $2000 now and would result in an expected increase in annual profit of 10%, or $50 per owner. The interest rate would have to fall below 2.5% for it to be rational for a single risk neutral owner to finance the investigation out of his own pocket. But if Doncam had only four owners, each with a 25% share, then any risk neutral owner could finance the investigation himself and recover the cost before the end of the second year. Management would be more intensely scrutinized if ownership were more concentrated.[9] In short, most of the stock in a large U.S. company is held by institutions who hold only a tiny fraction of its shares and who trade them frequently. This means that the majority of owners have only a very short-run interest in the company. And the executives themselves stay within the company for only five years on average. (In Japan it is typically a lifetime. Worker managed firms are springing up across the United States, and the worker–managers typically have a long-term interest in their business.)[10] Who, then, will put pressure on management to consider the long view? In the United States only 21% of research and development funding in the private sector is targeted for long-run projects; this contrasts with 47% in Japan, and 61% in Europe.[11]

An increasingly commonplace device for inducing performance that generates the maximum increase in the value of the company's shares is the *franchise* arrangement. A company provides a standardized product: hamburgers, fried chicken, automobile parts, retail drug outlets, etc. When another new outlet is opened, should the existing shareholders operate it themselves or license someone else (the franchisee) to do it according to the standard formula? If the shareholders operate it themselves they must hire a manager, in which case profit maximization cannot be taken for granted. The franchise arrangement requires the licensee (or franchisee) to put up her own capital and manage the outlet herself. Typically, the franchisee must also pay a substantial fee to the parent company in return for permission to use its brand label and enjoy the benefits of its reputation and national advertising. The parent is in the business of selling franchises instead of hamburgers (etc.). The franchise fees bring in more profit than would a chain of parent-managed outlets because managers would not perform as well under the latter system – because they would have less at stake personally. Why would an entrepreneur pay a fee to the parent *and* agree to follow the company formula strictly in return for the right to produce something that the entrepreneur could legally sell without paying the fee? Because the identification with the parent's brand is a source of extra profit, justifying the hefty licensing fee. But the extra profit depends on consumer confidence in the brand, which in turn depends on *other* outlets strictly adhering to the company formula, so each franchisee agrees to the limitations because the brand identification is not worth anything unless it is clear that the parent will enforce its standards generally. Nor will there be extra profit if the franchisee is not given the exclusive right to operate in a specified area, so the parent agrees not to allow anyone else to use the brand name in the franchisee's neighborhood. Without accepting this limitation the parent would have nothing valuable to sell. Each side agrees to restrict its activities because the configuration leads to maximum profit for all the participants.

There are many situations, however, in which franchising would not solve the problem of divorce between ownership (by shareholders) and control (by management). For example, the product may be produced at only a few locations, or sold only at the wholesale level. Most significantly, the firm may be too large to be purchased by a single individual, which is essentially what franchising accomplishes. (See sections 7.2 and 7.3.) Are there any other techniques that can be used to provide managers with appropriate incentives? One surprising possibility is *insider trading*. This term refers to the managers of firm *A* using important information about *A*'s prospects that is not available to the general public, or even to trading specialists. If this information is used to purchase or sell *A*'s shares in a way that benefits the manager or her friends we have an instance of insider trading. It seems very unfair for those on the inside to profit from their privileged position. Indeed, the U.S. Securities and Exchanges Commission declared insider trading unlawful in 1961 and the courts have ratified this position. (Insider trading is not unlawful if it is based on information that is available to the general public.) But why is it unfair? Or why is it harmful enough to others to warrant its prohibition?

One form of insider trading is clearly harmful to society in general. If managers were able to take short positions in the shares of their own company they would have a strong incentive to ensure that their firms did *badly*. Selling short consists in selling something you don't own (shares in this case) at a price agreed upon now for delivery at a specified time in the future. The person selling short is betting that the object will fall in value. When it is time to deliver the promised number of units of the object and the price *has* fallen, one simply buys the required number of units on the "spot" market and delivers them, collecting the high price specified in the original contract.

If managers could do this with shares in the companies that they run they could get rich by mismanaging their companies so that the stock falls in value. The flow of goods and service to consumers would be correspondingly diminished. It is clearly in our interest to have short sales by managers declared illegal. Short sales by insiders have been prohibited in the U.S. since 1936. (In July 1929 the head of the large Chase bank sold short over 42,000 shares of Chase stock in advance of the October crash. See Malkiel, 1981.)

What about ordinary (spot) trading by insiders? One argument in favor asserts that this gives managers a strong incentive to do their utmost for the shareholders. If the company performs substantially better than expected then the price of its shares will rise on the stock exchange. Once this superior performance is public knowledge the shares will be immediately bid up in price and it will be too late for a manager to benefit from purchasing her company's shares. But if the manager purchases her company's stock at the current price in the light of advance, inside information on the company's unexpected performance then substantial capital gains are made when the share price is bid up in the wake of public realization of the enhanced profitability. This suggests that insider trading – with short sales disallowed – can help align the interests of manager and shareholder. (You might ask yourself why stockholders do not insist that managers agree to abstain from insider trading as part of the contractual agreement between shareholder and manager.)

Takeovers may have value as a device for aligning the incentives of managers and shareholders. "Takeover" refers to the purchase of a controlling interest in a firm by a new shareholder.[12] If the firm is not maximizing profit then there is a profit opportunity for new owners to purchase the firm at a low price. The low price reflects the firm's record of low profits. The new owners can replace the incumbent manager with a more effective one. If there is a big increase in the flow of profits as a result, then the new owners will realize a handsome return, justifying the takeover. (The higher level of profit will increase the market value of the firm's shares.) The possibility of dismissal may provide an incentive for managers to maximize profit in the first place.[13] This argument is due to Manne (1965 & 1966). However, the owners appoint an agent in the first place because the organization and its environment are very complex, and it is costly to determine the profit maximizing strategy. To make things worse, managers often restrict the flow of information concerning the internal operation of the firm, making it even harder to determine its potential. Moreover, it often happens that the dismissed manager has a contract with the original owners that provides her with very substantial compensation (a 'golden parachute') in case she is fired as a result of a takeover. The fact that boards of directors offer this sort of compensation points to a weakness in directors' monitoring of managers. Some acquisitions serve the manager's interest in another way. Shleifer and Vishny (1988) report that managers sometimes initiate takeovers. If a manager has a strong reputation in the railroad industry, say, and her firm acquires a railroad then she will be much more valuable to the shareholders. She has strengthened her position at the head of the firm, even if the acquisition diminishes the present value of shareholder wealth.

There is a free rider problem that could undermine takeovers as a device to discipline managers. Existing shareholders stand to benefit from any improvement in the profitability of a firm that a takeover would bring. This could make them reluctant to sell to the takeover group at the current market price, or at a price low enough to render the takeover profitable to the new owners; it could become difficult or impossible to find enough current shareholders willing to sell their shares (Grossman and Hart, 1980). That is why the constitutions of many firms include a *dilution* provision. This allows the new owner to sell part of the firm's assets to another company owned by the new owner at terms that are beneficial to the takeover group and disadvantageous to the firm's minority shareholders. Dilution can also take the form of the new owners issuing themselves new shares. Why would the original owners of the firm place such a provision in their constitution when it is potentially to their disadvantage? Because it makes takeovers more credible and thus serves to discipline the firm's manager. If the discipline is strict enough then the incumbent manager will work assiduously to maximize profit, vitiating the need for dilution. A two-tiered offer can also eliminate the free rider problem. (See section 7.8 of Chapter 1.)

Managers have erected various defenses against hostile takeovers, and there is evidence that the defensive strategies often work (Jarrell et al., 1988). A *poison pill* can undermine the effectiveness of takeovers in disciplining management. Poison pills appeared for the first time in 1982. The term refers to a family of financial devices for imposing costs on the takeover group. By making hostile takeovers excessively costly, poison pills entrench management at the expense of shareholders, as Malatesta and Walking (1988) and Ryngaert (1988) have demonstrated. (Both papers are good introductions to the poison pill technique; in particular they have insightful examples.)

The wave of takeovers in the U.S. in the 1980s left a trail of data that should allow us to determine if takeovers have provided a significant corrective. Scherer (1988) is skeptical, but Lichtenberg (1992) finds strong evidence that a firm's total factor productivity increased after a takeover. And in a review of the empirical work on this question, Jarrell et al. (1988) conclude that takeovers induce a beneficial restructuring of real capital.

The spectrum of incentives that cause a manager to deviate from the path that would be mandated if she could be costlessly monitored are referred to as *agency costs* by Jensen and Meckling (1976). In section 7 this spectrum is collapsed to a single component – the amount of shirking chosen by the manager. This gives us a model that provides plenty of insight at fairly low cost.

Suggestions for further reading: Kotowitz (1989), Easterbrook (1985), Scherer (1988), Shleifer and Vishny (1988).

2 The savings and loan crisis

A savings and loan firm (*S & L,* or *thrift*), like a bank, takes in depositors' money, paying them an interest fee, and then lends their money for a fee. Its profit comes mainly from the difference between the interest rates on lending and borrowing. Loans by an S & L were essentially limited to residential mortgages until the Depository Institutions Act of 1982 eased restrictions. Maximization of general consumer welfare requires that borrowers be monitored to ensure that the funds are devoted to the installation of real capital equipment with the highest rate of return to society. And it is certainly in the interest of depositors as a whole to monitor their creditors to ensure that the funds will yield the maximum monetary return. However, no *individual* has an incentive to do the monitoring, as we will see.

A wave of S & L failures, beginning in the 1970s, has led to a crisis that will cost U.S. taxpayers tens of billions of dollars. The initial failures have their explanation in the drop in oil prices, which had serious implications for real estate values and business activity in the 'oil patch', particularly Oklahoma and Texas; a slump in real estate generally; a rise in interest rates that left many S & L's locked into long-term mortgages yielding low rates of return while paying high interest rates to current depositors; and other special features. In this section we are not going to examine the onset of the crisis. Rather, we will ask, "Why did a serious problem turn into a disaster?"

In 1981 there were almost 4000 thrifts in the U.S. that were insured by FSLIC, the federal program that guaranteed customers' deposits. (If a thrift failed, the FSLIC fund would cover any part of a deposit that couldn't be collected from the failed institution.) Of this 4000, 85% reported losses for the year, and the whole industry's net worth was negative – the market value of assets fell short of the dollar deposit liabilities. Here we had a clear warning sign. Yet in 1986 the President's Council of Economic Advisors was still trying to get the attention of the President, the Congress, and the country, calling for reform and warning of the potential bill that would be presented to taxpayers. Here is the key to understanding how we managed to pour gasoline on the flames: *Zombie* institutions – thrifts that were insolvent, and should have been pronounced dead – were allowed to *gamble for resurrection*.[14] They took in more money from depositors and sank it into risky investments in desperation. The risky investment would likely turn sour, but in the unlikely event that it succeeded it would restore the company to financial health. Let's look at this from the standpoint of incentives. Why did depositors entrust their wealth to zombie institutions? Why did the regulatory agency overseeing the thrift industry (the Federal Home Loan Bank Board) permit zombie thrifts to continue gambling? And finally, why did the owners of the S & L's want their firms involved in wildcat schemes?

First, why didn't depositors do a better job of monitoring the firms that borrowed from them? Because the federal deposit insurance program removed the incentive for depositors to do comparison shopping. Lenders still had a strong incentive to look for the highest interest on their deposit, but they had little reason to care about financial insolvency or imprudent thrift management. If the deposit were lost due to the thrift's insolvency then U.S. taxpayers, through the federal government, would replace the money.[15] The Canadian banking system did not have a formal deposit insurance scheme until 1967. The stability of the Canadian system before 1967 can be partly attributed to the incentive for monitoring by

lenders and to market discipline of the individual bank.[16] There is little incentive
for lenders to monitor U.S. banks – in addition to the family of savings and loan
institutions. Why was the crisis confined mainly to the thrift industry? Because
banks were subject to more stringent regulation.

Why was the regulation of the thrift industry much more permissive than that of
the banking industry? In particular, why did the Federal Home Loan Bank Board
(FHLBB) not put a stop to gambling for resurrection in the thrift industry?
Because Congress generally favored regulatory forbearance. Why would a federal
regulatory agency be sensitive to the mood of Congress? Because Congress can
restrict the powers of a regulatory agency, and it can cut the agency's budget. And
many who serve on the regulatory agency look forward to lucrative careers in
Washington when they leave the agency – counselling firms on how to approach
Congress, for example. So, even an independent agency is wary about defying
Congress. Moreover, the 1982 Depository Institutions Act changed the accounting rules to allow ailing S & L's to hide their insolvency, making them appear
healthy. Before we consider why Congress wanted a permissive regulatory climate, let's see why the owners of a thrift would be in favor of gambling for
resurrection in the first place.

Consider a prudent investment (*PI*). It requires an initial capital outlay of $1040
and it pays off exactly one year after the project is undertaken. With probability $\frac{1}{2}$
PI will provide a return of $1096 to the S & L, net of labor and materials costs.
And with probability $\frac{1}{2}$ the net return is $1092. If the S & L invests in the project
the owners will put up $40 of their own money, and the remaining $1000 will be
money entrusted to them by depositors. We assume that the market rate of interest
is 5%, so depositors will be paid $1050 before the owners can claim their profit.
The net return for the owners then is $46 = $1096 − $1050 with probability $\frac{1}{2}$,
and $42 = $1092 − $1050 with probability $\frac{1}{2}$. The average return to the share-
holders is $44 = $\frac{1}{2}$ × $46 + $\frac{1}{2}$ × $42. Since they put up $40 to begin with, their
return on capital is 10%. This is summarized in Table 1. The Society column is
just the total of the other columns and shows what happens to the economy as a
whole. The FSLIC column gives the amount that the insurer has to pay to depositors. Of course, the prudent investment does not require any outlay by FSLIC.
The owners might find *PI*'s 10% return attractive, but we have yet to compare *PI*
with *WS*, the wildcat scheme,[17] which is represented by Table 2. With *WS* the
high and low returns also occur with equal probability, but the low return of $150
does not come close to allowing the S & L to discharge its deposit liabilities. If
disaster occurs, the owners must turn over all of the $150 recovered to the
depositors. This is far short of their initial deposit, so the deposit insurance kicks
in and pays the remaining $900. The owners lose all of their invested capital, but
they do not have to tap into their private wealth to pay off depositors; the

Table 1. *Prudent investment*

	Depositors	Owners	FSLIC	Society
Initial outlay	1000	40	0	1040
High return	1050	46	0	1096
Low return	1050	42	0	1092
Average return	1050	44	0	1094
Rate of return	5%	10%		5.2%

Table 2. *Wildcat scheme*

	Depositors	Owners	FSLIC	Society
Initial outlay	1000	40	0	1040
High return	1050	400	0	1450
Low return	1050	0	−900	150
Average return	1050	200	−450	800
Rate of return	5%	400%		−23%

insurance fund does that. Therefore, the average return to the owners from *WS* is not

$$\tfrac{1}{2} \times \$400 + \tfrac{1}{2} \times -\$900 = -\$250,$$

which would be a negative rate of return of over 500%. With FSLIC covering the shortfall when investments turn sour, the average return to the owners is

$$\tfrac{1}{2} \times \$400 + \tfrac{1}{2} \times 0 = +\$200,$$

a *positive rate of return of 400%*. It is clear that the owners will prefer *WS*, although the return to society is negative (−23%) with *WS*, and it is a respectable plus 5.2% with *PI*.

The deposits that are used for either of the above schemes are fresh deposits, brought in to allow the S & L to undertake new investments. If the firm has outstanding deposit liabilities that it is unable to honor, and it is in danger of being shut down by the FHLBB, then the wildcat scheme offers the zombie S & L a last chance for financial health. In the unlikely event that the risky investments pay off, there will be plenty for everyone – depositors and owners. If they fail to pay off, the owners do not lose because the institution is already insolvent, and that means that they could not recoup any of the wealth they invested in their firm. Gambling for resurrection is exactly like the desperation pass thrown in the last seconds of a football game by a team trailing by four points. If the pass is intercepted and returned for a touchdown, the team that called the play will lose by ten points, but that's no worse than losing by four points. The pass could be successful, although that is unlikely. But there is no chance at all of winning without such a desperation move, and some slight chance with it. This logic made things tougher on responsible thrifts. The firms that were gambling heavily offered higher interest rates on deposits, in order to attract new funds to finance the wildcat schemes. Competition forced the responsible firms to pay higher interest rates too, making them more vulnerable. (The higher interest rates even influenced the size of the current national debt: See Shoven, Smart, and Waldfogel, 1992.) If depositors had cared how an S & L was managed, many would have accepted lower interest rates in order to have their money stored in a safer place.

Now, why would members of Congress want a milder regulatory climate? We have to assume that they failed to understand the impact on the efficacy of markets when the incentive for comparison shopping is diminished. And Congress itself would have had more incentive to work at understanding the banking industry if it had not been playing a version of the prisoner's dilemma game. To simplify, we suppose that a member of Congress simply has to choose between stringent regulation of the thrift industry and mild regulation. Consider the implications of these two strategies for the legislator's own constituency. With WS, U.S. taxpayers have to shell out $900 when the scheme fails. The scheme will fail half the time, so if there is a large number of gambling S & L's in the legislator's state the actual number of failures per investment will be close to the average. Therefore, we can assume that U.S. taxpayers have to contribute $450 per wildcat scheme. But only one-fiftieth of that will come out of the pockets of the legislator's constituents – the other forty-nine states receive 98% of the bill. So, when WS is successful it will rescue an S & L in the legislator's home state, and when it fails 98% of the costs are passed on to other states. This argument may explain the temptation that induced some members of Congress to intervene in the regulatory process on behalf of local thrifts, especially when it is coupled with the intense lobbying for regulatory forbearance by the thrift industry. However, it does not fully explain the creation of a milder regulatory climate via legislation. When it comes to the framing of legislation, we must think in terms of group decision making, rather than the independent individual choice that can lead to the prisoner's dilemma. (But we must not lose sight of the fact that legislation results from *individual* voting behavior.)

There is an important hidden characteristic element to the thrift debacle. The 1982 Depository Institutions Act broadened the scope of activities available to an S & L. At the same time the thrift regulators lowered the capital-asset requirements on individual thrifts. The new regulatory climate attracted entrepreneurs who saw an opportunity to raise easy money in order to finance their personal get-rich-quick schemes.[18] This is called the *adverse selection* phenomenon: the incentives are such that characteristics that are least beneficial to society are selected.

Suggestions for further reading: Milgrom and Roberts (1992, pp. 170–176); Mishkin (1992, chapter 11, 'The Crisis in Banking Regulation'); Romer and Weingast (1991); Litan (1991, a comment on Romer and Weingast).

Exercises

1   Would *WS* be more profitable than *PI* for the owners of a healthy S & L?
2   How would a private insurance carrier respond to a client that always took extreme risks and frequently submitted large claims?

3 Mandatory retirement

Mandatory retirement is the practice of preventing an employee from working beyond age sixty-five no matter how willing and able the individual is to work. Because many employees much prefer to continue working, mandatory retirement is often cited as an example of discrimination on the basis of age. Rather than debating this point we will discuss an economic rationale for mandatory retirement in a society in which there are hidden action and hidden characteristic problems on the job.

3.1 Posting a bond

Hidden action problems arise whenever work is performed in a team and it is difficult or impossible to identify the contribution made by a particular member of the team. This obviously applies to most manufacturing processes. In the long run, malingerers can be detected by a number of methods. But firing malingerers when they are identified is not by itself enough to discourage shirking if workers can switch jobs with impunity. But by accepting employment in a firm that pays its workers less than the competitive wage in the early years and more than the competitive wage in later years the worker is in effect posting a bond. The bond is forfeited if the worker is caught persistently shirking – i.e., she is fired.[19] (The competitive wage is the value of the marginal product.) In an economy that did not solve the hidden action problem, workers in general would perform poorly, total output would be unnecessarily low, and everyone's utility would be far below its potential.

Even when there is a single worker, such as a hired hand on a farm, it is impossible to determine the extent of the worker's contribution by observing output if that output is affected by random events (weather, insects, etc.) in addition to the worker's effort. Over a long period, however, the law of large numbers can be used by the employer to determine the worker's average effort from average output. The worker's actions do not remain hidden in the long run, and shirking is penalized by forfeiture of the "bond." Posting a bond in the form of deferred wages also brings the labor market closer to the efficient level of on the job training. An otherwise profitable investment in worker training will be unprofitable if workers leave the firm after the new skills have been acquired. This problem will be mitigated if the worker posts a bond with the firm that pays for the training.

Moral hazard remains a problem if effort levels are observable but not verifiable. It may be quite evident to a manager that a worker is shirking, even though the manager is unable to prove this by means of objective evidence that would convince a third party, say a judge. If that is the case, it will not be possible to employ contracts that directly penalize a worker for shirking. The contract could not be enforced because the employer could not prove to outside observers that shirking did in fact occur. A good example of observable but unverifiable shirking is discourteous behavior by a waiter to a restaurant customer.

There is a hidden characteristic element as well. Even if there were no shirking there would be talented and less talented workers. Again, team production makes it impossible to identify less talented workers in the short run. The less talented workers may know who they are but they will not voluntarily identify themselves and accept lower wages. However, if wages are below the competitive level in the early years and above the competitive level in later years a less talented worker will not accept a contract designed for a talented worker. Such a contract would be beneficial only if the worker collected the late-career high wages, but he would be dismissed or kept on at a lower wage when it became clear that he was not a high-quality worker. The wage profile can be used to sort less talented workers from talented workers even though the former have every incentive to conceal their identity. The wage profile induces the less talented workers to *self-select*. This also promotes efficiency.

The standard wage profile, paying below competitive levels early and above competitive levels later in one's tenure in the firm, has an economic rationale, then. However, this wage profile would be unprofitable for employers if workers were able to collect the high late-career wages without a time limit. Hence the mandated cut-off age of 65.

Although the U.S. Supreme Court restricted the practice in 1986, mandatory retirement has an economic rationale. Is it discriminatory nonetheless? The contract with low early-career wages, high late-career wages, and termination at age sixty-five is voluntarily chosen. Moreover, workers obviously care about the entire profile of lifetime earnings. If we compare lifetime wage profiles we can't find evidence of discrimination based on age. Now, let's give the economic argument for mandatory retirement more structure by means of the simple model of labor supply introduced in section 4 of Chapter 1.

3.2 The formal argument

There are two goods: X is leisure consumption and Y is a composite commodity – expenditure on all goods other than X. Let x and y denote the respective amounts consumed of the two goods. Consider consumer A with utility function $u(x, y) = B(x) + y$. We begin by showing that efficiency requires $B'(x) = f'(L)$, where $f(L)$ is a production function specifying the amount of Y produced when L units of labor are employed as input. If $B'(x) < f'(L)$ we can have this consumer supply an additional dL units of labor, resulting in the production of approximately $f'(L)dL$ additional units of Y, which we give to consumer A. This will increase utility, but the net change in utility must reflect the loss in leisure consumption of dL. If $dx = -dL$ then the reduction in the utility derived from leisure is approximately $-B'(x)dL$. The net change in utility then is

$$-B'(x)dL + f'(L)dL = \{f'(L) - B'(x)\} \times dL,$$

which is positive when $B'(x) < f'(L)$ and $dL > 0$. We have increased the utility of our consumer without affecting the utility of anyone else. The extra consumption of Y provided to consumer A was generated by increasing A's time on the job: no one else's consumption changed, and no one's hours of work changed. Similarly, if $B'(x) > f'(L)$ for A then we can increase A's utility without affecting anyone else by increasing A's leisure consumption by dx and letting A's consumption of Y fall by the resulting drop in output, which is $f'(L)dx$ because $dL = -dx$. Therefore, efficiency requires $B'(x) = f'(L)$ for each consumer. Let x^* be the solution of this equation. We can say that x^* is the efficient leisure consumption.[20]

Take 90 as the time endowment. That is, the individual anticipates living 90 years. Then the efficient labor supply is $90 - x^*$, which is represented as L^* on Figure 1. If B' falls as leisure consumption increases, then the marginal utility of leisure increases as L, measured along the horizontal axis, increases ($L = 90 - x$). The diagram shows $f'(L)$, the marginal product of labor, increasing early in the career, as the individual learns on the job, and then declining after a point, as age takes its toll.

If there were no hidden information problems, a wage equal to the marginal product of labor would induce the individual to retire at the efficient date L^*. Consider: W, the wage, equals $f'(L)$, the marginal product of labor, at each date L. (L is the number of *years* of labor supplied; when discussing the retirement issue it is convenient to measure time in years.) If the worker retires at date $L < L^*$ then $x > x^*$. Set $dL > 0$. (We'll have the individual worker longer.) We want to show that his utility will increase. The change in utility is

$$B'(x)dx + dy = dy - B'(x)dL$$

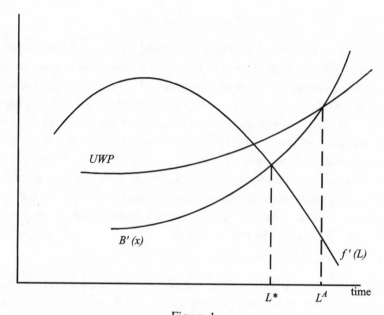

Figure 1

because we always have $dx = -dL$. Now $dy = WdL$, the wage multiplied by the additional time at work.[21] So, the change in utility is

$$\{W - B'(x)\} \times dL = \{f'(L) - B'(x)\} \times dL$$

because $W = f'(L)$. Therefore, the change in utility is positive when dL is positive. Similarly, we can increase utility by setting $dL < 0$ when $L > L^*$. The conclusion: If at each point in time the wage is equal to the marginal product of labor, then the utility maximizing consumer will choose to retire at the efficient retirement date L^*.

The wage profile represented by $f'(L)$, the marginal product of labor, in Figure 1 is rarely observed. Much more typical is the upward wage profile (UWP) represented by the curve labelled UWP in Figure 1. We can find an upward sloping UWP such that the consumer is indifferent between UWP and retirement at L^* on the one hand, and on the other hand always having a wage equal to the current marginal product of labor and retirement at L^*. Just find a UWP with the same present value as the marginal product wage schedule. (See section 3.3.) Even if the present value calculation is somewhat misleading, because the individual faces a different interest rate as a borrower than as a lender, for example, there is *some* UWP that gives exactly the same utility as the profile f'. If UWP is sufficiently low the individual will prefer f' and if UWP is sufficiently high he will prefer UWP. There must be some intermediate upward sloping wage profile to which the individual is indifferent, and this is represented in Figure 1.

At L^* the actual wage (located on UWP) is above $B'(x^*)$ and the individual will want to keep working at the current wage. To the extent that an upward sloping wage profile is in society's interest because it helps solve hidden information problems, leaving everyone with more utility, mandatory retirement is in society's interest because the upward sloping profile will not be offered by profit maximizing firms if workers continue on the job beyond L^*. Because UWP and the marginal product wage profile f' have the same present value *when each is truncated at* L^*, the firm will prefer the marginal product schedule to the UWP schedule if the worker chooses the retirement date. The worker will choose to retire at L^A with wage schedule UWP. Between L^* and L^A the wage is above the marginal product of labor and the firm loses the wage minus $f'(L)$ on each unit of additional labor employed. The overall outcome could be very unprofitable with UWP and no mandated retirement date. Therefore, the equilibrium will not include firms offering an upward sloping wage profile without specifying the retirement date. If we look at labor supply only, we see that the equilibrium could include firms that offer the marginal product wage profile with the retirement date chosen by the worker and contracts that offer an upward sloping wage profile with retirement mandated at L^*. Firms that employ the latter will be more profitable because they will have fewer hidden information problems. These firms will be able to set lower prices and drive the other firms out of the market. Therefore, when we look at labor demand as well as supply, we see that the equilibrium will feature only firms that offer an upward sloping wage profile with mandatory retirement at L^*.

The mandatory retirement story doesn't fit U.S. data perfectly. (See Stern and Todd, 1992.) For example, pension funds should be included in the model because they also play the role of bonds posted by the employees. (See Lazear, 1992.)

3.3 A primer on intertemporal choice

This section shows why there will be many wage profiles that provide a given worker with the same level of utility. Initially, assume that there are only two periods: period zero, the present, and period 1, which is one unit of time (year?) from now. Our study of a two period model will actually show us how to collapse a large number of periods – say 100 years – into two periods, giving us a model in which the two periods are 'now' and 'everything from next year on'. But first we assume only two periods: 'now' and 'next year'. Let C_0 be the number of dollars available for consumption now, and let C_1 be the number of dollars available for consumption one year from now. We assume an interest rate of r, which is the same for lenders and borrowers. To specify the budget constraint we need to know current income, which we denote by I_0, and income one year from now, I_1.

One way to derive the intertemporal budget constraint is to convert expenditure and income to present values, and then equate the present value of expenditure to the present value of income. But that is quite arbitrary; we would be equating present values merely because that's what economists say we should do. Instead, let's proceed from first principles: What does the *market* tell us to do? This point of view will enable us to *derive* present values from more primitive criteria. Now, let's put ourselves in the position of the consumer one year from now and ask simply, "How much money can I spend on goods and services in period 1?" If the consumer saved in period zero there will be

Savings + interest on savings + period 1 income.

Saving is, by definition, equal to the amount of income not spent on consumption. Therefore,

$$\text{Saving} = I_0 - C_0.$$

Interest earned on saving is the amount saved multiplied by the interest rate, which is

$$(I_0 - C_0) \times r$$

in this case. Therefore, the amount that a saver can spend on consumption in period 1 is

$$I_0 - C_0 + (I_0 - C_0) \times r + I_1, \quad \text{or} \quad (I_0 - C_0)(1 + r) + I_1.$$

Therefore, a saver is constrained by the following equation in period 1:

$$C_1 = (I_0 - C_0)(1 + r) + I_1.$$

What about someone who borrows initially? How much money can someone who borrowed in period 0 spend in period 1? The answer is clearly

Period 1 income − amount of the loan − interest on the loan.

The principal has to be repaid in period 1 in a two-period model, and so does the interest on the loan. It is easy to determine the amount borrowed: it will be equal to the amount spent on consumption in period zero in excess of period zero income. That is, borrowing $= C_0 - I_0$. The interest charge is the interest rate times the amount of the loan, or $(C_0 - I_0) \times r$. Therefore, the amount that a borrower can spend on consumption in period 1 is

$$I_1 - (C_0 - I_0)(1 + r)$$

and this is obviously equal to

$$(I_0 - C_0)(1 + r) + I_1.$$

Therefore, borrowers and savers are governed by the same intertemporal budget constraint:

$$C_1 = (I_0 - C_0)(1 + r) + I_1. \tag{1}$$

Of course, if the individual neither lends nor borrows in period zero we will have

$C_0 = I_0$ and hence $C_1 = I_1$, which also satisfies [1]. Therefore, [1] is *the* intertemporal budget constraint.

Let's gather the 'C' terms in [1] to the left hand side:

$$C_0(1 + r) + C_1 = I_0(1 + r) + I_1. \qquad [2]$$

We can express this as

$$P_0 C_0 + P_1 C_1 = P_0 I_0 + P_1 I_1,$$

where $P_0 = 1 + r$ and $P_1 = 1$. We have a standard budget constraint format in which the prices have a special interpretation. P_0 is the price of present consumption in units of C_1: every dollar of current consumption causes future consumption to fall by $1 + r$. Instead of using a dollar for current consumption, the individual could have saved (loaned) it at the interest rate r and had $1 + r$ dollars to spend one year from now. The price of consumption one year from now is utility, in the sense that a dollar's worth of consumption one year from now will cost a dollar one year from now. Therefore, P_0 and P_1 express the cost of consumption in periods zero and one, respectively, in terms of the amount of period one consumption sacrificed per unit of consumption. The budget constraint equates this with the market value of the income stream, $P_0 I_0 + P_1 I_1$. Now, let's take the intertemporal budget constraint [2] and divide both sides by $1 + r$. This yields.

$$C_0 + C_1(1 + r)^{-1} = I_0 + I_1(1 + r)^{-1}. \qquad [3]$$

We can express this as

$$V_0 C_0 + V_1 C_1 = V_0 I_0 + V_1 I_1,$$

where $V_0 = 1$ and $V_1 = (1 + r)^{-1}$. We refer to $(1 + r)^{-1}$ as the *present value* of one dollar received one year from now. No one would pay more than V_1 for the right to receive one dollar one year from now. Instead of paying $P > (1 + r)^{-1}$ for this right the investor could lend P dollars at the rate of interest r and have $P(1 + r) > (1 + r)^{-1}(1 + r) > 1$ after one year. Therefore, the market value of the right to receive one dollar one year from now cannot exceed $(1 + r)^{-1}$. On the other hand, no one would accept less than V_1 for an asset that paid one dollar one year from now. Instead of taking $P < (1 + r)^{-1}$ for the asset, the current owner keeps the asset and borrows P dollars now. One year from now, the loan would be paid back at a total cost of $P(1 + r) < 1$. The owner of the asset would be unambiguously better off, whatever her preferences, by holding the asset and borrowing to finance consumption if the price of the asset were less than $(1 + r)^{-1}$. Therefore, the market value of the right to receive one dollar one year from now can't be less than $(1 + r)^{-1}$. It cannot be higher, and it cannot be lower; it must be exactly $(1 + r)^{-1}$, which we can now call the present market value of one dollar payable one year from now.

We refer to [3] as the present value form of the intertemporal budget constraint. It equates the present value of expenditures with the present value of the income stream. Let's interpret it in terms of prices. V_0 is the price that one has to pay now for one dollar of consumption now. And V_1 is the price that one has to pay *now* for one dollar of consumption one year from now: If you put $V_1 = (1 + r)^{-1}$ dollars in a savings account now you will have $1 = (1 + r) \times (1 + r)^{-1}$ dollars in your account one year from now. Therefore, you have to reduce current consumption by V_1 dollars in order to finance one dollar of consumption next year, and if you spend V_1 dollars now you will have one dollar less to spend on consumption one year from now. We also refer to $(1 + r)^{-1}$ as the discount factor.

Now, consider two different assets I and J, yielding different income streams. Asset I pays I_0 dollars now and I_1 dollars in one year. Asset J pays J_0 dollars now and J_1 dollars one year from now. The budget constraints associated with the respective assets are

$$C_0 + C_1(1 + r)^{-1} = I_0 + I_1(1 + r)^{-1}, \quad \text{and} \qquad [4]$$

$$C_0 + C_1(1 + r)^{-1} = J_0 + J_1(1 + r)^{-1}. \qquad [5]$$

Let $PV(I)$ denote $I_0 + I_1(1 + r)^{-1}$, and let $PV(J)$ denote $J_0 + J_1(1 + r)^{-1}$, the respective present values of the income streams generated by the assets. Note that if $PV(J) > PV(I)$ then any C_0, C_1 pair that satisfies [4] will also satisfy [5] with room to spare. In other words, whenever $PV(J) > PV(I)$ and (C_0, C_1) satisfies [4] then there is some $\delta > 0$ such that $C_0 + \delta$ and $C_1 + \delta$ satisfy [5]. Therefore, *whatever one's preferences*, asset J will provide a higher level of utility than asset I. (This is known as the *separation theorem:* The preferred asset can be determined independently of preferences!) The utility maximizing basket on [5] may not have more of both goods than the utility maximizing basket on [4], but the fact that for any basket satisfying [4] there is one satisfying [5] with more of both goods shows that utility will always be higher with asset J. (See Figure 2.) Why? Because J has a higher present value, and that means that the budget constraint associated with J will have a larger number on the right hand side. Other things being equal, we want the right hand side of the budget constraint to be as large as possible.

Suppose there are $T + 1$ periods, where T is a large number. A generalization of the above argument, in which we look at the consumer's range of choice in period $T + 1$, will establish that

$$\begin{aligned} C_0(1 + r)^T + C_1(1 + r)^{T-1} + \dots C_t(1 + r)^{T-t} + \dots C_{T-1}(1 + r) + C_T \\ = I_0(1 + r)^T + I_1(1 + r)^{T-1} + \dots I_t(1 + r)^{T-t} + \dots I_{T-1}(1 + r) + I_T. \end{aligned} \qquad [6]$$

If we divide both sides of [6] by $(1 + r)^T$ we get

$$\begin{aligned} C_0 + C_1(1 + r)^{-1} + \dots C_t(1 + r)^{-t} + \dots C_{T-1}(1 + r)^{-T+1} \\ + C_T(1 + r)^{-T} = I_0 + I_1(1 + r)^{-1} + \dots I_t(1 + r)^{-t} \\ + \dots I_{T-1}(1 + r)^{-T+1} + I_T(1 + r)^{-T}, \end{aligned} \qquad [7]$$

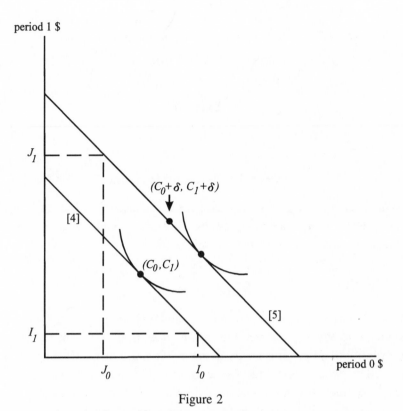

Figure 2

which can be read as "The present value of consumption equals the present value of the income stream." Moreover, we can let

$$y = C_1 + C_2(1 + r)^{-1} + \ldots C_t(1 + r)^{-t+1} + \ldots C_{T-1}(1 + r)^{-T+2} + C_T(1 + r)^{-T+1}$$

be the market value of future consumption as viewed from a vantage point one year hence. Y is a composite commodity representing expenditure on goods and services in all years from period 1, *discounted to period 1*. If x represents C_0 dollars spent on consumer goods and services now, then from our examination of the two-period model we know that the intertemporal budget constraint is

$$x + y(1 + r)^{-1} = m_0 + m_1(1 + r)^{-1} \qquad [8]$$

where $m_0 = I_0$ and

$$m_1 = I_1 + I_2(1 + r)^{-1} + \ldots I_t(1 + r)^{-t+1} + \ldots I_{T-1}(1 + r)^{-T+2} + I_T(1 + r)^{-T+1}.$$

That is, m_1 is the market value, discounted to period 1, of future income from the standpoint of next period. Note that [6] and [8] are equivalent (in the multiperiod model) if we employ the definitions of y and m_1 just given. Therefore, we have justified a two-period model in studying intertemporal choice.

Suggestions for further reading: Lazear (1979), Carmichael (1989).

Exercise

1   Derive [6] rigorously.

4 Moral hazard and insurance

Economists use the term "moral hazard" as a synonym for "hidden action" even though the term "moral hazard" traditionally referred to hidden action problems in the insurance industry, the subject of this section.

4.1 Overview

It has long been recognized that when an individual purchases insurance coverage his incentive to invest in preventive care is diminished. Preventive care reduces the probability of a loss. It is costly to the individual, however, while adding little to his welfare when losses due to carelessness or bad luck are covered by the insurance contract. It is not immediately obvious that 'underinvesting' in preventive care is a bad thing from society's standpoint: Preventive care is costly to society because it reduces individual utility to the extent that the resources required for extra care are diverted from the production of goods that contribute directly to utility. Preventive care also provides social benefits because it leads to a reduction in losses for the community as a whole, and the resources that would otherwise be required to replace the lost wealth are available for the production of commodities that enhance individual utility. The net effect on utility can be positive or negative. However, it is not too difficult to see that moral hazard leads to inefficiency. When an individual is insured, any increase in the loss that he suffers is financed by the pool of insured individuals generally and the individual's share of that increase will be negligible. In other words, preventive care by an individual will bring negligible benefit to that individual in terms of reduced insurance premiums. But the costs of preventive care are borne by the individual himself; we have another class of situations in which the social benefits of an individual action outweigh the social costs of that action, but the action is not taken because the costs to the individual exceed the individual benefits. But when every insured individual makes the same decision – failing to invest in preventive care – there is an appreciable increase in everyone's premium, reflecting the substantial reduction in the community's wealth, and it is often the case that each person has less utility than he would have enjoyed if each person had been forced to invest in preventive care. This is another instance of the prisoner's dilemma phenomenon. Before confirming this with a numerical example I will run through a few informal examples of moral hazard.

(You may feel that an individual has sufficient incentive to invest in preventive care because in most of the cases where insurance is available – burglary, fire, automobile insurance, etc. – there is also the potential for personal injury, or even loss of life. A lot of people jump to the conclusion that a person would employ every available device for minimizing the chance of accident and injury, independently of any financial incentive. But ask yourself this: Does every car buyer choose a new car with a driver's airbag? Are those of us who have recently purchased cars without airbags not concerned about our health or our families' health? Why are party-goers more likely to take taxis or appoint a 'designated driver' in communities where the police watch closely for drivers under the influence of alcohol? Because we can never tell for certain whether we are going to have an accident, it is not in our interest to spend money on all of the available preventive care measures. If we did, each household would want to live next to a hospital, and no one would ever take a vacation because the money saved on vacations could be devoted to increased fire protection for the home. Why not hire a night watchman for your home to reduce the probability that you will die in your bed in a fire? Or, consider the moral hazard problem associated with insurance that gave you protection against high home heating costs due to an unusually harsh winter.)

The most striking example of moral hazard is the case of an individual who commits suicide so that his family can collect the life insurance benefits. This particular moral hazard is in fact eliminated by the insurance contract which releases the insurance company from its obligation to pay off when death is the result of suicide. It is costly for the company to determine if the insured did commit suicide, but the cost is typically small relative to a potential claim. In most cases the costs of verifying moral hazard are too high for it to be part of the contractual relationship. Here are some examples: "Kevin and Sandy: I had to go out for an hour. The key is under the mat. Make yourself at home." Would you leave this note on your front door if you weren't covered by burglary insurance? Would it make a difference whether or not you were insured? Some homeowners with fire insurance will burn leaves in the driveway but would not do so if they were not insured against fire. When I lived in Ontario, which essentially provides full state coverage for medical expenses, I invested in much less preventive health care than I do in Virginia. You may be skeptical; I don't mean to say that I allowed my health to deteriorate when I lived in Ontario. Given that one has a health problem, there are often a number of ways of successfully treating it. If the alternative methods impose different burdens on the community's resources and these social costs are not reflected in the *private* costs incurred by the individual making the decision then the private decisions will not contribute to efficiency. For example, once on a trip with my family, I went to the emergency ward of an Ottawa hospital to get a prescription for our son's medication. We had forgotten the medicine at home. We're not that careless in Virginia because our Virginia health insurance company would not reimburse us for the visit to the emergency ward, and rightfully so. There need not be a hidden action problem in this case; my trip to the emergency ward was obviously not a true emergency, and a sensible insurance program would not allow me to pass the costs of that visit on to the community. (I'm not proud of this example.)

What exacerbates this problem are the facts, first, that physicians know patients will pass the costs of health care onto the insurance carrier *and*, second, that patients typically have almost no expertise in the treating of the condition that has sent them to the doctor. This can lead to the doctor's overprescribing medical care. According to one medical study, 20% of the heart pacemaker implants in the U.S. were not endorsed in retrospect as the most appropriate treatment, and 36% of the implants were recommended on the basis of an extremely optimistic fore-cast of expected benefits.[22] Medical practitioners in Western Europe rely more on drug therapy to treat heart disease than Americans who are more likely to recommend surgery. Of course, surgery is more expensive. Americans spend far more per capita on health care than Canadians, but have about the same health status.[23] (And virtually all Canadians are covered by some form of comprehensive health insurance, while 15% of Americans are not covered at all.) And because the direct cost to the recipient of medical services is typically very low, hospitals have very little incentive to compete on the price dimension. They tend to appeal to consumers by publicizing the acquisition of high-cost, high-tech equipment, even when it has little overall effect on citizens' health status. (For example, there is substantial excess capacity in organ transplant facilities in U.S. hospitals.) The equipment does have a big impact on health care cost, however.

Insurance companies try to mitigate moral hazard by requiring the insured party to pay a small fraction of the loss. Very often the patient will have to pay 20% of the health care costs while the insurance company pays 80%. This lightens the patient's financial burden considerably – compared to that of someone without any health care insurance – but at the same time imposes a charge on the patient that is proportional to the social cost of medical care. This makes it costly for an individual to incur expenses that add little to his utility. If medical care is free to the individual then he has an incentive to consume any health care service as long as it adds *something* to his utility, regardless of the cost to society. 'Deductibles' go a long way toward lining up private and social costs for small losses. A deductible clause in an insurance contract makes the insured party liable for any expenses under the deductible limit, which is usually around $200 for automobile collision coverage. The individual has protection against big losses, which is really what one needs, but for small losses, which are often the ones that are most easily avoidable, the individual suffering the loss pays. This means that private costs are equal to social costs for small losses – i.e., for losses below the deductible limit.[24] Automobile insurance companies use experience rating to encourage careful driving; drivers with poor records pay higher premiums. Some companies won't accept business at any price from drivers with poor records. This gives the individual a direct financial incentive to take preventive care. Health insurance companies now use experience rating to determine the amount of premium paid by firms that purchase group policies. Firms in industries in which the incidence of AIDS is unusually high sometimes cannot purchase health insurance at all. If insurance companies were able to sort us into risk categories with perfect precision and charge higher premiums to individuals in higher-risk groups they would do so. Any firm that didn't do this would not be very profitable if the other firms did sort. And if other firms did not sort, then a typical firm could increase its profit by sorting according to risk. Up to a point, sorting by risk is socially beneficial because it reduces the moral hazard problem. But if it is taken too far then each individual finds himself in a small risk group, unable to take advantage of the law of large numbers, and that would undermine the social benefit of insurance. When I am in a large pool of insured individuals and my annual premium equals the expected value of a loss then insurance increases my expected utility because I am risk averse and the premium varies very little because of the large numbers effect. But when I am in a small pool, the premium will be quite variable and therefore I am less insulated against risk. The expected utility of everyone in a small pool could be increased by aggregating the pools. (Similarly, I may find a particular investment unattractive in the sense that it would lower my expected utility. But one can easily construct examples for which it would benefit the individual to undertake a joint venture with, say nine others, each paying one-tenth of the costs and receiving one-tenth of the profit, or absorbing one-tenth of any loss. See exercise 6 at the end of Chapter 1.) Experience rating for health care insurance can go well beyond a due consideration of incentives. It is in society's interest to make individuals who choose to smoke pay higher health insurance premiums, but an individual with lung disease should be treated as a victim of bad luck, rather than as someone who made unwise choices in the past. As far as possible, we want to insure risks over the individual's lifetime, while preserving the insurance premium link between present behavior and future treatment costs. (See Diamond, 1992.)

If one were able to get more than 100% fire insurance coverage, the moral hazard problem would be particularly acute: if the building were completely destroyed by fire then the value of the insurance claim would exceed the market value of the building. The owner would have a strong financial incentive to torch his own building. This would definitely affect the probability of a loss and would have a big impact on the size of fire insurance premiums. Insurance companies will not give more than 100% coverage. This is clearly socially desirable for a lot of reasons. (How many can you cite?)

Very often the market system provides its own solution to a hidden action problem.[25] We have discussed the example of taxi fares (section 2 of Chapter 1). Here is another: Health maintenance organizations (HMOs) provide comprehensive medical care for a fixed annual fee. The link between the subscriber's health status and the profitability of the HMO is central, and HMOs emphasize preventive care in an attempt to reduce future expenditures for costly treatment of advanced illnesses. They pay for periodic medical examinations, for example.[26] Here is another interesting example: In the 1940s movie producers began giving major stars a share in the profits from their movies. This gave the stars an incentive to avoid the silly temper tantrums that cause production delays and escalate the costs of the movie. But when this became common practice some movie producers began disguising the profit earned by the most lucrative movies by shifting some of the profit to other movies. Contracts that offered the performers a cut of the profits were less rewarding as a result, and many responded by holding out for a percentage of the *gross* – i.e., they demanded a cut of the picture's revenue instead of its profit.

4.2 A formal treatment

We now investigate the conditions for efficiency under moral hazard by means of a simple model. There are only two commodities: X, which we will call wealth, and L, leisure. Let $B(w)$ be the utility of w dollars of wealth, and let ℓ denote the amount of leisure consumed. Hence, $U(w, \ell) = B(w) + \ell$, on the assumption that utility is quasi-linear. Uncertainty concerns the status of an individual's wealth endowment, which is either partially destroyed with probability π or remains intact with probability $1 - \pi$. Let a represent the value of an individual's wealth when there is an accident but no insurance is purchased, and let z represent the value of the same individual's wealth when there is no accident. Of course, $a < z$. The actual wealth level may be different from both a and z if insurance is purchased. Let x denote the individual's actual wealth when he suffers an accident, taking into account any insurance benefits that may be paid. Let y denote wealth when there is no accident but the individual has paid an insurance premium. The quantities x and y will be a function of the insurance contract chosen by the individual: y is equal to z minus the cost of purchasing insurance, and x is equal to a plus the net payment to the individual by the insurance company (net of the insurance premium). The amount of leisure is determined before the resolution of uncertainty. Therefore, the individual's utility is

$$u = \pi B(x) + (1 - \pi)B(y) + \ell.$$

We assume that the individual is risk averse, so $B' > 0$ and $B'' < 0$ at all levels of wealth. The probability of an accident, π, is a function of the amount e of preventive care taken by the individual. Of course $\pi'(e) < 0$. The derivative of π with respect to e is negative because preventive care reduces the probability of an accident. Preventive care is costly to the individual, and we take this into account by setting $\ell = \Omega - e$. That is, the amount of leisure is equal to the time endowment Ω (24 hours if the period is a day) less the amount of time devoted to preventive care. (You might prefer to let Ω represent time not spent at work.) Therefore,

$$u = \pi(e)B(x) + [1 - \pi(e)]B(y) + \Omega - e.$$

Let c denote the net insurance coverage. That is, $x = a + c$. And p is the cost of insurance per dollar of coverage.[27] Then pc is the premium on the policy, and $y = z - pc$. Now, the consumer will choose e and c to maximize utility,

$$V = \pi(e)B(a + c) + [1 - \pi(e)]B(z - pc) + \Omega - e,$$

subject to the constraints $0 \leq c \leq z/p$ and $0 \leq e \leq \Omega$. We will simply assume that the optimal value of c lies strictly between 0 and z/p.

Before examining the solution to the consumer's decision problem we determine p. We assume a competitive insurance market and (for convenience) zero administration cost. This means that the amount of money taken in in premiums will exactly equal the amount paid out in claims. And we take advantage of the law of large numbers to assume that the actual number of accidents is equal to the expected number, πn, where n is the number of policyholders. Obviously, npc is the total amount of premium income. Each accident victim will submit a claim of M dollars, so $x = a + M - T$, where T is the cost of the policy. (The premium has to be paid even when you have an accident.) This means that $M = c + pc$. Therefore, the zero profit condition is

$$npc = \pi n[c + pc],$$

the solution of which is $p = \pi/(1 - \pi)$. (We are also assuming, for convenience, that the n individuals are identical, so they make the same choices.) For *any* premium p (whether established under competitive conditions or not), the budget constraint is expressed by $x = a + c$ and $y = z - pc$. If you want to express this as a single straight line constraint, solve $x = a + c$ to get $c = x - a$ and then substitute this for c in $y = z - pc$, yielding $y = z - p(x - a)$.

Now let's find the solution to the consumer decision problem.[28] The *individual's* choice will not have an appreciable impact on the premium p, so the individual takes p as given. Of course, p is influenced by the amount of preventive care in the aggregate.

$$\partial V / \partial c = \pi(e)B'(a + c) + [1 - \pi(e)]B'(z - pc) \times -p$$
$$\partial V / \partial e = \pi'(e)B(x) - \pi'(e)B(y) - 1$$

where $\partial V / \partial c$ is the partial derivative[29] of V with respect to c, $\partial V / \partial e$ is the partial derivative of V with respect to e, $x = a + c$, and $y = z - pc$. Assuming an interior solution value for c, we have $\partial V / \partial c = 0$ and thus $0 = \partial V / \partial c = \pi B'(a + c) - p(1 - \pi)B'(z - pc) = \pi B'(a + c) - \pi B'(z - pc)$ because $p = \pi/(1 - \pi)$. But then $B'(x) = B'(y)$, which implies $x = y$ because $B'' < 0$ at all points. (See section 9 of Chapter 1.) Then $a + c = z - pc$ when $p = \pi/(1 - \pi)$, and hence

$$c = (1 - \pi)(z - a) \qquad \text{when } p = \pi/(1 - \pi).$$

Now, $\partial V / \partial e = \pi'(e)B(x) - \pi'(e)B(y) - 1$, but if $x = y$ we have $\partial V / \partial e = -1$, a negative number. This means that at the chosen basket, a reduction in e will increase V. Therefore, the consumer will optimize by setting $e = 0$. This is easy to explain. The cost of preventive care is positive. Preventive care also provides benefit in the form of a reduced probability of an accident, and the reduction in the probability (of not having an accident) is $-\pi'$, so the contribution to expected utility is $-\pi'B(y)$. Of course $\pi B(x)$ changes by $\pi'B(x)$, and the two terms offset when $x = y$. If $p > \pi/(1 - \pi)$, because of a lack of competition, then $\partial V / \partial e$ could be positive, and the individual could undertake protective care at equilibrium:

$$\partial V / \partial e = \pi'B(x) - \pi'B(y) - 1.$$

If $p > \pi/(1 - \pi)$ then $x < y$ and hence $B(y) > B(x)$. And $-\pi' > 0$. Therefore, $\pi'B(x) - \pi'B(y) > 0$ when $p > \pi/(1 - \pi)$. If p is sufficiently high then $e = 0$ is not consistent with expected utility maximization.

In summary, a risk averse individual will never invest in preventive care when he is insured by a firm in a competitive insurance industry. We discovered a special case of this in examining the S & L industry in section 2: Individual depositors do not monitor borrowers. Now we show that the equilibrium outcome $e = 0$ is typically inefficient. For concreteness, we set $\Omega = 1$ and

$$B(w) = 4\ln(w + 3), \qquad a = 24, \qquad z = 96, \qquad \Omega = 1, \quad \text{and} \quad \pi(e) = \tfrac{1}{2} - \tfrac{1}{4}e$$

with $0 \le e \le 1$. We have $B' > 0$ and $B'' < 0$ for all w, so the argument above applies. Check that $e = 0$ at equilibrium for all policyholders. Thus $\pi = \tfrac{1}{2}$ and $p = \tfrac{1}{2}/\tfrac{1}{2} = 1$. (This does not mean that a dollar of gross coverage costs a dollar; no one would buy such a policy. The policy pays $2c$ dollars in case of accident and costs c dollars, so $x = a + c = 24 + c$. A claim cheque for $2c$ dollars is issued, but after subtracting the premium the individual has c more dollars than if she were not insured.) If $p = 1$ and $x = y$, we have $a + c = z - c$, and therefore

$$c = \tfrac{1}{2}(96 - 24) = 36 \quad \text{and} \quad x = y = 60.$$

The competitive equilibrium insurance contract provides each policyholder with a utility of

$$\tfrac{1}{2}(4)\ln(63) + \tfrac{1}{2}(4)\ln(63) + 1 - 0 = 4\ln(63) + 1 = 17.573.$$

Let's determine if the competitive equilibrium is efficient. If we maximize the sum of individual expected utilities we will obtain an efficient outcome: If outcome A is feasible and gives one person more expected utility than outcome B, without giving anyone less utility than B, then the sum of utilities will be higher under A than B. Therefore, if we have already maximized the sum of expected utilities it will be impossible to find another feasible outcome that gives someone more utility without giving another person less. Therefore, maximization of the sum of individual utilities yields an efficient outcome. Assuming that we have n identical individuals, this will show us whether the competitive equilibrium is efficient. (Why?) The planner wants to maximize nG, where

$$G = \pi \times 4\ln(x + 3) + (1 - \pi) \times 4\ln(y + 3) + \Omega - e, \qquad [1]$$

which is individual expected utility. Maximizing nG is obviously equivalent to maximizing G.

Feasibility and efficiency impose restrictions on x and y. Feasibility requires that the policy will generate enough premium revenue to pay all of the claims submitted: The total wealth in the community will be

[Number of accidents] $\times a$ + [n − number of accidents] $\times z$.

The expected number of accidents is πn, the probability of an individual accident times the number of individuals, and the expected number can be assumed to be equal to the actual number, thanks to the law of large numbers. Therefore, the number of individuals who do not have an accident is $n - \pi n = (1 - \pi)n$. Therefore, the total wealth in the community is $n\pi a + n(1 - \pi)z$. The total wealth actually made available by an insurance policy provided by the planner is

[Number of accidents] $\times x$ + [n − number of accidents] $\times y$
$$= n\pi x + n(1 - \pi)y.$$

Feasibility requires that the total wealth made available by insurance is not greater than the actual amount of wealth in the community. Therefore, feasibility requires

$$n[\pi x + (1 - \pi)y] \leq n[\pi a + (1 - \pi)z].$$

If we actually had $n[\pi x + (1 - \pi)y] < n[\pi a + (1 - \pi)z]$ then the amount of wealth distributed by the planner would be less than the total amount available.

This is obviously inconsistent with efficiency. Therefore, feasibility and efficiency imply

$$\pi x + (1 - \pi)y = \pi a + (1 - \pi)z \qquad [2]$$

and we have fair odds. Hence maximization of G requires $x = y$ because each individual is risk averse. Set $x = y$ in [2] to obtain $x = \pi a + (1 - \pi)z = y$. If we set $x = y$ and $\Omega = 1$ in [1] we get

$$G = 4\ln(x + 3) + 1 - e.$$

This is a function of e because x depends on π which depends on e. Remember, $\pi = \frac{1}{2} - \frac{1}{4}e$. Now, maximize G.

$$G'(e) = \frac{4}{(x + 3)} \times \frac{dx}{de} - 1. \qquad [3]$$

Now, $x = \pi a + (1 - \pi)z = (\frac{1}{2} - \frac{1}{4}e)a + (\frac{1}{2} + \frac{1}{4}e)z$. Therefore, $dx/de = -\frac{1}{4}a + \frac{1}{4}z$. Therefore, [3] yields

$$G'(e) = \frac{4}{(x + 3)} \times [-\tfrac{1}{4}a + \tfrac{1}{4}z] - 1. \qquad [4]$$

If we set $G'(e) = 0$ we get $(z - a)/(x + 3) - 1 = 0$, or $z - a = x + 3$. (Confirm that $G'' < 0$ for all e.) We have $x = \pi a + (1 - \pi)z$ and $\pi = (\frac{1}{2} - \frac{1}{4}e)$, so

$$z - a = (\tfrac{1}{2} - \tfrac{1}{4}e)a + (\tfrac{1}{2} + \tfrac{1}{4}e)z + 3, \quad \text{or}$$

$$96 - 24 = 12 - 6e + 48 + 24e + 3,$$

which implies $e = \frac{1}{2}$. Let's confirm that $e = \frac{1}{2}$ gives everyone more utility than $e = 0$. If $e = \frac{1}{2}$ then $\pi = \frac{3}{8}$ and $1 - \pi = \frac{5}{8}$. We have $x = (\frac{3}{8})24 + (\frac{5}{8})96 = 69 = y$. Individual expected utility is

$$4\ln 72 + 1 - \tfrac{1}{2} = 17.607,$$

which exceeds 17.573, the utility realized when everyone sets $e = 0$. Why then *does* each consumer set $e = 0$? Because $e = 0$ maximizes individual expected utility given competitive insurance prices. Increasing e to $\frac{1}{2}$ increases individual utility only when everyone else also sets $e = \frac{1}{2}$. But an individual can only control his own level of preventive care. Can we have a competitive equilibrium where $e = \frac{1}{2}$ for everyone? No. $\partial V/\partial e < 0$ when $x = y$, regardless of the level of x and y. We have $G'(0) > 0$ for the planner's problem because the planner contemplates a simultaneous increase in e for everyone, and this will lower the premium p. The premium does not fall when a single individual changes his level of e.

Can the planner actually find an incentive scheme that will induce everyone to set $e = \frac{1}{2}$? If it were known that $e = \frac{1}{2}$ is efficient then the problem is a much easier one, but there is still the issue of verifying that the individual has in fact undertaken the socially optimal level of preventive care. In general, the planner will not know the socially optimal value of e because the utility-of-wealth function is a hidden characteristic, as is $\pi(e)$. Therefore, improving on the market outcome is problematic. What we have learned is that the standard efficiency claim made for the private ownership market economy is not always valid when there are hidden information problems. Private insurance companies provide incentive to take protective care by means of deductibles and copayments. Health insurance contracts often stipulate that the insured must pay a fraction, say 20%, of the treatment costs – the 20% is referred to as a copayment. A deductible, of say \$300, limits the insurance companies' obligation to expenses over \$300. The first \$300 is paid by the insured.

Exercises

1. For $\Omega = 1$, $B(w) = 10\ln(w + 1)$, and $\pi(e) = \frac{1}{2} - \frac{1}{4}e$ show that the individual will set $x = y$ and $e = 0$.

2. With $B(w) = \beta\ln(w + 1)$, $\pi(e) = \frac{1}{2} - \frac{1}{4}e$, and $u(x, y, \ell) = \pi B(x) + (1 - \pi)B(y) + \alpha\ell$. Find a condition on the positive parameters α, β, a, and z that implies inefficiency of the competitive equilibrium of the insurance market.

3. Find a condition that implies inefficiency of the competitive equilibrium of the insurance market when

$$u(x, y, \ell) = \pi\sqrt{x} + (1 - \pi)\sqrt{y} + \ell$$

and $\pi(e) = \frac{1}{2} - \frac{1}{4}e$.

4. Prove that the individual will set $x < y$ if $p > \pi/(1 - \pi)$.

5. If $B(w) = 4\ln(w + 3)$, $a = 24$, $z = 96$, and $\pi(e) = \frac{1}{2} - \frac{1}{4}e$, for what values of p will the *individual* set $e > 0$?

6. Prove that if $p < \pi/(1 - \pi)$ then the policy will not generate enough premium revenue to pay all of the claims submitted.

7. If an individual devotes e units of effort to preventive care then the probability of an accident is $1 - e$. Each individual has the expected utility function

$$\pi[0.2\sqrt{x}] + (1 - \pi)[0.2\sqrt{y}] + 1 - e$$

where π is the probability of an accident, x represents wealth if there is an accident, and y represents wealth if there is no accident. If there is no insurance then $x = 50$ and $y = 150$.

a Show how x depends on e (that is, display x as a function of e) assuming that the outcome is feasible and efficient and that $x = y$ at the same level for all households.

b Assuming that everyone can be made to employ the same level of preventive care, show that per capita expected utility is maximized when $e = \frac{1}{2}$.

c Explain briefly why the competitive equilibrium is not efficient. (A verbal argument will suffice, but a calculus-based explanation is also perfectly satisfactory.)

5 Partnerships

In this section we discover why few firms are organized as partnerships. A partnership is a firm in which the key workers are also the firm's owners, who share the profits. Sometimes one partner puts more capital into the firm than the others and receives a larger share of the firm's profits, but the essential point is that each partner shares in the income created by the effort of the other partners. By the same token, the partner receives only a fraction of the income generated by her own effort and, as we will see, each partner contributes less than the efficient amount of effort. There is an alternative contractual arrangement that results in each person's receiving a leisure–income package that she prefers to the one obtained in a partnership format. Why, then, are partnerships observed at all? We will provide the answer at the end of the next section. First we consider why production takes place in *teams*. Simply put, there is more output per worker when a production team is formed than when individuals work independently. That is, one-person firms generate less output per unit of labor input than do multiperson firms. We examine these issues by means of a simple model.

5.1 The model

There are two consumer goods, leisure and "income." By income we simply mean the total number of dollars available for expenditure on goods other than leisure. Let x be the amount of leisure consumed and let y be the income level. Then $u(x, y)$ represents the individual's utility function. Let Ω denote the number of hours available per period. ($\Omega = 168$ if the time period is a week.) The income generated by a production team depends on the amount of effort expended by each of the team members. If e is the amount of effort contributed by an individual then $x = \Omega - e$. Note that x is not just Ω less the number of hours "worked." An individual may show up for work but not put in much effort, consuming leisure on the job. This will affect the amount of output and income generated by the firm and also the individual's utility through its effect on leisure. Therefore, we need to keep track of effort, not hours on the job. (In most teams it is not just a question of how much effort is expended, but also of how the effort is employed, but in order to simplify the analysis we focus attention on only one dimension of the principal–agent problem: the incentive to work rather than shirk.)

All members of a production team share in the income generated by the team –

according to *some* formula, which may or may not constitute partnership. But the team income depends on the effort supplied by the members. Therefore, an individual's income is a function of the effort expended by all. One person cannot control the effort supplied by others, so we highlight an individual's effort supply decision by taking as given the effort contributed by everyone else, and working out the individual's income w as a function $w(e)$ of the effort that she herself supplies. The individual then chooses e to maximize $u(\Omega - e, w(e))$. That is, the individual supplies the level of e that maximizes $u(x, y)$ when $x = \Omega - e$ and $y = w(e)$, whether effort is observable or not. If effort is unobservable, how can a team member determine the effort supplied by others at equilibrium? By working out their utility maximizing responses to the incentives governing their behavior. Each team member is assumed to be aware of the contracts entered into by the others. Note that the individual can determine the *total* effort supplied by others simply by observing total output y, inferring the total effort supplied, and then subtracting her own.

When the individual works on her own (a one-person firm) the equation $y = \alpha e$ represents the technology of the firm. It expresses the income available when e units of effort are expended. The positive constant α is the income generated per unit of effort. Because $x = \Omega - e$ we can say that $y = \alpha(\Omega - x)$ in the case of a one-person firm. The individual chooses the package (x, y) to maximize u subject to the technology constraint $y = \alpha(\Omega - x)$, or $\alpha x + y = \alpha \Omega$. The chosen point $C^\alpha = (x^\alpha, y^\alpha)$, illustrated in Figure 3, is a point of tangency of the indifference curve and the technology constraint line L_α. In economic terms the marginal rate of substitution at C^α equals α, which is the opportunity cost of leisure – i.e., the amount of income sacrificed per hour of leisure consumed. (Note that an individual can always observe her own effort level.)

Now consider a two-person firm. Let β denote the income generated per unit of effort when two individuals cooperate in production. Let e_i denote the effort expended by i, x_i the leisure consumed by i, and y_i the income of individual i ($i = 1, 2$). Then $y_1 + y_2 = \beta(e_1 + e_2)$. Of course $\beta > \alpha$.

We will abstract from a lot of real-world phenomena in order to focus on the role of incentives. For one thing, we assume that the individuals in our firm have identical preferences, and $u(x, y)$ will again represent the individual's preference scheme. And we study only two-person firms, although the generalization to n persons is straightforward.

If the individuals have identical consumption then we will have $x_1 = x_2$ and $y_1 = y_2$, and hence $e_1 = e_2$. Then $y_1 + y_2 = \beta(e_1 + e_2)$ implies $2y_i = \beta(2e_i)$ and thus $y_i = \beta e_i$. This allows us to contrast the two-person firm with the one-person firm (Figure 3). Because $\beta > \alpha$ the technology line $y_i = \beta e_i = \beta(\Omega - x_i)$, denoted L_β, lies above its one-person counterpart L_α. Therefore, the two-person firm can

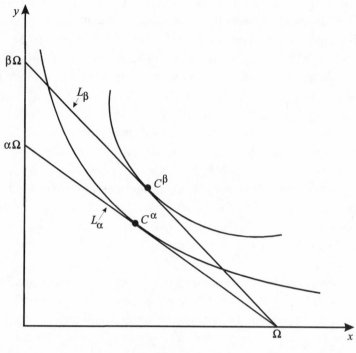

Figure 3

provide a higher level of per capita utility than the one-person firm. Let $C^\beta =$ (x^β, y^β) denote the utility maximizing bundle available with a two-person firm, assuming that the team members consume the same bundle. The marginal rate of substitution at C^β equals β, which is the opportunity cost of leisure per person in a two-person team.

We can call the outcome that gives each person the bundle C^β *fair* precisely because they have identical bundles and identical preferences. Because the outcome is also efficient it is a reasonable standard by which to measure the performance of a particular contractual arrangement.

Theorem *For any number of workers, the outcome that gives* C^β *to each person is fair and efficient.*

Proof As we have said, the outcome is fair by definition. To prove efficiency, let (x_1, y_1) and (x_2, y_2) be two bundles that give the respective individuals more utility than C^β. That is,

$$u(x_1, y_1) > u(x^\beta, y^\beta) \quad \text{and} \quad u(x_2, y_2) > u(x^\beta, y^\beta).$$

Now, C^β maximizes u subject to $y_i \leq \beta(\Omega - x_i)$ so anything that gives higher utility than C^β must violate the inequality $y_i \leq \beta(\Omega - x_i)$. Therefore

$$y_1 > \beta(\Omega - x_1) \quad \text{and} \quad y_2 > \beta(\Omega - x_2)$$

and hence $y_1 + y_2 > \beta(\Omega - x_1 + \Omega - x_2) = \beta(e_1 + e_2)$. Then the new outcome that assigns (x_i, y_i) to each i is not feasible: the total income allocated exceeds the total income $\beta(e_1 + e_2)$ generated by the effort that would be supplied. Therefore, an outcome that gives both persons more utility than C^β cannot be feasible. This proves that the outcome assigning C^β to each is weakly efficient – there is no feasible outcome that gives both persons more utility. (Complete the argument by showing that it is impossible to give one person more utility than provided by C^β without reducing the other person's utility below its level at C^β.)

Can C^β in fact be realized? C^β is feasible, but only when the two persons cooperate. But then person i's income depends on the total income of the firm, which in turn depends on the amount of effort contributed by *both* persons. Will there be incentive for each to contribute the required amount of effort? Let us consider the partnership example.

5.2 Partnership

The rules of partnership are simple. The partners share equally in the income that is created by their joint effort, and any losses are absorbed equally by the individual partners. Professional service industries employ the partnership method of team organization more than any other contractual form. Partnership is the typical form for accounting firms, law firms, and medical clinics. Apart from professional services, however, large firms rarely adopt the partnership contractual form.[30] Why are partnerships widely employed in the professional service industries but rarely in evidence elsewhere? In order to answer that question we need to determine the amount of effort contributed by a partner as a consequence of utility maximization. To determine the chosen level of effort, focus on partner 1. Person 1 chooses (x_1, y_1) to maximize $u(x_1, y_1)$ subject to the technology relationship $y_1 = \frac{1}{2}\beta(e_1 + e_2)$. Partner 1 cannot control e_2, so we will take it as fixed, at c. And $e_1 = \Omega - x_1$ so 1 endeavors to maximize $u(x_1, y_1)$ subject to $y_1 = \frac{1}{2}\beta(\Omega - x_1 + c)$. The constraint can be expressed as $\frac{1}{2}\beta x_1 + y_1 = \frac{1}{2}\beta(\Omega + c)$ ($L_{(1/2)\beta}$ in Figure 4). This is a budget line. The opportunity cost of good 1, leisure, to the individual is $\frac{1}{2}\beta$ under the partnership sharing rule. It is the ratio of the "prices" of the two goods. If person i consumes one more hour of leisure the *firm* loses one hour of effort and thus β dollars of income, but individual i loses only $\frac{1}{2}\beta$ dollars of income because the β dollars of income generated would have been shared with the other person. Therefore, utility maximization requires equality between the marginal rate of substitution and the opportunity cost $\frac{1}{2}\beta$. In deriving C^β, however, the constraint line was $y_1 = \beta e_1$, or $y_1 = \beta(\Omega - x_1)$, or $\beta x_1 + y_1 = \beta\Omega$. In that case the opportunity cost of leisure is β and at C^β the marginal rate of substitution equals β. Let $C^P = (x^P, y^P)$ be the individual's choice at equilibrium

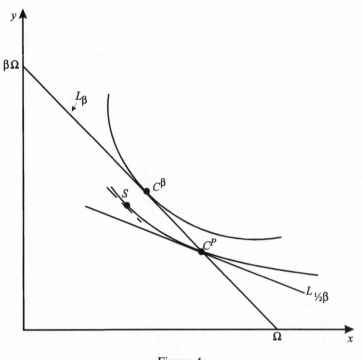

Figure 4

under the *partnership* arrangement. The partners will have the same consumption at equilibrium because they have the same preferences and are confronted with the same incentives. We know that $C^P \neq C^\beta$ because the marginal rate of substitution is $\frac{1}{2}\beta$ at C^P and double that at C^β. We also know that the utility of C^β exceeds the utility of C^P because C^β *maximizes* utility subject to $y \leq \beta e$ and C^P satisfies $y \leq \beta e$. To prove the latter claim note that $y^P + y^P \leq \beta(e^P + e^P)$ because the partnership outcome is feasible. (Recall that the partners make the same choices at equilibrium, and whenever we fail to employ a subscript it is implicit that the variable applies to each individual.) Therefore, $y^P \leq \beta e^P$. So the partnership outcome gives each person less utility than C^β, which is feasible. Not only that, C^P provides more leisure but less income than C^β. The reason for the increased consumption of leisure is that the opportunity cost of leisure to the individual in a partnership is half of the opportunity cost to the firm: Half of the β dollars lost to the firm when i consumes another unit of leisure would have been given to the other partner. To prove that leisure consumption is higher under C^P than C^β try placing C^P *above* C^β on L_β. Now draw the indifference curve through C^P. It has a marginal rate of substitution of $\frac{1}{2}\beta$ at C^P so the curve is flatter than L_β at C^P and bends up to the right of C^P. The marginal rate of substitution at C^β is equal to β, the absolute value of the slope of L_β, so the indifference curve through C^β bends up to the left of C^β. The two curves would have to intersect, and that is impossible. (A formal proof: Assume that both goods are normal. Find the point S in Figure 4 on the indifference curve through C^P at which the marginal rate of substitution is β. S will be northwest of C^P because the marginal rate of substitution at C^P is $\frac{1}{2}\beta$. That is, y is higher at S than at C^P. Now compare S and C^β. The marginal rate of substitution is β at both points. So, through either point one can draw a budget line with slope $-\beta$ that is tangent to the indifference curve through that point. The budget lines through S and C^β are parallel, but the line through S is lower because C^β yields more utility. Both goods are normal, so C^β provides more of both goods than S. Therefore, y is higher at C^β than at S. We already know that y is higher at S than at C^P. Therefore, y is higher at C^β than at C^P and hence x is lower at C^β than at C^P because C^β and C^P are on the same downward sloping line.)

Consider a specific example: Set $u(x, y) = xy$, $\alpha = 1$, and $\beta = 2$. For the single-person firm we maximize xy subject to $y = \Omega - x$. Then we want to maximize $x(\Omega - x)$. Set $f(x) = \Omega x - x^2$. Then $f'(x) = \Omega - 2x$. A maximum requires $f'(x) = 0$ because u is zero when x or y is zero. Then $x = \frac{1}{2}\Omega$. And $y = \Omega - \frac{1}{2}\Omega = \frac{1}{2}\Omega$. (Note that $f''(x) = -2 < 0$, which is the sufficient condition for a global *maximum*.) That is, $C^\alpha = (\frac{1}{2}\Omega, \frac{1}{2}\Omega)$.

Now, to find C^β we maximize xy subject to $y = 2(\Omega - x)$. The first order condition for a maximum of $x[2(\Omega - x)]$ is $2\Omega - 4x = 0$, or $x = \frac{1}{2}\Omega$. And $y = 2(\Omega - \frac{1}{2}\Omega) = \Omega$. $C^\beta = (\frac{1}{2}\Omega, \Omega)$. Note that $u(C^\beta) = \Omega^2/2 > \Omega^2/4 = u(C^\alpha)$.

To find C^P, the partnership equilibrium, we maximize $x_1 y_1$ subject to $y_1 = \Omega - x_1 + c$. That is, maximize $x_1(\Omega - x_1 + c)$. The first order condition[31] is $\Omega + c - 2x_1 = 0$, so $x^P = (\Omega + c)/2$. This depends on $e_2 = c$, but because persons 1 and 2 have identical preferences and face the same incentives they will make identical choices. Therefore, $c = e_2 = e_1 = \Omega - x^P$. Then $x^P = \frac{1}{2}(\Omega + \Omega - x^P)$, which yields $x^P = \frac{2}{3}\Omega = x_1 = x_2$. Thus, $e^P = \Omega - \frac{2}{3}\Omega = \frac{1}{3}\Omega = e_1 = e_2$. Then $y^P = 2e^P = \frac{2}{3}\Omega = y_1 = y_2$. (Verify: MRS $= y/x = \frac{2}{3}\Omega/\frac{2}{3}\Omega = 1 = \frac{1}{2}\beta$, and $y^P = \frac{1}{2}\beta[\Omega - x^P + \Omega - x^P]$.) Note that $u(C^P) = (2\Omega/3)(2\Omega/3) = 4\Omega^2/9 < \Omega^2/2 = u(C^\beta)$. The partnership is not efficient; there is another *feasible* outcome that would give each more utility than the partnership equilibrium. Let us consider how this outcome, C^β, might be implemented.

Exercises

1 Find the partnership equilibrium in a two-person firm with the following features: Each individual has the utility function

$$u_i = 5\ln(x_i + 1) + y_i$$

where x_i is i's consumption of leisure per day and y_i is i's daily income. Each dollar of income generated by the firm requires a total of two hours of effort per day as input. Defend your solution.

2   Determine the equilibrium of a two-partner firm in which each partner has the utility function $u(x, y) = 8\sqrt{x} + y$ (where x is the quantity of leisure and y is income), each has a total of 24 hours available to divide between effort and leisure, and the output/input ratio is 2. Show that the outcome is inefficient.

3   Determine the equilibrium of a two-partner firm in which each partner has the utility function $u(x, y) = 16\sqrt{x} + y$ (where x is the quantity of leisure and y is income), each has a total of 24 hours available to divide between effort and leisure, and the output/input ratio is 2. Show that the outcome is inefficient.

4   Consider a model of team production in which total income is four times the total amount of effort supplied. There are two individuals on the team and each individual i has the utility function $u_i(x_i, y_i) = x_i^2 y_i$, where x_i is i's consumption of leisure and y_i is i's income. There is a maximum of twenty-four hours of leisure available.

a Determine the commodity bundle that maximizes u_1 subject to the technology constraint and the requirement that $u_2 = u_1$.
b Determine the partnership equilibrium. Make sure you identify the amount of each good consumed by each person.

6 The owner–employee relationship

Suppose that person 1 is the sole owner of the two-person firm analyzed in section 5, and she hires individual 2 as the second member of the team. (We will employ the basic model of 5.1.) The two individuals work together as in a partnership but the reward scheme is quite different: Person 1 pays 2 an income of y_2 with the residual income going to the owner, person 1. That is $y_1 = \beta(e_1 + e_2) - y_2$. To determine e_1 and e_2 we need to be more explicit about the worker's contract. The owner agrees to pay the worker exactly y^β, no more and no less, provided that the worker, person 2, supplies *at least* e^β units of effort. (Both y^β and e^β, underlying the fair and efficient outcome C^β, are defined in section 5.1.) Otherwise, person 2 is not paid at all. In symbols, $y_2 = y^\beta$ if $e_2 \geq e^\beta$ and $y_2 = 0$ if $e_2 < e^\beta$. Assuming that utility is zero if income is zero and utility is positive if x and y are both positive, as is the case when $u(x, y) = xy$, it is in the worker's interest to supply exactly e^β units of effort and receive the income y^β.[32] Now consider the owner's situation. The owner wishes to maximize $u(x_1, y_1)$ subject to $y_1 = \beta(e_1 + e^\beta) - y^\beta$ and $x_1 = \Omega - e_1$. Recall that $y^\beta = \beta e^\beta$. Then 1 will maximize $u(x_1, y_1)$ subject to $y_1 = \beta e_1 + \beta e^\beta - y^\beta = \beta e_1 = \beta(\Omega - x_1)$. But $y_1 = \beta(\Omega - x_1)$ is the equation of the line L_β in Figure 3 and we already know that C^β is utility maximizing on this line. Therefore, it is in the owner's interest to choose C^β. We have designed a contract regime such that each person has an incentive to supply e^β units of effort and as a result each receives the bundle C^β, and this outcome is efficient. (Efficiency was proved in the theorem of section 5.1.)

Instead of a contract that pays the worker y^β if his effort is e^β or more and zero otherwise, the owner could simply offer a wage of β and let the worker choose his utility maximizing basket (x_2, y_2) subject to the budget constraint $\beta x + y = \beta\Omega$. The line representing this budget constraint is L_β of Figure 4. Therefore, the wage offer of β leads the worker to choose C^β as in the case of the "contribute e^β or else" contract. Either contract 'works', although they have slightly different monitoring consequences. (What are the differences?)

Why do the owner and employee receive the same level of utility, $u(x^\beta, y^\beta)$, at equilibrium? In our simple model the workers can reject a contract that doesn't give them $u(x^\beta, y^\beta)$ each and instead form their own firm in which they are the owners receiving at least $u(x^\beta, y^\beta)$ each.

We see why very few firms are organized as partnerships: Because each partner receives only a fraction (one nth if there are n partners) of the income generated by her own effort there is an incentive to undersupply effort, and hence the equilibrium leisure–income package consumed by each partner provides a lower level of utility than the ideal plan C^β, which can be realized by the owner–worker contractual regime. One can show that this utility differential is greater the larger is the number of partners. Then why do partnerships exist at all? The answer has to do with the costs of monitoring the worker to ensure that the threshold level of effort e^β has been supplied. There is a hidden action problem. In some production enterprises the manager (or her agent) need do little more than ascertain that the worker is on the job and at the appropriate work station to determine that there is no shirking (i.e., that $e_i \geq e^\beta$). If bicycle wheels are being produced and a sample reveals wheels with missing spokes it is a relatively easy matter to determine the source of the problem. The costs of monitoring are low and even when the per capita monitoring cost m is subtracted from C^β there is still substantially higher utility, $u(x^\beta, y^\beta - m)$, than is provided by the partnership outcome C^P. On the other hand, monitoring costs are very high when the firm uses sophisticated consulting or diagnostic services. Consider a team of accountants, lawyers, or physicians. If one member of the team is to verify that another has devoted considerable effort to a case then the former will essentially have to retrace the steps of the latter. In that case the technological income–leisure trade-off line *for the owner–worker regime* will be paralleled to L_β but strictly below it, the vertical distance between the two providing a measure of the per capita monitoring costs,

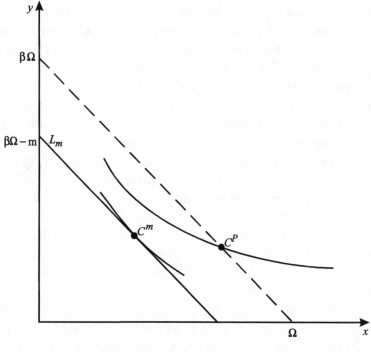

Figure 5

m. Let L_m denote the technological income–leisure trade-off when the per capita monitoring cost is *m*. In that case the utility maximizing bundle is C^m assuming that the two individuals receive the same bundle (Figure 5). The partnership scheme does not require monitoring so L_β remains the appropriate trade-off line in that case. Figure 5 shows that $u(C^P)$ will exceed $u(C^m)$ if *m* is sufficiently large. On the other hand, given the per capita monitoring cost *m*, the per capita partnership utility level $u(C^P)$ is lower the larger is *n*. Therefore, large firms are much less likely to be organized as partnerships than small firms.[33] To quantify, let $u(x, y) = xy$. If there are *n* partners then $y_1 = (1/n)[\beta(e_1 + e_2 + \dots + e_n)] = (\beta/n)(\Omega - x_1 + e_2 + e_3 + \dots + e_n)$. Then person 1 will choose x_1 to maximize $x_1(\beta/n)(\Omega - x_1 + e_2 + e_3 + \dots e_n)$. The first order condition is $(\Omega + e_2 + e_3 + \dots + e_n) - 2x_1 = 0$. Assuming identical preferences the individuals will make identical choices. Therefore $e_j = e_1 = \Omega - x_1$ for $j = 2, 3, \dots, n$. Then $n\Omega - (n + 1)x_1 = 0$ or $x_1 = n\Omega/(n + 1)$. If *n* is large then x_i is close to Ω, which means that very little effort is expended: $e_i = \Omega - x_i = \Omega/(n + 1)$. If $\beta = 2$ then $y_i = (2/n)(e_1 + e_2 + \dots + e_n) = 2\Omega/(n + 1)$ and thus $u(C^P) = [n\Omega/(n + 1)] \times [2\Omega/(n + 1)] = 2n(n + 1)^{-2}\Omega^2$. Recall that $C^\beta = (\frac{1}{2}\Omega, \Omega)$ when $\beta = 2$, and thus $u(C^\beta) = \Omega^2/2$. Therefore the differential between $u(C^P)$ and $u(C^\beta)$ is greater the larger is *n*. In fact, $u(C^P)$ is close to zero for large *n*.

Professional service firms do not require enormously large teams, in contrast to most manufacturing processes. Therefore, $u(C^P) > u(C^m)$ in the professional service field where the partnership format is employed. In fact, there will be some minimal monitoring in a partnership. Why would the partners in a medical clinic invest the time necessary to monitor each other even a little? The cost of malpractice can be very costly to the client, and hence to the partnership, and because the partners share losses as well as profits each member is very vulnerable to the shirking of the others. This gives the partners a strong incentive to monitor each other, in contrast to the position of senior executives in a limited liability corporation. By definition, and by law, the personal assets of an owner cannot be tapped in order to pay the liabilities of a limited liability corporation.

Exercises

1   Compute the equilibrium outcome for a firm that has ten workers, one of whom is the owner who manages the firm. The firm's net income (net of the cost of materials, etc.) is always five times the total amount of effort contributed. (The total effort includes the effort contributed by the owner.) Each individual has the utility function $u_i(x_i, y_i) = (x_i)^2 y_i$, where x_i is the number of hours of leisure consumed by i per week, and y_i is i's income per week. Assume that monitoring is costless.

2   Suppose that the owner of the firm described in question 1 offered each worker a contract that paid exactly \$230 per week as long as 40 units of effort or more were contributed, and paid \$0 if less than 40 units of effort were observed. Show that this is *not* an equilibrium contract.

3   Here is a more subtle version of question 2. Suppose that the owner of the firm described in question 1 offered each worker a contract that paid exactly \$200 per week as long as 40 units of effort or more were contributed, and paid \$0 if less than 40 units of effort were observed. Show that this is not consistent with *long-run* equilibrium.

4   Let the monitoring cost *per person m* be a function $m(n)$ of the number n of team members, with m increasing as n increases. How does this affect the analysis?

Suggestions for further reading: Alchian and Demsetz (1972).

7 Agency theory

We now consider a formal model of the principal–agent relationship, patterned on Ross (1973), Mirlees (1974), and Holmström (1979a). It abstracts from everything but the inability of shareholders to determine the amount of effort contributed by the manager of their firm even though effort is correlated with profit.

Because profit is also influenced by random forces, the correlation between managerial effort and the firm's profit is not perfect. The owner can only observe profit and thus has to offer the manager a wage schedule that features a dependence of the wage on profit alone, and will endeavor to design that schedule in a way that induces the manager to apply a high level of effort – not the highest possible level of effort, but the profit maximizing amount. Although we speak in terms of a manager in relation to the firm's owners, the analysis applies just as well to any principal–agent relationship. The principal can be a university designing a contract for its agent, a football coach. The manager of a privately owned firm is the principal when she employs a salesperson. Should the salesperson be paid on commission, and if so at what rate? The agent could be a professor hired by a university, the principal. And so on. In any principal–agent relationship there will be a wide variety of opportunities for shirking. For example, pickers in orange groves are paid a piece rate – a fee per box of oranges – to induce them to pick quickly. This solves one problem; if they were on salary they would have an incentive to dawdle. But it creates a new problem. The piece rate formula gives workers an incentive to pick the ground fruit first, although oranges on the ground are high in bacteria. Also there is a tendency to take the most accessible fruit from the branches and leave the rest to rot on the tree. These problems are handled by direct monitoring of the workers. (See McPhee, 1966, p. 55.) In spite of the fact that shirking is multifaceted, it is modelled here as a one-dimensional sacrifice of effort in return for increased leisure consumption. If you are unfamiliar with the elements of decision making under uncertainty you will need to read section 12 of Chapter 1 before continuing.

7.1 A diagrammatic introduction

Suppose that profit has no random component. (It will be easy to adapt the argument to cover uncertainty with risk neutral individuals when we have analyzed the deterministic case.) The firm's profit R is βe if the manager supplies e units of effort. (R is profit before deducting the manager's pay.) Figure 6 shows the profit function $R = \beta e$ as line L. The owner's net return N is the difference between R and the payment y to the manager. Profit maximization by the owner keeps the manager on the indifference curve u^0, representing the utility that would be realized by the manager in her best alternative. (This will be explained carefully in section 7.3.) The diagram shows three net return levels N_1, N_2, and N_3 corresponding to three possible budget constraints for the manager, B_1, B_2, and B_3. For any budget line B, the owner's net return N is the vertical distance between L and the point where B is tangent to the indifference curve; this measures $R - y$. If $-p$ is the slope of the budget line then it can be expressed as $px +$

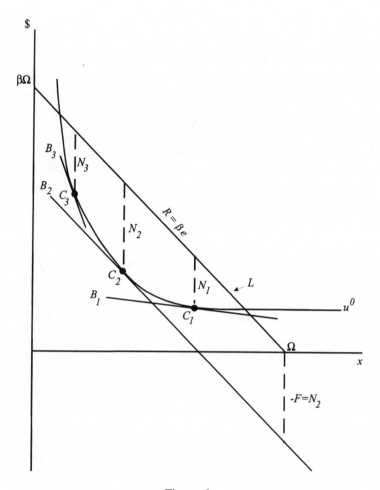

Figure 6

$y = K$, or $y = p(\Omega - x) + F$, where $F = K - p\Omega$. (K is a constant. Ω is the time endowment, and x is the manager's consumption of leisure. Of course $x = \Omega - e$. Although K and F are constants, they will have different values for different budget lines.) It is clear that the owners' net return is highest with the budget line B_2 parallel to L. Here's why. Assume for a moment that effort is observable and can be mandated in a contract offered by the owner. Consider B_1, which is tangent to u^0 at C_1. In other words, the manager will choose basket C_1 if her budget line is B_1. The owner's net return is N_1. Now, increase the manager's input of effort by changing the budget line, making it steeper, so that the manager has a new consumption plan C' along u^0 to the left of C_1. B_1 is flatter than L; this means that beginning at C_1, an increase in effort will increase income more quickly along L than along u^0. In other words, a reduction in x (caused by an increase in effort) will cause R to increase faster than y. (R is on L and y is on u^0.) This means that profit R increases faster than the manager's emolument y. Therefore, the owner's net return will increase. This argument applies at any point on u^0 to the right of C_2. Therefore, to the right of C_2 the owner's net return $N = R - y$ increases when the absolute value of the slope of the budget line increases and the manager's consumption plan moves along u^0 from right to left. Increasing p for budget line $y = pe + F = p(\Omega - x) + F$ is of course increasing the manager's reward per unit of effort supplied. But if we move beyond C_2 by making p larger than β, the owner's profit will fall. Why? Because u^0 is steeper than L to the left of C_2 and thus as we move the manager along u^0 to the left of C^2 the manager's consumption y will increase faster than R. Even though R increases, because the manager supplies more effort, y increases at a faster rate so the owner's net return falls to the left of C_2.

The owner's net return is highest with budget line B_2 parallel to L. (Exercises 4–6 at the end of this section take you through an algebraic proof.) L is the line $R = \beta e = \beta(\Omega - x)$. B_2 and L have the same slope, so B_2 has slope $-\beta$. Then we can write B_2 as $y = \beta(\Omega - x) + F = \beta e + F = R + F$, where R is the firm's realized profit. R depends on the manager's effort, and the manager knows the functional relationship between R and e. Therefore, the contract $y = R + F$ offered by the owner will induce the manager to supply the amount of effort that leaves N_2 for the owner, *even if the owner cannot observe and enforce* e. We can now drop the assumption that effort is observable, because the wage contract $w = R + F$ transfers all of the social gains or losses from a change in the manager's effort level directly to the manager, who is now the sole residual claimant on the firm's profit. In other words, $y = R + F$ is the efficient contract because the private cost of leisure consumption is equal to the social cost. By definition, the private cost is the drop in the income of the agent (the manager in this case) per unit increase in the agent's leisure consumption. The social cost of leisure consumption is the change in income (profit) to the economy per unit increase in the agent's leisure consumption. Note that F is negative (Figure 6). The manager pays a *franchise fee* of $-F$ to the owner and then keeps all profit, net of the fee.

The argument above applies to production with uncertainty as long as the manager and the owner are risk neutral and the expected value of the random component is zero. Suppose that $R = \beta e + \xi$, where ξ is a random variable with expected value zero. Then the expected value of R is βe, and we apply the analysis to the expected value of R, which the owner wants to maximize, net of the payment to the manager. And if the manager is risk neutral then y enters the manager's utility function linearly. That is $U(x, y) = B(x) + y$. If y is the expected value of the manager's pay then $B(x) + y$ is the manager's expected utility, and the argument above goes through.

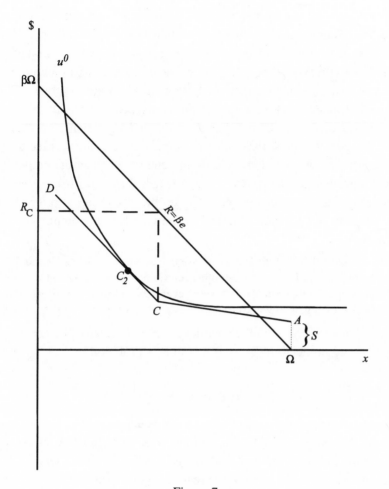

Figure 7

We can apply all of this to *any* of the firm's workers. The efficient contract requires a wage $w = R + F$, where F is negative. But would we really expect the worker to pay the employer? This incentive scheme would actually provide more utility for the worker. Because it induces efficiency there would be more output per capita in the economy, and competition among employers for workers would result in a higher u^0 (utility from alternative employment). But suppose there is a cash constraint preventing a payment by workers to employers, or hidden information problems standing in the way of a loan of F dollars from the owner to the worker. We can achieve the same outcome by means of *progressive piece rates*.[34] This is illustrated in Figure 7 with budget line *ACD*. The worker receives a basic salary of S. For output levels less than R_c the worker is paid p dollars per unit of additional effort supplied. (The slope of the budget line to the right of C is $-p$.)

For output above R_c the worker receives β dollars per unit of additional effort supplied. The contract would actually be written so that for output levels less than R_c the worker is paid p/β dollars per dollar of additional profit generated, and for output above R_c the worker receives the whole of each dollar of additional profit generated. This progressive piece rate system and the wage contract $y = R + F$ induce identical decisions for the agency problem represented by the diagram. But the progressive piece rate system has a serious hidden action defect that is not captured in Figure 7. Unless the quality of output can be easily verified the worker has an incentive to work quickly, sacrificing quality, to reach the output level R_c where the higher piece rate is available. Consider this report from a worker in a Baltic firm producing television sets. It describes conditions – prior to the collapse of communism – toward the end of the month as the employees strive to earn bonuses:

We never use a screwdriver in the last week. We hammer the screws in. We slam solder on the connections, cannibalize parts from other televisions if we run out of the right ones, use glue or hammers to fix switches that were never meant for that model. All the time the management is pressing us to work faster, to make the target so we all get our bonuses.[35]

There is no danger of this with the contract $y = R + F$ because the agent bears the full brunt of any production decision that affects profitability.

7.2 The basic agency model

The manager contributes a level of effort e that is unobservable. Before making a payment to the manager the firm's profit is $R(e, \xi)$, a function of the effort e supplied by the manager and of a random variable ξ. The firm offers the manager a wage w that is a function $w(R)$ of the realized profit. Although R will depend in part on e, the effort level e is unobservable so the wage contract will depend only on the actual, observable profit R. The manager can achieve an expected utility level u^0 by working elsewhere so the wage schedule must allow the manager to achieve a level of expected utility at least as high as u^0. We assume throughout that the owner of the firm is risk neutral; the manager may be risk averse. The manager's utility is $U(x, y)$, where x is her consumption of leisure and y is income.[36] Ω is the initial endowment of time, a constant, so $x = \Omega - e$. Note that y is a random variable, because it equals $w(R)$, and R depends on e and ξ. (Assume for convenience that the manager does not have an endowment of Y.) The manager will maximize her expected utility – i.e., the expected value of

$$U(x, y) = U(\Omega - e, w(R(e, \xi))),$$

subject to the expected utility being at least u^0 (the *participation constraint*). The maximization exercise induces a dependence of effort on the wage schedule, and the owner can use that relationship in selecting a profit maximizing wage schedule. For example, suppose that $U(x, y) = B(x) + y$ and the wage schedule is a member of the linear family $\theta R + F$, where θ and F are constants. (Think of θ as the commission rate paid to a salesperson, or the share of taxi revenues going to the driver, or the royalty rate paid to a textbook author. In each case, the individual in question shows up in our model as the manager.) As usual, we assume $B' > 0$ and $B'' < 0$ for all $x \geq 0$. The manager is risk neutral in this case, because x does not depend on the random variable ξ, so the manager's expected utility, $E[U(x, y)]$ is $B(x) + E(y)$, where E is the expectation operator. $E(y) = E(\theta R + F) = \theta E(R) + F$. Now, maximize

$$E(U) = B(\Omega - e) + \theta E[R(e, \xi)] + F.$$

The first derivative of $E(U)$, with respect to e, is $-B'(\Omega - e) + \theta dE(R)/de$, where $dE(R)/de$ denotes the derivative of $E(R)$ with respect to e. If $-B'(\Omega - e) + \theta dE(R)/de = 0$ we have

$$B'(\Omega - e) = \theta dE(R)/de. \qquad [1]$$

Assuming an interior solution, [1] is a property of the manager's decision. Given θ let e_θ be the solution to [1], the amount of effort supplied by the manager when facing the wage schedule $\theta R + F$. Now, let's increase θ. At the old level of e, [1] will not hold for the new value of θ because we have increased the right hand side. Suppose that $dE(R)/de$ is independent of e: For example, $R(e, \xi) = \beta e + \xi$ for positive constant β. (So $dER/de = \beta$.) Then having increased the right hand side of [1] by increasing θ we can restore equality only by increasing B', and that means that $\Omega - e$ will have to fall because $B'' < 0$. Thus, e will be higher. Therefore, for each θ there is one and only one optimal e for the manager, and a higher θ leads to a higher e. Even though the owner cannot observe e, he can employ this relationship between θ and e in designing a profit maximizing wage contract.

What is the owner's profit? The owner is risk neutral and supplies no effort, so the owner simply wants to maximize the expected value of R net of the payment to the manager, namely, the expected value of $R(e, \xi) - w[R(e, \xi)]$. From the owner's point of view, e depends on the wage schedule w, so the owner chooses w to maximize the expected value of

$$R[e^*(w), \xi] - w[R(e^*(w), \xi)] \qquad [2]$$

subject to $E(U) \geq u^0$, where e^* is the effort supplied as a function of the contract w. How does the owner solve for e? Effort depends on the wage schedule via the manager's optimization problem, but the owner's optimization problem causes the wage schedule to depend on the manager's supply of effort function. We'll start with an easy case, that of a risk neutral manager.

7.3 Risk neutral managers

$U(x, y) = B(x) + y$, with $B' > 0$ and $B'' < 0$ for all $x \geq 0$. Assume that the owner will choose from the family of linear wage schedules $\theta R + F$, where θ and F are constants. Then [1] will hold for the manager's choice of e. Given this constraint, and the participation constraint $E(U) \geq u^0$, the owner maximizes [2]. For convenience, assume $u^0 = 0$. Suppose that we actually have $E(U) > 0$. That is, $B(\Omega - e) + E(y) > 0$, where $E(y) = \theta E(R) + F$. Then the owner can lower F without affecting e and without violating the participation constraint. It is obvious that we can have a lower value of F and still satisfy $B(\Omega - e) + E(y) + F \geq 0$. Why will e be unaffected? Because the functions B and $E(R)$ are unaffected, and F is a constant, and hence the first order condition is unchanged. But if e is the same, then so is the expected value of R. The owner's profit will increase by precisely the drop in F. Even if F is already zero this argument applies. (As we will see, there are lots of examples of negative F, which signifies a lump sum payment by the manager to the owner.) Therefore, maximization of the owner's utility implies $B(\Omega - e) + E(y) = 0$, where y is the manager's income. Then $E(y) = -B(\Omega - e)$. Now, [2] can be written $R - y$, so the owner wants to maximize $E(R) - E(y) = E(R) + B(\Omega - e)$. Suppose $R(e, \xi) = \beta e + \xi$, where β is a positive constant. Suppose also that the expected value of ξ is zero. (Informally, high values of ξ are just as likely as low values.) Then the expected value of $R(e, \xi)$ is βe, and the derivative of $E(R)$ is just β. Therefore, [1] becomes $B' = \theta\beta$. The owner's expected profit net of the payment to the manager is

$$\beta e(\theta) + B(\Omega - e(\theta)) \qquad\qquad [3]$$

where $e(\theta)$ is the function of θ implicit in $B' = \theta\beta$. The owner then chooses θ to maximize [3]. The derivative of [3] with respect to θ is $\beta e'(\theta) - B'(x)e'(\theta)$, and if we set this equal to zero we get $\beta e'(\theta) - B'(x)e'(\theta) = 0$. Therefore, $\beta - B' = 0$ *if* $e'(\theta) \neq 0$ at the solution value of θ. But $B' = \beta$ along with $B' = \theta\beta$ implies that $\theta = 1$ maximizes the owner's net profit. We demonstrate this with a numerical example, which will allow us to calculate $e'(\theta)$. First, however, we employ a general approach that does not depend on differentiability of the functions and which is valid for corner solutions. By initially pretending that the owner can observe effort we can actually gain a lot of insight into the hidden action case.

The manager is risk neutral, so $U = B(x) + y$, but ξ can be any random variable, R can now be any function of e and ξ, and we place no restrictions on the wage schedule, although the profit maximizing schedule will turn out to be linear. Suppose that the effort level e can be mandated by the owners. (We know that it can't be mandated; we are investigating the implications of unobservable effort. We will identify the effort level that owners would mandate if they could costlessly observe effort and then show that an incentive scheme can be devised to elicit that level of effort.) With e observable the wage can be a function of e, so we let $w(e, R)$ represent the wage schedule. Given e, the manager's expected utility is $B(\Omega - e)] + E[w(e, R)]$, and this must be at least as large as u^0. Profit maximization implies that the owners will choose a wage schedule that equates the manager's expected utility with u^0. Why? We know that $E(U) \geq u^0$ must hold. If the manager's expected utility actually exceeded u^0 the owners could reduce the wage offered for each pair (e, R) without violating the participation constraint $E(U) \geq u^0$. This would increase profit. Therefore, at equilibrium we have

$$E[w(e, R)] = u^0 - B(\Omega - e). \qquad [4]$$

The shareholders wish to maximize expected profit net of the manager's pay – i.e.,

$$E[R(e, \xi)] - E[w(e, R)] = E[R(e, \xi)] - u^0 + B(\Omega - e). \qquad [5]$$

Let e^* be the value of e that maximizes [5]. Notice that the participation constraint is built in. Then e^* is the level of effort that would be required by the owners with full information – that is, with costless monitoring. This effort level can be elicited by the shareholders if they offer the manager a wage schedule $w(e, R) = R(e, \xi) - M$, where $M = E[R(e^*, \xi)] - u^0 + B(\Omega - e^*)$. Note that M is a constant, and that w does not require e to be known by the owner; only the realized profit R need be observed. Therefore, the wage schedule would give the manager the actual realized profit minus the constant M. To verify that it would be in the manager's interest to supply e^* *if* she accepted the contract let's compute the manager's expected utility for the wage schedule $w(R) = R - M$:

$$B(\Omega - e) + E[R(e, \xi)] - M.$$

Although the actual return R varies with ξ, M is a number – an expected value – so, any value of e that maximizes the manager's expected utility also maximizes the owner's profit by virtue of [5]. Because e^* was defined as the value of e that maximizes $B(\Omega - e) + E[R(e, \xi)]$ it is in the manager's interest to set $e = e^*$. *If* the manager accepts the contract she will choose the effort level e^*. But will she accept? By definition of M we have

$$B(\Omega - e^*) + E[R(e, \xi)] - M = u^0$$

so the wage contract $w(R) = R - M$ does allow the manager to achieve the expected utility level u^0. Note that the profit maximizing wage schedule is $w = \theta R + F$ for $F = -M$ and $\theta = 1$. In practice, the wage contract would offer slightly more utility than u^0 to ensure that the manager will accept the contract in preference to the best alternative, which yields a utility level of u^0.

The manager bears all the risk; the owners receive a constant return of M. This is equivalent to an arrangement in which the owners sell the firm to the manager for a price of M dollars. The incentive scheme that induces the optimal effort is equivalent to having the owner manage the firm herself. Is this plausible? Risk neutrality itself is plausible only if the manager's income from the firm is a small component of her portfolio (or income sources). In other words, the manager is diversified and $M represents a small fraction of her assets. This is implausible in the case of a typical firm and a typical manager. It is usually the other way around. The value of a typical firm is many times greater than a typical executive's wealth. (Franchises, however, are small relative to a modern corporation. The franchise situation, in which the manager pays a fee M to the parent and keeps the residual profit, comes close to the outcome outlined in this section.)

With risk neutral management, the equilibrium resulting from maximization of the manager's utility and of the owner's profit will be efficient. We have three ways of proving this: (1) Show that the equilibrium e^* maximizes the *sum* of the expected utilities. (There may be other efficient outcomes, but anything that maximizes the sum of utilities will belong to the set of efficient outcomes.) The owner's expected utility is just the expected value of y_1, the net return to the owner. The manager's expected utility is $B(x_2) + E(y_2)$, where y_2 is the payment from the owner to the manager, and $E(y_2)$ is its expected value. Therefore, we will find an efficient outcome by maximizing $E(y_1) + B(x_2) + E(y_2) = B(\Omega - e) + E(y_1 + y_2)$. Now, $y_1 + y_2$ is $R(e, \xi)$, the gross return to effort. We get an efficient level of e when we maximize $B(\Omega - e) + E(R)$. But this differs from [5] only by a constant, so the two functions are maximized by the same e^*. Hence, e^* is efficient. The value of e that solves society's maximization problem also solves the manager's decision problem when she is offered the profit maximizing wage contract. (2) Note that the social cost of leisure consumption equals the private cost of leisure consumption when $\theta = 1$. Equality between social and private cost is usually sufficient for efficiency. (See Chapter 8.) The social cost of leisure consumption is always the change in $E(R)$ when the manager reduces e by one unit. Of course, when $\theta = 1$ this is also the cost to the manager of an increase in her leisure consumption of one unit. (3) In any context, any solution to the problem "maximize u_1 subject to $u_h \geq u_h^0$ for all $h \neq 1$" is efficient. (u_h^0 is a constant for each h.)

Here is a simple example that allows us to solve explicitly for the manager's choice of e as a function of w and then to solve for the profit maximizing wage schedule w. Set $U(x, y) = 20x - \frac{1}{2}x^2 + y$. That is, $B(x) = 20x - \frac{1}{2}x^2$. The manager is endowed with 24 units of X and zero units of Y. We assume that the manager's best alternative is to consume 24 units of X, so $u^0 = 20(24) - \frac{1}{2}(24)^2 = 192$. (We could give the manager a positive endowment of Y, which represents expenditure on goods other than X, but it could simply be incorporated into F and u^0.) Initially, the owner chooses from the family of linear wage schedules $\theta R + F$, where θ and F are parameters, unaffected by the manager's behavior. Later, we will prove that this family contains the schedule that maximizes the owner's expected profit. Suppose $R(e, \xi) = 10e + \xi$, where ξ is a random variable with an expected value of zero. If u denotes the manager's expected utility then $u(x, y) = B(\Omega - e) + 10\theta e + F$.

Incentive compatibility is incorporated by assuming that the manager will respond to w by maximizing her expected utility. Because B does not depend on the random variable, the expected value of $B(x)$ is simply $B(x)$. Similarly, the expected value of the constant F is F. The expected value of $w = \theta[10e + \xi]$ is $10\theta e$ because the expected value of ξ is assumed to be zero. Therefore, the manager will maximize $V(e) = 20(24 - e) - \frac{1}{2}(24 - e)^2 + 10\theta e + F$. The first derivative of $V(e)$ is $-20 + 24 - e + 10\theta$. Note that $V''(e) < 0$ for all e, so the optimal value of e satisfies $V'(e) = 0$ as long as that is consistent with $0 \le e \le 24$. $V'(e) = 0$ implies $e = 4 + 10\theta$. Note that this satisfies $0 \le e \le 24$ for $0 \le \theta \le 1$. Therefore, the manager's effort supply function is $e = 4 + 10\theta$ as long as this yields an expected utility at least as high as $u^0 = 192$. As we will see, the owner will adjust F so that the participation constraint $u \ge u^0$ is satisfied. Therefore, we have indeed derived the effort supply function. Verify that e increases when θ does.

The owner's expected profit is the expected value of $R - w$, and the owner will choose w to maximize this, subject to the participation and incentive compatibility constraints. (The latter is incorporated by maximizing the manager's expected utility.) As long as $u > u^0$ the owner can increase his profit by reducing the wage for all realizations of R. Therefore, profit maximization implies $u = B(x) + E(w) = u^0$, where E is the expected value operator. The owner's expected profit is $E[R - w] = E(R) - E(w)$. But $B(x) + E(w) = u^0$, so $E(w) = u^0 - B(x)$, and hence

$$E(R) - E(w) = E(R) + B(x) - u^0.$$

Recall that $E(R) = 10e$. Assume for a moment that the owner can observe and mandate the effort level e. What e would he select? We just have to maximize $G(e) = 10e + B(x) - u^0 = 10e + 20(24 - e) - \frac{1}{2}(24 - e)^2 - u^0$. $G'(e) = 10 - 20 + 24 - e$, and $G''(e) < 0$. Therefore, we set $G'(e) = 0$ to maximize the owner's expected profit. And this yields $e^* = 14$.

Return to the case of unobservable effort. The effort supply function for the linear wage schedule is $e = 4 + 10\theta$. Therefore, when $\theta = 1$ the manager will supply the effort $e^* = 14$ that maximizes the owner's profit, even though the owner cannot observe or enforce e. Now, compute F under the profit maximizing contract. $E(w) = 10e + F = 140 + F$. And $x = 24 - 14 = 10$. Therefore, the manager's expected utility is

$$20(10) - \tfrac{1}{2}(10)^2 + 140 + F = 192.$$

Then $F = -98$. The manager pays the owner a license fee of \$98 and then keeps the remaining profit for herself.

Note that we have proved that the contract $w = R - 98$ yields a higher expected profit to the owner than *any* other contract. This is much stronger than merely proving that $w = R - 98$ is profit maximizing within the family of linear contracts. Nevertheless, you might benefit from solving directly for the profit maximizing values of θ and F within the linear family. The effort supply function is $e = 4 + 10\theta$ when $w = \theta R + F$. Profit maximization and the participation constraint imply $B(x) + E(w) = u^0 = 192$. Therefore,

$$
\begin{aligned}
E(w) &= 192 - B(x) = 192 - 20x + \tfrac{1}{2}x^2 \\
&= 192 - 20(24 - e) + \tfrac{1}{2}(24 - e)^2 \\
&= 192 - 20(24 - 4 - 10\theta) + \tfrac{1}{2}(24 - 4 - 10\theta)^2 \\
&\quad \text{because } e = 4 + 10\theta \\
&= 192 - 20(20 - 10\theta) + \tfrac{1}{2}(20 - 10\theta)^2.
\end{aligned}
\tag{6}
$$

Now, the owner wants to maximize $E(R) - E(w)$. Using [6] and the fact that $E(R) = 10e$,

$$
\begin{aligned}
E(R) - E(w) &= 10e - 192 + 20(20 - 10\theta) - \tfrac{1}{2}(20 - 10\theta)^2 \\
&= 10(4 + 10\theta) - 192 + 20(20 - 10\theta) - \tfrac{1}{2}(20 - 10\theta)^2.
\end{aligned}
$$

This is a function of one variable, θ. The first derivative is $100 - 200 + (20 - 10\theta)(10)$, and the second derivative is negative. Therefore, we achieve a maximum by setting

$$
-100 + 200 - 100\theta = 0
$$

and hence $\theta = 1$ maximizes the owner's expected profit. We solve for $F = -98$ as above. If the manager is risk neutral then the owner's profit maximizing contract has the manager paying the owner a fee that is independent of the firm's profit, with any residual profit going to the manager.

7.4 Risk averse managers

We now turn to the case of a risk averse manager of a large corporation. To give us a point of comparison, suppose (temporarily) that e can be observed by the owner and verified by a judge. This means that contracts can specify the effort level contributed by the employee. The owner can insist on a particular effort level e^*. Suppose that the manager's utility function is risk averse. If the manager is not offered a constant wage w, let $c = E[w(e^*, \xi)]$. If the manager had a choice between the actual w and a constant wage schedule that paid c whether profit was high or low then she would choose c because it has a higher expected utility. That follows from risk aversion and the fact that the constant wage c has the same expected monetary value as w but c offers complete certainty. Therefore, a constant wage of $c - \delta$ would yield a higher expected utility than the offered wage schedule if δ were positive but sufficiently small. And it would satisfy the participation constraint for δ sufficiently small, because $U(\Omega - e^*, c)$ is higher than the expected utility yielded by the initial wage schedule, which itself satisfies the participation constraint. The constant wage of $c - \delta$ would give the owner a higher expected profit than a schedule that paid an expected wage of c. Therefore, we would not have a variable wage at equilibrium if monitoring were costless.

With observable and verifiable effort, incentives play no role because the profit maximizing effort level can be mandated by the owner. Therefore, the manager receives a fixed payment (the constant wage), independently of random forces, and hence is fully insured. At the other extreme, with unobservable effort and risk neutral management, the *owner's* return is fixed and the manager bears the full brunt of the vicissitudes of nature. This gives the manager the optimal incentive, from the standpoint of both society and the owner. We expect that if the manager were just a tiny bit risk averse then there would be a small constant element to the wage, with the manager bearing almost all of the brunt of uncertainty. And as the degree of risk aversion increases, the amount of insurance afforded to the manager also increases. This means that there is a trade-off between incentives and insurance. Let's return to the model to investigate this.

We simplify the expression of the manager's expected utility, to make the model more amenable to the realistic case of costly monitoring of a risk averse manager. If w is a wage contract let $E(w)$ denote its expected monetary value. This expected value depends on the effort supplied by the manager, because effort influences profit R, which typically has a bearing on the manager's pay. Now, instead of explicitly writing utility in terms of x (the amount of leisure consumption) and y (income from w and a particular realization of the random variable ξ), we write

$$E(U) = E(w) - \theta^2 K - \tfrac{1}{2}e^2.$$

$E(U)$ is shorthand for the expression "the manager's expected utility." $E(w)$ is the expected monetary value of the wage contract, and that is affected by e. A contribution of e units of effort by the manager causes her utility to fall on that account, because leisure consumption falls by e. We subtract this loss of utility, $\tfrac{1}{2}e^2$, directly from the expected wage to determine the manager's net utility. Similarly, the manager's exposure to risk diminishes her utility, and the term $-\theta^2 K$ reflects the utility cost of this risk. ($K \geq 0$.) We are assuming that w has the form $w = \theta R + F$, where $R = 10e + \xi$. As usual, ξ is the random component and has expected value zero. The larger is θ the greater are the swings in the realized wage as the random variable moves up and down. Therefore, the larger is θ the greater is the negative impact of risk on utility. And, clearly, the larger is K the more risk averse is the manager.[37] Let's calculate the profit maximizing contract. (We will not specify the time endowment; instead, we simply assume that the first order condition yields a feasible value of e.)

Incentive compatibility is incorporated by maximizing the manager's expected utility. If $w = \theta R + F$ then $E(w) = \theta 10e + F$, so

$$E(U) = 10\theta e + F - \theta^2 K - \tfrac{1}{2}e^2,$$

which is a function $V(e)$ of e. $V'(e) = 10\theta - e$. Obviously, $V'' < 0$ at every point, so we want to set $V'(e) = 0$, and this yields $e = 10\theta$, the effort supply function. Of course, e increases as θ increases.

To calculate the owner's profit-maximizing values of F and θ we again recognize that profit maximization causes the participation constraint to be satisfied as a strict equality at equilibrium. Therefore,

$$E(w) - \theta^2 K - \tfrac{1}{2}e^2 = u^0, \quad \text{so} \quad -E(w) = -\theta^2 K - \tfrac{1}{2}e^2 - u^0.$$

And $E(R) = 10e$. Therefore, the owner's expected profit is

$$E(R) - E(w) = 10e - \theta^2 K - \tfrac{1}{2}e^2 - u^0$$
$$= 10(10\theta) - \theta^2 K - \tfrac{1}{2}(10\theta)^2 - u^0,$$

a function $G(\theta)$ of θ. $G'(\theta) = 100 - 2\theta K - 100\theta$ and $G''(\theta) < 0$ at every point. Therefore, we set $G'(\theta) = 0$. Then $100 - 2\theta K - 100\theta = 0$, which yields

$$\theta = \frac{100}{100 + 2K}. \qquad [7]$$

If the manager is not risk averse then $K = 0$ and hence $\theta = 1$. But for all $K > 0$ we have $0 < \theta < 1$. Let θ^* denote the solution to [9], the profit maximizing value of θ. Because $G'' < 0$, net profit rises as θ increases to θ^* and then falls as θ increases beyond that point (Figure 8). The expected return $E(R)$ is higher for θ greater than θ^* because more effort is supplied. But the manager is exposed to greater risk when θ is higher, and the participation constraint forces the owner to compensate the risk averse manager for the increased risk. The expected return is higher but the manager's pay is higher still when $\theta > \theta^*$. We no longer have maximum incentive ($\theta = 1$) because the owner has to trade off insurance and incentive. Note that θ falls as K increases: the greater is the degree of risk aversion the lower is the profit maximizing value of θ and the more insurance is provided to the manager by the profit maximizing owner. To determine F we return to the participation constraint, $E(U) = E(w) - \theta^2 K - \tfrac{1}{2}e^2 = u^0$ and $E(w) = \theta^* E(R) + F$. Expected gross profit $E(R)$ depends on e, which in turn is a function of θ, which equals θ^*. Therefore, with θ^* and u^0 specified we can pin down every term except F. That is, we can solve for F.

To summarize, when effort is unobservable the shareholders will have to provide the manager with an incentive to supply effort and this means that the

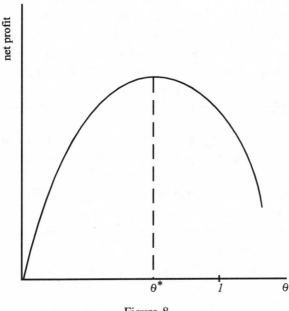

net profit

θ^* *1* θ

Figure 8

manager's payment must be correlated with observed profit. Because profit is influenced by random forces as well as the manager's effort the incentive effect prevents her from being fully insured against risk, even though the owners bear all the risk in the ideal case of costlessly observable effort. And because the manager is not fully insured, her expected wage bill must be higher than in the full information case in order to elicit her participation. Accordingly, the expected profit of the owners is lower. The manager is not fully insured, but does not assume all risk – much of it falls on the shoulders of the owners. To the extent that the manager is insured, the contract diminishes the manager's incentive to maximize the owner's expected profit. The agent is no longer the sole residual claimant. Because she is insured against bad outcomes she will work less assiduously to avoid bad outcomes. (This explains why managers are not paid solely in the form of stock options – see section 1.) In short, there is a trade-off between insurance and incentives.

Suggestions for further reading: Tirole (1988, chapter 1); McMillan (1992, chapters 8–10); Sappington (1991).

Exercises

1   A risk neutral manager has utility function $U(x, y) = 20\ln(x + 1) + y$, where x is leisure consumption and y is expenditure on all other goods.

Units have been chosen so that the individual is endowed with 3 units of X and 0 units of Y. (We could have a positive endowment of Y but we assume that it has been netted out of both F and u_0.) The manager's best alternative opportunity is to consume 3 units of leisure and not work. If the manager supplies e units of effort then the firm's profit R will be $10e + \xi$, where ξ is a random variable with expected value zero. (R is profit before deducting the manager's pay.)

a Suppose that the owner offers the manager the wage contract $w = \theta R + F$. Determine the manager's effort supply function. Show that e increases when θ increases.

b Solve for the contract that maximizes the owner's expected profit.

c What are the owner's expected profit, the manager's expected utility, and the effort supplied by the manager under the contract that maximizes the owner's expected profit?

d Is the outcome that maximizes the owner's expected profit efficient? Explain.

2   A risk neutral manager has utility function $u(x, y) = 2\sqrt{x} + y$, where x is leisure consumption and y is expenditure on all other goods. The manager is endowed with Ω units of X and 0 units of Y. The manager's best alternative opportunity provides a level of utility of $u_0 = 2\sqrt{\Omega}$. If the manager supplies e units of effort then the firm's profit R will be $\beta e + \xi$, where ξ is a random variable with expected value zero. (R is profit before deducting the manager's pay.)

a Suppose that the owner offers the manager the wage contract $w = \theta R + F$. Determine the manager's effort supply function. Show that e increases when θ increases.

b Solve for the contract that maximizes the owner's expected profit.

c What are the owner's expected profit, the manager's expected utility, and the effort supplied by the manager under the contract that maximizes the owner's expected profit?

3   Prove that any solution to the problem "maximize u_1 subject to $u_h \geq u_h^0$ for all $h \neq 1$" is weakly efficient in any context, where u_h^0 is a constant for each h. Now show that with a risk neutral manager and a risk neutral owner, the owner's profit maximizing contract solves "maximize u_1 subject to $u_2 \geq u_2^0$ where u_1 is the owner's expected utility and u_2 is the manager's expected utility."

4   This question features a manager whose utility function is nonlinear in Y but there are no random variables affecting production. The manager's utility function is $U(x, y) = xy$, and the manager's best alternative yields $U^0 = 1$.

Profit is $R = 4e$, where R is profit before deducting the manager's pay. The manager has an endowment of 2 units of X and 0 units of Y. Find the contract that maximizes the owner's profit. What are the owner's profit, the manager's consumption of X and Y, the manager's utility, and the effort supplied by the manager under the contract that maximizes the owner's profit?

5   Again we have a manager whose utility function is nonlinear in Y and no randomness in production. The manager's utility function is $U(x, y) = xy$, and the manager's best alternative yields $U^0 = 1$. Profit is $R = \beta e$, where β is a positive constant and R is profit before deducting the manager's pay. The manager has an endowment of Ω units of X and zero units of Y. Find the contract that maximizes the owner's profit. What are the owner's profit, the manager's consumption of X and Y, the manager's utility, and the effort supplied by the manager under the contract that maximizes the owner's profit?

6   This question features a manager whose utility function is nonlinear in Y but there are no random variables affecting production. Let $U(x, y)$ represent the manager's utility function. The manager's best alternative yields U^0. Profit is $R = \beta e$, where β is a positive constant and R is profit before deducting the manager's pay. The manager has an endowment of Ω units of X and zero units of Y. Show that the contract that maximizes the owner's profit has the form $w = R + F$, where F is fixed, independently of the profit R. *Hint:* Use the implicit function theorem and the participation constraint to solve for dy/dx in terms of the partial derivatives of U. Then compare the first order condition from the owner's maximization problem to the solution of

$$\max\ U(x, y) \qquad \text{subject to } P_1 x + P_2 y = B.$$

7   Solve for the profit maximizing wage contract in the model of section 7.4 with $R = 4e + \xi$, $K = 8$, and $u^0 = 5$. Calculate F as well as θ. What is the owner's expected profit?

8   Section 7.4 represents the agent's utility indirectly, as $y - C(e)$, where C is the cost of effort to the agent, and $C' > 0$ and $C'' > 0$. Show that this leads to the same behavior as when we take $U = B(x) + y$, with $B' > 0$, $B'' < 0$, and $x = \Omega - e$. In particular, show that in both cases, utility declines as effort increases and that the rate of decline is higher when effort is greater.

9   The manager of a firm has the utility $U = 50x - x^2 + y$, where x is consumption of leisure and y is the market value of other goods and services. The manager will cease to work for the firm if her utility falls below 624. She has a time endowment of 24 and her initial wealth is zero. The profit R realized by the owner, before deducting the manager's pay, is given

by $R = 30e + \xi$, where e is effort supplied by the manager and ξ is a random variable with an expected value of zero. The owner cannot enforce a contract that mandates a specific input of effort. Show that the owner's income is maximized if he offers the manager a contract that requires a payment of $196 from the manager to the owner with the manager keeping any additional profit realized by the firm.

3

Hidden characteristics

This chapter investigates ten different hidden characteristic problems, from voting to used car markets. We examine institutions that are already widely used; in Chapters 5 through 8 attention is also paid to the possibility of designing superior institutions or incentive schemes. In this chapter we will see that market forces have spawned contracts and other devices that induce agents to reveal their hidden characteristics, but that this does not mean that the equilibrium outcome is efficient. There are incentive schemes that *do* induce truthful revelation of the hidden information while bringing the system close to efficiency – the auction mechanism of section 2, in particular. Chapter 8 shows that the social cost pricing formula, implicit in the auction scheme of section 2, is essential for truthful revelation and efficiency. Most of the other examples of this chapter show how market forces do not foster social cost pricing when there is substantial monopoly (section 5), uncertainty (sections 7–10), or spillover benefits (section 4). I want to emphasize, though, that markets are wonderfully creative in circumventing hidden information problems. Warranties on consumer durables provide a nice example of the market system's generating its own solution to a hidden information problem. The producer of a shoddy appliance cannot afford to offer a substantial warranty. The point of producing a low quality item is to get more profit by keeping costs down, but if many appliances are being returned for refund or repair then costs will be high, not low. A producer that deliberately sets out to profit by misleading consumers about the quality of the product will not be able to offer the same kind of warranty as the producer of a high quality product. The producer of the high-quality item is signalling that high quality to the consumer by offering a substantial warranty.[1] (Reputable manufacturers will even make good on a warranty after it has expired, as long as the appliance is returned less than a month after the expiration.) We begin with a standard example of the hidden characteristic phenomenon.

1 Price discrimination

Price discrimination is an example of a hidden characteristic problem. Suppose that a firm's consumers can be divided into two categories, high demand elasticity and low demand elasticity. In that case the firm's profit can be increased by charging a higher price to the latter group. Because of this the low-elasticity customers cannot be expected to disclose their (elasticity) characteristic voluntarily. Firms often employ another statistic that is correlated with elasticity. Consider two simple examples:

1.1 Plane travel

On average, business travellers have a lower demand elasticity than vacationers. The former charge their fares to their companies (i.e., the shareholders), who in turn pass on part of the cost to taxpayers. And business trips often have an urgency that nonbusiness travel seldom does. All of this results in a relatively low elasticity of demand for plane tickets by business travellers. By charging a lower fare for travellers who stay over at least one Saturday night an airline company can force most business travellers to pay the higher fare. Most business trips do not extend through Saturday.

1.2 Equipment sales

The Xerox Corporation introduced the first push-button electrostatic copying machine in 1960 and for many years the company faced very little competition. Price discriminating profit maximization implies a higher charge for machines purchased by firms that intend to use them intensively. But these firms would not willingly admit that they are high intensity users. (And the machines can be resold anyway.) The chief rival to Xerox in the 1960s was Electrofax, which produced a copier that required a special coated paper. Initially, Electrofax held a monopoly on the sale of the special paper. By charging a price for the paper that was significantly above marginal cost, the company would, in effect, be charging a higher price for copying machines purchased by high intensity users – i.e., low demand elasticity users. A similar principle applies to the charges for Polaroid film during the period when Polaroid Corp. had a monopoly on the production of self-developing film and the complementary camera. And again in the case of the early IBM computers, the punch cards sold by IBM and used to enter input provided a way for IBM to meter the use of IBM machines. Initially, IBM had a monopoly on the sale of punch cards and they were priced above marginal cost, to allow IBM to extract more revenue from the high intensity users of its computing machines.

The Xerox copier did not require use of special paper, so the Xerox Corporation solved its hidden characteristic problem by refusing to sell the copiers; the machines had to be leased from Xerox. The rental fee was based on the number of copies made, so Xerox was able to meter its customers' usage and thus force high intensity users to pay more for the use of the copier. (See Phlips, 1981.)

There is a tension between price discrimination and extraction of consumer surplus. If all consumers had identical demand functions for the services generated by the machines and their variable input (paper, film, punch cards) then the monopolist would want to price the variable input at marginal cost in order to induce the buyer to use the equipment more intensively, thus in turn allowing a higher price to be charged for the equipment due to the larger consumer surplus. (One can show that profit is maximized when the price of the variable input is set at marginal cost and the price of the machine is set equal to the resulting consumer surplus. In this case there is only one demand curve to consider – the demand for the services of the machine.)

2 Auctions

Section 2 of Chapter 2 discusses the epidemic of failures of savings and loan institutions (S & L's) in the 1980s and the late 1970s. When a bank or S & L is taken over by the federal deposit insurance agency, or the Resolution Trust Corporation,[2] the bank's assets are typically sold to the private sector. The organization that sells these assets is an agent acting on behalf of taxpayers, who together constitute the principal. Are the principal's interests well served in this case? In particular, are the assets of failed S & L's sold to the private sector for the highest possible price? Sternberg (1991) argues that by soliciting *sealed bids* from potential buyers and awarding the asset to the high bidder at the bid price, the government agency is not maximizing the price at which seized bank assets are returned to the private sector. This first-price, sealed-bid auction requires each interested party to submit one bid in a sealed envelope. No one knows what others have bid, and the asset is sold to the highest bidder at a price equal to that high bid. There tend to be relatively few bidders in the case of the failed S & L assets, prompting speculation that the assets are being released too quickly. Moreover, Sternberg finds that the lack of competition, due to the fact the there are few bidders, who bid in secret, results in sales at prices that are millions of dollars below what would be realized with alternative selling strategies.[3] This section investigates the impact of a particular selling strategy on the buyer's behavior.

2.1 The seller's problem

Assume that a bank is to be sold, and there are several potential buyers. Each buyer attaches a different value to the bank, because the bidders have different opportunities for merging the bank with other companies that they own. This value, which we will refer to as the buyer's *reservation value,* is the maximum sum of money that the individual or institution would be willing to pay for the asset.[4] The reservation values are unknown to the seller. If they were known, the seller would simply sell the asset to the party with the highest reservation value for a price just under that reservation value. And because of that, buyers would not willingly and truthfully disclose their reservation values. The seller faces a hidden characteristic problem. Is there a scheme by which the seller could discover the individual reservation values and thereby sell the bank to the individual (or company) with the highest reservation value?

What about a conventional oral auction with ascending bids? The auctioneer calls out a price until someone accepts that price, whereupon the auctioneer raises the price again. She then asks for a new bid – i.e., acceptance of the new price – and so on, until no one is willing to accept the price, at which point the article is sold to the bidder who accepted the last price, which will be the price actually paid by the successful bidder. This is the standard *English auction.* This will induce more competition, and thus higher selling prices, than the first-price, sealed-bid auction, particularly if there are few risk averse bidders. But it is by no means straightforward to show this, and the result depends on crucial assumptions about what people know about the distribution of other bidders' reservation values, and what *these other bidders* know about the distribution of other bidders' reservation values. Instead, we will investigate the *second-price,* sealed-bid auction and show that it induces truthful revelation of an individual's reservation value.

2.2 The second-price, sealed-bid auction

The rules of the second-price, sealed-bid auction require the individuals to submit sealed bids. The asset goes to the highest bidder, who actually pays an amount of money equal to the second highest bid. It is thus in a person's self-interest to enter a bid equal to his true reservation value. Let's prove this. Consider a simple example. There are four bidders: *A*, with a reservation value of 100 ($100,000, if you like); *B*, whose reservation value is 50; *C*, with a reservation value of 40; and *D*, whose reservation value is 20. What should individual *B* bid? It might depend on what the others bid. Suppose *B* bids 75. If that were the highest bid and the next highest bid is 70 then *B* would be awarded the asset at a price of 70. *B* would pay $70 for something worth only $50 to him. So, submitting a bid above one's reservation value can be very unprofitable. Can it ever be beneficial? If B is awarded the asset and pays less than $50 for it, then B benefits, and his gain is $50 - P$, where P is the purchase price. If P is less than 50 then all bids other than B's were below 50. This means that a bid of 50, exactly equal to his reservation value, would also have been highest, and B would get the asset at the purchase price P, the second highest bid. This is the same purchase price paid by B as when he bids more than 50. In this case, bidding more than his reservation value leads to the same outcome as bidding an amount equal to his reservation value: B gets the asset at a price of P. Therefore, submitting a bid above one's reservation value can never help; it can only hurt. Suppose that B enters a bid of 30, which is below 50, his true reservation value. If the high bid is 40 then the asset goes to the person who bids 40. If B had bid 50 he would have been awarded the asset at a price of 40, the next highest bid, yielding a gain to B of $10 = 50 - 40$. By bidding below his reservation value B has forfeited a $10 profit. Can it ever be beneficial to enter a bid below one's true reservation value? If B submits a bid of 40 and it *is* the high bid then the high bid among B's competitors – call it P – must be less than 40. B gets the asset at a price $P < 40$. If B had entered a bid of 50 he would have been awarded the asset at the same price P: If B is the high bidder at 40, he would certainly be the high bidder at 50. The price P is the same in either case, because that depends on the bids submitted by others; P doesn't depend on B's bid, *given* that B has the high bid. The two strategies – bidding 40 and bidding 50 – yield the same outcome when B is the high bidder. Therefore, submitting a bid below one's reservation value can never help; it can only hurt. In short, no matter what the others bid, one can't improve on the strategy of entering a bid equal to one's reservation value! It is a simple matter to prove this in general.

Suppose that person X has a (true) reservation value of R and that H is the highest of all the bids except for X's own bid. What should X bid? Let S denote a bid that X considers making. Suppose that S is larger than R. There are three possibilities:

Case 1 $S > R > H$.

A bid of either R or S would secure the object for X and in either case the price paid would be H, the next highest bid. The gain to X would be $R - H$ in either case: the value of the object minus the price paid. It does not matter whether X bids R or S.

Case 2 $H > S > R$.

Whether X bids R or S the object will go to the person bidding H. Person X will pay nothing and will receive nothing with either bid, so again it does not matter whether X bids R or S. (It matters to the person bidding H, though, because he pays a price equal to the second highest bid. If that is S the object will be more costly to its recipient than when X bids R. But we are assuming that X is exclusively concerned with the payoff that he himself receives.)

Case 3 $S > H > R$.

If X bids R then the object will go to the person bidding H. X will receive nothing but will not have to pay anything either. X neither gains nor loses. If X bids S, however, he receives the object and will pay H for it although it is worth only R to him. There is a loss of $H - R$ in this case: X has paid \$$H$ for something worth only \$$R$. In this case it does matter to X whether he bids R or S; the outcome associated with R is much preferred.

We conclude that a bid above one's reservation value can only do harm; it will never do any good. Now consider the case $S < R$. There are again three subcases:

Case 4 $H < S < R$.

In this case X will receive the object with a bid of either S or R, and the price paid will be H in either case. The two bids have an identical impact on X's welfare.

Case 5 $S < R < H$.

The object goes to the person who bids H, whether X bids S or R. The two bids have the same effect on X's welfare.

Case 6 $S < H < R$.

If X bids R he receives the object and pays H, which is less than R. There is a profit of $R - H$ to X. If, however, X bids S the object will go to the person who bids H and there will be no gain to X. It is better for X to bid R in this case.

In any case a bid other than R can only hurt an individual. It can never help in a sealed-bid second-price auction. In practice one would not know H, the highest of all the other bids, and any bid above R exposes X to the risk of paying more for the object than it is worth. (If X bids $R + 50$ and the next highest bid is $R + 20$ then X will pay $R + 20$ for something worth only R.) Similarly any bid below R exposes X to the risk of losing the object when it could have been obtained for a price below R. (If X bids $R - 50$ and the highest bid is $R - 30$ then X could have bid R and obtained a profit of $R - [R - 30]$.)

Suppose the Resolution Trust Corporation used this auction to determine who is to receive an asset. Or consider any situation where the principal is attempting to promote the welfare of the group in question, aware of the possibility of inefficiency due to individuals independently pursuing their self-interest. Continue to assume that there is an object to be divided among n individuals. Let R_i be individual i's reservation value, and assume that the individuals have been labelled so that $R_1 > R_2 > R_3 \ldots > R_n$. If a sealed-bid second-price auction is used each individual i will bid R_i. The principal will then know each person's reservation value. The object will go to person 1 who pays R_2, providing a gain of

$R_1 - R_2$ to person 1. As we show in section 8 of Chapter 8, a necessary condition for efficiency is that the object be assigned to the individual with the highest true reservation value.

Note that a bid equal to one's reservation value is a *dominant strategy* for the sealed-bid second-price auction. A dominant strategy for person i with utility function U_i is defined to be a strategy S_i^* such that for any choice of strategies S_j ($j \neq i$) by the players other than i we have

$$U_i(S_1, S_2, \ldots, S_{i-1}, S_i^*, S_{i+1}, \ldots, S_n)$$
$$\geq U_i(S_1, S_2, \ldots, S_{i-1}, S_i, S_{i+1}, \ldots, S_n)$$

for every other strategy S_i available to i.

In the case of the second-price sealed-bid auction individual i's preference scheme is characterized by a reservation value R_i because i's utility function U_i is defined by

$$U_i = -P \qquad \text{if } i \text{ pays } P \text{ and does not get the object.}$$
$$U_i = R_i - P \qquad \text{if } i \text{ pays } P \text{ and gets the object.}$$

In particular, i's utility is zero if i pays nothing and does not receive the object. We have shown that a bid of R_i is a dominant strategy for individual i with reservation value R_i and utility function U_i. It is obviously the *only* dominant strategy. Any bid above or below R_i will be less profitable in some situation than a bid of R_i.

In terms of our specific example, A will bid 100, B will bid 50, C will bid 40, and D will bid 20. A will get the asset and pay 50 for it. But notice that our argument was completely general. It applies to the auctioning of any object among any number of individuals. And once the object is allocated it is not possible for two individuals to engage in a mutually beneficial trade because the object goes to the person who values it most.

Vickrey (1961) pioneered the study of auctions in economic theory and his seminal article anticipated important discoveries in the theory of public goods in addition to the contemporary literature on auctions and bidding. Section 5 of Chapter 5 explains the relation between the second-price sealed-bid auction and the question of preference revelation for public goods. See Milgrom (1987) for an introduction to auctions and bidding. Chapter 8 of this book shows that the second-price schedule is the *only* formula that guarantees truthful revelation and efficient outcomes.

Suggestions for further reading: Ashenfelter (1989), Milgrom (1989).

Exercises

1   A government agency is accepting tenders for the construction of a public building. There are n firms with an interest in undertaking the project. Each firm i has a minimum cost C_i that it would incur in construction. (C_i

includes the opportunity cost of capital.) The contract will be awarded by having the firms submit sealed bids. Firm i's bid B_i is the amount of money that it requires in order to undertake the project. The contract will be awarded to the firm submitting the lowest bid and that firm will be paid an amount of money equal to the second lowest bid. Prove that a bid of C_i is a dominant strategy for arbitrary firm i.

2   Show that the English oral auction has the same outcome as the second-price sealed-bid auction.

3   Consider the second-price sealed-bid auction in which the seller is allowed to submit a bid S. The object is retained by the seller if every other bid is below S.

    a   Show that the strategy of setting S equal to the seller's reservation value is not a dominant strategy for the seller if S is used to determine the price at which the asset is sold to the high bidder. (The price is equal to the second highest of all bids, including S.)

    b   Show that the strategy of setting S equal to the seller's reservation value is not a dominant strategy for the seller if the price at which the asset is sold is equal to the second highest of all bids *excluding S*.

3 Voting

The second-price sealed-bid auction of section 2 induces truthful revelation *assuming* that individual utilities belong to the special family $U_i = \alpha_i R_i - P_i$, where P_i is the money paid by i (if any), R_i is i's true reservation value, and α_i equals 1 if the object is assigned to i and zero otherwise. In this section we want to look at situations in which a group must make a decision that will be binding on all of its members. For example: a class has to determine a time for a review session; a town has to decide whether to build a new school; a nation has to elect a legislature. In this setting we can't rule out any ranking of the available options as a possible preference scheme for a member of the group. This makes it much harder to induce truthful revelation of the hidden characteristic, which in this section will be the individual's true preference ranking. We want the individuals to reveal enough information about their preferences to allow a Pareto optimal outcome to be identified.

Assume that there are three available alternatives; we want individuals to reveal their preference ordering of these alternatives. We won't worry about efficiency, however; it will be hard enough just to design a decision scheme for which it is in an individual's self-interest to reveal his ordering truthfully.

Although this section discusses voting procedures, the reader is encouraged to think of the candidates standing for election not as individuals seeking careers in government but as alternative packages of public projects. Candidate (or alternative) x may, for example, be a proposal to reduce expenditure on the space shuttle project by a specific amount and to use the proceeds to fund research on the production of energy by nuclear fusion. Alternative y may be a proposal to maintain the level of expenditure on the space shuttle while increasing federal expenditure on health care at the expense of grants to university professors. Other candidates or alternatives may present mixtures of x and y and each would be identified by its own label, $w, z,$ etc. The voters may be taken to be the members of the legislature or even the citizens themselves who are asked to vote directly for public projects. The fact that citizens do not presently vote directly on these matters should not stand in our way. The observation that a particular voting scheme is not widely used is not a persuasive argument against its introduction if it would serve society better than the methods presently in use. In this section we begin the discussion of voting systems in terms of how successfully they serve the community, although we do this in relation to one criterion only – the extent to which a voting procedure embodies incentives that induce individuals to mark their ballots to reflect their preferences in the way prescribed by the systems rules. Before discussing why this is of concern let's consider some specific examples. (The community could be very small – a college campus, for example.)

3.1 Majority rule

There are three mutually exclusive alternatives, $x, y,$ and z. The alternative that defeats each of the others by a simple majority is declared the winner. Suppose that it is known that individual preferences belong to the family of four preference schemes, or orderings, illustrated in Figure 1. For simplicity, suppose that there are only three individuals, whom we will call 1, 2, and 3. (Alternatively, assume three groups of individuals with the same number in each group and identical preferences within each group.) Then there will always be a unique majority rule winner. Before demonstrating this we define the majority rule process precisely. Alternative x, say, is declared the winner if it defeats y by a simple majority in an election where only x and y are candidates *and* x beats z by a simple majority in an election in which x and z are the only candidates.

Now, prove that a majority winner always exists when the preferences belong to the family of Figure 1. If two of the three individuals have identical preferences then whatever alternative ranks at the top of their common ordering must be the winner. If all three individuals have different preference schemes there are four cases to consider: (case 1) No one has the preference scheme R_1. Then it is easy to determine that y will be the majority winner. Anyone with preference scheme R_3 or R_4 will vote for y over x, and all three will vote for y over z. (case 2) No one has

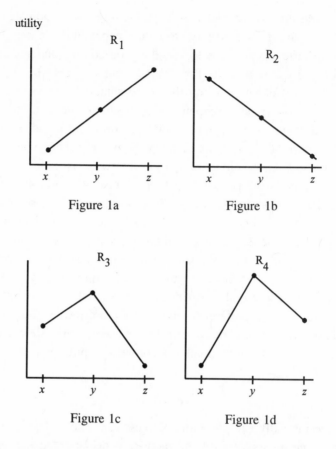

Figure 1a   Figure 1b

Figure 1c   Figure 1d

R_2. Everyone will vote for y over x and anyone with R_3 or R_4 will vote for y over z. Similarly, y is the winner when R_3 is absent (case 3) and also when R_4 is absent (case 4), as you can easily verify. Before considering what happens when other preference schemes are possible let us ask whether our subfamily (Figure 1) has some plausibility.

The graph of each of the preference orderings of Figure 1 shows only one peak. There is no instance of a graph dipping down and then back up, as would be the case with R_5 (Figure 2), which has z ranked at the top, then x, and y ranked last. There are situations for which we could plausibly argue that individual preferences would be single-peaked. For example, the alternatives represent levels of military spending, with z requiring the highest level of expenditure and x the lowest. Or x could represent a left-wing position, z a right-wing position, and y a moderate position. The important thing is that the alternatives can be arranged in a natural order, and while individual preference orderings of the alternatives may conflict, all single-peaked preferences have something in common – the two extremes x and z are not both preferred to the intermediate position y. Whenever

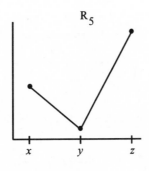

Figure 2

that is the case then there will always be a majority winner. (The winner will be y if the three individuals have different single-peaked preferences.)

Now, let's consider the issue of incentives. Suppose that each person reports his preference ordering to a referee, who then uses the reported preferences to compute the majority winner. Would a voter ever have an incentive to report anything other than his true preference scheme? The answer is "no" *if* we are using the majority rule scheme, and *if* each individual's true preference scheme belongs to the single-peak family of Figure 1, and *if* the referee disallows any reported preference scheme that is not a member of this family. It is easy to see why. Suppose that w is the outcome when individual i reports his true preference scheme. (Here w is just another name for "winner" and will be one of the three alternatives.) Suppose that ω emerges as the winner when i reports some false preference scheme and all other reports are unchanged. If $\omega \neq w$ then it must be the case that i truly prefers w to ω, in which case a departure from the truth would be harmful to i. How do we know that i prefers w to ω according to his true preference scheme? Because the change in outcome from w to ω can only occur when i changes the way he votes, and w is the result when i votes according to his true preferences. In particular ω defeats w when i votes untruthfully, and w defeats ω when i votes truthfully. Only the voting strategy of person i changes, so it must be the case that i truly prefers w to ω. There is no incentive to deviate from the truth.

What of situations where it is not reasonable to assume that all individual preferences belong to the single-peak family? This is typically the case when there are several criteria by which the policies are judged, effect on employment, for example, as well as the money cost. Suppose that the preferences are as described in Table 1. Person 1 has preference scheme R_2, person 2 has R_4, and 3 has the preference scheme R_5 represented in Figure 2. Then x beats y by two votes to one, y beats z by two votes to one, but z beats x by two votes to one. There is no

Table 1

1	2	3
x	y	z
y	z	x
z	x	y

Table 2

1	2	3
x	y	z
y	z	y
z	x	x

majority winner.[5] Let us augment the voting procedure by agreeing that the outcome remains the status quo – which we will take to be alternative z – if there is no majority winner. Now, suppose that the true preferences are as represented in Table 2. Each of these belongs to the single-peak family of Figure 1 and there is a clear majority winner, y. (Persons 2 and 3 vote for y over x, and 1 and 2 vote for y over z.) We emphasize that Table 2 represents the individuals' *true* preferences and that the winner is y *when* those true preferences are faithfully reported. Suppose that person 3 reports the preference scheme in column 3 of Table 1, instead of his true ordering. Suppose further that this ordering cannot be plausibly ruled out by the referee; it could be an individual's true preference ordering. Then there would be no majority winner and the outcome would be z, which is the most-preferred outcome according to 3's *true* preference scheme. An individual *does* sometimes have an incentive to misrepresent his preferences in this wider context. We say that individual 3 *manipulates*. (Note that we have not altered the reports of persons 1 and 2.)

Consider a slightly different situation. This time the true preference schemes are those represented by Table 1. The outcome is z, which is the least-preferred alternative in the case of individual 1. If person 1 reports the ordering in the first column of Table 3 below then the outcome is y, which 1 prefers to z according to his true preference. (We have not altered the preference of persons 2 and 3. Verify that y beats both x and z by a clear majority in Table 3.)

You may object that everyone can play this game; we cannot predict the outcome that results from strategic manoeuvering until we have identified the strategy that each voter will adopt. However, we are not attempting to *predict*

Table 3

1	2	3
y	y	z
x	z	x
z	x	y

the outcome at this point. We are merely proving that majority rule is vulnerable to manipulation if there is no a priori reason for restricting the preference schemes that individuals are allowed to report. Assume, on the contrary, that it *is* in everyone's self-interest to report his true preference scheme in every situation. It follows that persons 2 and 3 will report their preferences truthfully. We have just examined a case in which person 1 can gain by misrepresentation when 2 and 3 report truthfully, contradicting the claim that truthful revelation is in everyone's interest.

Consider an alternative formula for extending majority rule to cases where there is no clear majority winner. This time one individual will be appointed chairperson and that individual's most-preferred alternative will be adopted when there is no clear majority winner. There will still be opportunities for manipulation – i.e., for misrepresentation. Say that person 3 is chair and the true preferences are as set out in Table 2. If everyone reports truthfully alternative y is the clear majority winner. But, if person 3 deviates from the truth and reports the preference scheme in column 3 of Table 1 then z will be the outcome because there is no overall majority winner and z is the chair's most-preferred alternative because 3 prefers z to y according to his true preference ordering and he has an incentive to misrepresent. Let's see if we can avoid this phenomenon by means of some quite different voting schemes.

3.2 Plurality decision

With a plurality decision procedure the voters simply declare their most-preferred alternative and the one receiving the most votes is the outcome. If there is a tie then we have a second election involving only the first round winners. Table 4 shows how easily this scheme can be manipulated. There are five individuals and four alternatives. If everyone reports his most-preferred alternative truthfully then x will receive two votes and y, z, and t will receive one vote each. Then the outcome will be x, which is the alternative preferred least by person 5. If 5 deviates from the truth and claims y as his most-preferred alternative then there will be a tie between x and y. Alternative y will win the run-off, receiving votes

Table 4

1	2	3	4	5
x	x	y	z	t
y	y	z	y	z
z	z	x	x	y
t	t	t	t	x

from 3, 4, and 5, each of whom prefers y to x. Therefore, there are situations in which individuals have an incentive to misrepresent. Plurality decision is not immune to manipulation. (Note that the preferences of Table 4 belong to the family of single-peaked preferences *and* when 5 misrepresents he can claim to have the same preference ordering as person 3.)

3.3 The Borda or rank order method

There are four alternatives, $t, x, y,$ and z, but three individuals this time. Each person casts four votes for his most-preferred alternative, three votes for the alternative he ranks second, two votes for the alternative he ranks third, and one vote for the lowest ranking alternative in his preference scheme. The alternative receiving the largest total number of votes is the winner. (We will not have to consider ties.) Let the true preferences be as represented in Table 5. The winner is t, with nine votes, when everyone reports truthfully. If person 3 reports the preference scheme of column 3 in Table 6 then the outcome is x, which 3 prefers to t according to his true preference scheme (column 3 of Table 5). Again, there will be situations in which a voter has incentives to misrepresent his preferences.

3.4 The general case

A voting scheme for which truthful preference revelation is a dominant strategy is said to be *strategy-proof*. Here are two strategy-proof voting schemes. (1) Select two specific alternatives and label them x^* and y^*. The outcome is x^* unless the reported individual preference orderings have y^* ranking above x^* in a majority of cases, in which case y^* is the outcome. There may be many available alternatives other than these two but only x^* and y^* can ever be selected. Why is this scheme strategy-proof? If w is the outcome when i reports his preference scheme truthfully and $\omega \neq w$ is the outcome when i reports a different preference ordering then ω cannot be preferred to w according to i's true preference scheme. Therefore, i truly prefers w to ω and i has no incentive to misrepresent. In most situations there

Table 5

Preferences				Votes			
1	2	3		1	2	3	Total
t	z	y	t:	4	3	2	9
x	t	x	x:	3	2	3	8
y	x	t	y:	2	1	4	7
z	y	z	z:	1	4	1	6

Table 6

Preferences				Votes			
1	2	3		1	2	3	Total
t	z	x	t:	4	3	1	8
x	t	z	x:	3	2	4	9
y	x	y	y:	2	1	2	5
z	y	t	z:	1	4	3	8

are more than two alternatives to consider but with this voting scheme the outcome must be either x^* or y^* in every case. Suppose there is a third alternative z and everyone ranks z as most-preferred. The outcome will not be efficient; everyone prefers z to the winner, which must be either x^* or y^*. This procedure is strategy-proof but very unsatisfactory on efficiency grounds. Now we consider a procedure that is efficient. (2) There are any number of alternatives and the outcome is just m_1, the most-preferred alternative according to the reported preference scheme of person 1. No one other than 1 can affect the outcome so no one other than 1 has an incentive to manipulate. And it is in 1's self-interest to ensure the selection of his most-preferred alternative so 1 will always report truthfully. The procedure is strategy-proof. It is obviously dictatorial and therefore completely unsatisfactory.

If three or more alternatives are generated as winning outcomes, depending on the reported messages, and no individual preference scheme can be ruled out then *dictatorial schemes are the only ones that are strategy proof.* This remarkable theorem is due to Alan Gibbard (1973) and Mark Satterthwaite (1975). It is proved in Chapter 7.

Suggestions for further reading: Feldman (1988); Kelly (1988, chapter 10); Saari (1994, chapter 1).

Exercises

1 Does the following family of preferences over the three alternatives x, y, z have the single-peak property? Explain.

x	z	z	y
z	x	y	z
y	y	x	x

(There are four preference orderings, each represented by a column, and a higher alternative is preferred to a lower one.)

2 List all the logically possible linear orders on the three alternatives x, y, z. (A linear order is one that can be represented as a column, with the higher alternatives being more preferred; a linear order rules out the possibility that two distinct alternatives are indifferent to each other.) Now, identify all the families of single-peaked subsets of preferences.

3 This section presented a simple example of a majority rule cycle with three alternatives and three individuals. Explain how one can construct a cycle with three alternatives and any odd number n of individuals ($n \geq 3$).

4 There are three alternatives x, y, and z and three individuals. An outcome is determined by the simple majority rule process with alternatives competing in pairs – the winner is the alternative that defeats both of the others by a majority. If there is a cycle, and no majority winner emerges, then the outcome is person 1's most-preferred alternative. Show that someone will have an incentive to misrepresent his preference ordering in at least one situation.

5 Consider the following voting scheme defined for two individuals, 1 and 2, and three alternatives x, y, z: The individuals report a preference ordering of the three alternatives and if one alternative is ranked at the top of both reported preference orderings then that alternative is the winner, and otherwise person 1's top-ranked alternative is the winner. (Assume that two distinct alternatives are never indifferent in anyone's preference ordering.) Prove that truthful revelation is a dominant strategy for this voting scheme. Does this contradict the Gibbard–Satterthwaite theorem? Explain.

6 Consider the following voting scheme defined for two individuals, 1 and 2, and three alternatives x, y, z: The individuals report a preference ordering of the three alternatives and if there is a unique alternative that is ranked at the top of both reported preference orderings then that alternative is the winner, and otherwise person 1's top-ranked alternative is the

winner if there is a single alternative that is top-ranked by person 1. If there are two or more alternatives that are tied for top rank in person 1's reported preference scheme then the winner is person 2's more preferred alternative (according to 2's reported preference scheme) *in the set of top-ranked alternatives in the preference ordering reported by person 1*. If there are two or more alternatives that are top ranked in 1's reported preference scheme and within that set there is not a unique outcome that is highest ranked in 2's reported scheme then the outcome is x. Prove that truthful revelation is a dominant strategy for this voting scheme. Does this contradict the Gibbard–Satterthwaite theorem? Explain.

7   Consider the following voting scheme, or mechanism, for selecting an outcome from a set of three available alternatives, x, y, and z: Each individual reports her preference ordering to a referee. If according to the reported preferences one alternative defeats each of the two others by a majority then that alternative is the chosen outcome. If there is no such majority winner then the outcome is either x or y, whichever of those two alternatives defeats the other by a majority. Is reporting one's true preference ordering always a dominant strategy in the case of this particular mechanism? If it is, explain briefly why it is. If it is not, prove that truthful revelation is not a dominant strategy by means of an example.

8   Assuming that there are three available alternatives that can be arranged in a natural order in such a way that all individual preferences are single-peaked, prove that there will always be a majority winner. Suppose that the alternatives x, y, z have been arranged so that x is not ranked last by any individual. Prove that the majority winner will be x *if* the three individuals have *different* single-peaked preferences.

9   This section discussed three ways of modifying simple majority rule so that a unique winner would be declared even if there were a cycle. In each case an example was constructed for which at least one person had an incentive to misrepresent her preference scheme. For each case work out the Nash equilibrium that results when each person plays strategically. At equilibrium it will be the case that, *given the preferences reported by others*, no individual is able to modify her reported preference scheme in a way that elicits an outcome that she likes better according to her true preference scheme.

10   Suppose that three individuals have single-peaked preferences. Explain why the most-preferred alternative of the median voter – the one whose peak lies between the peaks of the other two voters – will defeat every other proposal by a majority of votes.

4 Public goods

Now we return to a model that has the richer structure of standard economic models. For the most part, the previous section assumed that any logically possible ordering of the three alternatives was a plausible preference scheme for an arbitrary individual. In an explicitly economic model, we are usually persuaded that there are some restrictive properties that individual preferences would exhibit. For example, if x offers everyone more of every good than y then we can rule out individual preferences that have y ranking above x. And indifference curves can often be assumed to be convex; this restriction disqualifies many other preference schemes. Perhaps such restrictions on the domain of admissible preferences lead to a model with more potential for truthful revelation of preferences. We begin the exploration of this question in a simple model with public goods. (Chapter 6 provides a more general treatment.)

A public good is a commodity from which everyone in the community jointly benefits. A pure public good is an ideal case in which every amount produced is consumed in equal measure by all, even though varying levels of benefit are realized. Consider for example street lights. In this case the community is the group of residents on one street. Street lights reduce crime. Consider the placement of lights on a typical city street. Would the residents be served best by having one light in front of each house, one light for the entire street, or some intermediate number? The decision *should* depend on householders' preferences. Preferences will in turn depend on the perceived benefits in terms of crime reduction from the various plans and on the nature of the goods and services – porch lighting, for example – that could be produced instead of a street lamp.

Let us consider the outcome that would be determined by the market system. Assume, therefore, that private firms produce light standards and sell them to private buyers at a price that is expected to maximize profit. Anyone desiring lighting on his street may purchase a lamp, hire a contractor to install it on his property, and pay the monthly electricity charges for its operation. Will this system serve the residents of our street very well? It is highly unlikely.

There is a *free rider problem*. Any householder will receive the benefit from a lamp installed by his neighbor and will have an incentive to avoid paying for a light on his own property in anticipation of getting the benefit of neighboring lights without paying for them. Of course, each resident has the same incentive, and it is likely that no street lights would be installed, but each resident would have been better off if lamps had been installed by the government, with each household paying a share of the total cost. In other words, the market outcome would not be efficient.

Having the government take the initiative for the project does not automatically solve the problem. One has to consider how the government is to discover the extent of household preferences for street lighting and for other goods and services that could be produced with the inputs required to manufacture a street lamp. This is by no means a simple matter. It is one virtue of the market mechanism that for a wide range or goods and services this process of accumulating essential information about household preferences is accomplished simply and neatly. (See Chapter 5.) In the case of any commodity for which the benefits are confined to one individual – such a commodity is called a *private good* – a consumer does not derive any benefit unless he pays for the good, and the higher the price, the higher the benefit that must be realized in consumption for the purchaser to justify the purchase decision. However, when the benefits of a commodity can be collectively enjoyed (as in the case of street lights), a very high level of community benefit can be sacrificed when each individual determines that *his* benefit is not great enough to justify *his* paying the purchase price.

Let us try to solve the problem of producing the efficient number of street lights by designing a mechanism that imitates the market system's success in the realm of private goods. We will have to face up to the issue of incentives.

Consider a scheme of contributions based on the degree of benefit received. Specifically, the residents of the street form a club and each household contributes to a fund that is to be used to purchase the lights and pay the monthly electricity bill. To imitate the role of prices in private goods markets, we can impose the rule that a householder's contribution to the fund be proportional to the benefit received and this will be called the *benefit tax scheme*. We will work through the implications of this scheme under five headings, presented as sections 4.1–4.5, in which we analyze a simple model of resource allocation with one public good and one private good.

4.1 The simple public goods model

There are two goods, a public good (street lighting perhaps) and a private good (labor/leisure). There are n households. Let x be the amount of the public good; its production requires $\frac{1}{2}x^2$ units of labor as input. Let y_i denote the amount of leisure consumed by individual i and let Ω_i be the total amount of this private good held by i initially. There is a total of n households. Then $\Omega = \sum_{i=1}^{n} \Omega_i$, a constant, is the total amount of labor available. Individual i's utility is given by the function $u_i = \alpha_i x + y_i$, which can also be written $u_i = \alpha_i x + \Omega_i - L_i$, where L_i is the amount of labor contributed by i to the production of the public good. We assume that $\alpha_i \geq 0$ holds, but the exact value of α_i is unknown to anyone but i. Of course, feasibility requires $\sum_{i=1}^{n} y_i \leq \Omega - \frac{1}{2}x^2$ and efficiency implies that $\sum_{i=1}^{n} y_i$

$< \Omega - \frac{1}{2}x^2$ does *not* hold. (Why?) Therefore a Pareto optimal – i.e., efficient – outcome will satisfy $\Sigma_{i=1}^{n} y_i = \Omega - \frac{1}{2}x^2$.

To find a Pareto optimal outcome we can maximize Σu_i:

$$\sum_{i=1}^{n} u_i = \sum_{i=1}^{n} \alpha_i x + \sum_{i=1}^{n} y_i$$

$$= \sum_{i=1}^{n} \alpha_i x + \Omega - \frac{1}{2}x^2.$$

(Anything that maximizes total utility must be Pareto optimal: see sections 5 and 11 of Chapter 1.) Because Ω is a constant, maximizing $\Sigma_{i=1}^{n} u_i$ is equivalent to maximizing $f(x) = \Sigma_{i=1}^{n} \alpha_i x - \frac{1}{2}x^2$. We have $f'(x) = \Sigma_{i=1}^{n} \alpha_i - x$ and $f''(x) = -1$. Because $f'' < 0$ setting $f' = 0$ will indeed give us a global *maximum*. Assuming that there will be an interior solution, $f' = 0$ is necessary and sufficient for a maximum. And $f' = 0$ implies $x = \Sigma_{i=1}^{n} \alpha_i$. Set $x^* = \Sigma \alpha_i$, which we refer to as *the* Pareto optimal level of the public good. (In the next section we show that Pareto optimality *implies* $x = x^*$.) But we have only shown so far that it is *one* Pareto optimal level of the public good. That is, the allocation $(x, y_1, y_2, \ldots , y_n)$ is efficient if $x = x^*$, $y_i \geq 0$ for each i, and $\Sigma y_i = \Omega - \frac{1}{2}(x^*)^2$: From an efficiency standpoint, it does not matter how the private goods are distributed as long as every amount of the private good not used in the production of the public good is made available for consumption. Formally, this is the equality $\Sigma y_i = \Omega - \frac{1}{2}(x^*)^2$. If this equality is satisfied and $x = x^*$ then the allocation in question maximizes the sum of individual utilities so it must be efficient.

4.2 Uniqueness of the Pareto optimal level of x

Maximization of Σu_i is equivalent to maximization of $f(x)$ as we have just seen, and this implies $f'(x) = 0$, which in turn implies $x = x^*$. Only one level of x is consistent with maximization of Σu_i but are there other levels of x consistent with Pareto optimality? (Maximization of Σu_i implies efficiency in any model, but efficiency does not imply maximization of Σu_i in general. In Chapter 5 we will encounter a simple two-person exchange economy with many Pareto optimal allocations that do not maximize Σu_i.)

Suppose that $f(x) < f(x^*)$. Let q be between x and x^*. Then $f(x) < f(q) < f(x^*)$. This follows from $f'(x^*) = 0$ and the fact that $f'' < 0$ holds at every point (the graph of f is a hill with its peak at x^*). Then

$$\Sigma \alpha_i q - \frac{1}{2}q^2 > \Sigma \alpha_i x - \frac{1}{2}x^2, \quad \text{or}$$

$$\Sigma \alpha_i q - \Sigma \alpha_i x > \frac{1}{2}q^2 - \frac{1}{2}x^2. \qquad [1]$$

We now use [1] to show that the allocation $(x, y_1, y_2, \ldots, y_n)$ is not Pareto optimal if it does not maximize Σu_i: that is, if x does not maximize $f(x)$. We can give everyone more utility by producing q and reducing each i's consumption of the private good by $[\alpha_i/(\alpha_1 + \alpha_2 + \ldots + \alpha_n)][\frac{1}{2}q^2 - \frac{1}{2}x^2]$. Note that $\frac{1}{2}q^2 - \frac{1}{2}x^2$ is the increase in the cost of producing public goods when the output level changes from x to q. (Of course, if q is less than x this will actually increase each y_i, because the input requirement will fall. That is, $\frac{1}{2}q^2 - \frac{1}{2}x^2$ will be negative.)

We want to show that $\Delta u_i = \alpha_i q + y_i - [\alpha_i/(\alpha_1 + \ldots + \alpha_n)][\frac{1}{2}q^2 - \frac{1}{2}x^2] - [\alpha_i x + y_i]$ is positive. It suffices to establish [2] for arbitrary individual h:

$$\alpha_h q - \alpha_h x > [\alpha_h/(\alpha_1 + \ldots + \alpha_2)][\frac{1}{2}q^2 - \frac{1}{2}x^2]. \qquad [2]$$

By multiplying both sides of [2] by $\Sigma \alpha_i/\alpha_h$ we can show that [2] is equivalent to

$$\Sigma \alpha_i\, q - \Sigma \alpha_i\, x > \frac{1}{2}q^2 - \frac{1}{2}x^2,$$

which is statement [1]. Therefore, $\Delta u_h > 0$ for each h. Each person receives more utility than under the outcome $(x, y_1, y_2, \ldots, y_n)$, which cannot, therefore, be Pareto optimal. Therefore, Pareto optimality *implies* maximization of Σu_i in the case of this particular model.[6] We proved this in general in section 11.1 of Chapter 1, but 11.1 did not bother to ensure that no one is assigned a negative amount of good Y by the new outcome. Let's verify this for the new allocation constructed in this section: If $y_i > 0$ for each i (each person initially has a positive amount of the private good) then we can be sure that replacing x by q and giving each person i exactly $y_i - [\alpha_i/(\alpha_1 + \ldots + \alpha_n)][\frac{1}{2}q^2 - \frac{1}{2}x^2]$ units of Y is feasible by making q sufficiently close to x, to ensure that each individual still winds up with a positive amount of Y. (But to guarantee $\Delta u_i > 0$ we have to have $x < q < x^*$ if $x < x^*$, and $x^* > q > x$ if $x^* > x$. Confirm that the new allocation collects enough of the private good from the household sector to provide sufficient input for the production of q units of the public good.)

4.3 The market equilibrium is not efficient

A firm produces the public good for profit at a price of P. Normalize and set the wage rate at unity. The firm's profit is $Px - \frac{1}{2}x^2$, which is maximized by setting the first derivative $P - x$ equal to zero. Therefore, $P = x$ at a market equilibrium. If $\alpha_i > 0$ for each i then $P = x^*$ implies $P > \alpha_i$ for each i. Therefore, if x^* emerges from a *competitive* private ownership market equilibrium we will have $P > \alpha_i$ for each i. Now, consider the consumer's utility maximization problem:

$$\text{Maximize } u_i = \alpha_i(q_i + \rho_i) + y_i$$
$$\text{subject to } Pq_i = \Omega_i - y_i + i\text{'s share of profit.}$$

Here, q_i is i's personal purchase of the public good; ρ_i is the total amount of the public good purchased by everyone other than i, which i treats as a constant; and

y_i is i's consumption of leisure, which means that i supplies $\Omega_i - y_i$ units of labor to the labor market. But $P > \alpha_i$. Therefore, $u_i = \alpha_i(q_i + \rho_i) + y_i = \alpha_i q_i + \alpha_i \rho_i + \Omega_i - Pq_i + R_i = C + (\alpha_i - P)q_i$, where R_i is i's profit income and C is a constant, and this is maximized by setting $q_i = 0$. Therefore, we cannot have $0 = \Sigma q_i = x^*$ $= \Sigma \alpha_i > 0$ at equilibrium. The next section actually identifies the market equilibrium and shows that it is *far* from Pareto optimal.

4.4 Private market equilibrium

To make it easier to compare the competitive market equilibrium for the public goods case to the Pareto optimal level of x, we modify the example. There are n individuals. We assume $u_i = 2\alpha_i\sqrt{x} + y_i$ and the cost function is simply x. To say that the cost function is x means that x units of the private good are required as input if the economy is to produce x units of the public good. This simple production process implies that profit is zero at equilibrium so we will not have to include profit income in the budget equation. Normalize, and let the wage rate be unity. Let P be the price of the public good, which we assume to be sold on the private market. Let q_i be the quantity of the public good purchased by i and let ρ_i denote the amount purchased by *everyone but* i. Then i will choose q_i to maximize

$$u_i = 2\alpha_i(q_i + \rho_i)^{1/2} + y_i, \text{ subject to } Pq_i = \Omega_i - y_i, \text{ and given } \rho_i.$$

This means that i will maximize

$$u_i = 2\alpha_i(q_i + \rho_i)^{1/2} + \Omega_i - Pq_i.$$

The firm will maximize $Px - x$. If $P > 1$ then profit is unbounded and supply will be unlimited. Therefore, $P \leq 1$ at equilibrium. If $P < 1$ the profit is maximized at $x = 0$, but the demand will be positive, so $P < 1$ is inconsistent with equilibrium. Therefore, $P = 1$ at equilibrium. This means that profit is zero at equilibrium.

Let V_i represent individual i's utility as a function of i's purchase decision q_i. That is $V(q_i) = 2\alpha_i(q_i + \rho_i)^{1/2} + \Omega_i - Pq_i$. The first derivative of V_i is $\alpha_i(q_i + \rho_i)^{-1/2} - P = \alpha_i(q_i + \rho_i)^{-1/2} - 1$. Because the second derivative of V_i is negative, setting the first derivative equal to zero gives us a maximum of u_i if it is consistent with $q_i \geq 0$. In that case $\alpha_i = (q_i + \rho_i)^{1/2}$ and hence $q_i = (\alpha_i)^2 - \rho_i$ if $q_i > 0$. But $q_i + \rho_i = x$ for all i, and this means that $\alpha_i = \sqrt{x}$ for all i if the first derivative of V_i is zero for all i. Then if the α_i are different we can have the first derivative of V_i equal to zero for at most one individual i. Suppose $\alpha_1 > \alpha_2 > \ldots > \alpha_n$. Then $\alpha_1 = \sqrt{x}$ implies $\alpha_i < \sqrt{x}$ for all $i > 1$. But this means that for $i > 1$, the first derivative of V_i is negative for all $q_i > 0$, and thus utility is increased by reducing q_i. Therefore, the market equilibrium has

$$P = 1, \quad q_1 = x = (\alpha_1)^2, \quad \text{and} \quad q_i = 0 \quad \text{for } i > 1.$$

To determine the Pareto optimal output of x just maximize $\Sigma u_i = \Sigma 2\alpha_i \sqrt{x}$ + Σy_i. Feasibility requires $\Sigma y_i = \Sigma \Omega_i - x$ so we want to maximize $g(x) = 2\Sigma \alpha_i \sqrt{x}$ $- x$. Note that $g'' < 0$ so $g' = 0$ gives a maximum. $g' = \Sigma \alpha_i / \sqrt{x} - 1$ and thus x^* $= (\Sigma \alpha_i)^2$, which is for larger than the market supply of $(\alpha_1)^2$ if $\alpha_2 + \alpha_3 + \ldots +$ α_n is large relative to α_1.

We can compute the market equilibrium to show that it is not Pareto optimal. Suppose $n = 3$ and $\alpha_1 = 5$, $\alpha_2 = 3$, and $\alpha_3 = 1$. That is, the utility functions are

$$u_1 = 10\sqrt{x} + y_1, \qquad u_2 = 6\sqrt{x} + y_2, \qquad u_3 = 2\sqrt{x} + y_3.$$

The market equilibrium is

$$P = 1, \qquad q_1 = x = 25, \quad \text{and} \quad q_2 = 0 = q_3.$$

This is far short of the efficient level of x, which is $(5 + 3 + 1)^2 = 81$. Let's produce 24 more units of X and see if we can make everyone better off.[7] The production of 24 additional units of X will require 24 additional units of Y as input. Therefore, we will have to reduce consumption of Y by a total of 24 units. Let's reduce each person's consumption of Y by 8 units. Now, compute the change in utility, Δu_i, for each individual i:

$$\Delta u_1 = 10\sqrt{49} + y_1 - 8 - 10\sqrt{25} - y_1 = 12.$$
$$\Delta u_2 = 6\sqrt{49} + y_1 - 8 - 6\sqrt{25} - y_1 = 4.$$
$$\Delta u_3 = 2\sqrt{49} + y_1 - 8 - 2\sqrt{25} - y_1 = -4.$$

We have made person 3 worse off, not better off. That's because of the equal cost shares: Person 3 receives relatively little benefit from the public good, but has to pay just as much to finance an increase in production as those who derive considerably more benefit. Let's try adjusting the cost shares so that they are proportional to benefit received at the margin. Individual's i's marginal benefit is proportional to α_i. Therefore, we want the cost shares to be proportional to the α_i, but we want these shares to sum to unity. If

$$t_1 = 5/(5 + 3 + 1) = 5/9, \qquad t_2 = 3/(5 + 3 + 1) = 3/9, \quad \text{and}$$
$$t_3 = 1/(5 + 3 + 1) = 1/9,$$

where t_i is i's cost share, then we will meet our criteria. Therefore, individual 1's contribution to the financing of the production of 24 more units of X is $5/9 \times 24$ $= 13\frac{1}{3}$; individual 2's contribution is $3/9 \times 24 = 8$; and 3's is $1/9 \times 24 = 2\frac{2}{3}$. Now, the changes in utility are

$$\Delta u_1 = 10\sqrt{49} + y_1 - 13\frac{1}{3} - 10\sqrt{25} - y_1 = 6\frac{2}{3}.$$
$$\Delta u_2 = 6\sqrt{49} + y_1 - 8 - 6\sqrt{25} - y_1 = 4.$$
$$\Delta u_3 = 2\sqrt{49} + y_1 - 2\frac{2}{3} - 2\sqrt{25} - y_1 = 1\frac{1}{3}.$$

We have made everyone better off this time, demonstrating that the market equilibrium is inefficient. The next section shows that it is naive to assume that individuals will reveal their benefit parameters to permit a government agency to use them in calculating cost shares as we have just done.

4.5 The benefit tax scheme

Assuming the preferences of section 4.1, each i reports a benefit parameter β_i and the government produces $z = \Sigma\beta_i$ units of the public good and requires that each i contribute $[\beta_i/(\beta_1 + \beta_2 + \ldots + \beta_n)]\frac{1}{2}z^2$ units of labor toward the production of z. *If* each i reports truthfully and reports $\beta_i = \alpha_i$ then $z = x^*$ and the outcome is Pareto optimal. If x were a private good and i could only obtain it by paying $(\alpha_i/(\alpha_1 + \ldots + \alpha_n))\frac{1}{2}x^2$ units of labor for x units of the good then i would order x^* units because x^* maximizes

$$u_i = \alpha_i x - [\alpha_i/(\alpha_1 + \ldots + \alpha_n)]\tfrac{1}{2}x^2.$$

Therefore, the mechanism imitates the market system. But *does* i have an incentive to set $\beta_i = \alpha_i$?

Suppose that each $j \neq i$ has reported β_j. What is the utility maximizing strategy β_i for i? His utility as a function of β_i is

$$V(\beta_i) = \alpha_i(\beta_i + \rho_i) - [\beta_i/(\beta_1 + \ldots + \beta_n)]\tfrac{1}{2}(\beta_i + \rho_i)^2,$$

where ρ_i is the sum of all β_j's *except* β_i. We refer to V as individual i's *value function* and write

$$V(\beta_i) = \alpha_i\beta_i + \alpha_i\rho_i - \tfrac{1}{2}\beta_i(\beta_i + \rho_i).$$

Note that $\alpha_i\rho_i$ is independent of β_i. Then

$$V'(\beta_i) = \alpha_i - \beta_i - \tfrac{1}{2}\rho_i.$$

Consider the value of V' at α_i. In words, $V'(\alpha_i)$ is the rate of change of i's utility as a consequence of a slight deviation from the truth. We have $V'(\alpha_i) = \alpha_i - \alpha_i - \tfrac{1}{2}\rho_i = -\tfrac{1}{2}\rho_i$. Therefore, $V'(\alpha_i)$ is negative as long as some other individual reports a positive benefit parameter. (Negative β_j's are not allowed.) Therefore, truthful revelation is not a dominant strategy. But we can say far more than that. Underreporting one's benefit parameter leads to a higher level of utility for an individual than does truthful revelation as long as the sum of everyone else's reported parameter is not zero. This means that an individual need not know very much about the preferences or activities of others to devise a strategy that gives more utility than truthful revelation.

Because $V'' < 0$ the condition $V' = 0$ identifies a maximum. $V' = 0$ gives $\beta_i = \alpha_i - \tfrac{1}{2}\rho_i$. But this may be negative, so utility maximization implies

$$\beta_i = 0 \qquad \text{if } \tfrac{1}{2}\rho_i \geq \alpha_i. \tag{3}$$

$$\beta_i = \alpha_i - \tfrac{1}{2}\rho_i \qquad \text{if } \tfrac{1}{2}\rho_i \leq \alpha_i. \tag{4}$$

If [4] holds for each i then summing over all i we have

$$\Sigma\beta_i = \Sigma\alpha_i - \tfrac{1}{2}\Sigma\rho_i \quad \text{or}$$

$$\Sigma\beta_i = \Sigma\alpha_i - \tfrac{1}{2}(n-1)\Sigma\beta_i \quad \text{or} \quad [(n+1)/2]\Sigma\beta_i = \Sigma\alpha_i.$$

Recall that $\Sigma\beta_i = z$ and $\Sigma\alpha_i = x^*$. Then $z = [2/(n+1)]x^*$, so for large n the actual value of x (namely z) is much smaller than the Pareto optimal value x^*.

We can compute the equilibrium strategies β_i in special cases. We will consider two of these. First, suppose $\alpha_1 = \alpha_2 = \ldots = \alpha_n$. Then there will be an equilibrium with $\beta_1 = \beta_2 = \ldots = \beta_n$. To simplify further, suppose that each α_i is unity. Then $x^* = n$ so $z = 2n/(n+1)$ and because $z = \Sigma\beta_i = n\beta_1$ we have $\beta_1 = 2/(n+1) = \beta_i$ for all i. Note that the equilibrium of the benefit tax scheme when individuals strategically misrepresent their preferences results in a little less than 2 units of X being produced. The competitive market equilibrium satisfies $P = 1 = x$. (Why?) Therefore, even the benefit taxation scheme outperforms the market, in the sense that it gets us closer to the efficient output of the public good.

Second, suppose $\alpha_1 > 2\alpha_i > 0$ for all $i > 1$. We will have an equilibrium with [3] holding for each $i > 1$ and [4] holding for $i = 1$. The first part of this claim implies $\rho_1 = 0$ and thus $\beta_1 = \alpha_1$ by the second part of the preceding sentence. This means that $\rho_i = \alpha_1$ for all $i > 1$ and thus $\tfrac{1}{2}\rho_i > \alpha_i$ for all $i > 1$. Therefore, $\beta_1 = \alpha_1$, $\beta_2 = \beta_3 = \ldots = \beta_n = 0$ simultaneously maximizes the utility of each individual i *given* β_j for all $j \neq i$. Note that 1 reports his *true* benefit parameter α_1 because each other agent reports zero and thus 1 pays the full cost of any public goods produced. It is optimal for individual 1 to report the truth because only his reported preferences influence x in this case. But the outcome is far from *Pareto* optimal: $z = \alpha_1 < x^* = \Sigma\alpha_i$.

(Be sure to distinguish the claim that zero is the *utility maximizing* benefit parameter for i to report when $\tfrac{1}{2}\rho_i \geq \alpha_i$ from the claim that reporting zero yields *more* utility than truthfully reporting α_i when $\rho_i > \alpha_i > 0$. Note that $\tfrac{1}{2}\rho_i \geq \alpha_i > 0$ implies $\rho_i > 0$ and thus $\rho_i > \tfrac{1}{2}\rho_i$, so $\rho_i > \beta_i$.)

Exercises

These questions pertain to the following simple economy with n persons, one firm, one private good, and one public good: $u_i = B_i(x) + y_i$, where y_i is household i's consumption of the private good and x is the amount of the public good made available to all. Assume that the first derivative of B_i is positive and that the second derivative of B_i is negative or zero for all $x \geq 0$. Each household i is endowed with Ω_i units of the private good and zero units of the public good. Let $c(x)$ denote the amount of the private good required to produce x units of the public good. Assume that $c'(x) > 0$ and $c''(x) > 0$ for all $x \geq 0$.

1   Characterize the set of Pareto optimal allocations. Explain why your con-
        dition does in fact identify the Pareto optimal allocations.
2   Explain briefly the failure of the mechanism in which each i reports B_i and
        is taxed at the rate $t_i(x')$, which is the ratio of i's marginal benefit at x',
        $dB_i(x')/dx$, to the sum of *all* marginal benefits at x', and where x' is the
        amount of the public good decided on by the planner on the basis of the
        reported benefit functions. (That is, x' is the Pareto optimal level of
        the public good associated with the *reported* B_i's.)
3   Prove that it is to person 1's advantage to report truthfully *if* 1 is certain
        that every other i will report that $B_i(x)$ is constant.
4   *Assuming that the functions B_i are known,* and that the current output of x
        is below the efficient level, show that it is always possible to increase
        everyone's utility by producing more X and assigning cost shares that are
        proportional to marginal benefit, just as we did in section 4.4 for a special
        case. What does this suggest for the case when x is greater than the
        efficient level?

    Questions 5–11 concern the following special case of our simple model: Indi-
vidual i's utility is given by $u_i(x, y_i) = \alpha_i x + y_i$. Production of x units of the
public good requires $\frac{1}{2}x^2$ units of the resource. An allocation is determined by
having each i report a benefit parameter β_i, producing $\beta_1 + \beta_2 + \ldots + \beta_n$ units
of the public good, and collecting a total of $\frac{1}{2}(\beta_1 + \beta_2 + \ldots + \beta_n)^2$ units of the
private goods from households. Specification of the mechanism is complete when
we determine by how much each household's consumption of the private good is
reduced in order to obtain the $\frac{1}{2}(\beta_1 + \beta_2 + \ldots + \beta_n)^2$ units that are needed for
the production of the public good.

5   Suppose that each individual i's consumption of the private good is re-
        duced by $\frac{1}{2}\beta_i(\beta_1 + \beta_2 + \ldots + \beta_n)$ units. Suppose that $\alpha_2 + \alpha_3
        + \ldots + \alpha_n = 2$. If $2 > \alpha_1 > 0$ then 1 is better off reporting a benefit
        parameter of zero than reporting the true parameter α_1. But what is 1's
        best strategy? What value of β_1, 1's *reported* benefit parameter, maxi-
        mizes u_1 given $\alpha_1 > 0$ and the fact that the benefit parameters reported by
        the others sum to 2?
6   Suppose that each individual i's consumption of the private good is re-
        duced by $\frac{1}{2}\beta_i(\beta_1 + \beta_2 + \ldots + \beta_n)$ units. Assume that $\alpha_1 = 3$ and $\alpha_i = 1$
        for all $i > 1$. Prove that we have a Nash equilibrium if 1 reports a
        benefit parameter of 3 and everyone else reports a benefit parameter of
        zero.
7   Assume that $\alpha_1 = \alpha_2 \ldots = \alpha_n$. Suppose that each individual i's con-
        sumption of the private good is reduced by $\frac{1}{2}[\beta_i/(\beta_1 + \beta_2 + \ldots + \beta_n)]x^2$

units if x units of the public good are produced. In section 4.5 we saw that a Nash equilibrium resulted in the production of $(2/(n + 1))x^*$ units of the public good, where $x^* = \Sigma_{i=1}^n \alpha_i$ is the Pareto optimal level of x. Suppose that the center anticipates this and changes the rules so that $[(n + 1)/2]\Sigma_{i=1}^n \beta_i$ units of the public good are produced. Work out a Nash equilibrium for this mechanism. Is it Pareto optimal? Does the equilibrium take the society closer to, or further away from, the equilibrium when $\Sigma_{i=1}^n \beta_i$ units of the public good are produced?

8   Assume that the required input of the private good is obtained by proportional taxation, with each household's tax bill proportional to its income, Ω_i. Assume also that n is odd and that $\alpha_1 > \alpha_2 > \alpha_3 > \ldots > \alpha_{n-1} > \alpha_n$. Find the level of the public good that would defeat every other level by a clear majority. Under what conditions would this majority equilibrium be Pareto optimal? Do you think that the conditions are likely to hold in the real world?

9   Assume that the required input of the private good is obtained by proportional taxation, with household i paying the fraction t_i of the total cost of whatever level of x is provided. Assume also that n is odd and that $\alpha_1 > \alpha_2 > \alpha_3 > \ldots > \alpha_{n-1} > \alpha_n$. Find the level of the public good that would defeat every other level by a clear majority. Under what conditions would this majority equilibrium be Pareto optimal?

10 Assume that $n = 2$ and that $u_1 = 4x + y_1$ and $u_2 = 3x + y_2$. $\Omega_1 = \Omega_2 = 20$. Each consumer has a one-half share in the ownership of the economy's only firm, which uses Y as input to produce X. Suppose that the public good is allocated by the private market system, so that the public good is supplied by a price-taking profit-maximizing firm to utility maximizing individuals. Show that $x = 4$ at equilibrium (i.e., competitive market equilibrium). (*Hint:* Begin by determining the firm's supply as a function of the price P of its output. For convenience, fix the price of the private good at unity.)

11 Set $\alpha_1 = \alpha_2 = 6$ and $\Omega_1 = \Omega_2 = 12$. The total supply of the private good is $12 + 12$. If we set $x = \alpha_1 + \alpha_2$ we will have $x = 12$, and this level of output requires 72 units of the private good as input. But the economy has only 24 units of the private good. What has gone wrong with our reasoning? Is $\alpha_1 + \alpha_2$ the efficient level of X in this case?

12 Consider a simple model of an economy with two goods, X and Y, and two households, 1 and 2. X is a public good and Y is a private good. Neither individual has any holding of X at the beginning of the period, but 1 has an endowment of 200 units of Y and 2 has an endowment of 100 units of Y. X is produced by a single firm which uses $1.5x^2$ units of the private good as

input to produce x units of the public good. Each individual owns 50% of the firm. The utility functions are

$$u_1(x, y_1) = 48\sqrt{x} + y_1 \quad \text{and} \quad u_2(x, y_2) = 30\sqrt{x} + y_2.$$

At a competitive equilibrium of the private ownership market economy we have the following:

The price of X is 12 and the price of Y is 1.

1 buys 4 units of X and 2 buys 0 units of X.

Find the values of y_1 and y_2 at equilibrium *and confirm that we do indeed have an equilibrium*.

13   Prove that the competitive market equilibrium of section 4.4 is truly an equilibrium by showing that each consumer is maximizing utility given his budget constraint, the firm is maximizing profit given the equilibrium price, and demand equals supply for each good.

14   Prove the claim at the end of section 4.5 (the third last paragraph). If each α_i equals unity then $x = 1$ at an equilibrium of the private ownership market economy.

5 The firm's quality choice

Never mind why the dinosaur perished, why is the Volkswagen Beetle extinct? The answer obviously has a lot to do with incomes rising over time, but there is more to the story. We will show that a manufacturer has an incentive to withdraw a product line even when it is very popular. This is a consequence of the fact that the consumer's quality preference is a hidden characteristic – hidden from producers. Assume that quality can be measured, with x_m representing the quality rating of model m. Of course, higher values of x represent higher quality. In fact, quality is multidimensional, particularly in the case of a sophisticated product like a car, and it is unrealistic to suppose that quality can be quantified in a way that would be compatible with everyone's tastes. But even a one-dimensional quality parameter gives us a model from which we can draw much insight. It is also possible to interpret x as the *quantity* of some good. We begin with that interpretation, and when the analysis is complete we will reinterpret our findings in terms of quality choice by the firm.

A monopoly is attempting to price discriminate by offering its output in the form of sealed packages with fixed prices. A package containing more output will bear a higher price tag, but the price is not a linear function of quantity. If package B has twice as much output as package A its price will be more than double that of A because the larger package is targeted for consumers who get more benefit from the good and are willing to pay proportionally more. This will generate more profit than a linear pricing schedule. (A linear schedule can be represented by a single number – the price. If Q units cost Q times as much as 1 unit let P denote the cost of 1 unit. For arbitrary Q the total cost is PQ; the seller merely has to announce P.)

There are two potential problems for a monopolist attempting to impose a nonlinear, price discriminating schedule. To illustrate the first problem suppose package A contains ten units of output and sells for $10, and B contains twenty units of output and is priced at $30. An arbitrageur can purchase two A packages and sell them for a total of $25 to someone who otherwise might buy a B package from the monopolist. Therefore, we need to confine our attention to goods that cannot be resold (or goods such as airline travel for which resale can be blocked by the seller, in this case by checking the traveller's identity). We will use the example of a public utility producing, say, electricity. It is possible to store electricity for future resale but it is very costly to do so. We can assume that our public utility monopoly does not have to worry about resale. The second difficulty arises from the fact that the monopolist cannot identify the consumers who are willing to pay more for electricity. They cannot be expected to disclose their identity voluntarily, knowing that they will be charged more when they do. In fact a consumer for whom the product provides a high level of benefit and for whom the B package is targeted can herself buy two "A packages." The monopolist can rule this out simply by offering each consumer an all-or-nothing proposition: "Either you buy one A package or one B package or we will not sell you anything." But there is a hidden characteristic problem. The firm cannot directly identify the individuals who derive a high level of benefit from the product. The best that the monopolist can do is to design the packages so that high benefit consumers will not want to buy package A even though it costs less per unit than B. They will want to purchase B at the proportionally higher price because it provides more of the good. Of course, they will not want B if the cost per unit is too high. Designing the packages and choosing the price tags are not simple tasks. The trick is to design the packages and select the prices so that a high-benefit customer will *choose* to buy the package intended for her. Because this is an example of a public utility monopoly we do not have to worry that the high benefit consumer will herself buy two A packages at a lower total cost. The monopoly controls delivery and will offer a consumer an all-or-nothing choice between the two packages. Let us examine this by specifying the cost of production and consumer preferences.

5.1 The model

Customer i's utility is $u_i = B_i(x_i) + y_i$ where y_i is the amount of money i "consumes" and x_i is the number of units of electricity delivered to i. (Think of money as a composite commodity, representing expenditure on goods other than electricity.) The benefit i derives from electricity is $B_i(x_i)$. That is, B_i is a benefit function, with $B_i'(x_i) > 0$ for all x_i and $B_i''(x_i) < 0$ for all x_i. Suppose that each individual is endowed with (begins with) Ω_i units of money. If i pays a total of C_i dollars for x_i units of electricity her utility will be $u_i = B_i(x_i) + \Omega_i - C_i$. Because Ω_i is constant we need only compute the change in utility, which is $\delta_i = B_i(x_i) - C_i$. If δ_i is positive then i will purchase the package (x_i, C_i), or some more attractive package if one is available, but if $\delta_i < 0$ then i will not purchase (x_i, C_i) because it would cause a decline in utility. Choose units so that one unit of electricity costs one dollar to produce. If each individual i purchases x_i units of electricity at a total cost of C_i then the monopolist's profit is $R = \Sigma_i C_i - \Sigma_i x_i$. Find an array of packages $(x_1, C_1), (x_2, C_2), \ldots, (x_n, C_n)$ that will maximize R.

5.2 Full information equilibrium

To give us a point of comparison, begin with the full information assumption that the monopolist knows each person's benefit function B_i. What package should be offered to person i? Let x_i° be the value of x_i that maximizes $B_i(x_i) - x_i$, which is the consumer's benefit less the monopolist's cost of producing x_i. That is, x_i° solves $B_i'(x_i) = 1$. (Note that the second derivative of the function that we are maximizing is negative, and hence the first-order condition is sufficient for a global maximum.) Suppose the monopolist offers i the package $(x_i^\circ, B_i(x_i^\circ) - \epsilon)$. That is, the total cost to i of x_i° units of electricity is $C_i^\circ = B_i(x_i^\circ) - \epsilon$. Here ϵ is a *very* small positive number, so the charge is just slightly less than the total benefit. Person i faces a take-it-or-leave-it proposition. Because $\delta_i = B_i(x_i^\circ) - C_i = B_i(x_i^\circ) - [B_i(x_i^\circ) - \epsilon] = \epsilon$, which is positive, the monopolist's offer will be accepted. This is the profit-maximizing strategy under the full information assumption that there is no hidden characteristic problem. Why is it profit maximizing? If $\delta_i < 0$ then i will not buy the package and the monopolist will receive zero profit from i. Therefore, the monopolist must respect the constraint $\delta_i \geq 0$, or $B_i(x_i) - C_i \geq 0$. As long as C_i is substantially below $B_i(x_i)$ the monopolist can raise C_i without violating $\delta_i > 0$, and sell the same x_i units at a higher price. Therefore, profit maximization requires C_i *almost* equal to $B_i(x_i)$. Let's approximate and set C_i exactly equal to $B_i(x_i)$. But we do not know what x_i is. The monopolist wants to maximize $C_i - x_i$ and if $C_i = B_i(x_i)$ this entails maximizing $B_i(x_i) - x_i$. Because x_i° denotes the level of x_i that maximizes $B_i(x_i) - x_i$ we have indeed found the profit maximizing set of take-it-or-leave-it offers.

Surprisingly, we have an efficient outcome even though the monopolist has succeeded in extracting all the benefit from the consumer. (Set $\epsilon = 0$ for convenience.) $\delta_i = B_i(x_i^\circ) - C_i^\circ = B_i(x_i^\circ) - B_i(x_i^\circ) = 0$. Therefore, each consumer pays a charge equal to the benefit *she* derives from the electricity received and there is no net gain in utility. Nevertheless, the outcome is efficient if all the profits are returned to the community. (The company's shareholders are members of the community.) To prove this, we show that any outcome satisfying $x_i = x_i^o$ for all i actually maximizes total utility, $\Sigma_i u_i$, as long as Σy_i, the total amount of Y consumed, equals the total amount left over after the required Σx_i^o units are used in the production of X. That is, as long as $\Sigma y_i = \Sigma \Omega_i - \Sigma x_i^o$ holds.

$$\Sigma u_i = \Sigma[B_i(x_i) + y_i]$$

$$= \Sigma B_i(x_i) + \Sigma y_i = \Sigma B_i(x_i) + \Sigma \Omega_i - \Sigma x_i$$

and this is maximized by setting $B_i'(x_i) - 1 = 0$ for arbitrary i, and x_i^o is the unique solution to this equation. Now set $\Sigma u_i = \Sigma[B_i(x_i^o) + y_i]$. Then $\Sigma u_i = \Sigma B_i(x_i^o) + \Sigma y_i$ and this total is preserved if we redistribute commodity Y among the consumers, as long as the total Σy_i is unchanged. Therefore, any outcome maximizes total utility if $x_i = x_i^o$ for each i and $\Sigma y_i = \Sigma \Omega_i - \Sigma x_i^o$. Therefore, any such outcome is efficient: If we could make one person's utility higher without lowering anyone else's we could make the sum higher, which is impossible. (See section 5 of Chapter 1 on this point.) In general, any outcome that has one of the agents extracting all of the surplus from the other agents is efficient. Once we specify formally what we mean by 'extracting all the surplus' it is easy to prove efficiency. Suppose that each agent i has some initial level of utility O_i. Agent 1 extracts all of the surplus from each of the other agents if, for all $i > 1$, the *final* level of utility is equal to O_i, the starting level. In symbols, agent 1 chooses the outcome so as to maximize U_1 subject to the constraint $U_i \geq O_i$ for all $i > 1$. (The solution to this problem must be efficient. Why?)

5.3 A special case

To bring more clarity to the exercise we suppose there are two types of consumers, H (high benefit) and L (low benefit). Suppose $u_H = 4\sqrt{x_H} + y_H$ and $u_L = 2\sqrt{x_L} + y_L$. Check that $x_H^o = 4$, $B_H(x_H^o) = 8 = C_H^o$, $x_L^o = 1$, and $B_L(x_L^o) = 2 = C_L^o$ at the full information profit maximizing equilibrium. Verify that $u_H + u_L$ is maximized however the total profit $(8 + 2 - 5)$ is divided between H and L. This special case will be the subject of our inquiry for the rest of section 5.

5.4 Asymmetric information equilibrium

We continue our investigation of the simple example but we now drop the full information assumption that the individual with utility function $B_H(x) + y$ can be identified. We do assume, however, that the monopolist knows the functional forms B_H and B_L; it just doesn't know which person has which function. An offer (α, β) is a specification of the amount α of electricity in the package and the price β of the package. What is the profit maximizing menu of offers? If the monopolist simply offers each person a choice of two offers $(1, 2)$ and $(4, 8)$ the H-types will choose the former:

$$\delta_H(1, 2) = 4\sqrt{1} - 2 = 2.$$
$$\delta_H(4, 8) = 4\sqrt{4} - 8 = 0.$$

The L-types will choose $(1, 2)$ also:

$$\delta_L(1, 2) = 2\sqrt{1} - 2 = 0.$$
$$\delta_L(4, 8) = 2\sqrt{4} - 8 = -4.$$

The monopolist's profit will be $2 + 2 - (1 + 1) = 2$, which is *not* a maximum even under the assumption that B_H and B_L cannot be identified by the monopolist. The monopolist can continue to offer $(1, 2)$, the contract that extracts all the surplus from the L-types, but design a contract (x_H, C_H) such that the H-types will not prefer $(1, 2)$ and it will extract as much surplus as possible. The first consideration requires

$$4\sqrt{x_H} - C_H \geq 4\sqrt{1} - 2.$$

This is called a *self-selection*, or *incentive compatibility*, condition. Then the monopolist will maximize $C_H - x_H$ subject to $4\sqrt{x_H} - C_H \geq 2$. If $4\sqrt{x_H} - C_H > 2$ then C_H can be increased without violating the self-selection constraint and without changing x_H. This will increase profit, so profit maximization requires $4\sqrt{x_H} - C_H = 2$, or $C_H = 4\sqrt{x_H} - 2$. Then the monopolist maximizes $4\sqrt{x_H} - 2 - x_H$. Setting the first derivative equal to zero yields $2/\sqrt{x_H} = 1$ or $x_H = 4$. (Does this actually give a maximum?) The same level of service is provided (this is a consequence of our simple utility functions) but this time at a charge of $C_H = 4\sqrt{x_H} - 2 = 6$. The monopolist's profit is $6 + 2 - (4 + 1) = 3$, which is lower than under the full information assumption of voluntary disclosure of one's type (5) but higher than 2, which is the profit that results when the "full information" solutions are packaged and the consumers are allowed to choose between them. This sophisticated solution, of offering $(1, 2)$ and $(4, 6)$ and letting the individual choose, is efficient: we have already shown that $x_L = 1$ and $x_H = 4$ maximizes $u_L + u_H$. We still haven't reached the maximum profit, however. Suppose the monopolist offers only one package, $(4, 8)$. Four units of electricity at a total cost of \$8, take it or leave it.

$$\delta_L(4, 8) = 2\sqrt{4} - 8 = -4.$$
$$\delta_H(4, 8) = 4\sqrt{4} - 8 = 0.$$

Consumer L will be better off not buying the package, and would not buy even if the cost were reduced slightly. Consumer H would gain slightly if the cost were reduced slightly: the cost will be slightly less than 8 and the profit will be very close to $8 - 4 = 4$, which is the highest profit yet, apart from the full information solution.

To show that we have maximized profit, we will maximize $C_L + C_H - x_L - x_H$ subject to the self-selection constraint $4\sqrt{x_H} - C_H \geq 4\sqrt{x_L} - C_L$ and the participation constraints $4\sqrt{x_H} - C_H \geq 0$ and $2\sqrt{x_L} - C_L \geq 0$. But first, why don't we have to worry about L's self-selection constraint? Because $2\sqrt{x_L} - C_L \geq 0$ and thus $2\sqrt{x_L} - C_L \geq 2\sqrt{x_H} - C_H$ is automatically satisfied if $2\sqrt{x_H} - C_H \leq 0$. If we have $C_H < 2\sqrt{x_H}$ then $C_H < 4\sqrt{x_H}$ and

$$2\sqrt{x_L} - C_L \geq 2\sqrt{x_H} - C_H > 0$$

so $C_L < 2\sqrt{x_L}$. This means that we can increase *both* C_L and C_H by the same amount (keeping x_L and x_H fixed) without violating the participation constraints: The left-hand and right-hand sides of each participation constraint will fall by the same amount. Profit will have increased without violating any of the constraints. Therefore, we will not have $C_H < 2\sqrt{x_H}$ at the profit maximizing outcome. Therefore, in searching for the profit maximizing decision we can ignore L's self-selection constraint. Now, if $2\sqrt{x_L} - C_L > 0$ then we can increase C_L without violating $2\sqrt{x_L} - C_L \geq 0$. If we don't change any of the other variables we will have increased profit, and the self-selection constraint will still hold as a consequence of increasing C_L alone. Therefore, profit maximization requires $2\sqrt{x_L} - C_L = 0$ and thus $C_L = 2\sqrt{x_L}$. Therefore, the self-selection constraint is $4\sqrt{x_H} - C_H \geq 4\sqrt{x_L} - 2\sqrt{x_L} = 2\sqrt{x_L}$. Then the self-selection constraint must hold as an equality. If $4\sqrt{x_H} - C_H > 2\sqrt{x_L}$ then profit could be increased by increasing C_H without changing x_H or x_L, and this could be done without violating the self-selection constraint. (Note that the participation constraint $4\sqrt{x_H} - C_H \geq 0$ will automatically hold if $2\sqrt{x_L} - C_L \geq 0$ and the self-selection constraint is satisfied.) Now we have $C_H = 4\sqrt{x_H} - 2\sqrt{x_L}$ and thus profit equals

$$2\sqrt{x_L} + 4\sqrt{x_H} - 2\sqrt{x_L} - x_L - x_H = 4\sqrt{x_H} - x_L - x_H.$$

Obviously, maximization of this expression requires $x_L = 0$ and hence the participation constraint implies $C_L = 0$. Then we want to maximize $4\sqrt{x_H} - x_H$ and this requires setting the first derivative equal to zero. Therefore, $x_H = 4$ and $C_H = 4\sqrt{x_H} - 2\sqrt{x_L} = 8 - 0$. To summarize, $x_H = 4$, $C_H = 8$, and $x_L = 0 = C_L$.

The profit maximizing solution is not efficient. We don't know the utility level of each individual because we don't know the share of profits received by each. But we can compute the change in utility for each as a result of an increase in the production of X by one unit if that unit is delivered to person L and at the same time L's consumption of Y is reduced by one unit. If we do not change x_H or y_H we have a feasible outcome. Certainly, H's utility will not change. The change in L's utility is $2\sqrt{1} - 1 = 1$, so L is better off and H's utility is unchanged. (How could we make *both* strictly better off?)

This is a special case of a general phenomenon. The incentive schedule that maximizes the principal's utility often involves distortions that take the system away from an efficient outcome.

There is a defect in the argument that the profit maximizing outcome can be improved. The argument implicitly assumed that the government or some central agency could identify the consumer with utility function u_L. But if this is possible then the firm can do so as well, and they will impose the full information profit maximizing outcome which *is* efficient.[8] Can we find a way of giving each individual more utility than he or she enjoys at the asymmetric information equilibrium (AIE) without employing the full information assumption? Let's try: Let R be the share of the AIE profit received by H. The AIE profit is $8 - 4 = 4$, so the share of the profit that goes to L is $4 - R$. The utility levels at the AIE are

$$u_L = 2\sqrt{0} + \Omega_L + 4 - R = \Omega_L + 4 - R \quad \text{and}$$
$$u_H = 4\sqrt{4} + \Omega_H + R - 8 = \Omega_H + R.$$

If we set $x_H = 4$ and $x_L = 1$ can we satisfy the self-selection constraints $4\sqrt{4} - C_H \geq 4\sqrt{1} - C_L$ and $2\sqrt{4} - C_H \leq 2\sqrt{1} - C_L$? Both will hold if and only if we have $2 \leq C_H - C_L \leq 4$. Set $C_L = 1$ and see what happens. Then $C_H = 4$ will satisfy the constraints, and we have each person paying for what she consumes. The government doesn't have to identify the individuals; it just has to make the two packages available, and in their self-interest consumer H will choose the package with 4 units of X and a price tag of \$4 and L will choose the package with 1 unit of X and a price tag of \$1. The resulting utility levels will be

$$u_L = 2\sqrt{1} + \Omega_L - 1 = 1 + \Omega_L \quad \text{and}$$
$$u_H = 4\sqrt{4} + \Omega_H - 4 = 4 + \Omega_H.$$

Do we have

$$1 + \Omega_L > \Omega_L + 4 - R \quad \text{and}$$
$$4 + \Omega_H > \Omega_H + R?$$

The inequalities hold if $3 < R < 4$, but how can R be determined? How can the government determine what share of the profit goes to the individual with utility function u_H under the asymmetric information assumption? Of course, after the individuals are observed to make their choices the government will know who's who. And then it can transfer some Y between the consumers to ensure that both have a higher level of utility than under the AIE. That is, the government can choose y_L and y_H so that

$$u_L = 2\sqrt{1} + y_L$$
$$u_H = 4\sqrt{4} + y_H$$
$$y_L + y_H = \Omega_L + \Omega_H - 5$$
$$2 + y_L > \Omega_L + 4 - R \quad \text{and}$$
$$8 + y_H > \Omega_H + R.$$

Set $y_H = \Omega_H + R - 7.5$. Now we have $u_H > \Omega_H + R$. (Assume $\Omega_H \geq 7.5$ to ensure $y_H \geq 0$.) Then $y_L = -y_H + \Omega_L + \Omega_H - 5 = \Omega_L + 2.5 - R$. Then $u_L = 2 + y_L = \Omega_L + 4.5 - R > \Omega_L + 4 - R$. So, we can find transfers that do the job. However, if the consumers know that the transfers are part of the utility enhancing change, and they know that the size and direction of the transfers depend on their choices, the incentives for each to choose the package targeted for her are undermined.

Asymmetric information induces an equilibrium that is not efficient, but we're not sure how to design modified rules of the game to guide the community to an efficient outcome that leaves everyone better off than under the profit maximizing asymmetric information equilibrium, or even if it is possible to do so.

The example of this section is based on Arrow (1984). Now interpret x_i as the model designed for the consumers in market group i, with the model identified by the 'amount' of quality that it provides. We can see why profit maximizing firms sometimes discontinue production of a popular model if it is at the low-quality end of the spectrum. In this case, low quality does not mean 'unreliable'; it simply means less luxurious. This gives a new interpretation to the automobile manufacturer's boast that features that used to be optional are now standard. Does the material in this section shed any light on why publishers of textbooks stop selling the first edition of a book after the second edition appears, even when they have a stock of first editions that could be sold at a discounted price?

Now, what about Volkswagen suspending exports of the Beetle to the United States and Canada at the height of its popularity? The decision came in the wake of legislation in both countries that introduced strict safety standards that would have substantially increased the cost of producing the Beetle. Exercise 5 asks you to show that an increase in the cost of production can result in the manufacturer's canceling a popular product line, retaining only the more expensive version.

Exercises

1    $U_H = 8\sqrt{x_H} + y_H$ and $U_L = 6\sqrt{x_L} + y_L$. The monopolist offers two packages on a take-it-or-leave-it basis. Package O_L is designed for consumer L and offers 9 units of electricity at a total cost of \$18. Package O_H is designed so that consumer H will not prefer O_L and O_H maximizes profit given that selection constraint. Derive O_H.

2   Electricity is provided by a monopoly. There are two consumers, H and L, with utility functions $U_H = 6 \ln(x_H + 1) + y_H$ and $U_L = 4 \ln(x_L + 1) + y_L$. Each unit of electricity costs \$1 to produce.

     a   Compute the full information equilibrium. Determine the monopolist's profit.

    b Assume that the monopolist continues to offer the package designed for consumer L in your solution to (a). What is then the profit maximizing package associated with consumer H, assuming that the monopolist cannot determine who H is or who L is? What is the associated profit?

    c Determine the asymmetric information equilibrium and the monopolist's profit.

    d Rank the three profit levels.

3   Rework question 2 when each unit of electricity costs \$2 to produce, leaving all other features of the model unchanged.

4   Prove the statement in parentheses at the end of section 5.2.

5   There are two consumers, H and L, with utility functions $U_H = 20\ln(x_H + 5) + y_H$ and $U_L = 15\ln(x_L + 5) + y_L$. It costs x dollars to produce x units of commodity X. Show that $x_L > 0$ at the AIE but $x_L = 0$ when the cost of production doubles. Is the framework of this section appropriate if commodity X is an automobile?

6 Publish or perish

Section 7 of this chapter investigates labor markets in which the hidden characteristic is the worker's quality. In this section we briefly consider a special case in which the worker is a university professor. The spotlight is on his or her hiring, promotion, and sometimes firing. The promotion regimen employed in colleges and universities in Canada, the U.S., and many other countries is an example of the *up-or-out* policy,[9] which is also used in most firms that are organized as partnerships. In the case of colleges and universities, a professor's performance is reviewed after six years by members of her own department. Outside evaluations of the candidate's research are obtained. Evidence of teaching effectiveness is also examined, but the candidate's contributions to scholarship are typically decisive in the promotion decision. If the decision is negative, the teacher must leave the university. Even if she offers to stay on at a big cut in pay, she will not be retained after a negative tenure decision. If the decision is favorable, the professor is granted lifetime tenure in the department. This means that she can never be fired for incompetence – only for moral turpitude. The only other way that a university can dismiss a tenured professor is to close down the entire department. Assuming no serious moral lapses, a tenured professor has a lifetime job; her position in the department is terminated only by death – her death (or retirement) or the department's, whichever comes first. But what benefit could come from a policy that prevented an employer from firing a worker for incompetence? And even if lifetime tenure is desirable, why base a teacher's promotion decision on her research output? We'll address the second question first.

Writing a paper for publication in a leading scholarly journal requires skills that are closely related to the talents needed for effective teaching at the university level: intelligence, thorough knowledge of one's field, intellectual discipline, creativity, and an interest in the subject. Less talented scholars take a lot longer to prepare an article that's suitable for the high-quality journals. Therefore, it is less costly for the "high quality" workers to signal their quality – in this instance, a signal is publication of an article in a high-prestige journal. Basing hiring, firing, and promotion decisions heavily on the individual's publication record has a rationale as a partial solution to a principal–agent problem, which has both hidden characteristic and hidden action elements. The university could not take the job applicant's word that he or she is a diligent scholar with a keen interest in the discipline, a determination to work long hours learning more about the subject, and the intelligence to keep up with the other scholars in the field. Even if the university and society in general had no interest in scholarly research there would be a signalling rationale for using publication records in employment decisions. (Of course, if research had no social value it would receive much less funding and there would be less of it.) If you wish to test the proposition that publication has its uses apart from the scientific value of the output, you need to go well beyond estimating the correlation between teaching ability and success in publishing in evidence at your own college. You want to compare the present situation with what you would expect to find if universities were unable to use a fairly objective quality signal such as publication.

But why grant lifetime tenure at all? Carmichael (1988) has an interesting answer. *Given* the roster of faculty members in a particular university department, it would seem to be in society's interest to allow the employer to fire low quality workers at any time and replace them with higher quality faculty. Research output could be used to rank the members of a department, so that the poor performers could be identified and released. However, if this policy were adopted by universities, the departments themselves would make different hiring decisions in the first place. The established department members would be reluctant to hire top notch young people. These high quality young people might outperform the original department members by such a wide margin that the university would want to reduce the pay of the incumbents, or even fire them. There would be a strong incentive for departments to hire low quality newcomers. The net result of allowing the university to fire low-quality professors at any time and replace them with higher-quality faculty would be departments with very low quality workers! The overall result of abolishing tenure could well be lower quality faculties. But why let the department members themselves hire their new colleagues? Because the members of the physics department are the only citizens of the university capable of judging the candidates for an opening in the physics department.

7 Job-market signalling

Sections 4 and 5 demonstrate how difficult it is to design an incentive environment in which individuals will truthfully reveal their hidden characteristic. Suppose, however, the hidden characteristic is a quality variable, and quality can be either good or bad. Owners of the high quality commodity would like to have the hidden characteristic revealed truthfully. They have an incentive to *signal* their quality. Would this incentive be strong enough to induce the market place to provide a signalling channel? The signal must be credible, which means that it is not to the advantage of a supplier of a low quality product to transmit the same signal as a high quality seller. When would this be possible? Typically signalling consumes resources, and it is substantially more costly for the holder of the low quality item to transmit the same signal as those who hold the high quality signal. Under the right conditions, the additional cost to those who have only low quality items to sell motivates them to provide a weaker signal and hence reveal their type. However, because the signal imposes real costs on the individual and on society, truthful revelation comes at a price: The resources consumed in signalling do not provide any direct utility. We will show that there is a range of signals consistent with equilibria, and often the same result could have been obtained with a lower investment in signalling. There are even cases in which everyone invests in signalling but the signalling doesn't distinguish the high quality from the low quality producers.

We consider a labor market example in this section. The signal is the amount of training that an individual has undergone. Training is costly and individuals who know themselves to be innately intelligent and hard working (relatively speaking) are more likely to graduate and be certified. Therefore, the population of graduates contains a disproportionately high number of individuals who are innately productive – i.e., intelligent and hard working. In other words, training can be used to sort workers into H-types, who have relatively high ability and productivity, and L-types, who have relatively low ability and productivity. A simple model will make the point more forcefully.

7.1 To make a long story short

High-quality (H-type) workers generate substantially more dollars of profit for the firm than low-quality workers (L-types) because H-types are more productive. Although individuals (and their parents) make choices during the formative years that help to determine a person's type, at the time an employer makes a hiring decision the worker's type has been determined. Therefore, the employer faces a hidden characteristic problem. To attract H-types a firm can offer a higher wage,

$W_H > W_L$, where W_H is the wage paid to H-types and W_L is the wage paid to L-types.[10] But we have a hidden characteristic problem. The L-types cannot be expected to identify themselves truthfully, claiming the lower wage, or salary, W_L. If we suppose that production takes place in teams in a setting that makes it impossible to identify the contribution of individuals then it is not possible for a manager to separate the L-types from the H-types directly. If, however, it costs H-types C_H dollars to graduate from a training program and it costs L-types a higher amount, C_L, then it is possible to induce the L-types to reveal themselves in spite of their narrow pursuit of self-interest. The firm simply pays a salary W_H to anyone who has a graduation certificate and a salary W_L to workers without a certificate. If $W_H - C_L < W_L$ the L-types will not pay the cost (C_L) necessary to obtain a certificate; it is more advantageous to obtain the lower salary W_L without training. (To simplify, we are assuming that training is not productive; it serves only to sort the two types.) If $W_H - C_H > W_L$ then H-types will incur the cost (C_H) of obtaining a graduate certificate, obtaining the higher net salary $W_H - C_H$. Note that both conditions hold if $C_H < W_H - W_L < C_L$. In particular, C_H must be less than C_L. (All monetary amounts are discounted present values.) If $W_H = 1000$ and $W_L = 600$ then $C_H < 400 < C_L$ is required for signalling to reveal a worker's characteristic. This gives a *range* of equilibria, many of which will be inefficient because the signalling could be done at lower cost to society. This phenomenon will be encountered in the more sophisticated models to follow.

Spence (1973) was the first to show how signalling could emerge as a solution to the asymmetric information (hidden characteristic) problem introduced into the literature by Akerlof (1970). Akerlof discussed the market for used cars; his contribution is outlined in the next section. Spence used the job market as his example. In another pathbreaking article, Rothschild and Stiglitz (1976) draw attention to some limitations in Spence's notion of equilibrium, using competitive insurance markets to illustrate. The Rothschild–Stiglitz analysis appears as section 10 of this chapter.

The argument above shows that workers can pay for and receive training in equilibrium, even when that training does not enhance productivity. What's missing from the story is a discussion of employer profit maximization, which will depend in part on employer beliefs about the relationship between the amount of training attained and the worker's ability. Therefore, we now consider a more elaborate model with an explicit role for firms. The new model will allow the amount (number of years) of training to have more than two values; and training can contribute directly to productivity.[11] Moreover, the more robust model will exhibit different kinds of equilibria, and equilibria with different levels of educational attainment.

7.2 A general model

There are two types of workers, H-types and L-types. It is common knowledge that the fraction ρ of the population is of type H. Worker i has the utility function

$$u_i(x, y) = B_i(x) + y$$

where x is leisure consumption and y is a composite commodity, dollars spent on all goods other than leisure. Assume that B_i has a positive first derivative and a negative second derivative at all points. If c is the amount of time spent by individual i in acquiring education, then $x = \Omega - c$, where Ω is the time endowment. This means that u_i will fall as c increases, and at an increasing rate. This allows us to simplify and write

$$u_i = w(e) - c_i(e),$$

where w is the wage rate, as a function of years of education e, and $c_i(e)$ is the amount of leisure sacrificed when e years of education are attained. The function $w(e)$ is the wage schedule posted by firms. Our assumption on the derivatives of B_i implies that the first and second derivatives of c_i are positive. In words, the marginal cost of education is positive, and the marginal cost increases as e increases. A key assumption is that $c_H(e) < c_L(e)$ for all e. It is more costly for an L-type to achieve a given education level because an L-type has to put in more hours studying (over more semesters, perhaps) than an H-type. For concreteness, we will set

$$c_H(e) = \tfrac{1}{2}e^2 \quad \text{and} \quad c_L(e) = \tfrac{3}{4}e^2.$$

Let $m_i(e)$ be the value of the marginal product of individual i. We can have m_i increasing with e, to reflect the fact that productivity increases with education. Assume that $m_H(e) > m_L(e)$ for all e.

Before turning to the case where education enhances productivity, let's take a final look at the polar case in which m_i is independent of e. Say, $m_L = m$ and $m_H = 2m$. What is the equilibrium? There are many equilibria; in fact there are two types of equilibria.

Case 1: Pooling equilibria All workers obtain the same number of years of schooling and are paid the same wage. What values of the wage and of e are consistent with worker utility maximization and firm profit maximization?

Recall that the proportion ρ of the population is H-type, so the expected (or mean) productivity is $\rho(2m) + (1 - \rho)m = m\rho + m$. Competition will ensure that $m\rho + m$ is paid to each worker at equilibrium *if* the same wage is paid to all. Consider the following wage schedule offered by each firm, based on a given critical level g of education:

Assume that the worker is L-type and pay her m if $e < g$.

If $e \geq g$, assume that the worker is H-type with probability ρ, and
    hence offer the wage $m\rho + m$.

What we have here is an equilibrium system of *beliefs* in addition to the usual
market clearance property of equilibrium. The employer's demand schedules for
workers are a function of their beliefs. At equilibrium, employer's beliefs are a
function of their observations, primarily of the amount of output, and these
observations depend on the wage schedule, which is a function of the demand
schedules. At equilibrium, we have a completed circle.

    What decision will an H-type individual make when confronted with this wage
schedule? There is no point in choosing $e > g$. (Why?) Therefore, H and L will
each set $e = g$ if the following two conditions hold for H and L, respectively:

$$m\rho + m - \tfrac{1}{2}g^2 > m,$$
$$m\rho + m - \tfrac{3}{4}g^2 > m.$$

Obviously, the first inequality will hold if the second does. Consider the case $\rho =$
$^1/_3$. Then the second inequality simplifies to

$$g^2 < (4/9)m, \quad \text{or} \quad g < \tfrac{2}{3}\sqrt{m}.$$

Suppose that $m = 9$. Then we have a pooling equilibrium for any value of g
satisfying $0 \leq g < 2$, with a wage of 12 to each worker. Each worker will be
optimizing by setting $e = g$ and taking a wage of 12 instead of 9. (Verify: Because
$g < 2$, u_H is greater than $12 - \tfrac{1}{2}(2 \times 2) = 10 > 9$ when $e_H = g$, and similarly u_L
is greater than $12 - \tfrac{3}{4}(2 \times 2) = 9$ when $e_L = g$.) Each firm is profit maximizing
under competitive conditions by paying a wage equal to 12, the expected value of
the per capita marginal product. The firm's subsequent observations confirm this
expectation. Everyone obtains g years of schooling, so the average productivity of
the group with g years of schooling will be observed to be 12. We are at equilibrium. This corresponds to a cohort of individuals with the same undergraduate
degree earning the same pay in spite of their different abilities.

    With full information, every worker would be required to set $e = 0$ for efficien-
cy, if education makes no contribution to productivity. With asymmetric information we can have an equilibrium with each worker spending a substantial amount
of time in higher education. (If average productivity per worker is 12, then $g = 2$
is a substantial investment in education.) But we're not finished with the analysis.
Continue to assume that education is not productive.

Case 2: Separating equilibria Suppose H-types obtain more education in equilibrium than L-types. The wage schedule is

Assume that the worker is L-type with probability 1 and pay m if
    $e < g$.
If $e \geq g$, assume that the worker is H-type with probability 1 and pay
    $2m$.

What is the worker's response? Setting $e > g$ just increases the worker's costs without any reward in terms of higher salary, so no worker will choose more than g years of schooling. Similarly, if $0 < e < g$ then the worker will receive the same wage as someone who sets $e = 0$. Therefore, regardless of type, the worker will set $e = 0$ or $e = g$. Consider the worker's decision:

$$u_H = 2m - \tfrac{1}{2}(g)^2 \quad \text{if } e = g \quad \text{and} \quad u_H = m \quad \text{if } e = 0.$$
$$u_L = 2m - \tfrac{3}{4}(g)^2 \quad \text{if } e = g \quad \text{and} \quad u_L = m \quad \text{if } e = 0.$$

A separating equilibrium then implies the following incentive compatibility constraints:

$$2m - \tfrac{1}{2}(g)^2 > m \quad \text{and} \quad m > 2m - \tfrac{3}{4}(g)^2 \quad \text{or}$$
$$\tfrac{3}{4}(g)^2 > m > \tfrac{1}{2}(g)^2, \quad \text{or} \quad \sqrt{12} < g < \sqrt{18} \qquad \text{if } m = 9.$$

The critical g has to be large, to discourage L-types from setting $e = g$, but not so large as to induce H-types to forgo higher education. If $\tfrac{3}{4}(g)^2 > m > \tfrac{1}{2}(g)^2$ then only H-types will obtain higher education (i.e., will set $e = g$) and firms' expectations will be confirmed. Again we have a range of equilibria in which there is investment in education even though education does not enhance productivity. In a model in which education *does* contribute to productivity, one would expect to find investment beyond the point justified by considerations of productive efficiency. This is indeed what we encounter in the next section.

7.3 When education is productive

Suppose $m_H(e) = 6e + K$ and $m_L(e) = 3e + K$, where K is a nonnegative constant. In both cases, value added increases with e, but an additional unit of higher education adds twice as much to the productivity of an H-type, compared to an L-type. Recall that the cost functions are $c_H(e) = \tfrac{1}{2}e^2$ and $c_L(e) = \tfrac{3}{4}e^2$. To establish a benchmark case, assume temporarily that the worker's type (ability) is directly observable. That is, let's determine the full information equilibrium before turning to asymmetric information. Set $K = 0$ for convenience. Each worker i will be confronted with the wage schedule $m_i(e)$, because the worker's type is known and competition ensures that the wage will equal the value of the *individual's* marginal product. Therefore, the H-type worker's utility maximizing decision is obtained by solving

$$\max w - c = 6e - \tfrac{1}{2}e^2.$$

The first derivative is $6 - e$. Because the second derivative is negative, utility maximization requires $e = 6$. Then w_H, the H-type's wage, is 36 because $m_H(6) = 36$ when $K = 0$. Similarly, the L-type worker solves

$$\max w - c = 3e - \tfrac{3}{4}e^2,$$

and the first derivative of the objective function is $3 - 1.5e$, so $e = 2$ at the maximum. Then $w_L = 6$ because $m_L(2) = 3 \times 2$ when $K = 0$. All of this is

Table 7

e	Wage	u_H	u_L
6	36	18	9
2	6	4	3

displayed in Table 7. Note that if we drop the full information assumption, an *L*-type would masquerade as an *H*-type because he prefers a wage of 18, even though it would cost $\frac{3}{4} \times 6 \times 6 = 27$ to obtain the six years of education necessary to pass as an *H*-type ($36 - 27 = 9$, which is greater than $6 - \frac{3}{4} \times 2 \times 2 = 3$). Therefore, the full information outcome is not an equilibrium in an asymmetric information world. The firms could not pay a wage of 36 to *everyone* with six years of higher education because, when $\rho = \frac{1}{3}$, the average value of marginal product is only $\frac{1}{3} \times 36 + \frac{2}{3} \times 18 = 24$ when everyone sets $e = 6$. Therefore, we need to work out the asymmetric information equilibrium.

7.4 Pooling equilibria with asymmetric information and productive education

Both *H*- and *L*-types choose g years of education, with g to be determined. Because education is the only observable variable that depends on ability, each worker is paid the same wage, the expected value of marginal product when everyone sets $e = g$. We need to work out the implications of worker utility maximization and firm profit maximization.

The fraction ρ of the entire population is *H*-type, so the expected productivity at $e = g$ is

$$\rho m_H(g) + (1 - \rho)m_L(g) = \frac{1}{3}(6g) + \frac{2}{3}(3g) = 4g.$$

When the wage is the same for each worker then each is paid $4g$ at equilibrium as a consequence of competition among firms for workers. Formally, the wage schedule offered by firms is as follows:

> Assume that the worker is *L*-type and pay $3e$ if $e < g$.
> Assume that the worker is *H*-type with probability ρ and pay $4g$ if
> $e \geq g$.

We already know the choice made by an *L*-type when the wage schedule is simply $3e$. The worker will set $e = 2$ and u_L will equal 3. (See Table 7 above.) This means that u_L increases as a function of e for $e < 2$ when the wage is $3e$. Therefore, if $g \leq 2$ worker *L* would not choose $e < g$ even with the wage schedule $3e$, and thus certainly not when he could receive $4e$. There is no private return to education beyond g with the posted wage schedule above, so an *L*-type will

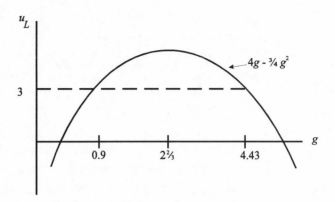

Figure 3

always set $e = g$ if $g \leq 2$. What if $g > 2$? The best that L can do by setting $e < g$ is $u_L = 3$ with $e = 2$. Therefore, if $g > 2$ then L will choose g only if $V(g) \equiv 4g - \frac{3}{4}g^2 \geq 3$. What restriction does this impose on g? Note that $V'(g) = 4 - 3g/2$ and $V'(2\frac{2}{3}) = 0$. Because the second derivative of V is negative, the graph of V rises until $g = 2\frac{2}{3}$ and then falls ever after (Figure 3). Therefore we need to solve $4g - \frac{3}{4}g^2 - 3 = 0$. We will have $4g - \frac{3}{4}g^2 \geq 3$ for all values of g between the solution values, which are 0.9 and 4.43. If $g > 2$ then 4.43 is the critical value of g: If $g > 4.43$ then L will choose $e = 2 < g$. Therefore, $g \leq 4.43$ is required for a pooling equilibrium.

An H-type will set $e = g$ if $4g - \frac{1}{2}g^2$ exceeds the highest utility attainable for an H-type when $e < g$ and the wage is $3e$. $F(g) = 4g - \frac{1}{2}g^2$ is maximized at $g = 4$. If $e < g \leq 4$ then $F'(e) > 0$ because $F'' < 0$ at all points, and thus

$$4g - \tfrac{1}{2}g^2 > 4e - \tfrac{1}{2}e^2 > 3e - \tfrac{1}{2}e^2 \qquad \text{if } e < g \leq 4.$$

Therefore, H will always choose g if $g \leq 4$. Because g is fixed, from the standpoint of the worker deciding how much to invest in education, we can have $4g - \frac{1}{2}g^2$ less than the maximum value of $3e - \frac{1}{2}e^2$ if $g > 4$. The maximum value of $3e - \frac{1}{2}e^2$ is clearly achieved at $e = 3$, in which case $3e - \frac{1}{2}e^2 = 4\frac{1}{2}$. What restriction does

$$4g - \tfrac{1}{2}g^2 \geq 4\tfrac{1}{2} \quad \text{and} \quad g > 4$$

impose on g? The function $4g - \frac{1}{2}g^2$ is maximized at $g = 4$ and the second derivative is negative at all points, so $4g - \frac{1}{2}g^2$ falls as g increases beyond 4. When does it equal $4\frac{1}{2}$? That is, what is the solution of $4g - \frac{1}{2}g^2 = 4\frac{1}{2}$? We get $g = 4 \pm \sqrt{7} = 1.35$ or 6.65. We can't accept $g = 1.35$ because we have to have $g > 4$ if H rejects the wage $4g$. Therefore, the critical value is $g = 6.65$ (Figure 4). In short, an H-type will not prefer setting $e < g$ and receiving a wage $3e$ as long as $g \leq 6.65$. Therefore, if we have a pooling equilibrium g must satisfy

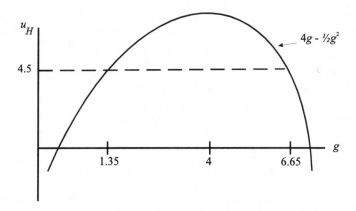

Figure 4

$$g \le 6.65 \quad \text{and} \quad g \le 4.43.$$

The first statement is redundant, so a pooling equilibrium exists if and only if $g \le$ 4.43. Whatever value of g emerges at equilibrium, we don't have the full information choices $e_L = 2$ and $e_H = 6$ that would be mandated by efficiency considerations alone.

7.5 Separating equilibria with asymmetric information and productive education

Suppose H-types obtain more education in equilibrium than L-types. Could we have $e_H = 6$ and $e_L = 2$ (the full information equilibrium choices from Table 7) at equilibrium? No. An L-type would prefer setting $e = 6$ and having a wage of 36, on the one hand, to $e = 2$ with a wage of 6, on the other hand. Everyone would choose $e = 6$. This cannot be sustained as an equilibrium because the average product is $1/3 \times 36 + \frac{2}{3} \times 3 \times 6 = 24$: Cost per worker (to the firm) is 36 and revenue per worker is 24. What are the possible equilibrium values of e_H and e_L? Separation requires that the worker's choice reveal his type. Hence, a worker choosing e_L will receive a wage of $3e_L$, and a worker choosing e_H will receive a wage of $6e_H$. Both are consequences of competition among producers for workers. The equilibrium will then have to satisfy the following *incentive compatibility constraints:*

$$6e_H - \tfrac{1}{2}(e_H)^2 \ge 3e_L - \tfrac{1}{2}(e_L)^2. \qquad [1]$$

$$3e_L - \tfrac{3}{4}(e_L)^2 \ge 6e_H - \tfrac{3}{4}(e_H)^2. \qquad [2]$$

Statement [1] says that an H-type prefers obtaining e_H years of training and a wage of $6e_H$ to a wage of $3e_L$ with e_L years of training. And [2] says that L prefers

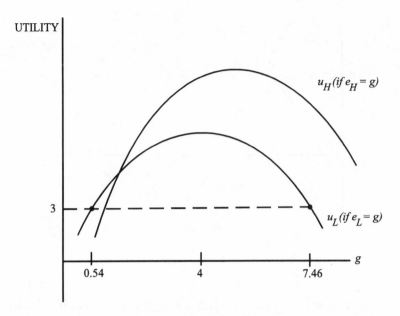

Figure 5

obtaining e_L years of training and a subsequent wage of $3e_L$ to e_H years of training with a wage of $6e_H$. In short, if [1] and [2] hold then no worker will have an incentive to conceal her true type. We already know that the maximum value of the left hand side of [2] is 3, which occurs when $e_L = 2$ (Table 7). If L-types did not get individual utility of at least 3 at equilibrium they could band together and set up their own firm. They could each set $e_L = 2$ in this new firm and pay themselves a wage of 6, yielding $u_L = 3$. If they received applications from H-types wanting to work for a wage of 6 the L-type owners of the firm would gladly welcome them aboard, realizing a profit of $6 \times 2 - 6 = 6$ per H-type worker.[12] Therefore, $u_L \geq 3$ at a separating equilibrium. The only way that an employer could provide $u_L = 3$ would be to offer a wage of 6 and insist on 2 years of training. (Why?) Therefore, the equilibrium must satisfy

$$3 \geq 6e_H - \tfrac{3}{4}(e_H)^2 \quad \text{and} \quad 6e_H - \tfrac{1}{2}(e_H)^2 \geq 3 \times 2 - \tfrac{1}{2} \times 2 \times 2 = 4. \qquad [3]$$

Now, maximize u_H subject to [3]. Consider the first restriction. The function $6e_H - \tfrac{3}{4}(e_H)^2$ is maximized at $e_H = 4$. Starting at $e_H = 4$, the function decreases as e_H increases *or* decreases (Figure 5). Now, $e_H = 0.54$ and $e_H = 7.46$ are the solutions to the equation $6e_H - \tfrac{3}{4}(e_H)^2 = 3$. Therefore, the first part of [3] will be violated if $0.54 < e_H < 7.46$, and it will be satisfied otherwise. Therefore, [3] can be replaced by

$$6e_H - \tfrac{1}{2}(e_H)^2 \geq 4 \qquad \text{and either } e_H \leq 0.54 \quad \text{or} \quad e_H \geq 7.46. \qquad [4]$$

The function $6e_H - \tfrac{1}{2}(e_H)^2$ is maximized at $e_H = 6$, and so u_H falls as e_H increases beyond 7.46 or falls below 0.54 (Figure 5). Therefore, if we maximize u_H subject to [4] we will have either $e_H = 0.54$ or $e_H = 7.46$. It is easy to see that 7.46 gives the higher value of u_H. (Besides, $0.54 < e_L = 2$.) We get $u_H = 6 \times 7.54 - \tfrac{1}{2} \times (7.54)^2 = 16.8$, so [4] is satisfied. We have a separating equilibrium: $e_H = 7.54$ and e_L is 2. Here is the wage schedule:

Pay a wage of $3e$ if $e < 7.54$, and pay $6e$ if $e \geq 7.54$.

What is the worker's response? Consider $V_L(e) = 6e - \tfrac{3}{4}e^2$. The first derivative is $6 - 1.5e$, which is negative for $e \geq 7.54$. Therefore, an L-type would never set $e > 7.54$. Similarly, the first derivative of $V_H(e) = 6e - \tfrac{1}{2}e^2$ is negative for $e \geq 7.54$. An H-type would not set $e > 7.54$. Therefore, an L-type's decision reduces to a choice between $e_L = 2$ (which provides the maximum utility available with the wage schedule $3e$) and $e_L = 7.54$. Now, $u_L(7.54) = 6 \times 7.54 - \tfrac{3}{4}(7.54)^2 = 2.6$, which is less than the utility of 3 realized by L when $e_L = 2$ and the wage is 3×2. If $e_H = 7.54$ then

$$u_H = 6 \times 7.54 - \tfrac{1}{2}(7.54)^2 = 16.8$$

which is larger than $3 \times 3 - \tfrac{1}{2}(3)^2 = 4.5$, the highest level of utility attainable by H with the schedule $3e$. Therefore, each H-type maximizes utility by setting $e_H = 7.54$ and each L-type maximizes by setting $e_L = 2$. If no firm wants to depart from the wage schedule "pay $3e$ if $e < 7.54$ and $6e$ if $e \geq 7.54$" then we are indeed at equilibrium. Each firm expects that a worker presenting a certificate confirming 2 years of training is an L-type, and that each worker presenting a certificate confirming 7.54 years of training is an H-type. If the firm hires n_L of the former and n_H of the latter it will expect its output to be $3 \times 2 \times n_L + 6 \times 7.54 \times n_H$ and of course that is exactly what it will be. Employers' expectations are confirmed, and they have no reason to modify the wage schedule.

We have an equilibrium, but is it the only separating equilibrium? We have already demonstrated that $u_L = 3$, and hence $e_L = 2$ and L's wage must be 6, at equilibrium. Could we have $e_H < 7.54$? No. If e_H were significantly less than 7.54 the L-types would set $e = e_H$, spoiling the equilibrium. How about $e_H > 7.54$. This would be unattractive to L-types. But $e_H > 7.54$ gives an H-type less utility than $e_H = 7.54$. (Why?) If the H-types don't get individual utility of at least $6 \times 7.54 - \tfrac{1}{2}(7.54)^2 = 16.8$ then they can form their own firm. If they each set $e_H = 7.54$ in this new firm and pay themselves a wage of 6×7.54 they could get higher utility (than with $e_H > 7.54$ and a wage $6 \times e_H$). There would be no job applications from L-types, because L-types get higher utility with $e_L = 2$ and a wage of 6. Therefore, $e_H \leq 7.54$ at a separating equilibrium. We have already ruled out $e_H < 7.54$.

Note that L-types make the same investment in education as in the full information efficient outcome, but H-types invest more than they would in full information. Asymmetric information results in more investment in education than can be justified by considerations of the return to society from enhanced productivity.

Suggestions for further reading: Riley (1989).

Exercises

1   Assume that $u_i(x, y) = B_i(x) + y$, as in section 7.2, with $x = \Omega - e$. Assuming that B_i has a positive first derivative and a negative second derivative at all points, show that the first partial derivative of u with respect to e is negative, and so is the second partial of u (taken with respect to e both times).

2   For the economy of section 7.4, show explicitly that there is a pooling equilibrium for $g = 1.5$. For $g = 3.5$.

3   When will the producer of a high-quality product be able to use a warrantee to signal that its output is superior to that of its low-quality rival even though consumers cannot directly determine quality?

8 The market for lemons

In this chapter there are several hidden characteristic problems for which the market system has not developed a completely satisfactory solution. In this section we examine another instance, the used car market. Many of these cars are "lemons" – that is, cars that frequently require expensive repairs. Individuals who purchase new cars often place them on the used car market when they are discovered to be lemons. For this reason the used car market contains a disproportionately high number of lemons. This depresses the price of used cars. As a result many car owners who would otherwise put their good cars on the used car market find that the selling price of their cars in that market is unacceptably low. In other words, they are better off continuing to drive their high-quality automobiles than selling them for a low price which reflects the low *average* quality in the used car market. This further lowers the average quality of used cars at equilibrium, resulting in an even lower equilibrium price. And so on. This is an example of market failure: There are owners of high-quality automobiles who would be willing to sell their cars at a price that buyers would be prepared to pay *if* they could be certain of the quality. However, one cannot distinguish high-quality cars from lemons *before* purchasing, so the price of high-quality used cars reflects the large fraction of lemons in the market and the buyer and seller of the high-quality car are (often) not able to strike a deal. The highest price that the seller could obtain is often below the seller's reservation price. The outcome is not efficient. To drive this point home – nice pun – consider what happens the day after you accept delivery of your new car. The car's value on the used car market is already well below the price you paid on the previous day and is thus below your reservation price. (Why has the car's market price fallen so much in one day? This question has already been answered.)

The difference between the job-market example (section 7) and the market for lemons is that *signalling* occurs in the former and this can induce efficient trades even where there is asymmetric information. (There is asymmetric information because the value of a transaction to the buyer depends on the seller's hidden characteristic which the seller knows but the buyer does not.) If it is possible for high-quality sellers to signal at a relatively low cost the market might force low-quality sellers to reveal themselves.

We conclude with a numerical illustration of market failure when there is no signalling. Assume that there are many more buyers in the used car market than sellers; competition among the latter will result in all sellers' charging the same price if there is no possibility of signalling (no warranties, etc.). Assume also that for a given quality level q the value to the seller is q and the value to the buyer is $1.5q$. Of course, the buyers, who are assumed to be risk neutral, do not know q and do not expect the owners of low-q automobiles to reveal q truthfully. Quality is uniformly distributed over the interval $[0, 1]$, the set of real numbers between zero and 1. Average quality is then $\int_0^1 q \, dq = 0.5$. In the absence of signalling all cars sell for the same price p. Therefore, if $q < p$ a seller will put her car on the market, receiving a payoff of $p - q$ if it is sold. If $q > p$ the seller will not offer the car for sale: a sale would cause a loss in utility of $q - p$. Therefore, at a price p buyers know that the average quality of used cars on the market is $\frac{1}{2}p$. To determine this, first compute the density function for the distribution of cars q satisfying $0 \leq q \leq p$. The density function for $0 \leq q \leq 1$ is $f(q) = 1$. Therefore, the density function for $0 \leq q \leq p$ is $p^{-1}f(q) = p^{-1}$, which is $f(q)$ divided by the probability that q falls between zero and p. (Verify: $p^{-1} \int_0^p dq = p^{-1}(p - 0) = 1$.) The average quality of cars on the market at a price of p is

$$p^{-1} \int_0^p q \, dq = p^{-1}[\tfrac{1}{2}q^2]_0^p = p^{-1}[\tfrac{1}{2}p^2 - 0] = \tfrac{1}{2}p.$$

Assuming that a buyer acts to maximize her average (or expected) payoff there is no sale at any positive price p, because the payoff to a buyer would be $\frac{3}{4}p - p$, a negative number. Therefore, the market clearing price is $p = 0$, even though every agent knows that mutually beneficial trades are possible in principle: The value of any owner's car is two-thirds of what it is worth to any buyer. *If* quality could be costlessly discerned then competition among buyers would bid up the price of a car of quality q to just about q and trade would take place. As it happens, the market is inefficient.

Suggestions for further reading: Akerlof (1970).

Exercise

1   "If used cars are either high-quality cars or lemons but only the seller knows which, then not only can the seller of a high-quality used car not sell it for its true value, she will not even receive a price equal to the average value of automobiles of the same age." Comment.

9 Bargaining

A risk neutral buyer and a risk neutral seller must agree on the price at which the seller is to deliver a single object to the buyer. The two agree that the object is worth more to the buyer than the seller but the buyer does not know the actual value of the object. The value is known to the seller, though. We have another hidden characteristic problem. Even though the seller knows the value of the object to himself before negotiation takes place, that value is determined by events beyond the seller's control and hence the value is a random value from the seller's standpoint. For example, the object in question may be a small firm that the seller owns. The buyer is a better manager than the seller, so the firm would generate more profit if it were managed by the buyer. But the actual profit depends upon a technological innovation for which the seller is seeking a patent and the seller knows much more about the discovery than the buyer.[13]

To be specific, let v denote the value of the object to the seller. The random variable v is assumed to be uniformly distributed on the interval [0, 1]. That is, v is uniformly distributed between the value zero and unity. The value to the buyer is assumed to be $1.5v$. Although both persons know that the value to the buyer is 50 percent higher than its value to the seller the buyer does not know v itself until the sale is complete and the object is in his hands. The seller knows v before negotiations take place, though.

The expected value of v is

$$\int_0^1 v \, dv = \tfrac{1}{2}[v^2]_0^1 = \tfrac{1}{2}[1^2 - 0] = \tfrac{1}{2}.$$

Suppose that the following simple bargaining scheme is adopted. The buyer submits a bid for the object which the seller either accepts or rejects. If the buyer's bid of b is accepted by the seller then the object changes hands at that price. The seller's payoff is b, the selling price, and the buyer's payoff is $1.5v - b$. If the buyer's offer is rejected there is no exchange and no further negotiation: the seller's payoff is v, the value of the object, which she keeps, and the buyer's payoff is zero – he pays nothing and receives nothing. Determine the expected value to the buyer from a bid of b. If $v > b$ the seller will keep the object and the buyer's payoff is zero. If $v \leq b$ the object will change hands and the buyer's profit is $1.5v - b$. The *expected* payoff to the buyer is

$$\int_0^b (1.5v - b)dv + 0 = [0.75v^2 - bv]_0^b = (0.75b^2 - b^2) = -0.25b^2.$$

Whatever the buyer bids, the expect value will be negative. This is because a bid of b is accepted by the seller only when v is below b, which means that the value to the buyer is $1.5b$ *at most*. However, the buyer pays \$$b$ for certain (when an offer of b is accepted). He pays \$$b$ for something worth less on average, a losing proposition. Therefore, the buyer will bid zero and the sale will never take place even though both parties are aware that the object is worth 50 percent more to the buyer than to the seller. This is surely inefficient. If *both* parties knew v then there would be no obstacle to a mutually profitable trade.

Let us consider another bargaining scheme applied to the same problem. This time the seller makes an offer s which the buyer can either accept or reject. When the seller makes her offer she knows v. Therefore, she will not set s below v. (If $s < v$ the seller would lose if the price were accepted by the buyer. She would receive s dollars for something worth v dollars to her. Therefore, $s \geq v$.) If $v < s < 1.5v$ then both parties gain by a sale at s dollars because the object is worth $1.5v$ to the buyer. The buyer does not know v but he knows that the seller knows that the object is worth $1.5v$ to the buyer. Then the buyer should accept s, anticipating that the seller will set s between v and $1.5v$. But this cannot be an equilibrium strategy. The seller has an incentive to charge a high s even when v is very low, relying on the buyer to *assume* that $v > s/1.5$. In fact, the expected value of the object to the buyer of accepting the seller's price of s is

$$\int_0^1 1.5v \, dv = 0.75.$$

The buyer pays s dollars for something worth 0.75 dollar on average so the expected payoff to the buyer is $0.75 - s$. At equilibrium the seller would have to be maximizing her utility and this implies $1 < s < 1.5$, which implies that $0.75 - s$, the expected payoff to the buyer, is negative. Here again, the buyer will not agree to any transaction and efficiency is lost.

Is there any scheme that will permit the realization of the gains from trade (which both parties know to be positive for each)? No! The most favorable scheme from the buyer's standpoint is the one where he makes a final offer which the seller has no authority to modify and can only accept or reject.

Suggestions for further reading: Samuelson (1984).

10 Competitive insurance markets

This section highlights the difficulties of achieving a satisfactory outcome when traders differ with respect to the information they possess concerning the likelihood of events. The hidden characteristic in this case is the probability that an individual will suffer a mishap – have a car accident, be burglarized, be hospitalized, etc. The probability of misfortune's befalling the individual is assumed to be known to that individual but not to anyone else. This probability is information that is hidden from others. Moreover, the individual cannot be expected to disclose his hidden characteristic willingly, especially if individuals who report a higher probability of accident are charged higher insurance premiums. Instead of looking at the design problem – the question of whether it is possible to design a scheme that induces individuals to reveal their private information – we investigate a model that is a reasonable approximation to the competitive insurance markets that operate in mature capitalist economies. We will see that the hidden characteristic problem can prevent the market from working out an equilibrium. When an equilibrium does exist, each individual will reveal her hidden characteristic by her choice of insurance contract. Nevertheless, the competitive equilibrium may not be efficient when it does exist, although it is not easy to determine when the market outcome can be improved upon.

10.1 The problem

Dorrit knows more about the likelihood of her having an accident in a certain situation than others do. This means that some of the information about the probability of Dorrit's having an accident is hidden from the company offering her an insurance contract. Think about automobile insurance. In fact, there is a lot of information about our driving habits that is available to insurance companies. Young men are more likely to be risky drivers than young women, and this observation is used by companies in determining rates. The correlation is far from perfect, however; but to the extent that a riskier driver is identified and charged a higher premium we can say that prices reflect costs to society – part of the cost in this case is the possibility that you or I will be the dangerous driver's victim. Driving records – information about speeding tickets and prior accidents – are used in determining automobile insurance premiums. This is called experience rating. Suppose that an insurance company has already used all available information to categorize drivers by risk and has determined that Dorrit and Shmuel are in the same risk category. There is additional private information that Dorrit has about her driving habits and Shmuel has about his, that is hidden from the insurance provider. Here is a good example of what I mean. I was driving home one day, correcting the manuscript for this section and wishing I had a better example of private information in this context. Then I realized that my practice of correcting manuscripts while driving is the perfect illustration. My insurance company would love to know about this dangerous habit.[14] (There is no chance that someone from the company will read this book.) So, within a particular risk category as determined by the evidence available to insurance companies there will be differences in risk that cannot be directly observed by outsiders, and it is these additional private characteristics that are the subject of this section.

To abstract from most of the other issues, assume that there is only one basic commodity, which we call wealth. Uncertainty concerns the status of an individual's wealth, which either is partially destroyed – by fire, say – or remains intact. We let a represent the value of an individual's wealth after an accident when no insurance is purchased, and let z represent the value of the same individual's wealth without insurance and also without an accident. The actual wealth level may be different from both a and z. If the individual buys insurance but there is no accident, then her wealth will be lower than z by the amount of the premium. And if she has an accident after buying insurance then her wealth will be higher than a because she will receive a claim cheque from the insurance company to compensate partly for the loss $z - a$. Let x denote the amount of wealth available to finance consumption when the individual suffers an accident; and let y denote the amount of wealth available for consumption when there is no accident. An insurance contract, or policy, P requires the purchaser to pay a stipulated fee (the premium) of f dollars before the resolution of uncertainty. If she does not have an accident then no further exchange takes place, but if she is involved in an accident then the insurance company pays her c dollars. The amount of the claim cheque is actually $c + f$, but the net claim is c because she must pay the annual premium whether she has an accident or not. Therefore, if the individual purchases policy $P = (f, c)$,

$$x = a + c \quad \text{and} \quad y = z - f.$$

We allow $f = 0 = c$, which represents the case when no insurance is purchased.

The number π is the probability that the individual has an accident (or a fire in his house, etc.). To make the model really simple, we assume there are only two possible values of π and hence only two types of individuals: low risk, L, and high risk, H, so we write π_L and π_H, respectively. The hidden characteristic is the value of π. Of course, $\pi_H > \pi_L$, $1 - \pi_L$ is the probability that an L-type does not have an accident, and $1 - \pi_H$ is the probability that an H-type does not have an accident. The individuals all have the same utility-of-wealth function $U(w)$. Individuals are assumed to be risk averse: $U''(w) < 0$ for all $w > 0$. And each has the same endowment allocation: a if there is an accident, and z if there is no accident.[15] Of course, $z > a$ because an accident destroys wealth. There are n_L low risk individuals and n_H high risk individuals. Although $U(w)$ is the same for each individual, it is not the case that expected utility is the same for an L-type and an H-type because the probabilities differ. Expected utility for L and H, respectively, is

$$u_L(x, y) = \pi_L U(x) + (1 - \pi_L)U(y) \quad \text{and}$$
$$u_H(x, y) = \pi_H U(x) + (1 - \pi_H)U(y).$$

The crucial assumption is that insurance companies cannot identify L-types and H-types directly but can separate them only by employing conjectures about their preferences (u_L and u_H) for insurance contracts and by observing their contract choices. Even within our very abstract framework, in which individuals are identical in all but one respect and only wealth available for consumption affects well-being, there are potential difficulties in terms of the satisfactory performance of competitive markets. We assume that U is monotonic: If $w > w'$ then $U(w) > U(w')$. Therefore, u_L will increase if x increases and y does not decrease, or if y increases and x does not decrease. The same can be said of u_H.

Assume that n_L and n_H are both large in absolute value, although one number might be small relative to the other. If n_L is large, then the total number of accidents suffered by L-types will be close to the expected number, $\pi_L n_L$. (This is the law of large numbers. If you haven't encountered this fundamental fact, convince yourself of its truth by tossing a coin. With a large number of tosses the fraction of heads will be very close to the expected number, one-half. I can safely make this claim, because the probability of its being contradicted is *very* small if the number of tosses is *very* large.) Then we can assume that the total number of accidents is always exactly equal to the expected number in order to avoid having to say that the results hold only approximately, or with high probability. Similarly, we assume that n_H is large and the total number of accidents suffered by H-types is always exactly $\pi_H n_H$. Let's also assume, for simplicity, that administration costs are constant and relatively small. This permits us to assume zero administrative costs without affecting the results. In that case, competition among insurance companies will ensure that the value of premiums taken in at equilibrium equals the value of gross claims paid out at equilibrium. Now we go on from here to examine the nature of a competitive insurance market equilibrium. Skip to section 10.5 if you merely want a worked example.

10.2 The number of contracts in equilibrium

H-types are identical to each other, so they will make the same choices. Suppose not, and some H-types choose policy P^1 and some choose P^2, which is different from P^1. If one yields a higher value of u_H than the other, we can't be at equilibrium. Some H-types will switch from the low-utility policy to the high-utility policy. Then $u_H(P^1) = u_H(P^2)$ at equilibrium. Further, P^1 and P^2 yield the same expected profit to the insurance company. If, say, P^1 provided higher expected profit per policy than P^2 then insurance companies would all offer P^1 in preference to P^2; their customers wouldn't object because $u_H(P^1) = u_H(P^2)$. Policy P^t charges a premium of f^t and pays a net claim of c^t, for $t = 1, 2$. Let's consider the expected profit to the insurance company generated by P^t. It is

$$f^t - \pi_H \times [c^t + f^t]$$

for $t = 1, 2$. (Each policy brings in a premium revenue of f^t with certainty and disburses a claim check of $c^t + f^t$ with probability π_H.) Then $f^1 - \pi_H \times [c^1 + f^1]$ $= f^2 - \pi_H \times [c^2 + f^2]$. Consider policy P^3 constructed by averaging P^1 and P^2. That is, P^3 charges a premium $f^3 = \frac{1}{2}f^1 + \frac{1}{2}f^2$ and pays a net claim of $c^3 = \frac{1}{2}c^1 + \frac{1}{2}c^2$. Then the expected profit per policy from P^3 is equal to

$$\tfrac{1}{2}f^1 + \tfrac{1}{2}f^2 - \tfrac{1}{2}\pi_H[c^1 + f^1] - \tfrac{1}{2}\pi_H[c^2 + f^2],$$

which is the average of the expected profits from P^1 and P^2. At equilibrium, P^1 and P^2 must yield the same profit. But if P^1 and P^2 generate exactly the same profit, and the profit from P^3 is the average of the profit from P^1 and P^2, then P^3, P^1, and P^2 must all yield the same profit. But P^3 *affords higher utility!* A glance at Figure 6 makes this quite evident. P^3 is on the straight line between P^1 and P^2, which are on the same indifference curve, and hence P^3 is on a higher indifference curve. (It is easy to confirm that the indifference curve has the shape given in the diagram. The marginal rate of substitution at (x, y) is

$$\frac{\pi_H U'(x)}{(1 - \pi_H) \times U'(y)}.$$

As we move along the indifference curve, increasing x and decreasing y, the derivative $U'(x)$ will fall and $U'(y)$ will increase because $U'' < 0$ at all points as a consequence of risk aversion. Therefore, we have diminishing marginal rate of substitution.)

Now, P^3 will yield the same profit as P^1 and P^2 but will afford more utility. Therefore, the insurance company could modify P^3 slightly, raising the premium and providing the same claim, c^3. This new policy will certainly bring in more

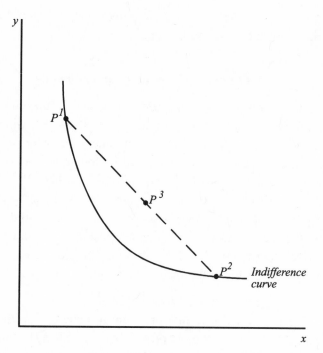

Figure 6

profit than P^1 or P^2 and H-types will prefer it to either P^1 or P^2 – as long as the increase in premium is not too large. Therefore, insurance companies and their clients will prefer this new outcome to the one in which only P^1 and P^2 were available. The original situation cannot have been in equilibrium.

We have proved that there is only one contract offered to the H-types in equilibrium. Obviously, the same argument will establish that the L-types will all choose the same contract at equilibrium. Therefore, if a contract has any buyers at all, it will have n_H, or n_L, or $n_H + n_L$ buyers. Now, let π denote the probability that an individual randomly selected from the entire population has an accident. Then π is the expected number of accidents divided by the total population. That is,

$$\pi = \frac{\pi_H \times n_H + \pi_L \times n_L}{n_H + n_L}.$$

Recall that $x = a + c$ and $y = z - f$ when an individual purchases policy $P = (f, c)$. Because the individual ultimately cares only about x and y, we will think of an insurance contract as a specification of x and y. If we need to, we can recover the premium and net claim by setting $f = z - y$ and $c = x - a$. The condition that all money taken in from a contract is paid out in the form of claim checks is

$$n(z - y) = \rho n(x - a + z - y) \tag{1}$$

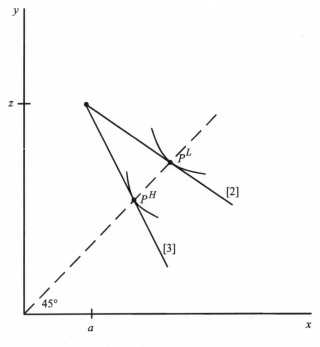

Figure 7

where $n = n_H$ (in which case $\rho = \pi_H$), or $n = n_L$ ($\rho = \pi_L$), or $n = n_H + n_L$ ($\rho = \pi$). The term on the left hand side of equation [1] is the total amount of money collected in premiums from policyholders, and the term on the right is the amount of the claim cheque (c, which equals $x - a$, plus f, which equals $z - y$) sent to each person having an accident multiplied by the number of accidents (ρn) by the company's policyholders. We can divide both sides of the equation by n and rewrite the zero profit conditions as

$$\pi_L x + (1 - \pi_L)y = \pi_L a + (1 - \pi_L)z. \qquad [2]$$

$$\pi_H x + (1 - \pi_H)y = \pi_H a + (1 - \pi_H)z. \qquad [3]$$

$$\pi x + (1 - \pi)y = \pi a + (1 - \pi)z. \qquad [4]$$

Equation [2] is the zero profit condition for a group composed exclusively of L types. It equates the expected market value of wealth with insurance to the expected market value of wealth without insurance. Why bother buying insurance then? Because (x, y) delivers higher utility than (a, z). Equation [3] is the zero profit condition for a group composed exclusively of H-types, and [4] is the zero profit condition for the entire community. Consider Figure 7. If the L-types had a contract that left them above line [2] then it would not generate enough premium income to pay all the claims. If they had a contract below line [2] then it would yield a positive profit because it takes in more premium income than required to honor the claims. The analogous statement holds for [3] with respect to H, of course.

10.3 Full information equilibrium

To establish a benchmark case, suppose that insurance companies are able to distinguish H-types from L-types. Assume, for instance, that each person can be relied on to answer truthfully when asked which risk group she belongs to. There is no cross-subsidization at equilibrium: All claims made by H-types are paid out of premiums contributed by H-types, and all claims made by L-types are paid out of premiums contributed by L-types. Here's why: We can't have L above [2] and H above [3] in Figure 7 because neither policies would collect enough revenue to pay the claims presented. What about a cross-subsidy? Say, have the L's below [2] and the H's above [3]. This means that the policy obtained by L-types collects more premium income than is required to finance claims by L-types. The surplus is used to finance the deficit from the H policy. But this is inconsistent with equilibrium. A company could offer a policy to L's that cut the surplus in half. This would be preferred by the L's and it would be profitable for the company offering it. (The company would not have to worry that H-types would buy it as well. We are assuming that insurance companies know who the H's are; they would not allow them to purchase the contract designed for the L's.) The original policy would quickly be driven off the market. Therefore, there is no cross-subsidy at equilibrium. (A similar argument will show that the H-types will not subsidize the L-types at equilibrium.) Because there is no cross-subsidization, H-types and L-types will buy different contracts at equilibrium, and thus equation [2] must hold for P^L, the contract obtained by L-types at equilibrium, and [3] must hold for the H-types' contract P^H. If the left side of equation [2] exceeds the right side, the contract is not feasible because the value of gross claims paid out will exceed the value of premiums collected. If the right side exceeds the left side, then insurance companies are earning excess profits and competition will force premiums to fall, and hence the original state was not in equilibrium. Similarly for [3]. Under these conditions, the best contract to offer a risk group is the one that maximizes its expected utility subject to its zero profit constraint. This is denoted in Figure 7 as P^H for the H-types and P^L for the L-types. Any other point P on [2] will give L less utility. A company could replace P with a policy that was the same as P^L but with a slightly higher premium. This would give the company more profit than P (all points on [2] yield the same profit, zero) and give customers more utility if the premium were not too much higher than the one at P^L. (Remember, H-types can be excluded in the full information world.) Then P is not consistent with equilibrium. Similarly for P^H. Let's determine P^L and P^H. Use [2] and [3] to solve for y. Then y is a function of x:

$$y = \rho a/(1 - \rho) + z - \rho x/(1 - \rho) \qquad [5]$$

for $\rho = \pi_H$ and $\rho = \pi_L$, respectively. In each case we want to maximize

$$u = \rho U(x) + (1 - \rho)U(y).$$

This can be treated as a function V of x because y is a function of x via [5]. The first-order condition for a maximum of V is

$$V'(x) = \rho U'(x) + (1 - \rho)U'(y)dy/dx = 0.$$

Now, $dy/dx = -\rho/(1 - \rho)$ and thus

$$V'(x) = \rho U'(x) - (1 - \rho)U'(y) \times [\rho/(1 - \rho)] = \rho U'(x) - \rho U'(y) = 0.$$

But we can't have $U'(x) = U'(y)$ unless $x = y$: Risk aversion implies that U' decreases as wealth increases. The optimal consumption can now be determined by setting $x = y$ in [2] and [3]. (See section 12 of Chapter 1.) This yields $x = y = \rho a + (1 - \rho)z$. As illustrated in Figure 7, H-types will consume $P^H = (x^H, y^H)$ satisfying $x^H = y^H = \pi_H a + (1 - \pi_H)z$, and L-types will consume $P^L = (x^L, y^L)$ satisfying $x^L = y^L = \pi_L a + (1 - \pi_L)z$. Because $x = y$ in each case, we have what is known as complete insurance. Wealth available for consumption is the same whether there is an accident or not. Competitive pricing (fair odds) is essential for this result.

Section 3.1 of Chapter 5 proves that the equilibrium that we have just derived – and that is depicted in Figure 7 – is Pareto optimal if each individual discloses his risk category truthfully. A problem arises only when there are two risk categories and the insurer does not know to which group a client belongs. This is the situation that insurers actually face. H-types have no incentive to reveal their true characteristic because they prefer the policy P^L intended for L-types to policy P^H. The former provides more of each good: If they masquerade as L-types, the H-types will have much more wealth. Everyone will declare himself to be in risk category L and will purchase P^L. This outcome is not feasible, however, because P^L yields zero profit only when H-types are excluded. If P^L is purchased by some H-types, who file more claims per dollar of premium than L-types, there will not be enough premium income to honor each claim. This is an instance of adverse selection.

10.4 Asymmetric information equilibrium

Assume from now on that high-risk individuals will not directly reveal their identity and only the individual knows his risk parameter π_i. There are only two possible equilibria: (1) The same contract is offered to both risk categories. This

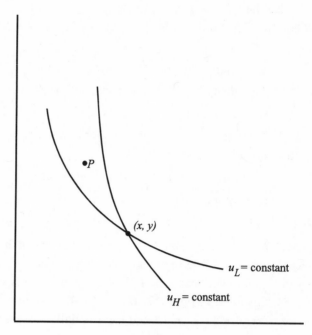

Figure 8

defines a *pooling equilibrium*. (2) The *H*-types are separated out by providing the *L*-types with a contract that is not preferred by the *H*-types to the one designed for them. This defines a *separating equilibrium*.

The constraint that incorporates feasibility and the zero profit condition for a pooling equilibrium is [4] above. Recall that π is the probability that an individual randomly selected from the entire population does not have an accident, and

$$\pi = \frac{\pi_H \times n_H + \pi_L \times n_L}{n_H + n_L}.\qquad [6]$$

Let MRS_H and MRS_L denote the marginal rate of substitution (ratio of marginal utilities) of an *H*-type and an *L*-type, respectively:

$$\mathrm{MRS}_H = \frac{\pi_H U'(x)}{(1 - \pi_H)U'(y)} \quad \text{and} \quad \mathrm{MRS}_L = \frac{\pi_L U'(x)}{(1 - \pi_L)U'(y)}.$$

Now, $\mathrm{MRS}_L < \mathrm{MRS}_H$ at any point[16] because $\pi_L < \pi_H$ and $1 - \pi_L > 1 - \pi_H$ (Figure 8). Intuitively, the high-risk types are willing to sacrifice more *y* (consumption in the "no accident" state) to get an additional unit of *x* (consumption in case of an accident) because the probability of an accident is higher for such individuals. Therefore, at the exchange rate $\xi = \frac{1}{2}\mathrm{MRS}_L + \frac{1}{2}\mathrm{MRS}_H$ there is a number δ small enough in absolute value so that

$$u_L(x - \delta, y + \xi \delta) > u_L(x, y) \quad \text{and} \quad u_H(x - \delta, y + \xi \delta) < u_H(x, y).$$

Suppose that we claim to have a *pooling equilibrium* with each consumer, regardless of type, obtaining the basket (x, y). If an insurance company offered a different contract $P = (x - \delta, y + \xi \delta)$ it would be preferred to (x, y) by L-types but not by H-types (Figure 8). The insurance company could offer P and be sure that L-types would purchase it in preference to (x, y), but H-types would not. Even though the company would not be able to distinguish an L-type individual from an H-type, by judicious contract design a company could rely on the H-types to reveal themselves by their behavior.

An insurance company that catered exclusively to L-type risks would have to pay claims to the fraction π_L of its policyholders. Before P was available, both types purchased (x, y) and the fraction π of policyholders filed claims. If $\delta > 0$ is small, then (x, y) and P are almost the same, but $\pi_L < \pi_H$, and a company offering P will pay a smaller fraction of its premium receipts in claims, though the premium and net claim per person will be almost the same as for (x, y). Therefore, P will yield more profit to the insurance companies offering it, and this means that the original situation in which each person purchased (x, y) is not in equilibrium. Companies would have incentive to offer a new contract P, and it would yield a profit if the individuals who preferred it to (x, y) purchased it. (We still won't have equilibrium when P is introduced because the viability of (x, y) depends, through equation [4], on its being purchased by L-types as well as by H-types, but the former will defect to P as soon as it is offered. The companies that continue to offer (x, y) will take a loss, and that is not consistent with equilibrium.)

What we have discovered is that an equilibrium must separate H-types from L-types by offering different contracts such that neither risk type would want to buy the contract intended for the other; the contract designed for L-types satisfies equation [2]; and the contract designed for H-types satisfies equation [3]. There must be separate contracts at equilibrium. And individuals of the same risk type will buy the same contract. Therefore, only two contracts will be offered at equilibrium since there are two risk categories. It is possible that the contract B^L available to L-types is below the line representing equation [2]. This would mean that the L-types are subsidizing the H-types. But this is inconsistent with equilibrium, because a new firm could enter and obtain a positive profit by offering a contract paying the same net claim as B_L at a slightly lower premium. This could be done in such a way that L-types prefer the new contract and H-types still prefer their original choice. Therefore, equation [2] must be satisfied at equilibrium by the contract designed for L-types. Similarly, equation [3] must be satisfied by the contract purchased by H.

Conditions [2] and [3] are represented geometrically as straight lines in Figures 7 and 9. Since (a, z) satisfies both equations, it is on both lines. Because the individuals are risk averse, we need not be concerned with any (x, y) for which x

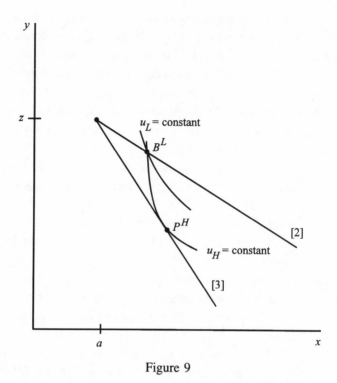

Figure 9

< a. (Why?) Is there any reason why the H-types cannot have their most-preferred contract subject to [3]? No. If any other contract were offered, a company would have incentive to offer the most-preferred contract P^H consistent with equation [3], and this would be purchased by H-types in preference to the one originally offered. Both would give rise to the same profit (zero), but because P_H is preferred, a company could raise the premium slightly and make more profit than with the original contract, and H-types would still prefer the new contract to the original. Therefore, P^H, depicted in Figure 9, is offered to H-types and chosen by them at equilibrium. Now, this imposes a constraint on B^L, the contract offered to L-types, which must satisfy

$$u_H(P^H) \geq u_H(B^L). \tag{7}$$

This is called the *incentive compatibility constraint*. At equilibrium B^L will maximize u_L subject to conditions [2] and [7]. This means that the L-types will not be offered their most-preferred contract P^L subject to [2], because that would be preferred by H-types to P^H, and P^L is feasible if and only if it is purchased exclusively by L-types. Note that the equilibrium pair of contracts is determined independently of n_H and n_L, the numbers of H-types and L-types, respectively.

The contract B^L offered to L-types at equilibrium is depicted in Figure 9. The striking thing is that H-types are exactly as well off as they would be if the L-types

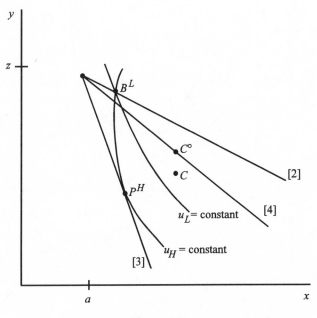

Figure 10

did not exist, but the *L*-types are worse off as a result of the presence of individuals with a higher risk of accident. Without the *H*-types the *L*-types would have P^L at equilibrium (Figure 7), but as it is, they wind up with B^L. The existence of a tiny group of *H*-types can have a strong negative impact on the welfare of the *L*-types, but the loss in welfare by the latter is not balanced by a gain in welfare by the former group.

The pair (P^H, B^L) of Figure 9 is the only candidate for equilibrium, but even this may not be an equilibrium. Suppose that n_H is relatively small. Then the line corresponding to equation [4] is close to the line depicting equation [2] as shown in Figure 10. Then there is a profitable contract *C* that the *H*-types prefer to P^H and the *L*-types prefer to B^L. Contract *C* in Figure 10 is profitable because it provides the same claim as C° but requires a larger premium than C°, which is on the zero profit line. Therefore, (P^H, B^L) is not an equilibrium. But we have just established that it is the only candidate for equilibrium. (We haven't got the *wrong* equilibrium; we've discovered that there is no equilibrium.) Therefore, we have proved the following:

> If $\pi_H > \pi_L$ *and* n_H/n_L *is sufficiently small, then there does not exist a competitive insurance market equilibrium.*

How small? The example of the next section shows that the ratio does not have to be tiny in order for equilibrium to be ruled out.

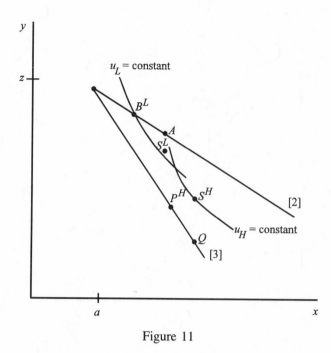

Figure 11

Consider the case in which a competitive equilibrium exists. Is the assignment of P^H to H and B^L to L Pareto optimal? Assuming knowledge of each individual's hidden characteristic – the risk parameter – it is not difficult to design a scheme that would make everyone better off. If L-types consume P^L and H-types continue to consume P^H then we have a feasible allocation that makes the former better off without affecting the utility of the latter, and we can modify this outcome slightly so that *everyone* is better off. But how would a planner or government offer P^L to low risk individuals without the high risk individuals claiming to be low risk and also lining up for P^L? Even though (P^H, P^L) Pareto dominates (P^H, B^L), it would be impossible to implement the former. Is there a superior allocation that could be implemented? Such an allocation exists if n_H/n_L is not too large. An example, giving S^H to the H-types and S^L to the L-types, is depicted in Figure 11. Note that H-types prefer S^H to P^H, but they also prefer S^H to S^L, so they would choose S^H if the government offered S^H and S^L; they would not choose to masquerade as low-risk individuals. Second, the low-risk individuals themselves prefer S^L to B^L and to S^H. Third, S^L yields a positive profit since it requires a higher premium than A, which pays the same claim and yields a zero profit. Finally, S^H entails a loss since it requires a lower premium than Q while paying the same claim as Q, which breaks even. But the government could use the profit from S^L to cover the loss of S^H as long as

$$n_L \times [\text{value of } y \text{ at } A - \text{value of } y \text{ at } S^L] \geq$$
$$n_H \times [\text{value of } y \text{ at } S^H - \text{value of } y \text{ at } Q]$$

and this will be possible if n_H/n_L is small enough. Note that the value of y at A less the value of y at S^L will be very small, because S^L must be near B^L to ensure that $u_H(S^H) > u_H(S^L)$. The pair (S^H, S^L) is not consistent with equilibrium in competitive markets: Cross-subsidization is not consistent with equilibrium. But the plan (S^H, S^L) could be implemented by a central authority if n_H/n_L is small. (Given n_L, the larger is n_H the more high-risk individuals there are to be subsidized by the low-risk group.) The plan (S^H, S^L) is feasible if the H-types choose S^H and the L-types choose S^L. As we have seen, the individuals do have an incentive to make these choices. Therefore, the competitive equilibrium is not Pareto optimal.

> *If $\pi_H > \pi_L$ and n_H/n_L is sufficiently small, then the competitive insurance market equilibrium is not Pareto optimal even if it exists.*

In determining whether the market outcome can be improved upon we have been careful to impose the same informational constraint on the government that private insurance companies face. What additional information would the government have to possess in order to be sure that (S^H, S^L) is feasible? It would have to know n_H and n_L to know if the surplus collected from the L-types were sufficient to cover the subsidy to the H-types. But how could it know the number of H-types without being able to identify the H-types? One answer is that the H-types reveal themselves by their choice of P^H at equilibrium. But suppose that insurance were provided by the government and not private insurance companies. The numbers n_H and n_L can actually be determined from data that are available to the government. Recall the definition of π from [6]. If we let n denote the total population, $n_H + n_L$, then the expected number of accidents for the population as a whole is πn. This will be very close to T, the actual number of accidents. Then $T = \pi_H n_L + \pi_L n_L = \pi_H n_H + \pi_L[n - n_H]$. T is known, and if π_H and π_L are known then we can solve for n_H, which will then also give us n_L. However, U will also have to be known, to ensure that the H-types will choose S^H in preference to S^L, and to ensure that each group is better off than it would be under a competitive equilibrium. It's not clear that the government can obtain the relevant information, but it is also not clear that the market outcome is the best that can be achieved, given the hidden information problem.

10.5 A worked example

In this section we develop the above ideas by means of a specific example. The probability that L has an accident is $\frac{1}{4}$, and $\frac{1}{2}$ is the probability that H has an accident. Then $\frac{3}{4}$ is the probability that an L-type does not have an accident, and $\frac{1}{2}$

is the probability that an H-type does not have an accident. Each individual has the utility-of-wealth function

$$U(w) = \ln(w + 1).$$

Then $U'(w) = (w + 1)^{-1}$ and hence $U''(w) = -(w + 1)^{-2} < 0$ for all $w \geq 0$, so individuals are risk averse. Each person's endowment is $a = 4$ if there is an accident, and $z = 12$ when there is no accident. The relevant utility functions are

$$u_L(x, y) = \tfrac{1}{4} \ln(x + 1) + \tfrac{3}{4} \ln(y + 1).$$
$$u_H(x, y) = \tfrac{1}{2} \ln(x + 1) + \tfrac{1}{2} \ln(y + 1).$$

Let's determine the basket $P^L = (x, y)$ that would be chosen by L-types if the amount of money they paid into insurance companies in premiums were paid out in claims. The premium per capita is $12 - y$ and the claim cheque per capita is $x - 4 + 12 - y$, the net claim plus the premium. Assuming that n_L is large, the total number of accidents suffered by L-types will be close to the expected number, $\tfrac{1}{4}n_L$. For convenience, assume that it is exactly equal to $\tfrac{1}{4}n_L$. Then we have

$$n_L \times (12 - y) = \tfrac{1}{4}n_L \times (x - 4 + 12 - y), \quad \text{or}$$
$$\tfrac{3}{4}(12 - y) = \tfrac{1}{4}(x - 4), \quad \text{or} \tag{8}$$
$$\tfrac{1}{4}x + \tfrac{3}{4}y = \tfrac{1}{4} \times 4 + \tfrac{3}{4} \times 12 = 10.$$

Note that equation [8] says that the expected market value of consumption with insurance equals the expected market value of wealth without insurance. That is what we would expect to see if all premium money received by insurance carriers were paid out as claims. Now, to find P^L we maximize u_L subject to [8]. We have $y = 40/3 - \tfrac{1}{3}x$ from [8], and substituting this into u_L yields

$$V(x) = \tfrac{1}{4} \ln(x + 1) + \tfrac{3}{4} \ln(40/3 - \tfrac{1}{3}x + 1)$$

which we want to maximize. $V'(x) = \tfrac{1}{4}(x + 1)^{-1} + \tfrac{3}{4}(y + 1)^{-1} \times (-\tfrac{1}{3}) = \tfrac{1}{4}(x + 1)^{-1} - \tfrac{1}{4}(y + 1)^{-1}$. Note that $V'' < 0$ at all points. Therefore, if $V'(x) = 0$ yields nonnegative values of x and y the equation $V'(x) = 0$ will characterize the solution to our problem. But $V'(x) = 0$ implies $x = y$, and substituting this into [8] yields $x = y = 10$. Therefore, $P^L = (10, 10)$, and $u_L(P^L) = 2.40$. This means that, subject to constraint [8], L would want a policy with a premium of $\$2 = 12 - 10$, and a net payment of $\$6 = 10 - 4$ in case of an accident. Note that the claim cheque would be for the amount of $\$8$ when L suffers an accident, but L still has to pay his premium in a year when he makes a claim, so the net addition to consumption is $\$6$.

Similarly, if we want to find P^H, the choice of H-types when the amount of money paid in as premiums by H-types was paid out in claims to H-types, we would maximize u_H subject to

$$\tfrac{1}{2}x + \tfrac{1}{2}y = \tfrac{1}{2} \times 4 + \tfrac{1}{2} \times 12 = 8. \tag{9}$$

We know we will have $x = y$ (the individuals are risk averse), in which case [9] implies $x = y = 8$. Therefore, $P^H = (8, 8)$, with $u_H(P^H) = 2.20$. The premium per capita is $12 - 8 = \$4$ and the net payment in case of accident is $8 - 4 = \$4$. Note that in the full information world, the H-types pay a higher premium and get less coverage than L-types.

Now, let's find the asymmetric information equilibrium. We know that there will be a separating equilibrium. And H-types will get the basket $(8, 8)$ at equilibrium. To find B^L, the basket obtained by L-types at equilibrium, we solve [8] and $u_H(x, y) = u_H(8, 8)$. That is

$\frac{1}{4}x + \frac{3}{4}y = 10$ and $\frac{1}{2}\ln(x + 1) + \frac{1}{2}\ln(y + 1) = \frac{1}{2}\ln(8 + 1) + \frac{1}{2}\ln(8 + 1)$.

The first equation yields $x = 40 - 3y$. Now substitute this value of x into the second equation and exploit the fact that the logarithm of a product is the sum of the logarithms.

$$(40 - 3y + 1)(y + 1) = 81.$$

Then $3y^2 - 38y + 40 = 0$ and hence $y = 38/6 \pm 31.048/6$. The smaller value won't do (why?) so we must have $y = 11.51$, and thus $x = 5.47$. $B^L = (5.47, 11.51)$, which gives H slightly less utility than P^H. $u_L(B^L) = 2.36 < 2.40 = u_L(P^L)$. $u_H(B^L) = 2.19685 < 2.1972 = u_H(P^H)$. Therefore, H would choose P^H in preference to B^L. H gets P^H and L gets B^L.

Now we turn things around. We show that both H and L prefer the basket $C = (9.8, 9.8)$ and determine the values of n_H and n_L, the number of H-types and L-types, respectively, that would allow each person to have basket C. Certainly, H prefers C to P^H because $C = (9.8, 9.8)$ provides more of each good than $P^H = (8, 8)$. And $u_L(9.8, 9.8) = \frac{1}{4}\ln 10.8 + \frac{3}{4}\ln 10.8 = \ln 10.8 = 2.3795 > 2.3617 = u_L(B_L)$. If there is a competitive equilibrium, then H will get P^H and L will get B^L, but each prefers C to her equilibrium basket. Therefore, if the outcome that gives each person the basket C is feasible, then there will be no equilibrium. Let $n = n_H + n_L$, the total number of individuals. Let π be the probability that an individual randomly selected from the entire population (of n persons) has an accident. Then the expected number of accidents each period is πn. If n is large, then the actual number of accidents will be close to the expected number with high probability. For convenience, assume that the number of accidents is *exactly* πn. The total amount of money paid out in net claims cannot exceed the total amount paid in as premiums. This is our feasibility condition, and it is expressed as follows:

$$\pi n \times (9.8 - 4 + 12 - 9.8) \le n \times (12 - 9.8), \quad \text{or} \quad 8\pi \le 2.2, \quad \text{or} \quad [10]$$

$$\pi \le 0.275. \qquad\qquad [11]$$

(Note that [11] is equivalent to $\pi x + [1 - \pi]y \le \pi 4 + [1 - \pi]12$ for $x = 9.8 = y$, which says that the expected consumption per individual cannot exceed an individual's expected wealth, $\pi 4 + [1 - \pi]12$, a condition that must hold if everyone winds up with the same basket.) Recall that

$$\pi = \frac{\frac{1}{2} \times n_H + \frac{1}{4} \times n_L}{n_H + n_L}.$$

Therefore, statement [11] becomes

$$(\tfrac{1}{2}n_H + \tfrac{1}{4}n_L) \leq 0.275(n_H + n_L), \quad \text{or}$$
$$2n_H + n_L \leq 1.1n_H + 1.1n_L, \quad \text{or}$$
$$n_H \leq n_L/9.$$

A small group of *H*-types (10% or less of the population in this case) can spoil the possibilities for a competitive equilibrium in the insurance market.

What condition would ensure the existence of equilibrium in the case of this example? We need an *L*-type indifference curve through B_L that lies above the line $\pi x + (1 - \pi)y = \pi 4 + (1 - \pi)12 = 12 - 8\pi$. This would mean that no feasible pooling contract is preferred by *L*-types to B^L. So, let's find the basket on

$$\pi x + (1 - \pi)y = 12 - 8\pi$$

that maximizes u_L. Solving the equation for *y* yields $y = (12 - 8\pi)/(1 - \pi) - x\pi/(1 - \pi)$. Then $dy/dx = -\pi/(1 - \pi)$. Set

$$V(x) = \tfrac{1}{4} \ln(x + 1) + \tfrac{3}{4} \ln(y + 1),$$

treating *y* as the linear function of *x* that we have just derived from the budget line. We have

$$V'(x) = \tfrac{1}{4}(x + 1)^{-1} + [\tfrac{3}{4}(y + 1)^{-1}] \times [-\pi/(1 - \pi)].$$

Confirm that $V''(x) < 0$ for all $x \geq 0$. If we set $V'(x) = 0$ we have

$$3\pi(x + 1) = (y + 1)(1 - \pi).$$

Now substitute $y = (12 - 8\pi)/(1 - \pi) - x\pi/(1 - \pi)$ into this equation and solve for *x*. We get $x = 3.25/\pi - 3$, and hence $y = (12 - 8\pi)/(1 - \pi) - (3.25/\pi - 3)\pi/(1 - \pi) = (8.75 - 5\pi)/(1 - \pi)$. These two values are functions of π, so we can state

$$x(\pi) = 3.25/\pi - 3, \quad \text{and} \quad y(\pi) = (8.75 - 5\pi)/(1 - \pi).$$

Recall that $u_L(B_L) = 2.36169$. We want $\tfrac{1}{4} \ln(x + 1) + \tfrac{3}{4} \ln(y + 1) < 2.36169$ for $x = x(\pi)$ and $y = y(\pi)$. That would ensure that $u_L(B^L)$ is higher than the utility of any basket satisfying the zero profit condition for the community as a whole. Try $\pi = 0.4$, which is close to $\pi_H = 0.5$. Confirm that

$$x(0.4) = 5.125 \quad \text{and} \quad y(0.4) = 11.25.$$

But $u_L(5.125, 11.25) = \tfrac{1}{4} \ln(6.125) + \tfrac{3}{4} \ln(12.25) = 2.3322$, which is less than $u_L(B^L)$, as desired. Now, $\pi \geq 0.4$ implies

$$(2n_H + n_L)/(4n_H + 4n_L) \geq 0.4$$

and hence $n_H \geq 1.5n_L$ is *sufficient* for existence of equilibrium. If for example, $n_L = K$ and $n_H = 2K$, an equilibrium exists, and it will be the one that gives each H the basket P^H and each L the basket B^L.

Let's see if we can find conditions under which the competitive equilibrium is inefficient. Set $S^L = (7, 10.8)$. That is, suppose that the government offers a contract that results in $x = 7$ and $y = 10.8$. If we set $x = 7$ in equation [2] and then solve for y we get $y = 11$. That is, $x = 7$ and $y = 11$ satisfies [8], the zero profit condition for L-types. Therefore, if L-types consume $x = 7$ and $y = 10.8$ they generate a surplus that can be used to subsidize the H-types. Are the L-types better off with S^L than with B^L? We have $u_L(B^L) = 2.36169$ and $u_L(S^L) = 2.37$, so the answer is "yes." What would it take to make the H-types better off than they would be with P^H? If we set $S^H = (8, 10)$ then we certainly have $u_H(P^H) < u_H(S^H)$ because S^H provides the same amount of x as P^H and provides 2 more units of y. But that also means that S^H is above the line representing equation [9]. In other words, S^H operates at a loss, and that will have to be covered by the surplus from S^L. If n_H is sufficiently small relative to n^L then no matter how small the per capita surplus from S^L it will cover the deficit from S^H. It remains to show that $u_H(S^H) > u_H(S^L)$ and that $u_L(S^L) > u_L(S^H)$. We have $u_H(S^H) = 2.2976 > 2.2738 = u_H(S^L)$ and $u_L(S^L) = 2.37 > 2.348 = u_L(S^H)$.

This example is unsatisfactory in one respect. It is clear that (S^L, S^H) leaves everyone better off than (B^L, P^H), and that the former is feasible if n_H is sufficiently small. But if n_H is very small (B^L, P^H) may not even be a competitive equilibrium.

Suggestions for further reading: Hirshleifer and Riley (1992).

Exercises

1   In section 10.2 we proved that a particular type will not purchase two distinct contracts in equilibrium. Prove that if each of $P^1, P^2, \ldots, P^K$ is purchased by at least one member of the risk group in equilibrium then $P^1 = P^2 = \ldots = P^K$.

2   Prove that if the expected profit per policyholder is the same for P^1 and P^2 then the expected profit per policy of $\frac{1}{2}P^1 + \frac{1}{2}P^2$ is identical to P^1's expected profit per policy.

3   Explain why

$$\pi = \frac{\pi_H \times n_H + \pi_L \times n_L}{n_H + n_L}$$

is the probability that an individual randomly selected from the entire population will have an accident.

4   Why don't we have to impose a participation constraint when analyzing the
        competitive insurance market? (*Hint:* Show that L's expected utility in-
        creases as we move along [2] and away from the endowment point, and
        similarly for H and [3].)

5   There are two types of individuals, and there are equal numbers of each
        type. The probability that one type has an accident is 0.10, and the proba-
        bility is 0.40 for the other type. Each individual has the utility-of-wealth
        function $\sqrt{w}$, where w is wealth. If an individual has an accident her wealth
        is 1000, but if there is no accident then wealth is 2000. This is true of either
        type.

   a   What is each type's expected utility function? Write down the competi-
        tive insurance provider's zero profit condition for a society consisting
        only of individuals with the probability of accident of 0.10. Write down
        the zero profit condition for a society consisting only of individuals with
        the probability of accident of 0.40. Now, give the zero profit condition
        for a competitive insurance market that offers everyone, regardless of
        type, the same contract.

   b   Find the full information competitive equilibrium. State the expected
        utility of each individual at equilibrium and the expected profit of the
        insurance companies.

   c   Determine the pooling contract P° for which $x = y$. Now find a new
        contract P that would provide positive expected profit for any firm offer-
        ing it if only P° were initially available. Show that the individuals pur-
        chasing P would have more utility than with P°. Calculate the expected
        profit for the firm selling P.

   d   Identify the competitive equilibrium. Calculate the expected utility of an
        individual of each type, and calculate a firm's expected profit. Explain
        why the equilibrium really is an equilibrium.

        Hint: Compare the expected utility at the endowment point with ex-
        pected utility at equilibrium for the relevant type. Now, starting at the
        endowment point, show that this type's expected utility falls as y in-
        creases. If you have to solve an equation of the form

$$ay + b\sqrt{y} + c = 0$$

        set $z = \sqrt{y}$ and $z^2 = y$ and use the formula for solving a quadratic
        equation:

$$z = \frac{-b \pm [b^2 - 4ac]^{1/2}}{2a}.$$

6   Show that at the separating equilibrium u_L increases as π_H falls.

7   Find the point in the derivation of the competitive equilibrium at which we

use the assumption that the two types have the same utility-of-wealth function. How would the argument be modified to handle the general case?

8   Each of n individuals has utility-of-wealth function $U(w) = 50w - w^2$. Let x represent wealth if there is an accident and let y denote wealth if there is no accident. If the individual buys no insurance then $x = 10$ and $y = 20$. (The utility derived from leisure is not needed for this question because we will assume that there is no opportunity for the individual to affect the probability of an accident by taking preventive care.)

a Is the individual risk averse? Explain.

b Show that when the odds are fair and the individual is risk averse she will set $x = y$. You may use a general argument, or the utility-of-wealth function $U(w) = 50w - w^2$.

c Find the competitive equilibrium insurance contract assuming that everyone has a probability of accident of 0.10. You may represent a contract as a combination of x or y, or in terms of the premium and net coverage. It's up to you, but expressing the contract in terms of x and y is probably easier.

d Find the competitive equilibrium insurance contract assuming that everyone has a probability of accident of 0.20.

e By means of a diagram, identify the competitive equilibrium when some individuals have a probability of accident of 0.10 and some have a probability of accident of 0.20. It is not necessary to calculate the equilibrium in this case – a diagrammatic analysis will suffice.

4

Reputation

A short-run decision can affect a firm or individual's long-run reputation, and that makes it easier to devise incentives under which the pursuit of narrow self-interest is socially optimal, or nearly so. In this chapter we study the effect of reputation on behavior by means of a few simple models. Therefore, we add a time dimension – something that is missing in the other chapters. However, the new models don't take us very far or very deep, compared to our informal, intuitive understanding of the role of reputation, based on observations. In part, this is because the notion of equilibrium in this setting has not been given a firm foundation – a firm foundation may not even be possible. Moreover, the situations that we are trying to model are very complex. We'll learn as much as we can from a few simple models that focus on the emergence of cooperation when competitors face each other in a *series* of confrontations. We will see that it is *possible* for cooperation to emerge in these settings even though a single encounter would produce self-defeating behavior, as in the prisoner's dilemma game. Only one of the models has a hidden characteristic element. Some economists reserve the term "reputation" for situations in which there is a hidden characteristic, and one or more players have something to learn about the type (characteristic) of other players. However, reputation effects are important in most situations in which the rivals know that they will face each other repeatedly, under similar conditions, and may live to regret actions that enhance their utility in the short run at great cost to their rivals. A player's reputation is simply the record of his or her performance in the past. We look at reputation informally in the next two sections before going on to a technical treatment.

1 Competition and reputation

The producer of a commodity has two sets of rivals. The obvious group consists of the other producers, but in a market economy consumers are also the firm's adversaries in the sense that the producer has an incentive to increase profit by misleading its customers – about product quality, in particular. Product quality has many dimensions – durability, versatility, performance, operating cost, maintenance cost – and there are many opportunities for the unscrupulous manufacturer to reduce cost by sacrificing quality while keeping up a good appearance. In a command economy, where profit maximization may not be firms' chief goal, the workers in a production plant can still gain by misleading consumers about quality because their task is easier if they do not have to maintain high quality.

What prevents a producer from succumbing to the temptation to gain at the expense of consumers? Regulation by a government agency sometimes plays an important role, even in a market economy. Far more important, typically, is the discipline of competition under capitalism. Modern technology requires a heavy initial capital outlay for the production of most goods and services. Competition among the owners of capital keeps the rate of return on capital low enough so that the initial expenditure can be recovered only after many (or at least several) years of sustained production and sales. Therefore, the firm is not just interested in profit now. High current profit will lead to heavy losses in the future, if present profits rest on duplicity which is discovered and broadcast to consumers by word of mouth, by consumer research firms, and by the media. When consumers have the option of buying from a firm's competitors, the temptation to sacrifice both consumer welfare and the firm's future is held in check to a great extent. Warranties also play a role. If other firms provide a comprehensive warranty in equilibrium, then firm X must do the same to stay afloat. If X were to deceive customers by manufacturing low-quality items and passing them off as high-quality products, then X would suffer heavy losses in the future as items were returned for replacement or repair under the warranty.

In some cases it is not easy to discover that the consumer has been misled. Consider housing construction. Defects may not show up for years, but when they do they can be extremely costly – wiring that causes fires, leaky roofs, etc. It will be very difficult for consumers to determine that construction company X produces houses that are more defect prone than those of other firms.[1] And warranties won't work well here. A meaningful warranty would have to be long lived, but that presents the construction firm with a hidden information problem. Warranties remain in force as long as the consumer undertakes routine maintenance. This is easy to monitor in the case of new cars, which can be taken back to the dealer for periodic inspections, but is very difficult in the case of new houses. More significant is the fact that it becomes harder to define "routine maintenance" the more time has elapsed since purchase. And if routine maintenance can't be specified, contracts cannot be written that are conditional on routine maintenance. But if the homeowner is not penalized for failure to keep the house in good repair then she has no incentive to exercise preventive care. A serious moral hazard problem prevents warranties from being offered. But for a wide range of goods and services, competition among producers forces the individual firm to be concerned with its *reputation*.[2] It is the lack of competition in the manufacture of appliances in the former Soviet Union that accounts for the explosion of thousands of television sets per year in Russia. (See Milgrom and Roberts, 1992, p. 13.)

Competition and reputation also have an important role to play in the political realm, of course. One reason why pollution reached grim proportions in Eastern Europe[3] by 1990 is that the lack of political competition made it relatively easy for ministers responsible for the environment to conceal problems and thus minimize the probability of being sacked. Politicians in multiparty, democratic countries also have an incentive to cover up, but political rivals and a competitive press make it much more difficult to escape detection. "It is significant that no democratic country with a relatively free press has ever experienced a major famine. . . . This generalization applies to poor democracies as well as to rich ones" (Sen, 1993, p. 43). A. K. Sen has demonstrated that even in severe famines there is enough food to sustain the entire population of the affected region, and that leaders who must seek reelection are far more likely to take the steps necessary to see that food is appropriately distributed (Sen, 1981; see also Drèze and Sen, 1989). The incentives confronting political leaders have life and death consequences for millions.

2 Basketball is a zero-sum game; so is football

Competition increases social welfare, as Adam Smith so cogently demonstrated. It is easy to cite examples. Competition among pharmaceutical companies leads to improved drugs and vaccines. Competition among medical researchers in nonprofit institutions[4] leads to breakthroughs that conquer disease. Competition among construction companies fosters the use of better quality materials at lower prices. Competition among automobile manufacturers leads to safety innovations. And so on. Enormous secular increases in output per worker, and thus in consumption per capita, can be attributed to individual firms striving to gain at the expense of their rivals by improving production techniques to reduce costs and hence prices, or to enhance product quality.[5] What about competition in organized sports? This brief section will assess the efficiency of existing incentives, rather than evaluate the response to incentives of the various players in our drama.

Many who follow competitive team sports care about more than just the win–loss record of a favorite team, but to the extent that a team's supporters do care only about the win–loss record, competition that increases coaching and scouting input and increases the time spent by athletes in training leads to high social costs that bring no corresponding social benefit. It is easy to identify the social costs: Labor is diverted from other activities to coaching and recruiting, and the athlete's training time has a high opportunity cost. Why is there no offsetting social benefit? Because for every victory there is a loss, and the win–loss ratio for the economy as a whole remains at 1. This is one of the few universal constants in economics.

In fact, competition that increases coaching and training costs generates some social benefit. Spectators care about the quality of the performance, in addition to their team's win–loss record. Increases in coaching and training input provide more thrilling athletic exploits.[6] But this also raises our expectations; it is not clear that spectators enjoy the contests more than in an earlier era when the performers were less well trained and coached.

As long as a high portion of the benefit derives from the win–loss record[7] of the spectator's team, the socially optimal amount of training and coaching will be much lower than the competitive outcome. But the socially optimal amount of input is very unstable. Given that a team's supporters care about the win–loss record, the individual team can benefit from increased coaching input and increases in the quality of its athletes, *given the input of its rivals*. This directly increases coaching input and creates a demand for better trained athletes. Therefore, coaching and training input increases substantially over time. To the extent that this gives a team an edge, its efforts will be matched by its rivals and all teams will increase coaching input and training demands. But the overall win–loss record will not change, even though the social costs will be substantial: We have another example of the prisoner's dilemma phenomenon. (An arms race is a good analogy.)

The training of professional athletes is intimately connected with high school and college athletic programs, especially in the case of basketball and football. The cost of training is not just the forgone present income. In far too many cases, the main cost is the lost opportunity for an education that would transform the student's life – materially and otherwise. (Athletic scholarships give many an opportunity to attend university, and many of these individuals make good use of the academic opportunity. This is to be counted on the benefit side, although one must be careful to determine if there is a *net* social benefit, as opposed to a redistribution of opportunities from one group to another.) In most cases, the time spent in athletic training pays off for only a few years, if at all. And if all athletes simultaneously reduced training costs there would be a substantial saving, with little or no reduction in benefit to society. This is not to say that competitive team sport provides little benefit to society: The benefit may be enormous. The argument here is that, given the matrix of teams, the payoff to *additional* training and coaching is very low although the social costs are very high. And there is very

Table 1

D	E	F	H	I	J
H	I	H	E	D	F
I	J	J	F	E	E
J	H	I	D	F	D

little that an individual university can do about the costs if it wants competitive sports teams. What can universities do collectively? The commission of NCAA university presidents has not been very successful in containing costs, or even agreeing on cost containment policy. (See Thelin and Wiseman, 1989, p. 73.) One important step would be to reduce recruiting costs by using the formula employed for decades by the medical community in matching interns and hospitals. They employ a simple algorithm[8] based on submitted individual preference rankings of hospitals by doctors and of doctors by hospitals. The algorithm has an important stability property: When the assignment is complete one cannot find a pair consisting of a hospital H and an intern D such that H would prefer D to the intern actually assigned to H, and D would rather work at H than at the hospital to which she was assigned. Here's how it works: We employ a simple example with three doctors, D, E, and F, and three hospitals H, I, and J. Table 1 gives the preference rankings.

Physician D prefers hospital H to the other two, and ranks I second. The columns for E and F are interpreted similarly. Hospital H ranks doctor E first and then F and then D. And so on. The algorithm that was tried first begins by searching for a hospital–intern pair such that each gives the other first place rank. There are no such pairs for Table 1, so we proceed to the second stage in which we search for a hospital that ranks a doctor second when that same doctor ranks that hospital first. There are two matches: E and I, and F and H. Then doctor E is assigned to hospital I, and F is assigned to H. By default J and D are paired. But hospital J is D's last choice. D would have fared better to have (untruthfully) ranked I in first place. Because this algorithm sometimes gives a physician incentive to misrepresent his or her first choice of hospital, it was revised in 1951. The rule that has been used since that time begins by searching for a hospital–intern pair for which each ranks the other first, as before. Again, there are no such pairs, but this time the algorithm searches for a match between a *hospital's* first choice and a *student's* second choice. The two matches this time are D and I, and F and J. These assignments are made, leaving E and H to be paired by default. Verify that none of the doctors has an incentive to misrepresent his or her first choice. And note that there is no hospital–intern pair that could upset the assignment by striking a mutually advantageous contract, with each preferring its new partner to the one assigned by the algorithm. (The algorithm can handle any number of participants.) Now, let's return to the issue of recruitment of athletes by universities.

How would high school athletes obtain information about college scholastic and athletic programs if this algorithm were employed? College guides are already widely used as a source of academic and social information; a similar guide could be produced for athletes. It could provide a lot of information, but there might be less available than with present recruiting methods. Nevertheless, the expenditure of resources on information transmission would be closer to the social optimum with the guides substituting for on-site visits. University coaches would obtain information about high school athletes from statistical summaries only, eliminating personal visits from recruiters. After all, we manage to turn out doctors, computer scientists, professors, etc., without a visit from university recruiters to students' homes, in spite of the fact that universities compete for good scholars. Colleges rely on statistical digests and resumés and students rely on college guides.[9] And remember, more intensive recruiting would not provide any productivity gains to the economy – the nationwide win–loss ratio is going to be 1 whatever anyone does. (Heavy recruiting input does generate a small gain to society if it produces better matches between schools and athletes. But it is not clear why this justifies costly recruiting in sports but not in academics.)

The use of the hospital–intern algorithm as a substitute for present recruiting methods requires monitoring, to eliminate on-site recruiting by coaches. But monitoring is already carried out by the NCAA, which has a long list of proscribed recruiting practices.

I'm not saying that competition on the playing field has no social value. The intense battle on the field is the ultimate source of the enjoyment of spectators, in spite of the emphasis on a team's win–loss record. It's the competition off the field that is the problem. In particular, the extreme input of time by athletes is socially costly. The system is often defended as an avenue of escape from poverty; and many scholarship athletes have used this escape route. But it's the cost of paving the highway to which I take exception. We would not endorse a policy of awarding college scholarships to students who spent 20 hours per week sitting on a flagpole during their high school careers. Encouraging young people to concentrate on the acquisition of skills that will be valued *if at all* for only a few years is a bad way of addressing the problem of poverty. (Some individuals turn the intensive training effort into an extremely lucrative professional career, but most of their income is rent that does not reflect a net contribution to social welfare. Anyway, the point here is not that individuals are responding inappropriately to incentives, but that the incentives invite inefficiency.)

Exercises

1   For the algorithm that has been used since 1951 to match interns and
     hospitals, prove that a physician never has incentive to rank her true most-
     preferred hospital lower than first.

2   Explain why your answer to the previous question does not contradict
     the Gibbard–Satterthwaite theorem. (See section 3 of Chapter 3 and Chap-
     ter 7.)

3 Subgame-perfect equilibria

Nash equilibrium has served us well to this point, but we need a more sophisticated notion of equilibrium for studying the effect of reputation. In particular, we
need to disqualify equilibria that are sustained by incredible threats, and to do that
we must go back to the beginning.

A *strategy* is much more intricate than an *action*. "Steal second base now" is a
simple instruction in a baseball game, and the attempted theft is the action. But a
strategy specifies an act as a function of every act made by every participant in the
game up to the present stage of the game. "Attempt a theft of second base if we
haven't reached the fifth inning, or if it is late in the game and we are behind by
two or more runs, provided that the batter has less than two strikes and the
probability of a pitch-out is less than 0.25, etc." is a strategy. We could specify a
single strategy for the manager of a baseball game for the entire game. It would
prescribe an act for each player (on the manager's side) for every situation that
could arise. Each act would be specified as a function of the history of the game to
that point; different histories would typically require different acts in a given
inning. Give a name, say S_1, to the strategy employed by the manager of team 1.
If we let S_2 denote the strategy chosen by team 2's manager then the pair (S_1, S_2)
uniquely determines the outcome of the game. If we display the payoffs awarded
to player 1 as a function of the strategies chosen by 1 and 2, and similarly for
player 2, we have what is called the *normal form* representation of the game.
There may be many points in the game at which a strategy calls for an act to be
selected randomly by means of a given probability distribution over a given set of
acts. Then the outcome will be random and the payoffs are expressed as expected
utilities. Uncertainty may even be *imposed* on the two players – the arrival of rain
during a ballgame, for example. Here, again, we will have to express the payoff to
a player as an expected utility, but we nonetheless have a single number as the
payoff. Therefore, the normal form payoffs are simply expressed as functions
$U_1(S_1, S_2)$ and $U_2(S_1, S_2)$ of the chosen strategies S_1 and S_2, for players 1 and 2
respectively. A *Nash equilibrium* is a pair of strategies (S_1, S_2) such that $U_1(S_1,$

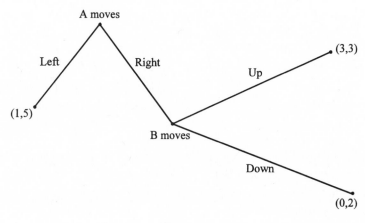

Figure 1

$S_2) \geq U_1(T_1, S_2)$ for every strategy T_1 available to person 1, and $U_2(S_1, S_2) \geq$ $U_2(S_1, T_2)$ for every strategy T_2 available to 2. We say that S_1 is a best response to S_2, and S_2 is a best response to S_1. It is helpful to think of the respective strategies S_1 and S_2 as being chosen simultaneously and submitted to a referee who then computes the outcome and assigns payoffs according to the rules of the game.

An *extensive* form representation of the game has much more structure than the normal form. The extensive form provides information about the sequences of moves – whose turn it is to move at each stage and what choices that person has. Consider, for example, the tree representation of an extensive form game in Figure 1. At the first stage player A has a choice of moving left or right. If A moves left the game is over and A receives 1 dollar and B receives 5 dollars. If player A moves right at the first stage then player B has the next move and can go up or down. If B chooses up, then each gets 3 dollars, but if B moves down, then A receives zero and B receives 2 dollars. Consider the normal form representation of the same game (Table 2). $R \to U$ represents the strategy "B moves Up if A has opened by moving Right," and $R \to D$ represents "B moves Down if A opened by moving Right." There are two Nash equilibria here: (Right, $R \to U$) and (Left, $R \to D$). The latter is not very plausible, however. It rests on B's threat to move down if A moves right. The Nash equilibrium pair of strategies (Left, $R \to D$) is properly identified this way: A announces his intention to move left whatever B proposes to do should B get a chance to move, and B announces his intention to move Down if A moves Right. If A believes that B is really committed to Down if B gets a chance to move, then Left is the rational choice for A: Left gives A a payoff of 1, but A gets zero if he moves right and B *carries out his threat* to move down. However, B's threat is not credible. If B *does* get a chance to move it will

Table 2

		S_B	
		$R \rightarrow U$	$R \rightarrow D$
S_A	Left	(1, 5)	(1, 5)
	Right	(3, 3)	(0, 2)

come after A's move and thus it can have no impact on A's choice. Therefore, the payoff maximizing move for B is Up, yielding a payoff of 3 instead of 2. A Nash equilibrium that does not depend on an incredible threat is termed a *subgame-perfect Nash equilibrium*. The word "subgame" refers to the game that would be defined if we were to begin play at some advanced stage of the game. The players are assumed to choose rationally. In the above example moving up is the only rational response for B at the second stage, so a threat to move down is not credible. The only subgame-perfect Nash equilibrium is (Right, $R \rightarrow U$).

Formally, a subgame of an extensive form game is a game obtained by separating the tree at one node and retaining only that node and all parts of the tree that can be reached from that node by going forward and not backward (in time). Figure 1 has five subgames, including the game itself: There are three trivial subgames corresponding to the three terminal nodes with respective payoff vectors (1, 5), (3, 3), (0, 2). The trivial subgames do not allow anyone to move, of course. There is only one proper and nontrivial subgame, obtained by eliminating the branches Left and Right. If the game itself includes moves in which the player moving is not perfectly certain of what has gone before, then a subgame must have an additional property: at the node N where the separation identifying the subgame occurs, any act A by the mover M (the player who moves at N) must be included in the subgame if there is *some* prior history of the game that would make A available to M *if* A is not ruled out by the information available to M at N. A subgame-perfect equilibrium is one that remains an equilibrium for all sub-games – with the equilibrium strategies amputated to fit the subgame. For *finite* games we locate such an equilibrium by backward induction: Begin with the proper subgames that are closest to a terminal node. In Figure 1, that would be the subgame beginning with B's move. Replace those subgames with their Nash equilibrium payoffs. For our example, we would have the game of Figure 2 below. For the proper subgame, B has a simple choice between Up, with a payoff of 3 to himself, and Down, which gives him a payoff of 2. He would choose Up, resulting in the payoff vector (3, 3). We replace the entire subgame with (3, 3), as illustrated in Figure 2. We continue by induction. Having reduced the size of the game by successively abbreviating the game by replacing subgames with their

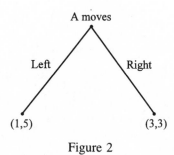

Figure 2

Nash equilibrium payoffs, we have a new game in which we identify the proper subgames that are closest to a terminal node of this new game. Then we replace those subgames with their Nash equilibrium payoffs. At some stage we will have reduced the game to one with a single move, as in Figure 2. The Nash equilibrium of that game gives us the subgame-perfect equilibrium of the original game. The unique Nash equilibrium of Figure 2 has A choosing Right in which she gets the higher payoff, 3 versus 1. Therefore, the unique subgame perfect equilibrium for the game of Figure 1 is (Right, $R \rightarrow U$).

Suggestions for further reading: Binmore (1992), Gibbons (1992), and Kreps (1990).

4 Partnerships

We reconsider the static model of section 5 of Chapter 2, this time allowing one partner to react to another partner who supplied less than the socially optimal amount of effort in a previous period. That is, we extend the model by allowing repeated play. This allows punishment of uncooperative behavior and conse-quently enlarges the set of outcomes that can emerge from the independent pursuit of self-interest. We begin by briefly reviewing the static model.

4.1 The static model

The two consumer goods are leisure and income, with x and y denoting the respective amounts consumed. The individuals have identical utility functions, $u(x, y) = xy$. Ω is an individual's time endowment – in plain words, the number of hours in one period. If e is the amount of effort contributed by an individual to the partnership enterprise, then $x = \Omega - e$. We assume two identical partners, so individual income y_h equals $\frac{1}{2}(y_1 + y_2)$, which in turn is a function of $e_1 + e_2$, the total effort contributed to the partnership. (The subscript identifies the individual.) Individual h chooses e_h to maximize $u(\Omega - e_h, \frac{1}{2}(y_1 + y_2))$. For convenience, we assume that each unit of effort results in one dollar of income to the partnership. Therefore

$$y_1 + y_2 = e_1 + e_2.$$

In the static model, individual 1 chooses e_1 to maximize

$$u(\Omega - e_1, \tfrac{1}{2}e_1 + \tfrac{1}{2}e_2) = (\Omega - e_1) \times (\tfrac{1}{2}e_1 + \tfrac{1}{2}e_2)$$

with e_2 treated as a constant – i.e., independent of 1's choice e_1. The first derivative of this function of e_1 is

$$\tfrac{1}{2}\Omega - \tfrac{1}{2}e_2 - e_1$$

and the second derivative is negative. The individuals are equal, so there will be a symmetric equilibrium with $e_1 = e_2$. Employing this equality after setting the first derivative equal to zero[10] yields $e_1 = e_2 = \tfrac{1}{3}\Omega$. But this is not the efficient effort level: The social cost of leisure in this model is 1. The consumption of one unit of leisure deprives the partnership of one dollar of income. But the partner consuming the leisure only loses half a dollar of income. In the static partnership model, the private cost of leisure is only half of the social cost, so from an efficiency standpoint there is overconsumption of leisure; equivalently, there is an undersupply of effort.

To determine the optimal symmetric outcome we set the marginal rate of substitution (MRS) equal to the *social* opportunity cost of leisure (unity). If $u = xy$ then the MRS is y/x. Therefore, $y/x = 1$ (or $y = x$) at an efficient outcome. And $y_1 + y_2 = \Omega - x_1 + \Omega - x_2$. If $y_1 = y_2$ and $x_1 = x_2$ then $y = x$ implies $x_1 = \tfrac{1}{2}\Omega = x_2$ and hence $e_1 = \tfrac{1}{2}\Omega = e_2$. It is easy to confirm that this outcome gives each individual more utility than the partnership equilibrium: From now on we set $\Omega = 24$ (a day). At the partnership equilibrium $e_h = 8$, $x_h = 16$, and $y_h = 8$. Therefore, individual utility is $16 \times 8 = 128$. But when $e_h = 12$, $x_h = 12$, and $y_h = 12$, individual utility is $12 \times 12 = 144$.

4.2 Dynamic analysis

There is an infinite number of periods, $1, 2, \ldots, t, \ldots$. Individuals care about lifetime consumption, and we represent their preferences by discounting the sum of the single period utilities. When making plans for the future in period 1, the utility that will be realized by the decision maker in period $t + 1$ is discounted by the factor δ^t. We simplify by assuming the same discount factor for each player. For example, $\delta = (1 + r)^{-1}$ where r is the rate of interest. This will give us $0 < \delta < 1$, which we assume whether or not δ is derived from the interest rate. Because $\delta < 1$, the discount factor will be close to zero if t is very large. This allows us to work with an infinite horizon – periods that are very remote will get almost no weight in the decision. If u^t is period t's utility, then the individual maximizes

$$u^1 + \delta u^2 + \delta^2 u^3 + \ldots + \delta^t u^{t+1} + \ldots$$

which we denote by $\Sigma \, \delta^t u^{t+1}$.

Here is an equilibrium pair of strategies for the partnership game that will induce both players to choose the cooperative outcome $e_h = 12$ each period: If player 1 deviates from $e_1 = 12$ in period t then player 2 will respond by playing $e_2 = 8$ in period $t + 1$ and in every period thereafter. Partner 1 makes the same threat to partner 2. But as long as partner h continues to set $e_h = 12$ the other partner will do the same. Let's see if this pair of strategies constitutes an equilibrium in which each chooses to play cooperatively ($e_h = 12$) each period.

With $e_1 = e_2 = 12$ each period we have $x_h = 12$ and $y_h = 12$, and individual utility is 144 each period. Then[11]

$$\Sigma \, \delta^t \, u^{t+1} = \Sigma \, \delta^t \, 144 = 144/(1 - \delta).$$

Now, suppose that player 1 deviates from cooperative play in period 1. What's the highest utility that 1 can achieve in period 1 given that $e_2 = 12$ in period 1? Choose e_1 to maximize $u = xy = (24 - e_1) \times (\tfrac{1}{2}e_1 + \tfrac{1}{2} \times 12)$. The first derivative is $12 - 6 - e_1$, which we equate to zero, so $e_1 = 6$ is our solution. Therefore, $x_1 = 18$, $y_1 + y_2 = 6 + 12$, and thus $y_1 = y_2 = 9$. Person 1's first period utility would be $18 \times 9 = 162$. *If* partner 1 sets $e_1 = 6$ in period 1 then the other partner will set $e_2 = 8$ in every subsequent period. We know from our analysis of the static case that the highest one-period utility for partner 1 is obtained by setting $e_1 = 8$ when $e_2 = 8$, in which case $u = 16 \times 8 = 128$. Therefore, if partner 1 deviates from cooperative play in period 1 her lifetime utility will be no greater than

$$162 + 128\delta + 128\delta^2 + \ldots + 128\delta^t + \ldots = 162 + 128\delta/(1 - \delta).$$

When is a period 1 deviation profitable for player 1? If and only if

$$162 + 128\delta/(1 - \delta) > 144/(1 - \delta)$$

and this will hold if and only if $\delta < 18/34$. If $\delta = (1 + r)^{-1}$ we would have to have $r > 16/18$ for a deviation to be profitable. Deviation from the cooperative strategy can pay off only when the interest rate is greater than 88 percent. So, if the discount rate δ is not too low, the discounted sum of utilities is higher when the individual does not deviate from cooperative play in the first period. What about a deviation in a subsequent period, say period T? Let's compute the utility from period T on when person 1 continues to play cooperatively, and also when 1 sets $e_1 = 6$ in period T. It is easy to see that in each case the discounted sum of utilities *from period* T *and beyond* is just δ^{T-1} times the corresponding discounted sum for $T = 1$. We reach the same conclusion: deviation will be profitable only for extraordinarily low discount rates. The cooperative outcome can be sustained if the partnership lasts many periods and the partners are not too impatient. We have not established that our Nash equilibrium strategies are subgame perfect. This is done at the end of section 6.2 for all such equilibria of repeated games.

4.3 Limitations

Why is the partnership method of organizing production not more widely used? Why is its use essentially confined to the provision of expert consulting and treatment services? There are at least two reasons for exercising caution in using the analysis of the preceding section to conclude that the partnership arrangement is an effective way of organizing teamwork. First, we proved that the cooperative outcome is *an* equilibrium in a multiperiod model. But there are many equilibria – an infinite number, in fact. The various outcomes can be sustained by means of a *trigger strategy*[12] similar to the one set out in the previous section: Any deviation from prescribed play by one partner induces the other to pull the trigger – i.e., punish the deviating partner. When will this be possible? It is clear from the analysis of the trigger strategy equilibrium of the previous section that the fact that $e_1 = 12 = e_2$ is efficient plays no role. As long as we have $u(24 - e_1, \frac{1}{2}e_1 + \frac{1}{2}e_2)$ $> 128 = u(16, 8)$ and $u(24 - e_2, \frac{1}{2}e_1 + \frac{1}{2}e_2) > 128 = u(16, 8)$ and $\delta < 1$ is sufficiently close to 1 we will have an equilibrium with the trigger strategy that has 1 playing e_1 and 2 playing e_2 each period until one partner deviates and then the other contributing 8 units of effort every period thereafter. Section 6 proves a general version of this result, first proved by Friedman (1971) for subgame-perfect Nash equilibria.

A second reason why the analysis of section 4.2 should be applied with great care is that we have assumed that each partner can observe the effort supplied by the other in the previous period. However, partnerships tend to be used in areas where monitoring is very costly. (If you were a member of a law firm, how would you determine if a partner were putting in the appropriate amount of effort on a case to which she was assigned?) All we have to do to get around this problem is to make the period long enough so that complaints of clients would get back to the firm. This does not provide complete information on a partner's effort level, but it is easier to accept that a partner could learn about the effort that his partners supplied in previous periods than to accept that one knows how much effort a partner is currently supplying.

Suggestions for further reading: Radner (1991).

Exercises

1   Work out the efficient symmetric outcome and the static equilibrium for the model of section 4.1, but with $u(x, y) = 8\sqrt{x} + y$ for each partner and $\Omega =$

24. Be sure that each solution respects the constraint $0 \leq x \leq 24$. Does the equilibrium reflect any real life situations in which you choose not to team up with a classmate for study purposes, even though teamwork is potentially more profitable?

2   Each partner has the utility function $u(x, y) = xy$, and each has the time endowment $\Omega = 24$. Consider the following the trigger strategy: Each partner supplies $e_i = 10$ each period until one partner deviates from this, and then the other contributes 8 units of effort every period thereafter. Find a condition on δ that guarantees that this strategy pair is a subgame-perfect Nash equilibrium.

3   Each partner has the utility function $u(x, y) = xy$, and each has the time endowment $\Omega = 24$. Let e_1 and e_2 be two effort levels such that $u(24 - e_1, \frac{1}{2}e_1 + \frac{1}{2}e_2) > 128 = u(16, 8)$ and $u(24 - e_2, \frac{1}{2}e_1 + \frac{1}{2}e_2) > 128 = u(16, 8)$. Find a condition on δ that guarantees that the trigger strategy that has 1 playing e_1 and 2 playing e_2 each period until one partner deviates, at which point the other "pulls the trigger" by contributing 8 units of effort every period thereafter, is a subgame-perfect Nash equilibrium.

5 The repeated prisoner's dilemma game

We briefly review the static (one shot) version of the prisoner's dilemma game discussed in Chapter 1. Each player wants to maximize his payoff, which is a function of his action and that of the other player. Each chooses whether to cooperate or to defect without knowing what the other has decided. The payoff for each of the four possible combinations of strategies is given in Table 3. The first number of each pair is A's payoff and the second number is B's payoff. When B cooperates then A can get \$20 by cooperating but \$30 by defecting. When B defects then A can get \$1 by cooperating and \$5 by defecting. In either case A's payoff A is higher when he defects, and similarly for B; defecting is a dominant strategy for each player. The incentive to defect is irresistible when the game is played only once. Now we consider the prospects for the emergence of cooperative play when the game is repeated a large number of times by the same two players.

We have to distinguish between a strategy and an action. In any period t a player has only two possible actions: cooperate or defect. A strategy for player A is a plan of action in each period as a function of the previous history of the game. A strategy allows a player to make his current action depend on what the opponent did in the previous period, or periods, *and to announce that fact*. We are still not assuming the possibility of binding agreements, however, so for an announcement to be credible it has to serve the interest of the person making it. We capture this

Table 3

		B's action	
		Cooperate	Defect
A's action	Cooperate	(20, 20)	(1, 30)
	Defect	(30, 1)	(5, 5)

by insisting that an equilibrium pair of strategies be subgame-perfect. First we assume an infinite horizon.

5.1 The infinitely repeated game

A and B simultaneously and independently choose whether to cooperate or defect in each of an infinite number of periods 1, 2, . . . , t, ... A's preferences are captured by the discounted sum of her payoff each period; period t's payoff is discounted by the factor δ^{t-1}. (Simplify by assuming the same discount factor δ for each.) If $\delta = (1 + r)^{-1}$ and r is the rate of interest then $0 < \delta < 1$, which we assume whether or not δ is derived from the interest rate. Because $\delta < 1$, the discount factor will be close to zero if t is very large; similarly for B. If both players cooperate each period, the payoff of each will be

$$\Sigma \, \delta^t u^{t+1} = 20 + \delta \, 20 + \delta^2 \, 20 + \delta^3 \, 20 + \ldots = 20/(1 - \delta).$$

One equilibrium pair of strategies that induces universal cooperation when δ is sufficiently close to 1 has each person cooperating in the first period and cooperating every period thereafter as long as his opponent cooperated in the previous period. If a player defects in period t then the opponent defects every period from $t + 1$ on. Do we have an equilibrium? Suppose that player A cooperates in periods 1, 2, . . . , $t - 1$, and defects in period t. According to the specification of the trigger strategy, B cooperates up to and during period t and defects every period thereafter. Now, compare A's payoffs discounted to period t from the trigger strategy and from the deviation. The deviation produces a payoff of 30 in period t and 5 in every subsequent period. Treating period t as "now," the discounted stream of payoffs, 30, 5, 5, . . . , 5, . . . is

$$30 + \delta \, 5 + \delta^2 \, 5 + \delta^3 \, 5 + \ldots = 30 + 5 \, \delta/(1 - \delta).$$

The trigger strategy, which has A and B cooperating every period, yields a discounted payoff of $20/(1 - \delta)$. Deviation from this is profitable for A if and only if

$$30 + 5 \, \delta/(1 - \delta) > 20/(1 - \delta)$$

which is equivalent to $\delta < 0.4$. If $\delta = (1 + r)^{-1}$ this is equivalent to $r > 1.5$: Only when the interest rate is greater than 150% can it be profitable for a player to deviate from the trigger strategy, which induces cooperation in each period. The cooperative outcome can be sustained as long as the players are not too impatient. To complete the argument, we need to show that we have a subgame-perfect equilibrium when each player uses the trigger strategy. Rather than do this for the prisoner's dilemma game, we consider the general case in section 6, where we see that almost any outcome can be sustained as a subgame-perfect equilibrium. So, we have an embarrassment of riches. Cooperation can be sustained at equilibrium, but why would we expect that to emerge instead of any of the other equilibria?

Exercises

1   Let A's discount rate be 0.9 and let B's be 0.7. Find a condition guaranteeing that cooperation every period by both players is the outcome of a subgame-perfect Nash equilibrium.

2   Prove that the Nash equilibrium in which each player uses the trigger strategy is subgame-perfect.

5.2 Finitely repeated prisoner's dilemma and reputation[13]

We begin with a two-period repetition of the one-shot prisoner's dilemma game, which is this time represented in general form as Table 4. We have $\ell < d < c < h$, with $\ell + h < 2c$. The second inequality rules out the possibility that the players do better overall by alternating between ℓ and h than by both cooperating each period. To make the analysis more transparent we will not discount; we assume that each player wants to maximize the sum of the payoffs over the lifetime of the repeated game.

A and B both know that play will end after two rounds. In each period the players simultaneously and independently choose between defecting and cooperating, and payoffs are then awarded according to Table 4. This is repeated at the second and last stage. At the last stage both will defect. There is no further play and thus no opportunity for their choices to affect future payoffs. Knowing that both will inevitably defect at the last stage, independently of what has happened previously, there can be no advantage to anyone who cooperates at the previous stage. In particular, it will not induce the opponent to cooperate in the last round, so both will defect in round one. We see that repetition by itself cannot sustain cooperation if the number of periods is finite and known. Following Kreps, Milgrom, Roberts, and Wilson (1982) we change the game by supposing that player A is one of two types, but B does not know which type A actually is when play begins. There is a positive probability π that A is a cooperative type who can

Table 4

		B's action	
		Cooperate	Defect
A's action	Cooperate	(c, c)	(ℓ, h)
	Defect	(h, ℓ)	(d, d)

Table 5

Period 1		Period 2
Opponent	Player	Player
D	D	D
D	D	C
C	D	C
C	D	D
D	C	C
C	C	D
D	C	D
C	C	C

only play the *tit-for-tat* strategy. Tit-for-tat cooperates in the first period and for every subsequent period duplicates the move made by the opponent at the previous stage. In that case we say that A is type T. With probability $1 - \pi$ player A is "rational" (type R), which means that R can play any strategy and R knows that this is also true of B. These strategies are implicit in Table 5. The player (R or B) can condition his period 2 move on the choices made by each in period 1. Each has two choices in period 1 so there are four possible histories for the first period, and for each of these a player has two choices for period 2. The first four cases will not arise when the player is type T because T always begins by cooperating. The tit-for-tat strategy is represented by the last two lines with T as the player. What will R do in equilibrium? R could begin by cooperating to fool B into thinking that A is type T. But in a two-period model this will not avail. R knows that B will defect in period 2. Therefore, R will defect in both periods. T will cooperate in the first period and select X in the second period, where X is B's first period choice. It remains to determine B's first period move X.

There are two possibilities: $X =$ coop (cooperate) and $X =$ def't (defect); for each of these R's move is uniquely determined in each period and so is T's move in each period. Therefore, there are $2 \times 2 = 4$ cases, represented in Table 6. If B cooperates in period 1 his payoff is $\pi(c + h) + (1 - \pi)(\ell + d)$, but if he defects at the outset his payoff is $\pi(h + d) + (1 - \pi)(d + d)$. Cooperation in period 1

Table 6

	Period 1		Period 2			
	A	*B*	*A*	*B*	*B*'s payoff	Probability
T	Coop	Coop	Coop	Def't	$c + h$	π
R	Def't	Coop	Def't	Def't	$\ell + d$	$1 - \pi$
T	Coop	Def't	Def't	Def't	$h + d$	π
R	Def't	Def't	Def't	Def't	$d + d$	$1 - \pi$

leads to a higher payoff for *B* when $\pi(c + h) + (1 - \pi)(\ell + d) > \pi(h + d) + (1 - \pi)(d + d)$, and this reduces to

$$\pi > \frac{d - \ell}{c - \ell} \qquad [1]$$

Set $\pi° = (d - \ell)/(c - \ell)$. As long as $\pi > \pi°$ the equilibrium strategies are as follows:

T: tit-for-tat

R: defect each period, whatever *B* does

B: cooperate in the first period, then defect, whatever *A* does

If we take the derivative of $\pi°$ with respect to ℓ we find that it is negative. Why? Consider $\ell = d - \epsilon$, with ϵ positive but very small. Then $\pi°$ will be arbitrarily small. That is, if we make ℓ sufficiently close to d we only need a tiny probability that *A* is tit-for-tat to sustain *some* cooperation in equilibrium.[14] That's because the cost to *B* of cooperating in the first period against someone who defects is very small if ℓ is close to d.

Consider a three-period replication. Now it is conceivable that *R* will open by cooperating in order to build a reputation for cooperating and so induce *B* to cooperate. We know that *R* and *B* will both defect in the last period, so there is no value to *R* in cooperating beyond the first period. Either *R* will defect every period, or else *R* will cooperate in period 1 and defect in the other two periods. But if *R* defects on the first move *B* will know for sure that he is not playing against *T* and will thus defect in each of the last two periods (because he will know that *A* will defect in each of the last two stages).

Let's see if cooperation by *R* on the first move can be sustained as an equilibrium. At equilibrium, *B* can cooperate for one or two periods and then defect, or defect every period. (Why?) But there is one decision to be specified for *R* – the first period move. There are two possibilities, and for each of these there are four possible moves for *B* (we know that *B* will defect on the last round). Therefore, there are $2 \times 4 = 8$ cases to consider, and they appear as Tables 7–14. An even

Table 7

	1	2	3	Payoff
T	C	D	D	$\ell + d + d$
B	D	D	D	$h + d + d$
R	C	D	D	$\ell + d + d$
B	D	D	D	$h + d + d$

Table 8

	1	2	3	Payoff
T	C	D	D	$\ell + d + d$
B	D	D	D	$h + d + d$
R	D	D	D	$d + d + d$
B	D	D	D	$d + d + d$

Table 9

	1	2	3	Payoff
T	C	D	C	$\ell + h + \ell$
B	D	C	D	$h + \ell + h$
R	C	D	D	$\ell + h + d$
B	D	C	D	$h + \ell + d$

Table 10

	1	2	3	Payoff
T	C	D	C	$\ell + h + \ell$
B	D	C	D	$h + \ell + h$
R	D	D	D	$d + h + d$
B	D	C	D	$d + \ell + d$

Table 11

	1	2	3	Payoff
T	C	C	C	$c + c + \ell$
B	C	C	D	$c + c + h$
R	C	D	D	$c + h + d$
B	C	C	D	$c + \ell + d$

Table 12

	1	2	3	Payoff
T	C	C	C	$c + c + \ell$
B	C	C	D	$c + c + h$
R	D	D	D	$h + h + d$
B	C	C	D	$\ell + \ell + d$

Table 13

	1	2	3	Payoff
T	C	C	D	$c + \ell + d$
B	C	D	D	$c + h + d$
R	C	D	D	$c + d + d$
B	C	D	D	$c + d + d$

Table 14

	1	2	3	Payoff
T	C	C	D	$c + \ell + d$
B	C	D	D	$c + h + d$
R	D	D	D	$h + d + d$
B	C	D	D	$\ell + d + d$

Table 15

Deviation	B's payoff
From Table 7	$\pi(h + 2d) + (1 - \pi)(h + 2d) = h + 2d$
From Table 9	$\pi(2h + \ell) + (1 - \pi)(h + \ell + d) = h + \ell + \pi h + (1 - \pi)d$
From Table 11	$\pi(2c + h) + (1 - \pi)(c + \ell + d) = c + \pi(c + h) + (1 - \pi)(\ell + d)$
From Table 13	$\pi(c + h + d) + (1 - \pi)(c + 2d) = c + d + \pi h + (1 - \pi)d$

numbered table differs from the one on its left only with respect to R's first period move – and the associated payoffs. Now we work out conditions on π such that Table 11 is observed at equilibrium. The strategies underlying this table are as follows:

S_R R cooperates in the first period and defects in each of the other two periods, whatever B does.

S_T T cooperates in the first period and then imitates B's previous move in each of the subsequent periods.

S_B B cooperates in period 1 and defects in the other two periods if A defects in period 1; if A cooperates in the first period then B will cooperate in the second period and defect in the last period.

Will it be profitable for R to deviate from S_R? If R defects in period 1 then B will know in period 2 that A is type R and will defect in periods 2 and 3. Therefore, a deviation by R will take us to Table 14. This deviation will be profitable for R only if $h + d + d \geq c + h + d$, and that is equivalent to $d \geq c$, which we rule out by assumption ($c > d$ is required for this to be a prisoner's dilemma game).

Will B deviate from the strategy S_B set out above? Table 15 above gives B's payoff from the possible deviations when R cooperates in the first period and defects in the other two, regardless of what B does. (The third line represents zero deviation.)

We have $c + \pi(c + h) + (1 - \pi)(\ell + d) > h + 2d$ as long as

$$\pi > \frac{h + d - \ell - c}{h + c - \ell - d}. \qquad [2]$$

We have $c + \pi(c + h) + (1 - \pi)(\ell + d) > h + \ell + \pi h + (1 - \pi)d$ as long as

$$\pi > \frac{h - c}{c - \ell}. \qquad [3]$$

And we have $c + \pi(c + h) + (1 - \pi)(\ell + d) > c + d + \pi h + (1 - \pi)d$ as long as

$$\pi > \frac{d - \ell}{c - \ell}. \qquad [4]$$

Therefore, we have an equilibrium with cooperation in the early stages of the game (for one period by R and two periods by B) as long as [2], [3], and [4] hold. Notice that [4] is the condition for cooperation by B in the first period of a two-period game.

We have examined reputation as a motivation for behavior that promotes social welfare. Is R building a *false* reputation by cooperating on the first move? No. Defecting every period is consistent with rationality only when there is a finite number of repetitions with a known terminal date and R's opponent knows that he is rational. But if B doesn't know A's type then the optimal strategy for rational A will be affected. In the two-period model it is only B that cooperates at all (for one period). But as the three-period case shows, if B can be induced to cooperate – because of her uncertainty about A's type – then A has an incentive to build a reputation as a cooperative player, even if A is actually type R.

Let's apply conditions [2], [3], and [4] to the payoffs of Table 3. We get $\pi > 7/22$, $\pi > 10/19$, and $\pi > 4/19$. Therefore, B has to believe that the probability of A's being tit-for-tat is greater than $10/19$ to be induced to cooperate in the first two periods. However, as the number of repetitions increases the greater the long-run payoff to cooperative behavior, and hence smaller values of π will sustain cooperation. Note that $\pi > 4/19$ is sufficient to induce B to cooperate in the first period of the two-stage game, while $\pi > 10/19$ is the sufficient condition for (S_T, S_R, S_B) to be an equilibrium in the three-stage game. Don't be misled into thinking that cooperation is *more* problematic when the time horizon is longer. We get *more* cooperation – two periods instead of one period – when $\pi > 10/19$.

Exercises

1   Show that the equilibrium of this section is subgame-perfect.
2   Rework the argument of this section using the specific payoffs of Table 3.
3   Does the analysis of this section change if we replace tit-for-tat by the strategy "cooperate every period whatever the opponent does"?

6 Friedman's theorem for infinitely repeated games

In this section we show that for any infinitely repeated version of a one-shot game, any payoff assignment that is feasible for the one-shot game can be sustained as a subgame-perfect equilibrium under repetition – provided that the discount rate is sufficiently high, and the payoff assignment does not leave any player below her security level. The security level is typically not very high. It is defined by selecting an arbitrary strategy for the player and then determining the lowest payoff she could realize with that strategy. The security level is the largest of all these minimal payoffs over the player's set of admissible strategies.

6.1 Formal statement and proof

We begin with a one-shot game involving two players, A and B, each of whom has to choose from an admissible set of actions. The actions are chosen simultaneously, and the actions available to A may be different from those available to B. For each combination of actions α and β, for A and B, respectively, there is a payoff $u_A(\alpha, \beta)$ to A and a payoff $u_B(\alpha, \beta)$ to B. This defines the *stage game*, which is a one-shot game. Now we are going to model the repeated play of this game. It will be played in each of an infinite number of periods 1, 2, . . . , t, ... An individual maximizes the discounted sum of utilities, and we continue to assume that they have the same discount rate δ. Individual i will endeavor to maximize the following sum:

$$\Sigma \, \delta^{t-1} \, u_i^t = u_i^1 + \delta u_i^2 + \delta^2 u_i^3 + \ldots + \delta^{t-1} u_i^t + \ldots$$

where u_i^t is the payoff to individual i in period t. This payoff is a function of the strategies chosen by the two players, of course. Let $(\alpha^\circ, \beta^\circ)$ be any Nash equilibrium of the stage game, and let v° and w° be the payoffs, to A and B, respectively, that result from $(\alpha^\circ, \beta^\circ)$. These strategies will be part of the trigger strategy in the infinitely repeated game. They will be used to sustain a subgame-perfect equilibrium. Let (α, β) be an arbitrary pair of strategies in the stage game, and let the resulting payoffs be v and w for A and B. As long as $v > v^\circ$ and $w > w^\circ$ there is a subgame-perfect equilibrium of the repeated game such that A receives v every period and B receives w every period. Here are the strategies:

S_A A plays α in the first period and α in each period t as long as B has played β in each of the first $t - 1$ periods. If B plays anything other than β at stage $t - 1$ then A plays α° in period t and in every subsequent period.

S_B Similarly, B plays β in the first period and in each subsequent period following the selection of α by A. If A plays anything other than α at stage $t - 1$ then B plays β° in all subsequent periods.

Let's see why this constitutes a Nash equilibrium pair of strategies for the repeated game.

Consider a deviation ϵ by A in period 1. This leads to a payoff of $\mu \equiv u_A(\epsilon, \beta)$ to A in period 1. B will respond by playing β° in every subsequent period. Because α° is a best response to β° the best that A can do after playing ϵ is to play α° in every period beyond the first. Therefore, the sequence of payoffs for A is

μ, $v°$, $v°$, ... $v°$, ... (or something that yields even less utility). The present value of this stream is

$$\mu + \frac{\delta v°}{1 - \delta}.$$

Compare this to the payoff from S_A. A will receive v every period, yielding a present value of $v/(1 - \delta)$. We will have

$$\frac{v}{1 - \delta} > \mu + \frac{\delta v°}{1 - \delta} \qquad [1]$$

if and only if

$$\delta > \frac{\mu - v}{\mu - v°}. \qquad [2]$$

If this holds then there is no period 1 deviation that will leave A better off than S_A, given B's strategy S_B. Would a deviation from S_A in some period $t > 1$ be profitable for A? No. The present value of the stream of payoffs yielded by S_A from period t on is $v\delta^{t-1}/(1 - \delta)$, and a deviation in period t will generate a stream of payoffs from t on that has a present value of at most $\mu\delta^{t-1} + v°\delta[\delta^{t-1}]/(1 - \delta)$. The deviation will be profitable if and only if [1] holds. (Multiply both sides of [1] by δ^{t-1}.)

Now, if ϵ is the deviation that maximizes A's first period payoff then $\mu \geq v$. And we are assuming $v > v°$, and thus $\mu - v < \mu - v°$, so we can have $\delta < 1$; if δ is sufficiently large then S_A maximizes the present value of A's payoff stream given that B employs S_B. Similarly, there will be a number $d < 1$ such that $\delta > d$ implies that S_B maximizes the present value of B's payoff stream given that A employs S_A. Therefore, for δ sufficiently large the pair (S_A, S_B) constitutes a Nash equilibrium. Is it subgame-perfect? We show that it is by considering the subgame beginning in any period t, assuming that δ satisfies [2] and its counterpart for player B. There are three cases. First, suppose A and B have played α and β, respectively, in every period prior to t. Are the truncated strategies a Nash equilibrium for the truncated game? Yes, because we are back at the original game: an infinite number of repetitions of the stage game. When we truncate S_A and S_B we obtain the same trigger strategies, which we have just shown to constitute a Nash equilibrium. Second, suppose that A played $\alpha°$ and B played $\beta°$ in period $t - 1$. When we truncate S_A and S_B in this situation we get A playing $\alpha°$ and B playing $\beta°$ in every period from t on. This is a Nash equilibrium for the truncated repeated game because $(\alpha°, \beta°)$ is a Nash equilibrium for the stage game. Have we completed our examination of what would happen off the equilibrium path, in order to verify that the equilibrium is not supported by incredible threats? Suppose that one player, say A, deviated from S_A in period $t - 1$ although A and B played S_A

and S_B, respectively, up to that point. But this is not consistent with S_A, so we have indeed established that (S_A, S_B) is subgame-perfect. To bring out the significance of Friedman's theorem we explore a version of the prisoner's dilemma game that gives rise to an infinite number of subgame-perfect Nash equilibria in the infinite replication game, even though the stage game has a single dominant strategy equilibrium.

6.2 The continuum dilemma

We illustrate the significance of Friedman's theorem by considering a version of the prisoner's dilemma game that allows each player to choose any level of cooperation between zero and one – not just the extreme points, zero (defect) and one (full cooperation). In the stage game player A selects a fraction α ($0 \le \alpha \le 1$) and B selects a fraction β ($0 \le \beta \le 1$). Each person's fraction expresses the degree of cooperation chosen. The payoffs are defined so that $\alpha = 0$ is a dominant strategy in the stage game for A, and similarly, $\beta = 0$ is a dominant strategy for B. Set

$$u_A(\alpha, \beta) = 2\beta - \alpha \quad \text{and} \quad u_B(\alpha, \beta) = 2\alpha - \beta.$$

These payoff functions can be given a simple interpretation. A and B are neighbors, and each is bothered by the amount of debris that motorists deposit as they drive by. If either A or B supplies e units of effort to cleaning up the trash then *each* will receive $2e$ units of utility from the improved appearance of the neighborhood. But clean-up is costly, and for each unit of effort expended by A there is a utility cost of 3 units. Similarly for B. Then if A devotes α units of effort to clean up while B contributes β, then A's utility is $2(\alpha + \beta) - 3\alpha$ and B's utility is $2(\alpha + \beta) - 3\beta$. This gives us the payoff functions above. Whatever the value of β, player A can increase u_A by reducing α. Therefore, $\alpha = 0$ is a dominant strategy for A in the stage game. Similarly, $\beta = 0$ is a dominant strategy for B.

What are the feasible payoff vectors for this game? They comprise the entire diamond *OKLM* in Figure 3 (including the interior). Consider point x, which is a convex combination of $(-1, 2)$ and $(1, 1)$. That is, $x = \lambda(-1, 2) + (1 - \lambda)(1, 1)$ for some value of λ between zero and unity. In plainer terms, the first component of x (A's payoff) is $\lambda(-1) + (1 - \lambda)(1)$ and the second (B's payoff) is $\lambda(2) + (1 - \lambda)(1)$. Can we have

$$2\beta - \alpha = -\lambda + (1 - \lambda) \quad \text{and} \quad 2\alpha - \beta = 2\lambda + (1 - \lambda)?$$

The solution of these equations is $\alpha = 1$ and $\beta = 1 - \lambda$, and both are admissible strategies.

Consider $y = \lambda(1, 1) + (1 - \lambda)(2, -1)$. Set

$$2\beta - \alpha = \lambda + 2(1 - \lambda) \quad \text{and} \quad 2\alpha - \beta = \lambda - (1 - \lambda).$$

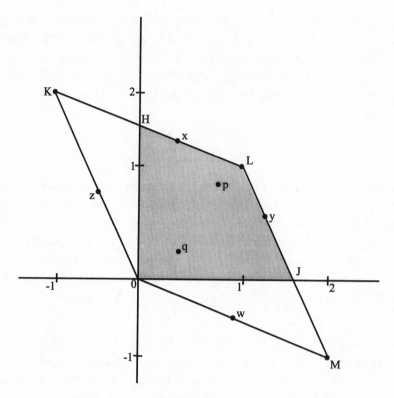

Figure 3

The solution is $\alpha = \lambda$ and $\beta = 1$; both are admissible. Verify that:

$z = \lambda(-1, 2) + (1 - \lambda)(0, 0)$ results from $\alpha = \lambda$ and $\beta = 0$.

$w = \lambda(2, -1) + (1 - \lambda)(0, 0)$ results from $\alpha = 0$ and $\beta = \lambda$.

$p = \lambda(-1, 2) + \theta(1, 1) + (1 - \lambda - \theta)(2, -1)$ if $\alpha = \lambda + \theta$ and

$$\beta = 1 - \lambda.$$

$q = \lambda(-1, 2) + \theta(2, -1) + (1 - \lambda - \theta)(0, 0)$ if $\alpha = \lambda$ and $\beta = \theta$.

In each case $0 \leq \lambda \leq 1$, and for p and q we have $0 \leq \theta \leq 1$ and $0 \leq \lambda + \theta \leq 1$ as well.

To summarize, any point in the diamond $OKLM$ in Figure 3 is a feasible payoff assignment for the one-shot version of the game. Friedman's theorem says that any point (u_A, u_B) in the shaded part of the diamond, excluding the lines OH and OJ, can be sustained as a subgame-perfect Nash equilibrium in which A gets u_A each period and B gets u_B each period in the infinitely repeated game. At least, that will be the case if the discount rate is sufficiently high. We have seen why these payoffs can be supported by a subgame-perfect Nash equilibrium. The trigger strategy permanently reduces an opponent to a utility of zero if he once deviates from the equilibrium degree of cooperation. It is easy to see why a point outside the shaded area cannot be sustained, even with infinite replication and a high discount rate. Outside the shaded area one person receives less than zero, but a player can always guarantee a payoff of at least zero per period by selecting a cooperation level of zero each period.

Any infinitely repeated game has a subgame-perfect equilibrium for every strategy pair (α, β) from the stage game that gives each player a larger payoff than some Nash equilibrium of the stage game. Therefore, full cooperation is *an* equilibrium of the infinitely repeated game if the discount rate is sufficiently high. Although we can show how full cooperation might be sustained in the infinitely repeated continuum dilemma game, we certainly have not been able to show that full cooperation is inevitable. Limitations in the information processing capacity of the players can eliminate a lot of Nash equilibria, appearing to make cooperation more likely in the prisoner's dilemma case. In particular, see Rubinstein (1986) and Binmore and Samuelson (1992).

Exercise

1   State and prove Friedman's theorem for $n > 2$ players.

5

Resource allocation: private goods

In this chapter we examine a hidden characteristic problem of great significance: the design of a resource allocation mechanism that will elicit private information about individual preferences and firm production recipes in a way that allows a Pareto optimal menu of private goods and services to be identified and implemented. We assume away all hidden information problems other than the dispersion of knowledge of individual consumer preferences and individual firm production recipes. In particular, we assume that every consumer knows the quality of every firm's output, every employer knows the abilities of every prospective employee, every manager can be relied on to maximize profit – in fact there is no shirking by anyone – every lender knows the probability of default of every creditor, and so on. This still presents the economy with an impressive challenge: to induce truthful revelation of the remaining hidden information – the preferences and production functions. In fact, the first four sections even assume away this hidden information problem, highlighting instead the transmission of information. We model the private ownership market economy as a computing algorithm that asks each agent to report partial information about the private characteristic. Specifically, if P_1 is the current price of commodity X and P_2 is the price of Y then each consumer is asked to identify a basket of goods at which her marginal rate of substitution between X and Y equals P_1/P_2; and each firm must declare a production plan for which its marginal rate of transformation of X into Y is equal to P_1/P_2. This provides the algorithm (economy) with only limited, partial information about preferences and production recipes. Nevertheless, this allows an efficient (or Pareto optimal) outcome to be identified at equilibrium in a wide range of circumstances. An outcome is efficient if there is no other arrangement of production and consumption activities that makes one person better off without lowering the utility of anyone else. Identification of an efficient outcome would seem to require an enormous amount of information about all of the private characteristics. Therefore, even with most of the hidden information problems assumed away, identification of an efficient outcome by the market system is a remarkable accomplishment. Social cost pricing is the key, as we will see.

Our principal is a fictitious planner who designs the algorithm, or mechanism. The agents are the consumers and the managers of firms, who are motivated by self-interest. If the mechanism is well designed the individual pursuit of self-interest will not be self-defeating, and the equilibrium outcome will be Pareto optimal.

1 A simple model of resource allocation

We will look at a simple two-commodity model and identify some key conditions that are necessary for efficiency. These will be properties of the outcome, or *allocation*, not of individual behavior. In this section we (naively) assume firms will maximize profit *given* the market prices and each consumer will maximize his utility without considering that his demands may affect prices. Sections 5 (Price taking behavior) and 6 (Implementation) take a more sophisticated look at the behavior of an individual agent.

There are two goods, named X and Y, with x and y denoting the respective amounts of the two goods. It may help to think of X as leisure and Y as some good that is manufactured by employing labor. Commodity X cannot be produced but it can be used as an input to produce Y. When X is used as an input we will let L denote the number of units of X employed.

1.1 Consumers

A typical consumer's utility function is $u(x, y) = B(x) + y$, where B is a real-valued function such that $B'(x) > 0$ (i.e., positive marginal utility for X) and $B''(x) < 0$ (diminishing marginal utility) for all x. We don't know the form of the function B, which reveals the level of benefit that the individual receives from consuming x units of commodity X, but we do know that it is independent of the amount of Y consumed. We also know that the benefit obtained from Y is a simple linear function of y which is added to $B(x)$ to determine the overall level of utility enjoyed by the individual. The consumer is endowed with Ω units of X and zero units of Y. In other words, before trading and production begin the individual has Ω units of commodity X, and this can be disposed of as he wishes. He can consume all or part of it or transfer his ownership of it to another agent. There-fore, if nothing is produced the individual's utility will be $u(\Omega, 0) = B(\Omega) + 0$.

$B'(x)$ denotes the marginal benefit at x, the first derivative of $B(x)$. Suppose that the individual always buys a positive amount of both goods X and Y. Let P_1

represent the price of X, with P_2 denoting the price of Y. Then we have $B'(x^*) = P_1/P_2$ if the basket (x^*, y^*) maximizes u subject to the budget constraint

$$P_1 x + P_2 y = \text{Income}.$$

To prove this, suppose that $B'(x) > P_1/P_2$. Then the purchase of one more unit of X can be obtained without violating the budget constraint by simply reducing Y consumption by P_1/P_2 units. The loss of P_1/P_2 units of Y causes utility to decline by P_1/P_2 units, but the addition of one unit of X causes utility to increase by $B'(x)$ units. The overall change in utility is $B'(x) - P_1/P_2$, which is positive when $B'(x) > P_1/P_2$. (In fact a change in X consumption of one unit may be too large. But there is some $\delta > 0$ such that $B(x + \delta) + y - \delta P_1/P_2 > B(x) + y$ holds if the inequality $B'(x) - P_1/P_2 > 0$ holds. In general, if f is a differentiable function of x then $df = f'(x)dx$ approximates $f(x + dx) - f(x)$ for dx sufficiently small.) Therefore, utility maximization implies that we cannot have $B' > P_1/P_2$ at the consumer's chosen basket. Suppose that we have $B'(x) < P_1/P_2$. Then utility can be increased by reducing the consumption of X. The net change in utility as a result of adding P_1/P_2 units of Y to the basket and eliminating one unit of X is $-B'(x) + P_1/P_2$, which is positive when $B'(x) < P_1/P_2$. (At least, for $\delta > 0$ small enough the change in utility is arbitrarily close to $-B'(x)\delta + \delta P_1/P_2$.) Therefore, we can't have $B'(x) < P_1/P_2$ either when the consumer has optimized. Consequently, $B'(x^*) = P_1/P_2$ is characteristic of consumer choice (when both goods are purchased at equilibrium) in this simple model with individual preference belonging to the family of preference schemes that can be represented by a utility function of the form $u(x, y) = B(x) + y$.

It is necessary to distinguish one consumer from another, so we let u_i denote the utility function of consumer i. Then we can write $u_i(x_i, y_i) = B_i(x_i) + y_i$. Note that the subscripts on x and y enable us to distinguish the amounts consumed by different individuals.

1.2 Production

The employment of L units of input results in the production of $f(L)$ units of Y. We refer to f as a production function. Assume that f is twice-differentiable, with $f(0) = 0$, $f'(L) > 0$ (i.e., positive marginal product) and $f''(L) < 0$ (diminishing marginal product) for all L. The first derivative of the production function, $f'(L)$, is called the marginal product of labor. By definition, if exactly L units of labor are currently employed then the input of a small amount dL of additional labor would lead to the production of (approximately) $f'(L) \times dL$ additional units of commodity Y.

1.3 Pareto optimality

Now we characterize a Pareto optimal outcome for this economy and show that a competitive equilibrium of the private ownership market economy is Pareto optimal (or efficient). Note that the change in individual i's utility as a result of an increase in the consumption of X by δ units and a decrease in the consumption of Y by $\xi\,\delta$ units is approximately $[B'_i(x_i) - \xi]\delta$ and the change in i's utility as a result of a decrease in the consumption of X by δ units and an increase in Y of $\xi\,\delta$ units is approximately $[-B'_i(x_i) + \xi]\delta$.

Claim 1 Efficiency implies that $B'_i(x_i)$ is identical for all consumers i. (In general, the marginal rate of substitution between any two goods X and Y must be the same for every two individuals who consume both X and Y.)

Proof Suppose that we have $B'_1(x_1) > B'_2(x_2)$. For example, $B'_1(x_1) = 7$ and $B'_2(x_2) = 3$. Then individuals 1 and 2 can trade with each other in a way that leaves both better off without affecting the welfare of anyone else. It is obvious that if any trade is going to work we must have person 1 importing X and exporting Y because 1 places a higher intrinsic value on X than does 2. And 1 must give up less than 7 units of Y per unit of X imported if she is to realize a higher level of utility. That is because the change in utility for person 1 is approximately

$$B'_1(x_1) - \text{export of } Y = 7 - \text{export of } Y$$

for every unit of X imported from person 2. But if 2 receives less than 3 units of Y per unit of X exported by 2 then she will suffer. This follows from the fact that the change in 2's utility is

$$-B'_2(x_2) + \text{import of } Y = -3 + \text{import of } Y$$

for every unit of X exported to person 1. On the other hand, as long as the exchange rate ξ is between 3 and 7 then both persons will enjoy an increase in utility if person 1 delivers ξ units of Y to individual 2 in exchange for one unit of X. This means that the original outcome was not Pareto optimal. Therefore, efficiency demands that $B'_i(x_i)$ is identical for all individuals i. (Exercise: Make this argument rigorous by using arbitrarily small changes in the consumption of X and Y with ξ units of Y exchanged per unit of X.)

Claim 2 Efficiency implies that $B'_i(x_i) = f'(L)$ for all individuals i. (In general, any individual's marginal rate of substitution between any two goods X and Y must be equal to the *real* marginal social cost of producing X as defined by the amount of Y that could have been produced with the resources used to produce a unit of X at the margin.)

Proof Suppose to the contrary that $B'_h(x_h) > f'(L)$. For example, $B'_h(x_h) = 2$ and $f'(L) = 1$. The marginal product of labor is 1. In other words, the consumption of an additional unit of X will result in the loss of one unit of Y. Suppose then, that we increase h's consumption of X by 1 unit by reducing her contribution to production by 1 unit of input. Then the total amount of Y produced in the economy will fall by 1 unit. If we reduce h's consumption of Y by 1 unit then no one else's consumption will be changed in any way. *Provided that everyone's utility is independent of the consumption of others (no pollution or other externalities) and is also independent of the production activities of firms (no pollution or other externalities)* there will be no change in the utility of any individual other than person h as a result of the proposed change in her production and consumption activities. How is h's utility affected? The change in her utility is $2 - 1$, which is positive: She gains 1 unit of X and the marginal utility of X is 2; she loses 1 unit of Y and the marginal utility of Y is 1. We have made one person better off without affecting the utility of anyone else. Therefore, the original outcome was not Pareto optimal. In general, if we increase h's consumption of X by 1 unit and reduce her consumption of Y by $f'(L)$ units then no one else's utility will be affected, the change in h's utility is $B'_h(x_h) - f'(L)$, which is positive if $B'_h(x_h) > f'(L)$: Person h gains 1 unit of X, which adds $B'_h(x_h)$ to her utility; she loses $f'(L)$ units of Y, which diminishes her utility by $f'(L)$. We have made h better off without affecting the utility of anyone else. Therefore, a configuration of production and consumption activities is not Pareto optimal if $B'_i(x_i) > f'(L)$ for any individual i.

Suppose that $B'_i(x_i)$ is actually less than $f'(L)$, say $B'_i(x_i) = 2$ and $f'(L) = 5$. Then the consumption of the last unit of X by person i has added only 2 to her utility but has resulted in a drop in Y production of 5 units. That 5 units of Y could have added 5 to i's utility. By reducing her consumption of X by 1 unit and having her contribute an additional unit of input to the production process we can increase her utility by $-2 + 5$ without affecting the consumption of anyone else. This means that the original outcome is not Pareto optimal. In general, if we reduce i's consumption of X by 1 unit and have her contribute an additional unit of input to the production process we can increase the production of Y by $f'(L)$ units. If we give all of this additional output of Y to h we will not affect anyone else's consumption or utility (assuming away externalities), and i's utility will change by $-B'_i(x_i) + f'(L)$, which is positive if $B'_i(x_i) < f'(L)$. Therefore, $B'_i(x_i) < f'(L)$ is inconsistent with Pareto optimality.

Pareto optimality rules out $B'_i(x_i) < f'(L)$ and also $B'_i(x_i) > f'(L)$, proving Claim 2.

Claim 3 Assume that both marginal product (f') and marginal benefit (B'_i) decline as L and x_i increase, respectively. If $B'_i(x_i) = f'(L)$ for each consumer i and the total amount of X consumed is equal to the total endowment of X minus the amount required to produce $\Sigma \, y_i$ units of Y then the outcome is Pareto optimal.

We will not prove this in general; section 1.6 establishes the result for a special case and section 3 proves that a competitive equilibrium is Pareto optimal in general. What is relatively easy to demonstrate is that the equilibrium of the private ownership market economy will satisfy the efficiency requirement of Claims 1 and 2. This follows from budget-constrained utility maximization and *competitive* (i.e., price taking) profit maximization. Consider the consumer's budget constraint. If a market period lasts Ω units of time and consumer i enjoys x_i units of leisure then her labor income is $\Omega - x_i$ times the wage rate. That is, income equals $P_1(\Omega - x_i) + R_i$, where R_i is the share of profits going to person i. Then i's budget constraint is

$$P_2 y_i = P_1 \Omega - P_1 x_i + R_i \quad \text{or} \quad P_1 x_i + P_2 y_i = P_1 \Omega + R_i.$$

We know that the consumer will purchase a basket of X and Y that satisfies $B_i'(x_i)$ $= P_1/P_2$. Because P_1/P_2 is the same for all consumers the marginal benefit of X, $B_i'(x_i)$, will be identical for all i. This establishes that the property of Claim 1 is satisfied by the private ownership market economy. (We're assuming that each consumer i consumes a positive amount of X and Y.)

One unit of Y requires $1/f'(L)$ units of labor as input and at a wage of P_1 the production of an additional unit of Y requires the expenditure of $P_1/f'(L)$ additional dollars. Therefore, the firm's marginal cost at output level y is $P_1/f'(L)$, where L is the total number of units of labor required to make y units of Y. A *competitive* firm sets the price of its output Y equal to marginal cost so we have $P_2 = P_1/f'(L)$, which obviously yields $f'(L) = P_1/P_2$. Because $B_i'(x_i) = P_1/P_2$ we also have $B_i'(x_i)$ $= f'(L)$ for all consumers. This establishes that the private ownership market economy satisfies the efficiency property of Claim 2. You might prefer the following argument: The firm will maximize profit,

$$P_2 f(L) - P_1 L,$$

given the prices. The first derivative is $P_2 f'(L) - P_1$, and setting this equal to zero yields $f'(L) = P_1/P_2$.

1.4 Social cost and social benefit

With quasi-linear utility function $u = B(x) + y$ the consumer will choose a consumption plan at which the marginal utility of X equals the price ratio P_1/P_2 of the respective prices. For this preference scheme $B'(x)$, the marginal utility of X, is equal to the marginal rate of substitution. (Why?) In general, the consumer will choose a consumption plan at which the marginal rate of substitution (MRS) between goods X and Y is equal to P_1/P_2. Therefore, the price ratio signals to consumer A the benefit (MRS_c) that consumer C would derive from an additional unit of X, as measured by the amount of Y that consumer C would be willing to sacrifice to obtain another unit of X. The opportunity cost incurred by A when she orders a unit of X is P_1/P_2: It costs P_1 dollars to buy a unit of X; each dollar will buy $1/P_2$ units of Y, so P_1 dollars spent on X could have been used to purchase P_1/P_2 units of commodity Y. Consumer A takes the opportunity cost P_1/P_2 of X into consideration in determining her optimal consumption plan. Because P_1/P_2 equals consumer C's marginal rate of substitution, consumer A is being forced to take C's preferences into consideration when A formulates her consumption plan. Every unit of X consumed by A is worth MRS_c to consumer C, in the sense that $MRS_c = P_1/P_2$ is the amount of Y that C would need to compensate for the loss of a unit of X. We can say that MRS_c is the cost to society of A's taking a unit of good X for herself. This means that P_1/P_2 signals the cost that one imposes on society by consuming a unit of good X.

P_1/P_2 is also the amount of Y that could have been produced, given available technology, with the resources required to provide to consumers a unit of X at the margin. The consumption of one unit of leisure deprives the economy of one unit of labor input. Therefore, for our simple model, it takes one unit of input (X) to produce one unit of X for consumption. P_1 is the wage rate and at equilibrium P_1/P_2 is the marginal product of labor – i.e., output of Y per unit of labor at the margin. Therefore, the consumption of an additional unit of leisure deprives the economy of P_1/P_2 units of commodity Y. This is another sense in which P_1/P_2 can be viewed as the cost an individual imposes on society by ordering a unit of commodity X for her own use. We have shown that social cost pricing can be used to guide the economy to an efficient outcome. Chapter 8 proves that it is the only device that will do this if truthful revelation of the private characteristics cannot be taken for granted.

1.5 Subsidy

Consider a special case of our simple model: There is one consumer with utility function $u(x, y) = 10 \ln(x + 1) + y$, and one firm with production function $f(L) = L$. The consumer is endowed with 12 units of X ($\Omega = 12$) and zero units of Y. We have $f'' = 0$ at every point, but the second derivative of $10 \ln(x + 1)$ is negative everywhere, so $B' = f'$ is still necessary for efficiency. (Can you prove this?) $B(x) = 10 \ln(x + 1)$ and thus $B'(x) = 10/(x + 1)$, which equals $f'(L) = 1$ when $x + 1 = 10$. Therefore, $x = 9$ is necessary for efficiency. Then $L = 12 - 9 = 3$, and thus $y = 3$. Utility is $10\ln 10 + 3 = 26.026$. The market equilibrium has $B'(x) = P_1/P_2 = f'(L) = 1$. Therefore, $P_1/P_2 = 1$. In fact, any price system in which the price ratio is unity is an equilibrium for this economy. (Confirm this.) Let's set $P_1 = 1 = P_2$.

Suppose that the government subsidizes the consumption of Y to the extent that the price paid by consumers is now $\frac{1}{2}$, although firms still receive \$1 per unit of Y sold. The equilibrium will no longer be efficient because the price signal to which consumers now respond understates the true social marginal cost of Y. The consumer will set $B'(x) = P_1/P_2 = 1/\frac{1}{2} = 2$. Therefore, $10/(x + 1) = 2$, and thus $x = 4$. We have $y = L = 12 - 4 = 8$. Utility is $10\ln 5 + 8 = 24.094$. Although the consumer demands – and hence consumes – more Y because its price is lower, her utility falls. The price ratio does not correctly signal the social cost of consumption. The only information about preferences and production recipes comes via the prices. If this information is inaccurate we cannot expect the economy to generate an efficient outcome.

1.6 Efficiency of competitive equilibrium

Let's take a brief look at a simple example of an economy with many consumers, to see why the market equilibrium is efficient (or Pareto optimal) when each person's utility depends only on his own consumption and the market prices are not diverted from their competitive equilibrium values by either private monopoly power or government mandate. (Section 3 provides a general proof.) We assume $f(L) = L$. There are n consumers.

Normalize and set $P_1 = 1$. Then we must have $P_2 = 1$ at equilibrium. If $P_2 > 1$ then the firm makes a profit of $P_2 - 1$ on every unit of output sold. (One unit of X is required as input, and this costs \$1. A unit of input is converted into one unit of Y, which is sold for P_2 dollars.) Profit can be made arbitrarily large by producing an arbitrarily large amount of output. Then the supply of Y will exceed the demand, and the demand for X by the firm will exceed the amount supplied by the household sector. This is obviously inconsistent with equilibrium. Therefore, we can't have $P_2 > 1$. If $P_2 < 1$ then the firm *loses* $1 - P_2$ on every unit of Y sold. In that case profit maximization requires $L = 0$, with zero units of Y produced. But Y is inexpensive, so there will be a positive amount of Y demanded. And there will certainly be a positive amount of X supplied by consumers. Again, we are not at equilibrium. Therefore, we must have $P_2 = 1$ at equilibrium.

If $P_1 = 1 = P_2$ each individual's budget constraint is $y_i = \Omega - x_i$, where x_i is the amount of Y chosen by i and y_i is the amount of X. There is no profit income. (Why?) Let x_i^O and y_i^O denote the amounts of X and Y chosen at equilibrium. These choices constitute the competitive equilibrium E. Consider some other outcome G that makes everyone better off. Let x_i^N and y_i^N denote the amounts of the two goods consumed by i under this new outcome G. We have said that individual i prefers basket (x_i^N, y_i^N) to basket (x_i^O, y_i^O). Why, then, did i choose the latter at equilibrium? The former must not have been affordable. That is, $y_i^N > \Omega - x_i^N$. Therefore, $\Sigma_i y_i^N > \Omega n - \Sigma_i x_i^N$, where $\Sigma_i y_i^N$ is the total amount of Y consumed in the community under G, Ωn is the total amount of X initially available (there are n households), and $\Sigma_i x_i^N$ is the total amount of X retained for consumption under outcome G. Therefore, $\Omega n - \Sigma_i x_i^N$, which we denote by L^N, is the total amount of X available as input under G. Therefore, $\Sigma_i y_i^N$ exceeds L^N, which is impossible: The production technology only allows L^N units of Y to be produced with L^N units of input. Therefore, G is not feasible; it attempts to provide consumers with more Y than the economy is capable of producing given the amount of X consumed under G. Therefore, there is no *feasible* outcome that will make everyone better off than under the competitive equilibrium E. Therefore, E is Pareto optimal. (Explain why there is no feasible outcome that will make one person better off than under E without making someone else worse off. Note that our argument is valid for any type of individual preference. Preferences do not even have to be representable by utility functions.)

Exercises

1   Consider a simple model of an economy with two private goods, X and Y, and many consumers. Each individual has a utility function of the form $B_i(x_i) + y_i$. Let P denote the price of Y. Choose units so that the price of X is one dollar. Good X can either be consumed or used to produce Y, and when one unit of X is used as input exactly one-third of a unit of Y is obtained as output.

      a What is the equilibrium price of Y if the two goods are produced in a private ownership market economy with competitive firms?

      b Suppose now that the government decides to subsidize the consumption of Y by paying one dollar for each unit of Y consumed. That is, consumers pay $\$P - 1$ per unit for Y but firms receive $\$P$ per unit. What will P be in this case? Will the outcome be Pareto efficient? If so, explain why; if not, prove it with a numerical example in a one-consumer economy with $B_i = 2\sqrt{x_i}$ and $\Omega = 24$.

2   Consider a simple model of an economy with two private goods, Y and X, and many consumers. Each individual has a utility function of the form $B_i(x_i) + y_i$. Let P denote the price of Y. Choose units so that the price of X is one dollar. Good X can be either consumed or used to produce Y, and when one unit of X is used as input exactly one-third of a unit of Y is obtained as output.

a What is the equilibrium price of Y if the two goods are produced in a private ownership market economy with competitive firms?

b Suppose now that the government decides to tax the consumption of Y by collecting one dollar for each unit of Y consumed. That is, consumers pay $\$P + 1$ per unit for Y but firms receive $\$P$ per unit. What will P be in this case? Will the outcome be Pareto efficient? If so, explain why; if not, prove it with a numerical example in a one consumer economy with $B_i = 2\sqrt{x_i}$ and $\Omega = 24$.

3 Prove Claims 1 and 2 of section 1.3 by exploiting the fact that when everyone has quasi-linear preferences the maximization of total utility is equivalent to efficiency. (See section 11.1 of Chapter 1.)

4 Make the proof of Claim 2 of section 1.3 rigorous by using arbitrarily small changes in the consumption of X and Y with ϵ units of Y exchanged per unit of X.

2 The Arrow–Debreu economy

We investigate the efficiency properties of an abstract model of an economy – the Arrow–Debreu economy, named after K. J. Arrow and G. Debreu, who first worked out the fundamental properties of general equilibrium in market economies.[1] We begin by examining a pure exchange version of the Arrow–Debreu economy: There are n consumers, indexed by $i = 1, 2, \ldots, n$, and ℓ commodities, $c = 1, 2, \ldots, \ell$. A commodity bundle for individual i is a plan (vector) $x_i = (x_{i1}, x_{i2}, \ldots, x_{i\ell})$ that assigns x_{ic} units of commodity c to individual i. T_c specifies the total amount of each commodity c available to the society. (Production has already taken place and there is a total of T_c units of commodity c to be divided among the n individuals.) An *allocation* x is an assignment of a commodity bundle x_i to each individual i. Allocation x is *feasible* if $x_{1c} + x_{2c} + \ldots + x_{nc} \le T_c$ for each commodity c. The preference scheme of individual i is represented by a utility function u_i. Individual i prefers bundle x_i to bundle y_i if and only if $u_i(x_i) > u_i(y_i)$.

Now that we have the basic ingredients, we define the Arrow–Debreu exchange economy, which is an abstract representation of the market mechanism. Each individual i has an *endowment* Ω_i which is an ℓ-vector of commodities owned by i. Of course $T_c = \Omega_{1c} + \Omega_{2c} + \ldots + \Omega_{nc}$ for each commodity c. An auctioneer announces a price system $p = (p_1, p_2, \ldots, p_\ell)$ and each consumer i responds by announcing a bundle x_i that maximizes u_i subject to the budget constraint

$$p_1 x_{i1} + p_2 x_{i2} + \ldots + p_\ell x_{i\ell} \le p_1 \Omega_{i1} + p_2 \Omega_{i2} + \ldots + p_\ell \Omega_{i\ell}.$$

A *competitive equilibrium* of this economy is a pair (p, x) such that for each i, x_i maximizes u_i subject to the budget constraint and $x_1 + x_2 + \ldots + x_n = \Omega_1 + \Omega_2 + \ldots + \Omega_n$ (demand equals supply for each good).

Suggestions for further reading: Campbell (1987, pp. 39–41, and appendix 2).

Exercises

1   The consumer's utility function is $u(x, y) = \min\{2x, y\}$. Determine the individual's demand function.

2   What are the broadest conditions under which we can claim that a bundle of two goods maximizes utility subject to the budget constraint if and only if

    a the marginal rate of substitution equals the price ratio and
    b the market value of the bundle is equal to the consumer's income?

    Explain briefly.

3   Characterize the choice of a single consumer who takes prices (and income) as given. For convenience, you may assume only two commodities but you must be explicit about any assumptions you make, explaining (briefly) their significance.

4   Solve the following two-person, two-commodity exchange economy for the competitive equilibrium.

$$u_1 = ab \qquad \Omega_1 = (1, 1)$$
$$u_2 = xy + y \qquad \Omega_2 = (1, 0)$$

Of course, person 1 consumes the basket (a, b) and person 2 consumes the basket (x, y). Is the equilibrium outcome Pareto optimal? Explain briefly.

5   Present a simple example to show that a competitive equilibrium may not exist if preferences are not convex.

6   Consider a one-person exchange economy with two goods, a and b. Let $u_1 = a^2 + b^2$ and $\Omega_1 = (1, 1)$ be the utility function and endowment, respectively. Prove that this economy does not have a competitive equilibrium. In a sentence or two, explain why this is so.

7   Find the Pareto optimal allocation or allocations in the following simple *one-person* exchange economy:

$$u_1(x, y) = x^2 + y^2 \quad \text{and} \quad \Omega_1 = (1, 1).$$

Is there *any* price system and income level at which the consumer will choose the Pareto optimal outcome? Explain your answer.

8   Compute the competitive equilibrium of the two-person, two-commodity exchange economy with utility functions

$$u_1(a, b) = a^2b \quad \text{and} \quad u_2(x, y) = xy^2$$

and endowments $(0, 3)$ for person 1 and $(3, 0)$ for person 2. Of course, person 1 consumes the basket (a, b) and 2 consumes (x, y).

3 The first welfare theorem

We prove that a competitive equilibrium of the Arrow–Debreu economy is Pareto optimal if there is a market for every commodity that affects individual utility – the *completeness of markets* assumption. Completeness of markets means that for every realization ξ of every random event there is a market in which one can purchase or sell a unit of any good contingent on ξ. The complete markets assumption also means that for every future date t there is a market in which anyone can purchase or sell a unit of any good for delivery at time t. This would require a literally astronomical number of markets. We never have anything close to completeness in the real world.[2] Nevertheless, the Arrow–Debreu economy with complete markets is a valuable framework within which to study resource allocation. It is also an important benchmark case. For one thing, it helps us identify what has gone wrong when the economy is not efficient. (Complete markets also entail the unrealistic assumption that if A's consumption generates spillover benefits or costs then there is a competitive market in which the spillover is priced and entered into A's budget constraint.)

3.1 Proof of the first welfare theorem for an exchange economy

Suppose that (p, x) is a competitive equilibrium and y is an allocation that is preferred to x by everyone. That is, $u_i(y_i) > u_i(x_i)$ for all i. Because x_i maximizes u_i subject to the budget constraint we must have

$$p_1 y_{i1} + p_2 y_{i2} + \ldots + p_\ell y_{i\ell} > p_1 \Omega_{i1} + p_2 \Omega_{i2} + \ldots + p_\ell \Omega_{i\ell};$$

otherwise i would have chosen y_i in preference to x_i. Therefore,

$$\Sigma[p_1 y_{i1} + p_2 y_{i2} + \ldots + p_\ell y_{i\ell}] > \Sigma[p_1 \Omega_{i1} + p_2 \Omega_{i2} + \ldots + p_\ell \Omega_{i\ell}]$$

where summation is taken over all individuals i. This is inconsistent with the inequality

$$\Sigma[y_{i1} + y_{i2} + \ldots + y_{i\ell}] \leq \Sigma[\Omega_{i1} + \Omega_{i2} + \ldots + \Omega_{i\ell}],$$

which is implied by the feasibility condition $y_{1c} + y_{2c} + \ldots + y_{nc} \leq \Omega_{1c} + \Omega_{2c} + \ldots + \Omega_{nc}$ for each c. Therefore, the only allocations that make everyone better off than x are infeasible. (Finish the proof by showing that we can't make one person better off without reducing the utility of someone else.)

Note this proof is valid even when one or more consumers is at a corner of his budget line, with marginal rates of substitution unequal to the equilibrium price ratio, and even when marginal rates of substitution are not defined. The proof does not even depend on the representation of individual preference by a utility function: If individual i prefers y_i to x_i, and x_i was chosen at equilibrium then y_i must have been too expensive. The rest of the proof follows without modification.

It is a *very* general argument. The key assumptions are that agents take prices as given and that there is a complete set of markets.[3]

3.2 General equilibrium with production

The proof for the general case, with production taken into consideration, is not much more difficult but it does require substantially more notation. There are ℓ commodities, n households, and m firms. Let $I = \{1, 2, \ldots, n\}$ denote the set of households and let $J = \{1, 2, \ldots, m\}$ denote the set of firms. A price system p specifies a nonnegative price p_c for each commodity c. An allocation $a = (x, y)$ consists of a consumption assignment x and a production assignment y. The consumption assignment x specifies a consumption plan x_i for each household i, where x_i assigns the amount $x_{ic} \geq 0$ of commodity c ($c = 1, 2, \ldots, \ell$) to i. The production assignment y specifies a production plan y_j for each firm j, where y_j specifies a positive or zero or negative number y_{jc} for each commodity c. If $y_{jc} > 0$ then the production plan y_j yields y_{jc} units of commodity c as output, but if $y_{jc} < 0$ then the plan y_j requires $|y_{jc}|$ units of commodity c as input. This sign convention allows us to distinguish inputs and outputs, and to compute profit quite easily.

If z specifies a number z_c for each c then we let pz denote the market value of z at the prices specified by p. That is,

$$pz = p_1 z_1 + p_2 z_2 + \ldots + p_c z_c + \ldots + p_\ell z_\ell.$$

Then py_j is the profit generated by firm j's production plan y_j under price regime p.

$$py_j = p_1 y_{j1} + p_2 y_{j2} + \ldots + p_c y_{jc} + \ldots + p_\ell y_{j\ell}.$$

If y_{jc} is positive then $p_c y_{jc}$ is firm j's revenue from the sale of commodity c when it uses production plan y_j and the prevailing prices are given by p. If y_{jc} is negative then $p_c |y_{jc}|$ is the cost to firm j of using the input of commodity c required by production plan y_j. And $p_c y_{jc} = -p_c |y_{jc}|$, so when we add in the term $p_c y_{jc}$ we are subtracting the cost of employing commodity c as input from the revenue realized by the firm from the production plan y_j. Therefore, py_j is the firm's total revenue less its total cost with production plan y_j at price system p.

Focus on a particular commodity c. The net output of c is given by $\Sigma_{j \in J}\, y_{jc}$ when y is the production assignment. Because y_{jc} is a negative number when j uses c as an input, the expression $\Sigma_{j \in J}\, y_{jc}$ gives us the total output of c by the production sector less the total amount of c used as input by firms. Therefore, $\Sigma_{j \in J}\, y_{jc}$ is indeed the net output of commodity c. It is possible to have $\Sigma_{j \in J}\, y_{jc} < 0$. This would be inevitable if c were labor: all firms use labor as an input but it is not produced by any firm. Labor would be supplied by households, of course, and if Ω_{ic} denotes household i's endowment of labor then $\Sigma_{i \in I}\, \Omega_{ic} + \Sigma_{j \in J}\, y_{jc}$ is equal to the total endowment of labor in the economy less the total amount used as input. Therefore, $\Sigma_{i \in I} \, \Omega_{ic} + \Sigma_{j \in J} \, y_{jc}$ is the total amount of labor available to households for consumption (as leisure). And $\Sigma_{i \in I} \, x_{ic}$ is obviously the total amount of leisure consumed by the household sector. Therefore, any allocation $a = (x, y)$ must satisfy

$$\sum_{i \in I} x_{ic} \leq \sum_{i \in I} \Omega_{ic} + \sum_{j \in J} y_{jc}$$

if commodity c is labor. Consider another commodity c for which $\Sigma_{j \in J} \, y_{jc}$ is positive. Then the production assignment y leads to a net output of c and this can be added to the household sector's total endowment $\Sigma_{i \in I} \, \Omega_{ic}$ of c (if any) to determine the total amount of commodity c available for consumption. This total again is $\Sigma_{i \in I} \, \Omega_{ic} + \Sigma_{j \in J} \, y_{jc}$ and again we see that an allocation must satisfy

$$\sum_{i \in I} x_{ic} \leq \sum_{i \in I} \Omega_{ic} + \sum_{j \in J} y_{jc}. \tag{1}$$

Therefore, [1], the *material feasibility* condition, must hold for every commodity c.

An allocation must also satisfy the *individual* feasibility conditions. Firm j's technology must be capable of turning the inputs specified by y_j into the outputs specified by y_j. Let Y_j denote the set of production plans that are technologically feasible for firm j. If y_j belongs to Y_j there is no guarantee that j will actually be able to obtain the inputs required by y_j. There might be excess demand for one input, making it unavailable to some firms. This will not happen if the material feasibility condition holds, but that condition is sure to hold only at equilibrium.

An economy e is described by specifying the utility function u_i of each household i, the endowment Ω_i of each i, the share α_{ij} of each firm j owned by i, and the technology set Y_j of each firm j. The Arrow–Debreu model of the market system is simply one in which firms maximize profit given prices and their technology sets and consumers maximize utility given their budget constraints. At equilibrium the demand for each good equals the supply. In symbols, market clearance condition is

$$\sum_{i \in I} x_{ic} = \sum_{i \in I} \Omega_{ic} + \sum_{j \in J} y_{jc} \tag{2}$$

for each commodity c. Profit maximization is easy to characterize: y_j must belong to Y_j and we must have $py_j \geq pz_j$ for all z_j in Y_j. Derivation of the consumer's budget constraint requires a little work. Expenditure is clearly px_i if the prices are given by p and x_i is i's consumption plan. What is i's income? Income from the sale of i's endowment is just $p\Omega_i$, but i may also have profit income. Household i owns the fraction α_{ij} of firm j so i will receive that fraction of j's profit and hence will receive $\alpha_{ij} py_j$ in total from firm j. If we add this term over all firms j we will get i's total profit income, namely $\Sigma_{j\in J} \, \alpha_{ij}py_j$. Therefore, i's total income is $p\Omega_i$ $+ \Sigma_{j\in J} \, \alpha_{ij}py_j$ and hence i's budget constraint is

$$px_i \leq p\Omega_i + \sum_{j\in J} \alpha_{ij}py_j.$$

A competitive equilibrium of the Arrow–Debreu economy is a price regime p and an allocation $a = (x, y)$ such that

For each household i, x_i satisfies i's budget constraint

$$px_i \leq p\Omega_i + \sum_{j\in J} \alpha_{ij}py_j$$

and no consumption plan satisfying that budget constraint gives a higher level of utility than x_i.   [3]

For each firm j the production plan y_j belongs to Y_j and no member of Y_j gives a higher profit than y_j *given* the price regime p.   [4]

All markets clear; this means that

$$\sum_{i\in I} x_{ic} = \sum_{i\in I} \Omega_{ic} + \sum_{j\in J} y_{jc} \qquad \text{holds for each commodity } c. \qquad [5]$$

Theorem *If there is a complete set of markets but no externalities then a competitive equilibrium is Pareto optimal.*

Proof Let (p, x, y) be the competitive equilibrium. Suppose that the allocation a' $= (x', y')$ is feasible and gives everyone more utility. Feasibility of a' implies

$$\sum_{i\in I} x'_{ic} \leq \sum_{i\in I} \Omega_{ic} + \sum_{j\in J} y'_{jc} \quad \text{for each commodity } c$$

and that the production play y'_j belongs to Y_j for each firm j. If a' gives everyone more utility than the equilibrium allocation then we have $u_i(x'_i) > u_i(x_i)$ for each i. But x_i maximizes i subject to the budget constraint. This means that x'_i cannot satisfy the budget constraint that governed i's choice at equilibrium. Therefore,

$$px'_i > p\Omega_i + \sum_{j\in J} \alpha_{ij}py_j.$$

This is true for each i, so it will remain true when we sum up over all households. That is,

$$\sum_{i\in I} px'_i > \sum_{i\in I} p\Omega_i + \sum_{i\in I} \sum_{j\in J} \alpha_{ij}py_j.$$

Now $\Sigma_{i\in I} \Sigma_{j\in J} \, \alpha_{ij}py_j$ is equal to $\Sigma_{j\in J} \, py_j \, \Sigma_{i\in I} \, \alpha_{ij}$. But for any firm j the sum $\Sigma_{i\in I} \, \alpha_{ij}$ is the sum of all the ownership shares in firm j and that total must equal 1. Therefore, $\Sigma_{i\in I} \Sigma_{j\in J} \, \alpha_{ij}py_j$ equals $\Sigma_{j\in J} \, py_j$, which is the total profit in the economy at equilibrium. Therefore, we can state,

$$\sum_{i \in I} px'_i > \sum_{i \in I} p\Omega_i + \sum_{j \in J} py_j. \qquad [6]$$

Now, y_j maximizes j's profit given p and y'_j belongs to Y_j so we must have $py_j \geq py'_j$ for each firm j. Therefore, $\sum_{j \in J} py_j \geq \sum_{j \in J} py'_j$. This inequality and [6] give us

$$\sum_{i \in I} px'_i > \sum_{i \in I} p\Omega_i + \sum_{j \in J} py'_j. \qquad [7]$$

But $\sum_{i \in I} x'_{ic} \leq \sum_{i \in I} \Omega_{ic} + \sum_{j \in J} y'_{jc}$ holds for each commodity c and thus by virtue of the fact that $p_c \geq 0$ we have

$$p_c \sum_{i \in I} x'_{ic} \leq p_c \sum_{i \in I} \Omega_{ic} + p_c \sum_{j \in J} y'_{jc}$$

for each c. When we add up over all commodities c we contradict [7], because $p \sum_{i \in I} x'_i$ is equal to $p_1 \sum_{i \in I} x'_{i1} + p_2 \sum_{i \in I} x'_{i2} + \ldots + p_\ell \sum_{i \in I} x'_{i\ell}$, and the other terms of [7] can be similarly expressed. We have shown that any allocation that gives everyone more utility than the competitive equilibrium must violate one of the feasibility conditions. In other words, there is no feasible allocation that would give everyone more utility than the market equilibrium. (Show that there is no feasible outcome that could make someone better off without lowering someone else's utility.)

3.3 Externalities

Let's see why the theorem does not go through if there are externalities. Consider an exchange economy with two goods and two consumers. Person 1 consumes the basket (a, b) and 2 consumes the basket (x, y). The endowments are $\Omega_1 = (0, 1)$ and $\Omega_2 = (1, 0)$. Set

$$u_1 = ab - x \quad \text{and} \quad u_2 = xy + a.$$

Person 1's utility is adversely affected by the other person's consumption of the first good and person 2's utility is favorably affected by 1's consumption of the first good. Person 1 cannot control the choice of person 2 so when 1 maximizes utility he must take x as given. That is, x will be treated as a constant in 1's decision making. Similarly, 2 will treat a as a constant when determining his demands.

The values of a and b that maximize $ab - x$ with x treated as a constant are the same numbers that maximize ab, and vice versa. Therefore, it suffices to maximize ab subject to $p_1 a + p_2 b = p\Omega_1 = p_2$. We can set $b = 1 - p_1 a / p_2$ (from the budget constraint) and hence person 1 will maximize $V(a) = a(1 - p_1 a / p_2)$. We will have $0 < a < p_2 / p_1$ at the solution value a. (Why?) Hence $0 = V'(a) = 1 - 2p_1 a / p_2$. Thus $a = \frac{1}{2} p_2 / p_1$. Then $b = 1 - \frac{1}{2} = \frac{1}{2}$. Similarly, person 2 will maximize $x(p_1/p_2 - p_1x/p_2) \equiv G(x)$, and $G'(x) = 0$ implies $x = \frac{1}{2}$ and $y = \frac{1}{2}p_1/p_2$. At equilibrium $a + x = 1$. Then $\frac{1}{2}p_2/p_1 + \frac{1}{2} = 1$. This implies $p_1 = p_2$, which is also implied by $b + y = 1$. When $p_1 = p_2$ we have $a = b = x = y = \frac{1}{2}$. This is the competitive equilibrium.

Is the equilibrium Pareto optimal? Because 1's utility increases when 2's consumption of the first good falls and 2's utility increases (ceteris paribus) when 1's consumption of the first good increases, it should be possible to make both persons better off than they are at the equilibrium by transferring some of the first good from person 2 to person 1. In order to shed light on the first welfare theorem we actually construct a *trade* that increases the utility of both households.

Person 1's utility at equilibrium is $u_1 = \frac{1}{2}(\frac{1}{2}) - \frac{1}{2} = -\frac{1}{4}$ and 2's utility is $u_2 = \frac{1}{2}(\frac{1}{2}) + \frac{1}{2} = \frac{3}{4}$. Now, transfer 0.3 units of the first good from person 2 to 1, and transfer 0.4 units of the second good from person 1 to 2. The new utility levels will be

$$u_1 = (.8)(.1) - .2 = -0.12 \quad \text{and} \quad u_2 = (.2)(.9) + .8 = 0.98.$$

Both individuals have a higher level of utility than at equilibrium, proving that the equilibrium allocation was not Pareto optimal.

When there are consumption externalities the proof of the first welfare theorem breaks down right at the start. If u_i depends on the consumption of other individuals as well as on i's consumption then it is no longer true to say that if i prefers the assignment x' to x then the market value of x_i must exceed i's income at equilibrium. It may be changes in the consumption of others, changes that are beyond i's control, that make x' superior to x in i's estimation. For example at the equilibrium prices $p_1 = p_2$ the basket $(0.8, 0.1)$ is *cheaper* for person 1 than his equilibrium basket $(0.5, 0.5)$. But the latter was the best that 1 could do given his budget constraint *and* given the choice $(0.5, 0.5)$ of person 2. But 1 prefers x' to the equilibrium consumption assignment because of the changes in the other person's consumption.

In general, negative externalities are created when the decision of a consumer or firm imposes costs on society that are not costs to the decision maker. In most cases the market system uses prices to transmit information about social costs and benefits. But when an agent's decision imposes a cost on society that is not incorporated in the price that the agent pays, then vital information, necessary for efficiency, is not transmitted to the decision making agent. Even if the agent receives the information from other sources, if it does not reduce his spending power then he has no *incentive* to take those costs into consideration. Consider what happens when social costs *are* incorporated into the price: Labor accounts for about 75% of all costs of production in mature capitalist economies. The labor used by a firm is clearly a cost to society – if it were not used by the firm it could be productively employed elsewhere. The firm using the labor has to pay a wage bill that is a function of its workers' potential contribution to production in general – a consequence of all firms' bidding for the use of productive factors. That gives the firm incentive to economize on the use of labor. This contributes to efficiency. More strikingly, the firm has a strong incentive to reduce the size of its wage bill (75% of total cost) by research into labor saving equipment. If capital equipment lowers the labor requirement per unit of output, it raises the total output of a given labor force. And of course, output per worker, and hence consumption per worker, has risen dramatically over the decades and centuries. And all because the firm's use of labor is a cost to society that is brought to bear on the firm's decision by means of a price – the wage rate.

If the costs of pollution could be incorporated into the prices that confront firms and consumers, the same powerful force for innovation would be unleashed. Each household would strive to avoid the social costs of its polluting: by altering activities to reduce the amount of waste discharged into the water and air, and by purchasing products that lower cost overall because they incorporate pollution reduction technology. Knowing this, firms would have a strong incentive to invent pollution controlling technology, and to invest in that technology when it became available. And to the extent that the activities of firms result in waste being discharged into the water and air, if this cost to society were converted to a cost paid by the polluting firms there would be a strong incentive for firms to avoid these costs by investing in technology to reduce waste byproducts.

The presence of significant *positive* externalities also results in an inefficient market equilibrium. For example, when I purchase fireworks for a private independence day celebration, I don't take into consideration the benefit that my neighbors will derive from the display. But that spillover benefit should clearly be counted – by someone – as a benefit to society. But the decision maker considers only the benefit to himself. Here is a numerical example: X is a *pure public good* – any amount of it provided for one person or group benefits everyone in the community. Let Y be a conventional private good that can be consumed directly or used to produce X. Each unit of X requires one unit of Y as input. If we let the price of Y be unity then the price of X will also be unity in a competitive equilibrium, because the marginal cost of producing Y is constant at 1. Therefore, the price ratio is 1. Now, suppose that there are three consumers, each is endowed with 50 units of Y and 0 units of X, and each has the utility function $6\sqrt{x} + y_i$, where x is the amount of the public good produced and y_i is the amount of Y consumed by individual i. If the public good X – e.g., fireworks – were only available on the private market then each consumer would optimize by equating marginal benefit and the price ratio. Therefore, $3/\sqrt{x} = 1$ at equilibrium. We can solve this for $x = 9$. The total amount of X purchased in the community is 9 units, and everyone benefits from each of the 9 units, whether he purchased much or little of the good. Each individual might buy 3 units of X, for example. Is this outcome efficient? Individual utility is

$$u_i = 6\sqrt{9} + 50 - 3 = 65$$

for each i. However, if the community could somehow arrange for $x = 81$ and have each i's consumption of Y reduced by $\frac{1}{3} \times 81 = 27$ to collect the input necessary to produce 81 units of X then $u_i = 6\sqrt{81} + 50 - 27 = 77$, which is much higher *for each individual* than utility at the private market equilibrium. The market equilibrium is not efficient.

Suggestions for further reading: Campbell (1987, pp. 41–43, section 7.1, appendix 2, and pp. 140–143, 109–114).

Exercises

1   The *second* theorem of welfare economics asserts that under certain "convexity" conditions on preferences and production functions, every Pareto optimal allocation is a competitive equilibrium allocation *for some redistribution of initial endowments and profit shares*. Verify the second welfare theorem for the following two-person, two-commodity exchange economy:

$$u_1(a, b) = a \qquad \Omega_1 = (0, 1)$$
$$u_2(x, y) = xy \qquad \Omega_2 = (1, 0)$$

That is, identify all of the Pareto optimal allocations and then prove that each is a competitive equilibrium outcome for some distribution of the total endowment $(1, 1)$.

2   Present a simple example to show that the first welfare theorem is false in general when there are externalities.

3   Consider the following two-person, two-commodity exchange economy:

$$u_1 = a + b, \ \Omega_1 = (1, 1), \ u_2 = 2x + y, \ \Omega_2 = (1, 1).$$

a Characterize the set of Pareto optimal allocations.

b Show that the allocation that assigns $(a, b) = (1, 2)$ to person 1 and $(x, y) = (1, 0)$ to person 2 is Pareto optimal.

c Show that the allocation of (b) is a competitive equilibrium outcome for some price system and some distribution of wealth.

4   Consider the following simple two-person, two-commodity exchange economy:

$$u_1(a, b) = ab \qquad \Omega_1 = (0, 1)$$
$$u_2(x, y) = x + \ln y \qquad \Omega_2 = (2, 2)$$

(Recall that $\ln y$ is the function whose first derivative is y^{-1}.) Find the competitive equilibrium for this economy. Is the competitive equilibrium allocation Pareto optimal? Explain.

5   Consider the following simple two-person, two-commodity exchange
     economy:

$$u_1 = ab - x \qquad \Omega_1 = (0, 1)$$
$$u_2 = xy + a \qquad \Omega_2 = (1, 0)$$

Here, (a, b) is the basket consumed by person 1 and (x, y) is the basket
consumed by person 2.

a Explain carefully why $p_1 = 1 = p_2$ and $a = b = x = y = \frac{1}{2}$ define a
   competitive equilibrium.

b Is this competitive equilibrium allocation Pareto optimal? Explain your
   answer.

6   What are the broadest conditions under which we can claim that an alloca-
     tion that provides each person with a positive amount of each good is Pareto
     optimal if and only if

a the individual marginal rates of substitution are identical and

b the allocation has the material balance property?

Explain briefly.

7   This question pertains to a two-person, two-commodity exchange economy
     with utility functions

$$u_1(a, b) = ab + x \quad \text{and} \quad u_2(x, y) = xy - \tfrac{1}{2}b.$$

Person 1's endowment is $(0, 1)$ and 2's endowment is $(1, 0)$. Person 1
consumes the basket (a, b) and 2 consumes (x, y).

a Explain why we have a competitive equilibrium when each person consumes $\frac{1}{2}$ a unit of each good and the price of each good is unity.

b Prove that the competitive equilibrium is not efficient.

4 Nonconvex economies

What can we say about economies in which individual preferences do not have the
diminishing marginal rate of substitution property? The proof of the first welfare
theorem does not require any assumption about marginal rates of substitution. It
just says that if there are complete markets and no externalities then a *competitive
equilibrium is Pareto optimal. But will a competitive equilibrium exist?* There will
always be a competitive equilibrium if preferences have the diminishing marginal
rate of substitution property at every point,[4] but not necessarily otherwise. The
easiest way to demonstrate the difficulties that can arise when diminishing marginal rate of substitution does not hold is to examine a *one-person* exchange
economy with two commodities.

Suppose that the individual consumes the basket (a, b) and the utility function
is $u_1 = a^2 + b^2$. Draw a few indifference curves (or use calculus) to show that the
marginal rate of substitution is increasing at every point. Suppose that the con-

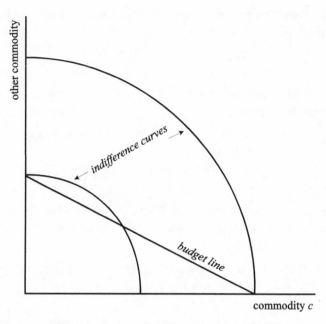

Figure 1

sumer is endowed with one unit of each good. "Demand equals supply" will require a price system at which the consumer demands one unit of each good. It is easy to show that there is no such price system.

Everything hinges on the fact that $(\alpha + \beta)^2 > \alpha^2 + \beta^2$ if α and β are both positive. This has implications for the individual's demand curve; he will want to spend all of his income on one of the goods. Accept the truth of this assertion for a moment. Then there can be no equilibrium at any price regime: The demand for one of the goods will be zero but there is a supply of one unit of that good – Figure 1. (And there will be excess demand for the commodity on which the consumer spends all of his income.) Therefore, our demonstration will be complete once we show that all of the income will be spent on one good.

Suppose that good c is the cheaper of the two goods. (It doesn't matter which of the goods you pick if the prices are identical.) Let α be the demand for good c and let β be the demand for the other good. Then utility is $\alpha^2 + \beta^2$. If $\beta > 0$ then the individual can increase his consumption of good c by β units and can reduce his consumption of the other good by β units without violating the budget constraint. (The price of good c is less than or equal to the price of the other good.) The new level of utility will be the square of the amount of good c consumed and this will equal $(\alpha + \beta)^2$, which will be higher than the original level of utility if α and β are positive, because $(\alpha + \beta)^2 = \alpha^2 + 2\alpha\beta + \beta^2$, which exceeds $\alpha^2 + \beta^2$ when $2\alpha\beta > 0$. Therefore, we have proved the following: if the individual's utility function is $u_1 = a^2 + b^2$ then he will spend all of his money on the cheaper good, and if the prices are equal he will not care which good he buys but he will prefer either extreme to any affordable consumption plan with a positive amount of each good. He will never demand a positive amount of both goods, but the supply of each is positive. Therefore, there can be no price system at which demand equals supply in this simple economy. More important, there does not exist a price system at which supply and demand are approximately equal in each market: Let the two goods be denoted commodity c and commodity k. (That, is, either $c = 1$ and $k = 2$, or else $c = 2$ and $k = 1$.) If $p_C < p_k$ then the consumer will spend all of his income on commodity c. The demand for k will then be zero, but the supply is 1. The consumer's income is $p_C + p_K$, so the consumer will buy $(p_C + p_K)/p_C$ units of c. Therefore, the demand for the good c will be $(p_C + p_K)/p_C = 1 + p_K/p_C$, which exceeds 2 because $p_K/p_C > 1$. And if $p_1 = p_2$ the consumer will get 2 units of one good and zero unit of the other. For any price system, the demand for one of the goods will be zero, which is well below the supply, and the demand for the other good will be at least double the supply (Figure 1).

It is remarkable that we can exhibit a failure of markets to clear at any price regime, even in an approximate sense, by means of a simple economy having only one consumer and two goods. It is easy to extend the above example to one that has many commodities, and the reader is invited to do so. But how special is the fact that there is only one consumer? This is far from realistic. Is it essential for the nonexistence of equilibrium? Consider an economy with *two* consumers, each endowed with one unit of each good, and with utility functions $u_1 = a^2 + b^2$ and $u_2 = x^2 + y^2$. Person 1's consumption plan is represented by (a, b) and 2's plan is represented by (x, y). If $p_1 = p_2 = 1$ then each person has an income of \$2, all of which he will spend on one good. If Person 1 buys only the first good and person 2 buys only the second good then both markets will clear. We will have $a = 2 = y$ and $b = 0 = x$. The total demand for the first good is $2 + 0$, which equals supply. The total demand for the second good is $0 + 2$, which equals the supply of the second good. So, with two consumers, each with the nonconvex preference scheme represented above, there will exist a market clearing configuration of prices.

Now consider an economy with *three* consumers, each endowed with a unit of each good and each with the utility function $u_i = a^2 + b^2$. (There is no danger of confusion at this point if we let (a, b) denote the consumption plan of whichever individual we are discussing.) Suppose we have $p_1 > p_2$. Each consumer will spend all of his income on the cheaper good. The total demand for the first good will be zero, which is well below the total supply of 3 ($= 3 \times 1$). Individual income is $p_1 + p_2$, and the consumer will get $(p_1 + p_2)/p_2$ units of the second good when he devotes all of his income to the purchase of that good. Therefore, the total demand for the second good will be $3 \times (p_1 + p_2)/p_2 = 3 \times (p_1/p_2 + 1)$, which is greater than 6 because $p_1/p_2 > 1$. This is more than double the total supply of 3. Similarly, if $p_1 < p_2$ then everyone will spend all of his income on the first good and the total demand for that good will be more than double the supply. Therefore, we must have $p_1 = p_2$ if both markets are to clear even approximately. Recall that individual income is $p_1 + p_2$, and the consumer will get $(p_1 + p_2)/p_C$ units of commodity c when he devotes all of his income to the purchase good c. But $p_1 = p_2 = p_c$, so each person will get exactly 2 units of the good that he buys. Consider the total demand for both goods as a function of the number of individuals who purchase the first good. This is given in the following table.

Number of consumers of good 1	Demand for X	Demand for Y
0	0	6
1	2	4
2	4	2
3	6	0

The closest we can come to matching demand and supply is achieved by the second and third lines of the table. In either case, demand exceeds supply for one of the goods by one unit, and supply exceeds demand for the other good by one unit. At least the gap between demand and supply has been reduced to $33\frac{1}{3}\%$. When there was only one consumer, the closest the market could come to balancing demand and supply left a gap of 100%.

Now, consider a large number t of consumers, each identical to those of the above economies. For reasons that must now be clear, an equilibrium requires $p_1 = p_2$, with each consumer buying exactly two units of one of the goods and none of the other. The consumer doesn't care which good he receives when the prices are identical. If t is even then $\frac{1}{2}t$ consumers can buy the first good, resulting in a total demand of $2 \times \frac{1}{2}t = t$ units, which equals the supply of that good. And the remaining $\frac{1}{2}t$ consumers buy the second good, resulting in a total demand of $2 \times \frac{1}{2}t = t$ units, which equals supply. Both markets clear exactly. Suppose that t is odd. Then $\frac{1}{2}t$ is not an integer. The next table shows how close we can get to market clearance.

Number of consumers of good 1	Demand for X	Demand for Y
$\frac{1}{2}t - \frac{1}{2}$	$t - 1$	$t + 1$
$\frac{1}{2}t + \frac{1}{2}$	$t + 1$	$t - 1$

You can see that with either configuration of plans we have a very good approximation to clearance in both markets. The difference between demand and supply is one unit, which is a very tiny fraction of the total supply of t units when the number t is large: If the number of traders is large then we are guaranteed a general equilibrium in a practical sense, if not in an exact sense, regardless of the nature of individual preferences. (Verify that when t is an odd number then we cannot have an exact equilibrium in the economy we have been discussing.)

5 Price taking behavior

Now we consider whether consumers will be motivated to reveal their private information truthfully. A consumer's hidden (private) characteristic is her preference scheme. What does misrepresentation of preference mean in the context of the market system? Consumers are never asked to report their utility functions. They *are* asked to submit a list of demands that maximize individual utility given the current prices, however. If a consumer misrepresents her preferences by demanding a basket of goods that is not utility maximizing, there will be no way for the system, or any referee, to detect this misrepresentation. Therefore, she can get away with it. But will she ever want to? If the false demands cause prices to change in a way that leaves her with more utility than she would have realized with truthful revelation, then she will have an incentive to deviate from the rules of the game. So, it all comes down to the ability of the consumer to influence prices by altering her demands. The intuition is that this power is negligible when there is a realistically large number of consumers. We are about to support this with analysis. We begin by showing how misrepresentation can be profitable when the number of consumers is small. This will prepare us for the large numbers case by clarifying what is meant by misrepresentation of preference.

Consider the following simple exchange economy with two households and two commodities: Person 1's endowment is $\Omega_1 = (0, 1)$ and 2's endowment is $\Omega_2 = (1, 0)$. The utility functions are given by

$$u_1 = ab \quad \text{and} \quad u_2 = xy$$

assuming that a typical allocation assigns the consumption plan $\theta_1 = (a, b)$ to person 1 and the plan $\theta_2 = (x, y)$ to person 2. The competitive equilibrium is easy to compute:

Individual 1's marginal rate of substitution is b/a and individual 2's marginal rate of substitution is y/x.

$$\text{MRS}_1 = \frac{(\partial u_1 / \partial a)}{(\partial u_1 / \partial b)} = \frac{b}{a} \qquad \text{MRS}_2 = \frac{(\partial u_2 / \partial x)}{(\partial u_2 / \partial y)} = \frac{y}{x}.$$

(The MRS is the marginal utility of the first good divided by the marginal utility of the second good. Marginal utility is computed by taking the derivative of the utility function with respect to that commodity while treating the amount consumed of the other commodity as a constant.) If the price of either good is zero then there will be unlimited demand for that good and demand will certainly exceed supply. Therefore, both prices will be positive at equilibrium. Therefore, each individual will have a positive income and hence can afford a positive amount of each good and that means that utility will be positive. If individual i consumes zero units of some good then u_i will be zero. (Zero times any number is zero.) But that can't be a utility maximizing strategy. Therefore, both persons will consume a positive amount of each good at equilibrium. Therefore, each person's MRS will equal the price ratio at equilibrium.[5] That implies, $b/a = y/x$. But $a + x = 1$ and $b + y = 1$ at equilibrium (market clearance). Therefore,

$$b/a = (1 - b)/(1 - a),$$

and if we cross-multiply we get $a - ab = b - ab$, which implies $a = b$. Now, (a, b) and the endowment point $(0, 1)$ are both on 1's budget line, so the slope of the line is $(b - 1)/(a - 0)$ and this is the negative of the price ratio which will equal person 1's MRS at equilibrium. Therefore,

$$b/a = -(b - 1)/a,$$

which implies $b = \frac{1}{2}$, and therefore $a = \frac{1}{2}$ because $a = b$. Therefore, $x = y = \frac{1}{2}$. The equilibrium price ratio is equal to the marginal rates of substitution at equilibrium, and $b/a = 1$ so the price ratio equals 1 at equilibrium. That is $p_1 = p_2$. For convenience, set each price equal to unity. We have found the competitive equilibrium (p^*, θ^*). The equilibrium price system is $p^* = (1, 1)$ and the equilibrium allocation θ^* assigns the consumption plan $(\frac{1}{2}, \frac{1}{2})$ to each household. Note that each individual's income at equilibrium is unity.

By definition of a *competitive* equilibrium, each person takes the price regime as given. That is, $(\frac{1}{2}, \frac{1}{2})$ is the unique utility maximizing consumption plan of all those plans (a, b) satisfying the budget constraint $1a + 1b = 1$. But each individual has a monopoly in the supply of one of the goods, and each individual supplies one-half of a unit at the competitive equilibrium. An individual can be expected to know that the price ratio will change if he changes his supply. That is, the individuals will surely not behave as price takers in this economy – our price taking assumption is unfounded. We offer a proof by contradiction.

Suppose that person 2 always acts as a price taker. This means that 2's demand vector (x, y) will always be the one that maximizes u_2 subject to the budget constraint $p_1 x + p_2 y = p_1$. (Why is 2's income equal to p_1?) Let's see if person 1 can profit from misrepresenting his preferences. The intuition is simple. If 1 demands the vector v_1 and at that point he demands more of good 2, the good that he supplies, than the straightforward utility maximization exercise would predict, then the price of good 2 will be kept high. This will be utility maximizing in a more sophisticated sense. Let's see why. Suppose that 2 demands v_2 and both markets clear. This means that $v_1 + v_2 = \Omega_1 + \Omega_2 = (1, 1)$. If 1 were to move to

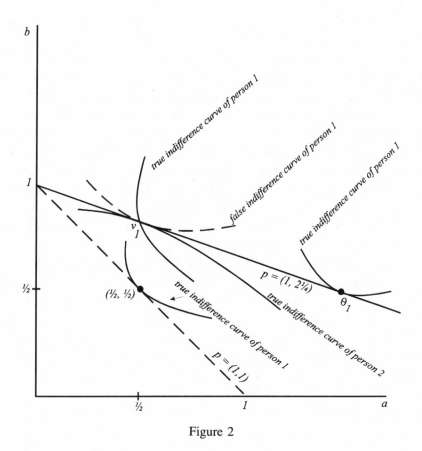

Figure 2

the competitive demand vector θ_1 then $u_1(\theta_1)$ would be greater than $u_1(v_1)$. *If 1 could be sure of having his order θ_1 filled* then ordering θ_1 would be 1's best strategy. But 1 can be sure that his order θ_1 *won't* be filled. Markets clear when 1 undersupplies the second good by ordering v_1 for himself, and because θ_1 specifies a lower demand (i.e., higher supply) for the second good we will have excess supply of the second good when 1 orders θ_1 and 2 orders v_2. The price of the second good will have to fall and this means that individual 1 can't have θ_1 after all. This argument is illustrated by Figure 2. *Figure 2 represents person 2's utility in terms of person 1's consumption* (a, b). This means that an indifference curve for person 2 is the set of plans (a, b) such that $u_2(1 - a, 1 - b)$ is constant. In the present case, $u_2 = xy$, so an indifference curve for person 2 is the set of plans (a, b) such that $u_2(1 - a, 1 - b)$ is constant. In the present case, $u_2 = xy$, so an indifference curve for person 2 is the set of plans (a, b) such that $(1 - a) \times (1 - b)$ is constant.

The *competitive* equilibrium allocation gives each person the basket ($\frac{1}{2}$, $\frac{1}{2}$). The associated equilibrium price vector is $p^* = (1, 1)$. At a higher price for good 2, say $p_2 = 2\frac{1}{4}$, person 2 will demand less of good 2. Person 2's demand under price system $p = (1, 2\frac{1}{4})$ is v_2, which is identified by the point v_1 in Figure 2: v_1 would be what is left over for person 1 if person 2 were given the basket v_2. If 1 were to demand the vector that maximizes u_1 given the price vector $p = (1, 2\frac{1}{4})$ then 1 would demand θ_1 shown in Figure 1. As we have seen, markets won't clear when 1's consumption plan is θ_1 and 2's plan is v_2. If 1 continued to behave competitively – i.e., take prices as given – then the economy would wind up back at the competitive equilibrium with each person receiving $(\frac{1}{2}, \frac{1}{2})$. But if 1 were to demand v_1 under price system $p = (1, 2\frac{1}{4})$ when 2 demands v_2 then both markets would clear. That is because v_1 is defined as the total supply minus v_2. The economy would be in equilibrium because there would be no tendency for prices to change: Demand and supply would be equal in both markets. And because markets clear, each consumer would be able to carry out her plan. Moreover, v_1 gives individual 1 more utility than $(\frac{1}{2}, \frac{1}{2})$ according to 1's true preferences! To make this even more concrete, let's work out v_2 and θ_1. To obtain v_2 we want to maximize $u_2 = xy$ subject to $1x + 2.25y = 1$. (Note that person 2 has one unit of good 1 to sell at a price of $1.) Clearly, utility maximization implies $MRS_2 = y/x = p_1/p_2 = 1/2.25 = 4/9$. Then $y/x = 4/9$ or $9y = 4x$. And $1x + 2.25y = 1$, which is equivalent to $4x + 9y = 4$. Therefore, $4x + 4x = 4$, which implies $x = \frac{1}{2}$. Then $y = 4(\frac{1}{2})/9 = 2/9$. Therefore, $v_2 = (1/2, 2/9)$. Therefore, if 1 demands $v_1 = (1/2, 7/9)$ when $p = (1, 2\frac{1}{4})$ and 2 demands v_2 then both markets will clear and 1's utility will be

$$u_1 = (1/2)(7/9) = 7/18,$$

which is more than

$$u_1 = (1/2)(1/2) = 1/4,$$

the utility that 1 receives when he announces his true utility maximizing demand at every turn.

Had person 1 reported her true utility maximizing demand θ_1 when $p_1 = 1$ and $p_2 = 2\frac{1}{4}$ she would have set $b/a = 1/2\frac{1}{4} = 4/9$. Hence $9b = 4a$. 1's budget constraint at this price regime is $a + 2.25b = 2.25$, or $4a + 9b = 9$. Then $8a = 9$, so $a = 9/8$. Hence $b = \frac{1}{2}$. This plan yields $u_1 = (9/8) \times \frac{1}{2} = 9/16$, which is even greater than $7/18$. But 1 could never realize the utility level $9/16$ because markets wouldn't clear. If person 1 continued to take prices as given, the excess demand for good 1 when 1 demanded $(9/8, \frac{1}{2})$ would cause the price of the first commodity to rise relative to the second, pushing the price regime toward the equilibrium where $p_1 = p_2$. But when the two prices are equal person 1's utility is considerably less than $7/18$.

We say that a trader behaves *sincerely* if he always demands a basket that maximizes his utility *given* the price regime. We have just discovered that sincere behavior is not a dominant strategy. Now we show that the gain from deviating from sincere behavior is virtually zero if the number of consumers is large. Specifically, we show that the gain from deviating from sincere behavior goes to zero as the number of traders gets arbitrarily large. Consider an economy with t type 1 persons identical to person 1 and t type 2 persons identical to person 2. That is:

$$t \text{ persons have } u_i = ab \quad \text{and} \quad \Omega_i = (0, 1) \quad \text{and}$$
$$t \text{ persons have } u_j = xy \quad \text{and} \quad \Omega_j = (1, 0).$$

We prove our result by demonstrating that the ability of a single type 1 person to manipulate prices becomes more and more negligible as t becomes larger and larger. We need to determine the demand functions: For convenience, let's normalize and set the price of the second good equal to unity, with P denoting the price of the first good. A type 1 person's MRS is b/a, and we will have $b/a = P$ if a type 1 person demands the basket that maximizes u_1 *given* P. (We know that a and b will both be positive, so there will be an interior solution.) Then $b = Pa$. The budget constraint is $Pa + b = 1$. (A type 1 person sells one unit of the second good at a price of \$1 so her income is \$1.) If $b = Pa$ we have $2Pa = 1$, or $a = 1/2P$. Then $b = P(1/2P) = 1/2$. Therefore, the *true* demand functions of a type 1 person are:

$$a = 1/2P \quad \text{and} \quad b = 1/2.$$

A type 2 person's MRS is y/x, and we will have $y/x = P$ if she demands the basket that maximizes u_2 *given* P. (There will be an interior solution.) Then $y = Px$. The budget constraint is $Px + y = P$. (A type 2 person sells one unit of the first good at a price of P dollars, so her income is P dollars.) If $y = Px$ we have $2Px = P$, or $x = 1/2$. Then $y = P(1/2) = P/2$. Therefore, the *true* demand functions of a type 2 person are

$$x = 1/2 \quad \text{and} \quad y = P/2.$$

If $P = 1$ then each person demands half a unit of each good, which means that the aggregate demand for each good is t, which equals supply. That is, $P = 1$ is the equilibrium price *assuming* price taking behavior by each agent. (Notice we get the same equilibrium as the one that we have already determined for the two-person economy with $t = 1$.)

Suppose that everyone takes price as given and announces her true utility maximizing demand vector *except* for one type 1 person, whom we will refer to as person m. Then the aggregate demand for the first good is at least $(t - 1)(1/2P) + t(1/2)$. The total supply of the first good is exactly t, so even before we add on the demand of person m we must have

$$(t - 1)(1/2P) + t(1/2) \leq t. \tag{1}$$

If $(t - 1)(1/2P) + t(1/2) > t$ then supply will exceed demand, whatever m announces, and we cannot be at equilibrium. But [1] is equivalent to

$$P \geq (t - 1)/t. \tag{2}$$

Similarly, the aggregate demand for the second good is at least $(t - 1)(1/2) + t(P/2)$. The total supply of the second good is exactly t, so even without the demand of person m we must have

$$(t - 1)(1/2) + t(P/2) \leq t, \tag{3}$$

and this is equivalent to

$$P \leq (t + 1)/t. \tag{4}$$

Putting [2] and [4] together gives us

$$(t - 1)/t \leq P \leq (t + 1)/t$$

even before we add on person m's demand. If t is very large then both $(t - 1)/t$ and $(t + 1)/t$ will be very close to unity, so the actual price will be very close to the *competitive* equilibrium price, regardless of what person m decides to do. Therefore, an individual's potential utility gain from any departure from sincere behavior is very tiny when the number of suppliers of each good is large. This small positive benefit is more than offset by the cost of acquiring enough information to enable the individual to manipulate prices *advantageously*. We can expect everyone to behave sincerely when the number of suppliers of each good is large. (See Roberts and Postlewaite, 1976, for the general argument.)

Exercises

1   Consider an economy with t persons identical to person 1 ($u_1 = ab$, $\Omega_1 = [0, 1]$) and t persons identical to person 2 ($u_2 = xy$, $\Omega_2 = [1, 0]$). Show that the ability of *person 2* to manipulate prices becomes more and more negligible as t becomes larger and larger.

2   Consider an exchange economy with two goods and $n = 2t$ individuals. The first t individuals have the utility function $u_i = a_i^2 b_i$ and endowment $\Omega_i = (1, 0)$. The other individuals have the utility function $u_i = x_i y_i$. Show that the ability of a single individual to influence the price ratio p_1/p_2 is negligible if t is large.

6 Implementation

The previous section demonstrated that it is rational for each individual to reveal her utility function truthfully if there is a large number of suppliers of each good and allocation is determined by the market system. In real-world market economies there are many goods that are produced by only a handful of firms. In such cases, the individual firm deviates from sincere play by taking into account the effect of its own supply on the market price.[6] Are there other devices for inducing truthful revelation of hidden characteristics at equilibrium even when there are few agents? We now take a brief look at this question.

A *game* is a structure that specifies a set S_i of strategies from which player i is permitted to choose; an outcome function g which determines an outcome $x = g(s_1, s_2, \ldots, s_n)$ for each profile $s = (s_1, s_2, \ldots, s_n)$ of strategies, one for each of the n players; and a payoff function u that determines the payoff $u_i(x)$ that i receives at outcome x. Strictly speaking, this is a game in *normal form*. A strategy profile s is simply a specification of the strategy s_i played by each person i. A strategy profile s^* is a Nash equilibrium if for each person i, playing strategy s_i^* is a best (utility maximizing) response to the strategies s_j^* played by each $j \neq i$. Formally, s^* is a Nash equilibrium of the game if for each player i, s_i^* belongs to S_i and

$$u_i(g(s^*)) \geq u_i(g(s_1^*, s_2^*, \ldots, s_{i-1}^*, s_i, s_{i+1}^*, \ldots, s_n^*))$$

for all s_i in S_i.

A *mechanism* (or game form) is a framework that specifies a strategy set S_i for each player i and an outcome function $g(s_1, s_2, \ldots, s_n)$. This generates a *game* for each specification of the payoff functions.

Consider the following simple example. There are two players and two possible outcomes x and y. In this case we only need to know whether an individual prefers x to y, or the converse. It is not necessary to know the utility derived from each outcome. (For simplicity we ignore the possibility that i is indifferent between x and y.) Then there are four possible individual preference regimes, θ:

$$\theta = (x, x) \quad \text{or}$$
$$\theta = (x, y) \quad \text{or}$$
$$\theta = (y, x) \quad \text{or}$$
$$\theta = (y, y).$$

Note: $\theta = (a, b)$ means that 1 prefers a to the other alternative and 2 prefers b to the other alternative. (We don't need to know the utility levels. Why? When only the order of preference matters we refer to the list of payoff functions as a preference profile.) Within this simple framework, we can show how demanding is the requirement that an equilibrium exist for every specification of individual preferences and that every equilibrium give rise to an efficient outcome. This is accomplished in the next section, 6.1. The theorem and proof are due to Hurwicz and Schmeidler (1978).

6.1 The Hurwicz–Schmeidler theorem

Let (S_1, S_2, g) be a mechanism that satisfies the following *existence* and *optimality* criteria: For each player i, S_i is the set of strategies available to i; $g(s_1, s_2)$

belongs to $\{x, y\}$ and is the outcome when 1 plays s_1 in S_1 and 2 plays s_2 in S_2; and for each preference profile θ a Nash equilibrium exists, and every Nash equilibrium for θ is Pareto optimal for θ (and this is to hold for all θ). Then the mechanism is dictatorial. Person i is a dictator if for each outcome x there is a strategy s_i^x in S_i such that $g(s) = x$ whenever $s_i^x = s_i$: In words, person i can control the outcome.

Proof Let (s_1, s_2) be a Nash equilibrium for $\theta = (x, y)$. Assume that $g(s_1, s_2) = x$. The proof for $g(s_1, s_2) = y$ is analogous. Because it is an equilibrium and 2 prefers y to $g(s_1, s_2)$ we must have $g(s_1, \beta) = x$ for all β in S_2. Let (t_1, t_2) be an equilibrium for $\theta' = (y, x)$. If $g(t_1, t_2) = y$ then we must have $g(t_1, \beta) = y$ for all β in S_2 because (t_1, t_2) is an equilibrium and 2 prefers x to y under θ'. Therefore, 1 can ensure that the outcome is x by playing s_1 and can guarantee that the outcome is y by playing t_1, in which case 1 is a dictator. Suppose, then, that $g(t_1, t_2) = x$. We have

$$(s_1, s_2) \text{ is an equilibrium for } \theta = (x, y) \quad \text{and} \quad g(s_1, s_2) = x$$
$$(t_1, t_2) \text{ is an equilibrium for } \theta' = (y, x) \quad \text{and} \quad g(t_1, t_2) = x.$$

We will show that (s_1, t_2) is an equilibrium for $\theta'' = (y, y)$, *and* that $g(s_1, t_2) = x$, contradicting Pareto optimality. Now, if $g(\alpha, t_2) = y$ for some α in S_1 then (t_1, t_2) is not an equilibrium for $\theta' = (y, x)$. Therefore, $g(\alpha, t_2) = x$ for all α in S_1. In particular, $g(s_1, t_2) = x$. If $g(s_1, \beta) = y$ for some β in S_2 then (s_1, s_2) is not an equilibrium for $\theta = (x, y)$. Therefore, $g(s_1, \beta) = x$ for all β in S_2, and we have established that (s_1, t_2) is an equilibrium for $\theta'' = (y, y)$, although $g(s_1, t_2) = x$. Therefore, existence and optimality of equilibrium require $g(t_1, t_2) = y$ and hence person 1 is a dictator.

6.2 Subgame-perfect Nash equilibria

In a resource allocation context there are far more than two feasible outcomes. This allows us to design more sophisticated mechanisms in which one person can use threats to prevent another from employing a strategy that would precipitate a sub-optimal outcome. But a threat has to be credible if we are to take the resulting equilibrium seriously. Accordingly, we will employ subgame-perfect equilibrium. (See section 8 of Chapter 1.) We'll start with ordinary Nash equilibrium, though, to reveal why incredible threats can block the achievement of a welfare optimum.

We assume two persons and two *commodities* (private goods). The individuals have classical economic preferences. (This example is taken from Moore and Repullo, 1988.) Suppose there are two possible payoff functions.

Case C Both individuals have the Cobb–Douglas utility function $u_C(x, y) = xy$.
Case L Both individuals have the Leontief utility function $u_L(x, y) = \min\{x, y\}$.

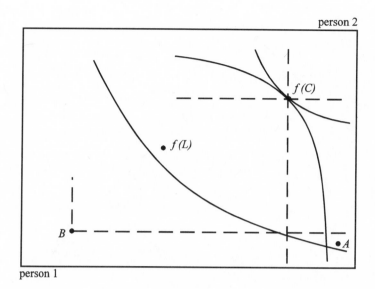

person 2

f (C)

f (L)

B

A

person 1

Figure 3

Suppose that the welfare criterion *f* designates *f(C)*, identified in Figure 3, as socially optimal in case *C* and *f(L)* in case *L*.

Suppose that (S_1, S_2, g) is a mechanism that implements *f*. That is, ordinary Nash equilibria always exist and are always optimal according to *f*. Let (s_1^*, s_2^*) be an equilibrium for case *C*. Then $g(s_1^*, s_2^*) = f(C)$. But (s_1^*, s_2^*) must be an equilibrium for case *L* as well. If $g(\alpha, s_2^*)$ gives person 1 higher utility than $g(s_1^*, s_2^*) = f(C)$ according to u_L then that must be true for u_C also, contradicting the fact that (s_1^*, s_2^*) is an equilibrium for case *C*. Consult the Edgeworth box, Figure 3, to prove this: the upper contour set for u_L is contained in the upper contour set for u_C, at allocation *f(C)*. Similarly, we cannot have $g(s_1^*, \beta)$ giving 2 more utility than *f(C)* according to u_L. Therefore, (s_1^*, s_2^*) is a Nash equilibrium in case *L*, contradicting the claim that the mechanism implements *f*: $g(s_1^*, s_2^*) = f(C) \neq f(L)$. A more elaborate framework – the extensive form of a game – will provide us with a way out of this difficulty.

We show that optimality criterion *f* can be implemented by an *extensive form* mechanism – one that generates an extensive form game once the payoff function is specified – with subgame perfection as the equilibrium concept. The following extensive form game (mechanism) does implement *f* in *subgame-perfect* Nash equilibrium. That is, subgame-perfect equilibria exist in both cases and these equilibria are always optimal according to *f*.

Stage 1 *Person 1 announces either* L *or* C.

> If 1 announces *L* the outcome is *f(L)* and there is no further play. If 1 announces *C* then player 2 makes a move at . . .

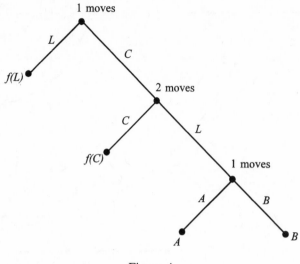

Figure 4

Stage 2 *Person 2 agrees or disagrees with player 1.*
    If 2 agrees that case *C* is the true state then the outcome is $f(C)$ and there is no further play. If 2 disagrees then player 1 makes the next move at . . .

Stage 3 *Person 1 chooses A or B to be the outcome.*

The scheme is represented as Figure 4.

Analysis

1 The true state is *L* and both persons have Leontief preferences. Person 1 prefers $f(C)$ to $f(L)$, but if he announces *C* at stage 1 then player 2 will challenge, knowing that 1 will choose *B* over *A* at stage 3 because 1 prefers *B* to *A* in case *L*. Because 2 prefers *B* to $f(C)$ in case *L* the challenge would be the profitable strategy for him. *If* 1 threatened to choose *A* in stage 3 then 2 would be forced to accept $f(C)$ and we have a Nash equilibrium. But it is not subgame-perfect – i.e., it is not in 1's interest to carry out this threat if stage 3 were actually reached. The only subgame-perfect Nash equilibrium results in $f(L)$. It has 1 announcing *L* at stage 1 and declaring that he would choose *B* if stage 3 were reached, while 2 declares his intention to challenge in stage 2.

2 The true state is *C*. Person 1 has no incentive to announce *L* and take $f(L)$ unless he fears that 2 would challenge at stage 2. But then 1 would be forced to choose between *A* and *B* and he would pick *A*, which gives more utility than *B* according to u_C, and *A* is worse for 2 than $f(C)$. Therefore, even if both *A* and *B* are worse for player 1 than $f(L)$, a threat by 2 to challenge *C* at stage 2 unless 1

announces L in stage 1 would not be credible, because if push came to shove the challenge would precipitate A, which gives 2 less utility (in terms of u_c) than $f(C)$. Therefore, the only subgame-perfect equilibrium in this case results in $f(C)$. This is sustained by having 1 announce C at stage 1, declaring that he would choose A if stage 3 were reached, while 2 announces that he would accept C at stage 2.

7 Common property resources

Suppose that n entrepreneurs all have free access to a resource from which they can extract a marketable commodity, say fish. If we assume that the amount harvested by any entrepreneur depends on the effort expended by that agent *and* also on the effort of all others, and if we assume in addition that output per unit of effort declines as the total effort of all fishers increases, then we have the classical common property resource model in which the pursuit of self-interest leads to an inefficient rate of extraction in the short run and insufficient conservation in the long run. Let's focus on the short-run problem.

First, we need to identify the efficient rate of extraction. Let e_i be the effort expended by entrepreneur i on the lake, which we take as the common resource. Then e_i denotes the number of hours of fishing per week spent by the workers in boat i. Let $e = e_1 + e_2 + e_3 + \ldots + e_n$ denote the overall level of effort. For simplicity, assume that effort is undertaken at a constant opportunity cost of c. That is, one hour of fishing on the lake involves the sacrifice of c fish that could have been obtained by fishing in the ocean for one hour. (Or c could be the opportunity cost of leisure.) If $T(e)$ denotes the total number of units of X harvested by all entrepreneurs as a function of total effort then $A(e) = T(e)/e$ is the average product, which we assume declines as e increases. Therefore, marginal product $M(e)$, the first derivative of T, is less than $A(e)$ for each level of e.[7]

The efficient level of effort e^* is that value of e that equates marginal cost and opportunity cost. This is depicted in Figure 5, where the intersection of the marginal product curve $M(e)$ and the constant opportunity cost line c identifies the efficient level of effort e^*. The efficient rate of extraction of fish is $x^* = T(e^*)$.

Proof If e is the actual amount of effort expended and $M(e) < c$ then one unit of effort transferred *from* the lake *to* the ocean will increase the community's consumption of fish by $c - M(e)$, and if $M(e) > c$ then one unit of effort transferred from the ocean to the lake will also increase fish consumption by $c - M(e)$. In neither case will there be any increase in overall input employed. Therefore, everyone can be made better off by distributing the gain $c - M(e)$ over the community. This means that $M(e) = c$ must hold if the outcome is efficient.

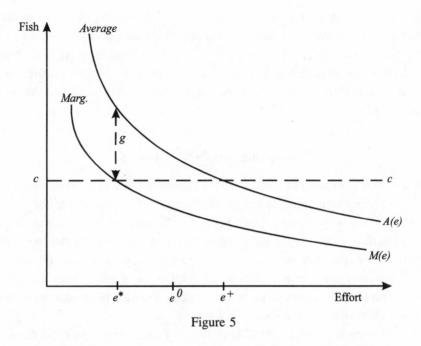

Figure 5

We have proved that equality of marginal product and marginal cost is required for efficiency. Now let's determine the actual extraction rate when the resource is available to anyone without a user charge, in which case the only cost to an individual entrepreneur as a result of expending e units of effort in extraction is the opportunity cost of ce. It turns out that the equilibrium occurs at e^+ in Figure 5 where *average* product equals marginal cost, *above* the efficient level of input (or effort). Let's see why. Suppose that the current total input level is some amount e^0 which is below the point where $A(e)$ equals c. Suppose that entrepreneur i now increases his input slightly. The addition to the total catch per unit of additional input will be $M(e^0)$, the marginal product at e^0. *Society* would be better off if that additional unit of effort were employed in fishing the ocean, where the yield would be c fish per unit of effort instead of $M(e^0)$. But the individual entrepreneur has no incentive to maximize social welfare. In the case of a common property resource the harvest per person tends to be the average harvest. Even though the average harvest falls as a single individual increases his input level, the total harvest tends to be shared evenly by the entrepreneurs. If the individual takes home the average output then it pays *him* to increase his effort or input level as long as the private gain at the margin – which will be close to the average output – is above the private cost at the margin – which is c in this case. Therefore, harvesting will continue until average product is equal to marginal cost, or $A(e) = c$. This defines the equilibrium e^+ in Figure 5.

If the government imposes a user charge of g dollars per hour spent fishing on the lake then the private marginal cost to an individual will now be $c + g$, and self-interest will drive entrepreneurs to harvest up to the point where average product equals $c + g$. In other words, $A(e) = c + g$ characterizes the equilibrium that results when there is a user charge of g. If g is set equal to $A(e^*) - c$ then $A(e) = c + g$ implies $e = e^*$ and the efficient outcome is attained. (See Figure 5 again.)

The same equilibrium would be realized if the lake were owned by a profit maximizing firm. The owner of the firm need not be a single individual; it could be the entire community. Let's see what the profit maximizing fee f would be. Assume that the costs of setting and collecting the fee are independent of the intensity of economic activity on the lake. That is, the costs of the lake owner are fixed, at k, say. Then the lake owner's profit is $fe - k$. Maximizing fe will give us the same value of e that maximizes $fe - k$. Let's determine what the value of e would be at equilibrium when the users of the lake must pay a user charge of f to the private owner: They will harvest up to the point where $A(e) = c + f$. Therefore, $f = A(e) - c$ at equilibrium, and thus $fe = A(e)e - ce$. Because $A(e)e$ is just total product, $T(e)$, the owner of the lake will want to maximize $T(e) - ce$, which is just total product minus total variable cost. This will be maximized when marginal product equals marginal cost: The first derivative of $T(e) - ce$ is $T'(e) - c$, and if $T'' < 0$ at all points then $T'(e) = c$ is necessary for maximization of $T(e) - ce$. Profit maximization requires $M(e) = c$ and we already know that this is satisfied by e^*. Therefore, profit maximization by the owner of the lake leads to the socially optimal outcome. On the other hand, free, unrestricted use of the lake will not precipitate a socially optimal outcome.

Notice that the social optimum can be realized by private ownership or by government directive. (Verify that $f = g$.) Which does a better job of promoting social welfare? Perhaps it doesn't matter whether society chooses the public or private remedy for correcting the inefficiency. They both yield the same outcome, e^*. Is there any difference between the two regimes?

In both cases the principal delegates the crucial job to an agent. In the case of the public approach, with the state imposing a user fee, the principal is the society and the agent is a government body that is given the job of computing the efficient fee g and enforcing it. Let's call this government agency a regulator. Acquiring the necessary information about marginal and average product is not an easy task. What assurance is there that the regulator will devote the necessary effort to this task? Who monitors the regulator? We can ask the same question of the private solution. It works only if the owner of the lake maximizes profit. But owners typically hire an agent, called a manager, to carry out this task for them. The manager's personal welfare is her chief concern, and that is not perfectly aligned with the interests of the owners. In a capitalist economy the manager is monitored by the capital market. If her activities are not providing the rate of return that the capital equipment and resources at her command are capable of earning then a takeover will be profitable for anyone who has access to an agent who *can* get the most out of the inputs.[8] Moreover, there is usually better information on the performance of agents in the private sector than in the government sector. Almost all of the relevant data can be reduced to a single number: rate of return on capital. Another reason why government agents can be harder to regulate is that their budget constraints are typically softer than those that govern firms in the private sector. (But recall the government assistance given to Chrysler in the late 1970s, and the 'too big to fail' rationale for government assistance to banks in the 1980s.) This is just a very preliminary look at the question of public versus private regulation, but it gives an indication of the kind of issues that have to be settled before one can decide whether the public or private remedy is better for society in a particular case.

Suggestions for further reading: Ostrom (1990).

Exercise

1   Show that the constant opportunity cost assumption is critical to our demonstration that profit maximization will lead to efficiency.

6

Resource allocation: public goods

This chapter explores a very simple model of resource allocation with one pure public good X and one pure private good Y. Although the model is extremely simple it incorporates enough features of resource allocation with public goods to enable us to bring out all the strategic nuances and complications that economists have uncovered in studying pure public goods. As in the previous chapter, hidden action problems are assumed away, to enable us to focus on the preference revelation problem. But preference revelation has a different twist in this chapter because of the presence of a pure public good. By definition, any amount of a public good that is made available to one individual or group can be simultaneously enjoyed by everyone in the community, although not everyone receives the same level of benefit. An individual who makes no contribution to the financing or production of public good X is said to be a *free rider,* because that individual consumes the same amount of X as someone who did contribute. This makes truthful preference revelation particularly tricky, because production of X will have an inescapable impact on the consumption of private goods, as resources are diverted to the production of X. Efficiency requires that the production of X be a function of reported preferences. But this means that one's consumption of the private good is a function of the information that one provides about her benefit from the public good. If one's consumption of the private good is negatively correlated with the amount of benefit one claims to derive from the public good, there will be a strong incentive to be a free rider. A successful allocation mechanism will have to eliminate this incentive. To study this problem, we employ a very simple model in which the marginal utility of the private good is constant and identical across individuals. Moreover, this information is common knowledge. Only the individual's benefit function for the public good is private (hidden) information.

Each individual i is endowed with Ω_i units of the private good Y at the beginning of the period and zero unit of the public good. The private good can be either consumed or used as an input in the production of the public good, X. The production of x units of X requires $g(x)$ units of Y as input and X itself is not used as an input in any production process. Consumer i's utility function has the quasi-linear form $u_i(x, y_i) = B_i(x) + y_i$, where x is the amount of the public good made available and y_i is the amount of the private good consumed by i. By definition of a pure public good any amount consumed by one individual is equally available to all so the total amount of the public good produced, x, enters everyone's utility function. Let $B_i'(x)$ denote the first derivative of $B_i(x)$ evaluated at x. We assume that $B_i'(x)$ falls as x increases.

A typical public project F specifies the amount x_F of the public good produced and the amount $c_i(F)$ by which i's consumption of the private good falls as a result of the fact that some of the private good is diverted from consumption to use as input in producing the public good. $U_i(F) \equiv B_i(x_F) + \Omega_i - c_i(F)$ is the utility derived from project F by individual i. Clearly, i will prefer project F to project G if and only if $U_i(F) > U_i(G)$. In words, i prefers F to G if and only if F yields more benefit to i net of the effect on i's consumption of the private good. We don't at this point specify how i's private consumption is reduced when X is produced, but to the extent that resources are diverted in order to produce X there will have to be a reduction in the total community consumption of Y and this will inevitably be borne by individuals, although there is a great variety of ways in which the distribution of this burden can be determined. (By means of a fixed income tax formula, as the result of some type of election, by having individuals voluntarily contribute to the financing of x and then producing whatever level of x has been funded, etc.)

The next three sections, as well as sections 5, 6, and 7, can be interpreted without the supposition that a project specifies the output level of some public good along with a detailed specification of its implications for the consumption of the private good. One can interpret F and G abstractly as two public options that provide arbitrary individual i with the respective utility levels $U_i(F)$ and $U_i(G)$ and the center wants to induce the individuals to reveal these true utility numbers so that it can adopt the outcome that yields the larger total utility.

We begin by looking at conventional voting, but our search for a successful mechanism will lead us to social cost pricing. You might resist the notion that one's vote can have a social cost, but if person A's vote changes the outcome, and the aggregate net utility of everyone else in the community falls as a result, then the decline in overall net utility (excluding A) is the cost that A's participation in the election imposes on others.

1 Plurality voting

Consider two projects F and G and a community of three individuals. Individual preferences are revealed by Table 1. If the two projects come up for election then

Table 1

	Max	Sam	Liz
$U_i(F)$	5000	100	150
$U_i(G)$	3000	105	160

Table 2

	Max	Sam	Liz
$U_i(F)$	5000	100	150
$U_i(G)$	3000	105	160
$U_i(H)$	4800	200	250

G will win because Sam and Liz both prefer G to F. (If you like, you can suppose there are three million individuals, with each voter of Table 1 belonging to a group of one million individuals with identical preferences.) Outcome G is inefficient, however. If Max were to compensate the other two individuals by paying them each \$100 for throwing their support to F we have a new outcome H, which everyone prefers to G, as illustrated by Table 2. We have uncovered a general principle: *In this simple model*, if F and G are two feasible projects and $\Sigma_{i=1}^n U_i(F)$ exceeds $\Sigma_{i=1}^n U_i(G)$ then project G is not efficient. (For a general proof see section 3 of this chapter. $N = \{1, 2, \dots, n-1, n\}$ is the set of all individuals and $\Sigma_{i=1}^n$ indicates that we sum over all individuals i in the community.)

The reason why plurality voting can select an inefficient outcome is that an individual who cares very little about the choice between two projects is given the same number of votes as an individual who has a great deal at stake. There is no mechanism for recording the intensity of an individual's preference and therefore no way to ensure that $\Sigma_{i=1}^n U_i$ is maximized. To correct this defect we consider a voting scheme that allows individuals to cast a variable number of votes.

2 Elections with a variable number of votes

Define a new voting mechanism in which individual i is required to report $U_i(F)$ and $U_i(G)$ when F and G are the two projects on the ballot. The net benefit figure reported by i can be interpreted as the number of votes cast by i for the project in question and each individual is required to cast a number of votes equal to his or her net utility. If the project that receives the largest total vote is selected *and* individuals report truthfully then an inefficient outcome will not survive the

Table 3

	Max	Sam	Liz
$U_i(F)$	5000	100	150
$U_i(G)$	3000	5105	160

voting process with this new mechanism because project F's total vote will be $\Sigma_{i=1}^{n} U_i(F)$ and the project with the highest total vote is selected.

Of course individuals have a strong incentive not to report truthfully. Suppose Table 1 gives the true utility levels. If Sam declares that her net utility from G is 5105 (i.e., casts 5105 votes for G) and in all other cases each individual reports truthfully then Table 3 gives the observed voting pattern. Inefficient outcome G will receive the most votes. Of course this voting pattern does not constitute an equilibrium. Every individual has an incentive to overstate his preference for the project he prefers, however slight his intensity of preference for one option over the other, and there is no limit to the number of votes an individual will be willing to cast for his preferred outcome in the case of this voting mechanism.

Suppose that we modify the mechanism by imposing a limit. Let's consider the implications of a cap of 10,000 on the number of votes that one can cast for an outcome. An individual is asked to cast a number of votes for an alternative in accord with the net utility that he would receive from that alternative, but in no case can he exceed 10,000 votes. Each individual will cast exactly 10,000 votes for the option that he prefers and zero vote for the other project, so the mechanism imitates the plurality decision rule of section 1. (The number of votes cast has no effect on the tax formula used to finance the winning project – the financing formula is part of the definition of a project.) Each alternative will now receive 10,000 times as many votes as under plurality rule, so the two mechanisms yield the same decision. The problem with this new scheme is that there is no restraint on an individual's desire to overstate the benefit from his preferred alternative, even if there is only a very slight advantage to him in having one outcome over another. Therefore, we next consider a modification of the variable number of votes model in which there is a built-in restraint. Before doing that it is necessary to characterize the efficient allocations. This we do in the next section; then section 4 works out a numerical example.

3 Pareto optimality

Let $g(x)$ denote the amount of good Y required in order to produce x units of the public good. Assume that $g'(x) > 0$ and $g''(x) > 0$ for all $x \geq 0$. Because $g(x)$ is the real cost of producing x units of X, we are saying that marginal cost is positive and increasing. Similarly, we assume that $B_i'(x) > 0$ and $B_i''(x) \leq 0$ for all $x \geq 0$. In words, marginal utility for the public good is always positive, but it is (weakly) decreasing. (Marginal utility may fall as x increases, or it may remain constant, but it cannot increase.) Now we turn to the task of characterizing the set of Pareto optimal allocations.

We can always find at least one Pareto optimal allocation by maximizing the sum of individual utilities subject to the resource constraint. In this case, $\Sigma u_i = \Sigma B_i(x) + \Sigma y_i$ and the solution must satisfy $\Sigma y_i \leq \Sigma \Omega_i - g(x)$. Pareto optimality obviously implies that this inequality will be satisfied as an equality; that is, we will have $\Sigma y_i = \Sigma \Omega_i - g(x)$. We can substitute this into the expression for the sum of utilities, obtaining

$$\Sigma u_i = \Sigma B_i(\text{x}) + \Sigma \Omega_i - g(x)$$

which is a function of x. Let f denote this function. That is, $f(x) = \Sigma B_i(x) + \Sigma \Omega_i - g(x)$. We want to maximize this function, but there are still two constraints that have to be respected: $x \geq 0$ and $x \leq M$, where M satisfies $g(M) = \Sigma \Omega_i$. Assume that preferences and technology are such that we have a maximum of f at an interior point, by which we mean a value of x satisfying $0 < x < M$. Then $f'(x) = \Sigma B_i'(x) - g'(x) = 0$ is a necessary condition for a maximum. It is also sufficient because $f''(x) = \Sigma B_i''(x) - g''(x) < 0$ for all $x > 0$. Clearly, $f'(x) = 0$ implies $\Sigma B_i'(x) = g'(x)$, which is known as the *Samuelson efficiency condition*. Let x^* denote the value of x satisfying the Samuelson condition. Then x^* is unique because $f''(x) < 0$ for all $x \geq 0$. The fact that the second derivative is negative means that f' strictly decreases as x increases. Because $f'(x^*) = 0$ we must have $f'(x) < 0$ for all $x > x^*$. And $x < x^*$ implies $f'(x) > f'(x^*)$ and hence $f'(x) > 0$. Therefore, if a function has a negative second derivative at every point it can have a zero first derivative at one point at most.

If $x = x^*$ and $\Sigma y_i = \Sigma \Omega_i - g(x^*)$ then Σu_i is maximized subject to the resource constraint and thus the allocation is Pareto optimal. In words, *any* allocation that provides exactly x^* units of the public good and uses exactly $g(x^*)$ units of Y in producing the public good and redistributes the remaining amount of Y to consumers is Pareto optimal. Are there any other Pareto optimal allocations? The rest of the section consists in proving that there are no other interior Pareto optimal allocations. (An interior allocation is one that gives each individual a positive amount of Y. In symbols, an allocation is interior if $y_i > 0$ for each i.)

Suppose that an interior allocation satisfies $x < x^*$. Because $f'(x^*) = 0$ we have

$$\Sigma_i B_i'(x) - g'(x) > 0. \qquad [1]$$

Now, look at individual utility. Let

$$t_i = \frac{B_i'(x)}{B_1'(x) + B_2'(x) + \ldots + B_n'(x)} \qquad [2]$$

be individual i's tax rate. (There are n households.) The initial allocation provides everyone with x units of the public good and leaves each i with y_i units of the private good. Let's increase x to z (where $x < z < x^*$) and reduce individual i's consumption of Y by $t_i \times [g(z) - g(x)]$. Individual i's utility as a function of z is

$$V_i(z) = B_i(z) + y_i - t_i[g(z) - g(x)].$$

Then $V_i'(z) = B_i'(z) - t_i g'(z)$. For $z = x$ we have

$$V_i'(x) = B_i'(x) - t_i g'(x). \qquad [3]$$

Compare [3] and the left hand side of [1]. Multiplying the left hand side of [1] by t_i yields [3], and thus $V_i'(x) > 0$ for each i. Therefore, we can increase everyone's utility by increasing x and obtaining the necessary input by reducing i's consumption of Y in proportion to the i's marginal benefit for X. (Note that t_i is proportional to $B_i'(x)$, and $t_1 + t_2 + \ldots + t_n = 1$.) Feasibility requires $y_i - t_i[g(z) - g(x)] \geq 0$, but if $y_i > 0$ for each i we can ensure that the new level of consumption of Y will be positive for each i by having z sufficiently close to x – i.e., by having a sufficiently small increase in the production of X.[1]

If, on the other hand, we have $x > x^*$ at the initial allocation then $f'(x^*) = 0 > \Sigma_{i=1}^n B_i'(x) - g'(x)$. With t_i given by [1], we *reduce* x to x^* and increase individual i's consumption of Y by $t_i \times [g(x) - g(x^*)]$. An argument parallel to the one of the previous paragraph will show that everyone's utility will increase. The new level of consumption of Y is guaranteed to be positive, because this time we are reducing the amount of Y that is used in producing X, and this adds to an individual's private good consumption.

The tax rates specified by [1] are critical if we are to increase everyone's utility by moving from x toward x^*. If tax rates are equal, then those who derive little marginal benefit from X will suffer a net decline in utility when we increase x. And with equal tax rates, individuals who have a high marginal benefit from X will find their net utility falling when x is reduced. But if $x \neq x^*$ there is *some* system of tax rates that will allow everyone to benefit from a move toward x^*. To summarize: If an allocation gives each individual a positive amount of the private good Y then it is Pareto optimal *if and only if* $x = x^*$ and $\Sigma y_i = \Sigma \Omega_i - g(x^*)$.

Exercises

Exercises 1–6 pertain to the following simple model of pure public goods production and consumption: X is the public good and Y is a private good which can be either consumed or used in the production of the public good. There are three households. Each household has an endowment of 10 units of the private good and zero units of the public good.

1   Individual 1's preferences are represented by the utility function $\sqrt{x} + y_1$. Individual 2's preferences are represented by the utility function $2\sqrt{x} + y_2$. Individual 3's preferences are represented by the utility function $3\sqrt{x} + y_3$. Let P denote the price of X. Normalize so that the price of Y is \$1. When one unit of Y is used as input exactly one-third of a unit of X is obtained as output.

    a What would be the equilibrium price of X in a private ownership market economy with both goods being allocated by the market system?

    b Will the competitive equilibrium outcome be Pareto efficient? If so, explain why; if not, prove it with a numerical example.

2   Individual 1's preferences are represented by the utility function $\sqrt{x} + y_1$. Individual 2's preferences are represented by the utility function $2\sqrt{x} + y_2$. Individual 3's preferences are represented by the utility function $3\sqrt{x} + y_3$. Each unit of the X produced requires one unit of Y as input.

    a Characterize the allocation that is defined by transferring all of the private good to person 3 and then choosing x to maximize 3's utility subject to the production constraint.

    b Is this allocation Pareto optimal? Explain.

    c Does this allocation satisfy the Samuelson condition? Support your answer with a simple proof.

    d Explain how an allocation can be Pareto optimal without satisfying the Samuelson condition.

3   Consider the economy of question 2. If we maximize u_2 subject to the constraint $y_2 \le 30 - x$ we get the allocation $x = 1$, $y_2 = 29$, and $y_1 = 0 = y_3$. This allocation is Pareto optimal. Why? Are there any other Pareto optimal allocations for which $x = 1$? Support your answer with a proof.

4   Each individual's preferences can be represented by the utility function $5\ln(x + 1) + y_i$. When one unit of Y is used as input exactly one-third of a unit of X is obtained as output.

    a What is the marginal social cost of X?

    b Is an allocation for which $x = 2$ Pareto optimal if each individual has a positive amount of the private good? If so, explain why; if not, prove it with a numerical example.

    c Is an allocation for which $x = 9$ Pareto optimal? If so, explain why; if not, prove it with a numerical example.

5   Individual 1's preferences can be represented by the utility function $\alpha_1\sqrt{x} + y_1$. Individual 2's preferences can be represented by the utility function $\alpha_2\sqrt{x} + y_2$. Individual 3's preferences can be represented by the utility

function $\alpha_3 \ln(x + 1) + y_3$. The production of one unit of X requires δ units of Y as input.

   a What is the marginal social cost of X?

   b Express the Samuelson condition as simply as you can and then further simplify the condition for the case $\delta = \alpha_3$.

6   Individual 1's preferences can be represented by the utility function $\sqrt{x} + y_1$. Individual 2's preferences can be represented by the utility function $4\sqrt{x} + y_2$. Individual 3's preferences can be represented by the utility function $5\ln(x + 1) + y_3$. The real cost of production is given by the function $g(x) = 5x$.

   a What is the marginal social cost of X?

   b Characterize the set of Pareto optimal allocations.

7   State the efficiency condition for a pure public good. Explain why that condition would not be satisfied at equilibrium if the level of the pure public good were determined by demand and supply forces in a competitive market – i.e., if it were allocated the way private goods are allocated in the market system.

4 Fireworks

We use a specific example to investigate the problem of allocating resources when one of the commodities is a pure public good. A fireworks display is a nice example because cost per unit is small enough to allow us to consider what would happen if the event were left in the private domain. The community in this case is a small town rather than the entire nation. Let's assume that there are ten families in the community. Let x be the number of units consumed; that is, x is the number of Roman candles ignited in the community on a public holiday. Assume that the marginal cost of production is constant and equal to 50. Assume, also, that Roman candles are produced under competitive conditions, so the market price will be 50.

The only additional information that we require is the utility function of each household. We will assume that the households have identical preferences, and $u_i(x, y_i) = 70x - \frac{1}{2}x^2 + y_i$. This means that preferences are quasi-linear, with $B_i(x) = 70x - \frac{1}{2}x^2$ for each household i. Then each household's marginal benefit function, B_i', is given by $B_i'(x) = 70 - x$. Although we said that there would be no resource allocation problem if everyone had the same preferences, this would be the case only if everyone *knew* that his preference scheme was the same as everyone else's. The assumption of identical preferences here is just a convenience; if we also assume that no one knows very much about anyone else's preferences, the society still faces the task of discovering what the individual preferences are and thus what the efficient level of x is.

Let's see what happens when the good is not provided by a central agency but instead it is left to the private ownership market economy to allocate fireworks. Budget-constrained individual utility maximization will always lead to an equilibrium in which each individual i sets the marginal benefit of the amount of X *consumed* by i (not the amount purchased by i) equal to its price. Therefore, in the case of individual purchase of fireworks we will have $B_i' = 50$ for each person because the price is $50. Does this mean that each consumer sets $70 - x = 50$ and thus buys 20 Roman candles? Certainly not. If each household ignited 20 Roman candles then each household would consume 200 units of X because fireworks are public goods. And when $x = 200$ the marginal benefit of each consumer is negative, taking us well beyond the point where an individual consumer could justify the purchase of fireworks in terms of his self-interest.

In order to find the market equilibrium we focus on a particular consumer whom we will call Max, and we let Q denote the number of Roman candles that he purchases. Let R be the total number of candles purchased by all other households. Then Max will purchase an amount Q to satisfy the equation

$$70 - (R + Q) = 50.$$

To prove this, maximize $70(R + Q) - \frac{1}{2}(R + Q)^2 + y_i$ subject to $y_i = \Omega_i - 50Q$ with R constant. Because the individuals are identical we can have an equilibrium where everyone purchases the same number of fireworks. This means that $R = 9Q$, which gives us the equilibrium condition

$$70 - 10Q = 50$$

and therefore, $Q = 2$. Each individual buys 2 Roman candles and the total consumption is 20. Note that $B'(20) = 70 - 20 = 50$, which equals the price, and we are indeed at equilibrium.

Each individual is better off than if fireworks were not consumed at all. To prove this just compare utility levels. If no public goods are produced then each i's utility is

$$u_i(0, \Omega_i) = \Omega_i$$

where Ω_i is i's endowment of the private good. At the market equilibrium we have

$$u_i(20, \Omega_i - 100) = 1200 + \Omega_i - 100$$

which, of course, is larger than Ω_i.

The private market equilibrium is not efficient because the good in question is a public good: The market equilibrium equates individual marginal benefit and marginal social cost. Marginal social cost is 50 in this example. If the marginal benefit is 50 for each individual then the *sum* of the marginal benefits is 10 times

50, which is much larger than marginal social cost, so the Samuelson efficiency condition is not satisfied. The level provided by the market is far below the efficient level.

If the marginal benefits sum to 50 then $10(70 - x) = 50$ and thus $x = 65$. This means that 65 is the efficient level of output of fireworks. Let's use benefit taxation to determine each individual's contribution to the purchase of \$3250 worth of fireworks. Because individuals have identical marginal benefit schedules the tax rates will be identical: each will pay one-tenth of the cost. So, $c_i = 50x/10 = 50(65)/10 = 325$. Therefore, $u_i(65, \Omega_i - 325) = 2112.5 + \Omega_i$ for each i at this efficient outcome, and this is substantially higher than the utility provided by the market equilibrium.

Even though we used benefit cost taxation to locate a feasible outcome that everyone prefers to the market equilibrium, I do not claim that benefit taxation would work in practice. We have just used it to prove that the market equilibrium is not efficient. We have not by any means proved that there does exist some scheme for generating an efficient output of a public good. The problem is one of incentives. If preferences are unknown then the efficient level of output is unknown, and a successful public decision scheme would have to elicit the necessary information about individual preferences in order to identify efficient outcome. But the outcome affects the consumption of private goods too – via taxes, etc. – and inevitably, there is a relationship between the taxes that the individual pays and the information he provides about his preferences for public goods. An individual may misrepresent his private information in order to reduce his tax burden. As section 4 of Chapter 3 demonstrated, benefit taxation is particularly vulnerable on this account. Before giving consideration to the incentive problems associated with the public provision of public goods we conclude this section with another look at the performance of the market system.

At the market equilibrium we have each household enjoying the output of the public good that is financed by other households and in that sense there is free riding. We can illustrate free riding by supposing that Samantha is much wealthier than anyone else in the community. It is plausible that she would not wait to see how many Roman candles were purchased by others and would purchase 20 candles for her own display. Next year[2] this would be anticipated by the other households, who would not devote any money to expenditure on fireworks. With the 20 units that Max consumes thanks to Samantha's purchases, Max has equated his marginal benefit and price (even though he didn't purchase anything). Max has no incentive to add to his consumption of X by purchasing more on the private market. We have $x = 20$ and marginal benefit is equal to price for *each* consumer. Even though Samantha finances the community's entire consumption of the public good she has no incentive to change her behavior. The appropriate marginal condition for selfish budget-constrained utility maximization is satisfied in her case as in everyone else's. "Marginal benefit = $70 - x = 70 - 20 = 50$ = price" for each individual. Everyone but Samantha is getting a free ride because each consumes the public good provided by Samantha but contributes nothing. (Note that we have inadvertently discovered that there is more than one market equilibrium when public goods are allocated by the market system. Are there any equilibria other than the two that we have uncovered?)

Are there any public decision schemes that perform better than the market system with respect to the allocation of public goods? The rest of this chapter is devoted to this question. Although the model that we use is extremely simple it incorporates enough features of resource allocation with public goods to enable us to bring out all the strategic nuances and complications associated with the provision of public goods.

5 Benefit taxation

A conventional plurality election can precipitate an inefficient outcome because intensity of individual preference plays no role (section 1). We attempted to remedy this by allowing individuals to vary the number of votes cast for each option on the ballot – section 2 – but found that there is no cost to the individual who overstates his intensity of preference for a project. In other words, we do not get truthful revelation of utility functions, so we don't get efficient outcomes either. Benefit taxation does impose a cost on the individual that increases with the amount of the public good 'demanded', but the cost is too high. The typical individual will *understate* the benefit derived from a project.

The benefit tax scheme requires an individual to report the gross benefit that she receives from each option, before subtracting the reduction in her consumption of the private good due to the tax. In other words, each i is asked to report the function $B_i(x)$. The center then derives each i's marginal benefit schedule $B_i'(x)$ and then determines the level x° that equates the sum of the marginal benefits to the marginal real cost of producing X. In order to remove the incentive for i to overstate the benefit that she derives from her most-preferred output level of X she is assessed a tax that is proportional to her declared marginal benefit. That is, i's tax rate is

$$t_i = \frac{B_i'(x)}{B_1'(x) + B_2'(x) + \dots + B_n'(x)}$$

evaluated at $x = x^\circ$. Obviously, t_i depends on the reported benefit schedules of all individuals. We have $t_i \geq 0$ and $\Sigma_{i=1}^n t_i = 1$. Individual i's total tax bill is t_i times the cost of producing x°. By design, this scheme will yield the efficient level of output *if* individuals report their benefit schedules truthfully, but now there is a strong incentive for an individual to *understate* B_i. Suppose for example that $B_i(x) = 2\sqrt{x}$ for each i, and each unit of X requires one unit of Y as input. Then $B_i'(x) = x^{-1/2}$, and the equation $\sum_{i=1}^{n} B_i'(x) = 1$ reduces to $nx^{-1/2} = 1$, where n is the number of individuals. Therefore, $x^* = n^2$ is the efficient level of x. Each i pays the average cost of financing X because the individuals are identical, and that means that they have identical tax rates. That is, $t_i = 1/n$ and i's total tax bill is $x^*/n = n$. Therefore, if each individual were to report B_i truthfully each i's utility level would be $u_i = 2(n^2)^{1/2} + \Omega_i - n = n + \Omega_i$. If individual 1 were to report instead that she received zero benefit from any amount of the public good then the value of x that equated the sum of the reported marginal benefits to unity would be $x^\circ = (n - 1)^2$. This assumes that the other individuals continue to report truthfully. Because i's tax rate would be zero if she declared $B_i \equiv 0$ she would pay no tax and her level of utility would be $u_i = 2[(n - 1)^2]^{1/2} + \Omega_i = 2(n - 1) + \Omega_i$ and this is larger than $n + \Omega_i$ as long as n is larger than 2. The differential, $n - 2$, will be extremely large for large n. Therefore, it is far from optimal for an individual to report truthfully under the benefit taxation scheme: Even if no other individual misrepresents her preferences, individual i has a strong incentive to do so.

Evidently, we have made the penalty for claiming to derive a substantial benefit from a public project too great; the present scheme fails to provide an efficient outcome in practice because individuals will understate their benefit levels. It is important to get the incentives just right. We now introduce a scheme that induces truthful reporting of the benefit schedules.

Exercises

1   For each $i = 1, 2, \ldots, n$ we have $B_i(x) = 2\sqrt{x}$. Find the equilibrium level of x under benefit taxation when *each* individual reports the benefit function that gives him the maximum utility given the reports of others.

2   Suppose that $u_i(x, y_i) = \ln(x + 2) + y_i$ for each $i = 1, 2, \ldots, n$. The number of individuals n is at least three. Let $g(x) = x$, the input of y required to produce x units of X.

    a   Find the Pareto optimal level of x.

    b   Show that the situation in which each individual reports a benefit function with a constant marginal benefit of zero constitutes a Nash equilibrium if benefit taxation is employed to determine the output of the public good. Is this Nash equilibrium outcome Pareto optimal? (Extend the definition of benefit taxation so that when everyone's marginal benefit is constant at zero then no public goods are produced and no taxes are levied.)

6 The Groves–Clarke mechanism

We have looked at a scheme for which the cost of overstating one's utility is too low (section 2), and one for which the cost is too high (section 5). Now we look at a mechanism for which the cost is *just right* – namely, the cost to the individual is equal to the cost to society. This scheme was discovered independently by Groves (1973) and Clarke (1971). (See also Tideman and Tullock, 1976.) Before defining the Groves–Clarke mechanism we recall the role played by social cost pricing in Vickrey's second-price, sealed-bid auction allocation rule (section 2 of Chapter 3). There are n individuals $i = 1, 2, \ldots, n$ who are eligible for the indivisible object, and person i's reservation value for this object is R_i. Suppose that $R_1 > R_i$ for all $i > 1$. We know from the analysis of Chapter 3 that submitting a bid equal to one's reservation value is a dominant strategy, so that each R_i will be known to the auctioneer after the bids have been recorded. If the object is a very old painting then the costs of production are zero, and we don't have to worry about taxing the community to underwrite its production. But giving the painting to individual i entails an opportunity cost because others are denied the utility that the object would have provided. The cost to the community is R_1 when the painting is given to anyone but person 1, because R_1 is the maximum utility that can be generated by an alternative assignment. If 1 does get the object then the cost to the rest of the group is R_h, where h denotes the individual with the second highest reservation value. And according to the second-price auction rules, R_h is the price that will be paid by 1 when everyone submits a bid equal to his true reservation value. We can interpret the auction this way: Each individual submits a sealed bid. With no other information to go by, the auctioneer does the best that she can by assuming that the bids are equal to the reservation values. Efficiency then demands that the auctioneer award the object to the individual submitting the highest bid, but to give each individual an incentive to take into consideration the cost that his participation imposes on the rest of the community, the one who receives the object must pay a fee equal to that cost – i.e., the fee is equal to the second highest bid. The cost to the rest of the community of a bid that is not highest is zero because the outcome would not have been any different if that individual had not participated in the auction. In other words, each person pays a surcharge equal to the cost that his participation imposes on the rest of the group. This gives each individual the incentive to report his benefit function truthfully. That is exactly what the Groves–Clarke mechanism does in the case of allocation with public goods. All we need to do now is apply the surcharge formula to public goods. This takes a little work because the benefit functions are much more complicated than for the problem of allocating a single indivisible object. In the auction model, once we know R_j we know j's entire benefit function. This means that the auctioneer only has to ask each individual to report his reservation value, and the surcharge formula induces each person to report truthfully. Let's see how we can apply this insight to the problem of allocation with public goods.

To introduce the allocation scheme we return to the original framework in which two options are presented to the community for consideration. Once we understand how the mechanism works in this setting we will examine the case where a value of x is chosen from a continuum of possible values. The two proposals are F and G and each individual is asked to report the net benefit that he receives from each project. That is, i is asked to report $V_i(F) = B_i(x_F) - c_i(F)$ and $V_i(G) = B_i(x_G) - c_i(G)$, where x_P is the level of x specified by project P and $c_i(P)$ is that part of the cost of financing P that is borne by i. ($P = F$ or G.) Project F is adopted if $\sum_{i=1}^n V_i(F) = \sum_{i=1}^n B_i(x_F) - \sum_{i=1}^n c_i(F)$ exceeds $\sum_{i=1}^n V_i(G) = \sum_{i=1}^n B_i(x_G) - \sum_{i=1}^n c_i(G)$; otherwise G is adopted. Clearly, this does not lead to the selection of an inefficient project provided that each individual i reports $B_i(x_F) - c_i(F)$ and $B_i(x_G) - c_i(G)$ truthfully. To induce truthful revelation we impose tax surcharges that make misrepresentation too costly. Note that $\sum_{i=1}^n V_i(F) > \sum_{i=1}^n V_i(G)$ holds if and only if $\sum_{i=1}^n U_i(F) > \sum_{i=1}^n U_i(G)$ because $\sum_{i=1}^n U_i(F) - \sum_{i=1}^n V_i(F) = \sum_{i=1}^n \Omega_i = \sum_{i=1}^n U_i(G) - \sum_{i=1}^n V_i(G)$.

Without loss of generality, assume that $\sum_{i=1}^n B_i(x_F) - \sum_{i=1}^n c_i(F) > \sum_{i=1}^n B_i(x_G) - c_i(G)$. Any individual i for whom $\sum_{j \neq i}[B_j(x_F) - c_j(F)] > \sum_{j \neq i}[B_j(x_G) - c_j(G)]$ holds does not pay a tax surcharge; even if i had not participated outcome F would have been selected. This is true whether $B_i(x_F) - c_i(F) < B_i(x_G) - c_i(G)$ or $B_i(x_F) - c_i(F) \geq B_i(x_G) - c_i(G)$ holds. And no individual for whom $B_i(x_F) - c_i(F) < B_i(x_G) - c_i(G)$ holds is required to pay a surcharge. (But this is already implied by the first two sentences of this paragraph.) If, however, $B_i(x_F) - c_i(F) > B_i(x_G) - c_i(G)$ *and* $\sum_{j \neq i}[B_j(x_F) - c_j(F)] < \sum_{j \neq i}[B_j(x_G) - c_j(G)]$ then i pays a tax surcharge equal to the cost imposed on the rest of society by his participation. That cost is $\sum_{j \neq i}[B_j(x_G) - c_j(G)] - \sum_{j \neq i}[B_j(x_F) - c_j(F)]$, which is the total decline in utility experienced by the rest of the community as a result of i's participation, which changes the outcome from G to F. Thus i's tax surcharge is $T_i = \sum_{j \neq i}[B_j(x_G) - c_j(G)] - \sum_{j \neq i}[B_j(x_F) - c_j(F)]$. If $B_i(x_F) - c_i(F) > B_i(x_G) - c_i(G)$ but $\sum_{j \neq i}[B_j(x_G) - c_j(G)] < \sum_{j \neq i}[B_j(x_F) - c_j(F)]$ then i pays no tax surcharge because i's participation did not affect the outcome.

Consider the following example involving three persons, Max, Sam, and Liz, and the two public projects F and G. The first two rows of Table 4 give the benefit V_i derived by each person from each project – that is, the benefit net of

Table 4

	Max	Sam	Liz
Project F	10	19	30
Project G	15	10	40
Tax surcharge	0	0	4

the taxes assessed in order to command the resources necessary to construct the project. If each individual reports truthfully project G will be adopted because it yields a total net benefit of 65, versus 59 for F. Although Max prefers G to F he does not pay a tax surcharge because G would still win (by one vote) without Max's participation. Sam does not pay a tax surcharge because the outcome she prefers was not selected. But Liz pays a tax surcharge because without her participation the outcome would have been F, which yields a total net benefit to the rest of the community of 29, versus 25 for G. The surcharge that Liz pays is the difference, which is 4. Clearly, Max has no incentive to deviate from the truth: His preferred outcome is selected without his having to pay a surcharge. He can only change the outcome by causing F to be selected and then he would have to pay a surcharge (of one). Sam could cause her preferred outcome F to be selected by overstating her preference for F so that it garnered the most votes, but then Sam would have to pay a tax surcharge of $(15 + 40) - (10 + 30) = 15$. Sam's net utility is 10 when G is selected and it would be $19 - 15 = 4$ if she misrepresented her preference to ensure the victory of F. Clearly, this would not be to her advantage. Liz could avoid the tax surcharge of 4 by understating her preference for G (or overstating her preference for F) but her net utility when she tells the truth is $40 - 4 = 36$, which is greater than her net utility when she misrepresents her preference to avoid the surcharge. (Her net utility from F is only 30.)

Now let's see if anyone has an incentive to misrepresent his preference under any circumstance. Without loss of generality, assume that F is selected when everyone reports truthfully. Recall that $V_i(F)$ denotes $B_i(x_F) - c_i(F)$, the net benefit to i from project F, and $V_i(G)$ denotes $B_i(x_G) - c_i(G)$. We examine individual i's decision in three cases.

Case 1 $V_i(F) > V_i(G)$ and $\Sigma_{j \neq i} V_j(F) \geq \Sigma_{j \neq i} V_j(G)$.

This means that individual i sees his preferred project selected, without having to pay a tax surcharge, when he reports truthfully. There is no incentive to change his report to ensure the selection of G. That would lower i's utility even if he did not have to pay a tax surcharge, although he would surely have to if $\Sigma_{j \neq i} V_j(F) > \Sigma_{j \neq i} V_j(G)$.

Case 2 $V_i(F) > V_i(G)$ and $\Sigma_{j \neq i} V_j(F) < \Sigma_{j \neq i} V_j(G)$.

When i reports truthfully then project F, which i prefers, is selected and individual i pays a tax surcharge of $\Sigma_{j \neq i} V_j(G) - \Sigma_{j \neq i} V_j(F)$. Because the tax surcharge does not depend on i's report there is nothing that he can do to reduce it *except* to modify his report so much that G is selected as the outcome. He could certainly cause this to happen by sufficiently overstating the net benefit that he receives from G. The question that we have to answer is "Is $V_i(G)$ greater than $V_i(F) - [\Sigma_{j \neq i} V_j(G) - \Sigma_{j \neq i} V_j(F)]$?" This cannot be the case because F is selected when i reports truthfully and this means that $V_i(G) + \Sigma_{j \neq i} V_j(G) < V_i(F) + \Sigma_{j \neq i} V_j(F)$, which in turn implies that $V_i(G) < V_i(F) - [\Sigma_{j \neq i} V_j(G) - \Sigma_{j \neq i} V_j(F)]$. Therefore, an individual who sees his preferred project adopted when he reports truthfully cannot gain by deviating from the truth even if he has to pay a tax surcharge.

Case 3 $V_i(G) > V_i(F)$.

Individual i would prefer to see G adopted but if he were to overstate the benefit that he received from G he would surely have to pay a tax surcharge if G were selected. That is because F wins when i reports truthfully, even though $V_i(G) > V_i(F)$, and so it must be the case that $\Sigma_{j \neq i} V_j(F) > \Sigma_{j \neq i} V_j(G)$ and thus i would have to pay a tax surcharge equal to $\Sigma_{j \neq i} V_j(F) - \Sigma_{j \neq i} V_j(G)$ if G were selected. Because $V_i(F) + \Sigma_{j \neq i} V_j(F) > V_i(G) + \Sigma_{j \neq i} V_j(G)$ we have $V_i(G) - [\Sigma_{j \neq i} V_j(F) - \Sigma_{j \neq i} V_j(G)] < V_i(F)$. Even if i's preferred project is rejected when he reports truthfully he cannot gain by misrepresentation.

Exercises

1   In the case of two available (i.e., feasible) options, does the Groves–Clarke mechanism always select the option that is preferred by a majority? Explain.

2   Consider the case of three individuals, Max, Sam, and Liz, and two public projects, F and G. The following table gives the benefit derived by each person from each project – that is, the benefit net of the taxes assessed in order to command the resources necessary to construct the project.

	Max	Sam	Liz
Project F	10	20	30
Project G	15	10	40

   a What project would be undertaken if the Groves–Clarke mechanism were employed *and* individuals reported the above benefit figures truthfully?

   b Show that none of the three individuals has an incentive to misrepresent his benefit schedule in the setting of question (a). What does it mean to say that truthful revelation of preference is a dominant strategy in this case?

c What is the size of the government budget surplus associated with your answer to question (a)?

3   Consider the case of three individuals, Max, Sam, and Liz, and two public projects, *F* and *G*. The following table gives the benefit derived by each person from each project – that is, the benefit net of the taxes assessed in order to command the resources necessary to construct the project.

	Max	Sam	Liz
Project *F*	4	30	24
Project *G*	10	20	30

a What project would be undertaken if the Groves–Clarke mechanism were employed *and* individuals reported the above benefit figures truthfully?

b Show that none of the three individuals has an incentive to misrepresent his benefit schedule in the setting of question (a). What does it mean to say that truthful revelation of preference is a dominant strategy in this case?

c What is the size of the government budget surplus associated with your answer to question (a)?

7 The budget surplus

The tax surcharges provide just the right incentive for individuals to report their benefit schedules truthfully. The surcharge makes it costly for *i* to overstate his preference for his preferred outcome in an attempt to prevent the other from being selected. And because the surcharge is independent of *i*'s report, *as long as it does not cause the outcome to change,* there is no incentive to understate one's benefit as there is with benefit taxation. But the surcharges result in the accumulation of a government budget surplus. (The surplus is 4 in the example of Table 4.) This budget imbalance is inevitable if the incentive to report truthfully is to be maintained! The government could return the surplus to the community but that would alter the incentives and would in fact cause truthful revelation to be inferior to some other strategy in some situations. We can demonstrate this by means of the example of Table 4 from the previous section. Suppose that the budget surplus were shared equally by the three voters. If Sam were to report $V_{SAM}(F) = 24$ and $V_{SAM}(G) = 10$ then *G* would still be selected, this time by 65 votes to 64. However, the surcharge paid by Liz would increase by 5 to 9 and Max would have to pay a surcharge of $24 + 30 - (10 + 40) = 4$. This means that Sam would

Table 5

	Max	Sam	Liz
$V_i(F)$	20	30	40
$V_i(G)$	30	25	31
Tax surcharge	0	1	5

receive a one-third share of a $13 surplus instead of a one-third share of a $4 surplus and her utility would increase from $10 + 4/3$ to $10 + 13/3$. Therefore, misrepresentation pays in this case. If, however, she overestimates the support for G from the rest of the community and claims a net benefit of 26 from F (instead of 19, her true net benefit) then F would be selected (by 66 to 65) and her net utility would be $19 - (55 - 40) + 5 = 9$, which is less than the net utility that she receives when G is selected, even without considering her share of the budget surplus when G is selected. By reporting a net benefit of 26 she will obtain a net benefit from F (19), but will pay a tax surcharge of 15 although one-third of that will be returned to her when the budget surplus is paid out to the community.

There are situations in which an individual can profit from misrepresentation if he knows that the budget surplus is to be returned to the community but does not know what net benefit levels the others are likely to report. Consider, for example, the situation represented in Table 5. This table reveals the true net benefit levels for the three individuals and the two projects. With truthful revelation project F will be selected (90 votes to 86). If the budget surplus of 6 is not returned to the community then Max cannot benefit by swinging the election to G because he would have to pay a tax surcharge of 14 ($= 70 - 56$). If, however, the budget surplus were distributed to the individuals in equal shares then Max could afford to cast up to fifteen votes more for G than for F. Let D represent the votes cast for G by Max minus the votes cast for F by Max. As long as $D \leq 15$ Max stands to gain by misrepresenting his benefit levels, and in any case he can do no worse than when he reports truthfully. Here's why: Max would pay a surcharge only if G were elected and this could happen only if $\Sigma_{j \neq \text{MAX}} [V_j(F) - V_j(G)] < D$. Therefore, $D \leq 15$ would result in Max's paying a surcharge of at most 15 and if one-third of that were returned when the government budget surplus was rebated then the net surcharge would be at most 10. If it were exactly 10 then Max's net utility from causing G to be selected would be $30 - 10 = 20$; on the other hand, his net utility from truthful revelation is 20 (his net utility from F). Therefore, without knowing anything about the votes likely to be cast by others, Max cannot be left worse off by misrepresenting his preferences as long as $D \leq 15$, and within the range $0 \leq D \leq 15$ he has the best chance of profiting by setting $D = 15$. $D =$

15 maximizes the probability of G being selected (subject to the constraint $D \leq 15$). With the present example, if Max reported $V_i(G) = 35$ and $V_i(F) = 20$ then G would win (91 votes to 90). Max would pay a surcharge of 14 (= 70 − 56) and one-third of that would be rebated so the net utility to Max from this misrepresentation would be $30 - 14 + 14/3 = 20 + 2/3$, which is higher than Max's net utility from truthful revelation.

Exercise

1   Suppose that the surplus were returned to the community by giving each individual an equal share. *By means of a specific numerical example,* show that truthful revelation is no longer a dominant strategy in the case of the Groves–Clarke mechanism applied to the examples of questions 2 and 3 in section 6.

8 Shortcomings of the Groves–Clarke mechanism

We have seen that truthful revelation is a dominant strategy only when the government budget surplus is not rebated to the community. This means that the Groves–Clarke mechanism does not yield Pareto optimal outcomes even though it satisfies the Samuelson equation: The other efficiency requirement, $\sum_{i=1}^{n} y_i = \sum_{i=1}^{n} \Omega_i - g(x)$, is violated because the tax surcharges by individuals are payments over and above what is required to purchase the input needed to produce the public good. By definition, the government budget surplus is the sum of the individual tax surcharges. Now, $g(x)$ units of Y are needed to produce x units of X, but $\sum_{i=1}^{n} y_i$ falls short of $\sum_{i=1}^{n} \Omega_i - g(x)$ by the amount of the surplus, which is positive or zero. However, if the number of individuals is large then the surplus will be close to zero on average – because the probability that an individual's participation changes the outcome will be low if the number of voters is large. (This was proved by Rob, 1982. Green and Laffont, 1979, have a simpler proof but they make stronger assumptions about the probability distribution of voter utilities.)

More serious is the fact that the Groves–Clarke mechanism can leave someone worse off than if the mechanism had not been used at all. Consider again the example of Table 5. Suppose that F is the status quo, with no government provision of public goods, and G is the consequence of a government project to land on Mars. The fact that $V_{\text{LIZ}}(G) < V_{\text{LIZ}}(F)$ means that after paying her share of the cost of funding the Martian project Liz would be worse off. The status quo will be retained if the Groves–Clarke mechanism is used to elicit information about individual preference, but the surcharges that are necessary to induce truthful revelation leave Liz worse off than if proposal G had not been considered.

Table 6

	Max	Sam	Liz
$V_i(F)$	20	30	30
$V_i(G)$	40	25	25
Tax surcharge	10	0	0

Table 7

	Max	Sam	Liz
$V_i(F)$	20	300	300
$V_i(G)$	40	25	25
Tax surcharge	0	0	0

There is no change in the status quo but it costs Liz one-eighth of her initial utility (five dollars) for the Groves–Clarke mechanism to determine that the status quo was efficient all along. As we will see in section 10, this is unavoidable.

Another problem is that the mechanism is vulnerable to manipulation by *coalitions*. Consider Table 6, which gives the true net benefit figures. If individuals reported truthfully then *G* would win, with 90 votes to 80, even though the majority prefers *F* to *G*. The efficient *project* is selected with the Groves–Clarke mechanism and truthful revelation. (The entire *outcome* is inefficient because of the surplus of 10.) If Sam and Liz collude and each agrees to cast 300 votes for *F* then *F* will be selected without either Sam or Liz having to pay a surcharge. This is confirmed by Table 7. Sam does not pay a surcharge because *F* would win without her, and Liz does not pay a surcharge for the same reason. Each gets a net utility of 30 as a result of this ploy, and that is 20% higher than the utility that each receives with truthful revelation and the outcome *G*. So, although a single individual cannot manipulate the Groves–Clarke mechanism, it is too vulnerable to manipulation by a pair of individuals acting in concert. Sam and Liz could successfully collude even if there were millions of other voters.

9 The Groves–Clarke mechanism with a continuum of options

In this section a 'project' is a specification x of the level of the public good along with a specification of the reduction $c_i(x)$ in the private good consumption of each person i that is required in order to obtain the input of Y needed to produce x. Of course, $\Sigma_{i=1}^{n} c_i(x) = g(x)$, where $g(x)$ is the amount of the private good Y required as input to produce x units of the public good. We wish to elicit an individual's entire benefit function $B_i(x)$ so that the level of x that maximizes $\Sigma_{i=1}^{n}[B_i(x) + \Omega_i - c_i(x)]$, or total net benefit, can be identified. Refer to $\Sigma_{i=1}^{n}[B_i(x) + \Omega_i - c_i(x)]$ as the function $f(x)$. *If* everyone reports his true benefit function then the value of x that maximizes $f(x)$ will satisfy the Samuelson condition of section 3. This follows from the fact that $\Sigma_{i=1}^{n} c_i(x) = g(x)$ and hence

$$f(x) = \Sigma_{i=1}^{n} B_i(x) + \Sigma_{i=1}^{n} \Omega_i - \Sigma_{i=1}^{n} c_i(x)$$
$$= \Sigma_{i=1}^{n} B_i(x) + \Sigma_{i=1}^{n} \Omega_i - g(x).$$

Therefore, the value of x that maximizes $f(x)$ is the same value that maximizes $\Sigma_{i=1}^{n} B_i(x) - g(x)$, and this will occur where $\Sigma_{i=1}^{n} B_i'(x) - g'(x) = 0$. As usual, let x^* denote the level of x that satisfies this condition. We can refer to x^* as *the* Pareto optimal level of x. We want to induce individuals to reveal their true $B_i(x)$ functions so that the community can identify x^*. We assume that the function c_i is known by individual i, and of course by the center, so it is only necessary for i to report his benefit function. Let $\beta_i(x)$ denote the benefit function *reported* by i, while B_i is i's true benefit function. As in the two-alternative case, individual i will pay a surcharge S_i which is equal to the cost that his participation imposes on the rest of society. When the individuals submit their reported benefit functions $\beta_i(x)$ the center produces the value of x that maximizes $\phi(x) = \Sigma_{i=1}^{n} \beta_i(x) - g(x)$. Alternatively, we could say that the center produces the value of x that satisfies the Samuelson condition for the *reported* benefit functions. Let x^β denote that value of x. Individual i's tax bill is $T_i = c_i(x^\beta) + R_i - \Sigma_{j \neq i}[B_j(x^\beta) - c_j(x^\beta)]$. The term R_i is defined as $\Sigma_{j \neq i}[B_j(x^i) - c_j(x^i)]$ with x^i set equal to the value of x that maximizes $\Sigma_{j \neq i}[B_j(x) - c_j(x)]$. In words, x^i is the output of X that would have been selected if i had not participated. Therefore, $R_i - \Sigma_{j \neq i}[B_j(x^\beta) - c_j(x^\beta)]$ is the cost imposed on the rest of society by i's participation, which results in x^β being produced instead of x^i. The tax surcharge $S_i = R_i - \Sigma_{j \neq i}[B_j(x^\beta) - c_j(x^\beta)]$ paid by i can be zero or negative, but in the continuum case everyone 'pays' a surcharge according to the formula S_i. Individual i's utility is

$$\mu_i(x) = B_i(x) + \Omega_i - c_i(x) - \{R_i - \Sigma_{j \neq i}[B_j(x) - c_j(x)]\}$$

when x is produced and each voter $j = 1, 2, \ldots, n$ reports $\beta_j(x)$. We can't differentiate μ_i with respect to x to determine i's utility maximizing strategy because x is a function of i's report β_i. But notice that R_i does not depend on x; it does depend on x^i but that is treated as a constant by i because it is unaffected by anything that i says or does. To determine i's utility maximizing strategy – *will i report $B_i(x)$?* – we examine the function $\mu_i(x)$. We can write

$$\mu_i(x) = B_i(x) + \Sigma_{j \neq i} \beta_j(x) - c_i(x) - \Sigma_{j \neq i} c_j(x) + \text{Constant},$$

where 'Constant' refers to terms that cannot be affected by i's report. Because $\Sigma_{i=1}^{n} c_i(x) = g(x)$ we can write

$$\mu_i(x) = B_i(x) + \Sigma_{j \neq i} \beta_j(x) - g(x) + \text{Constant}.$$

Therefore, the value of x that maximizes μ_i is identical to the value of x that maximizes $B_i(x) + \Sigma_{j \neq i} \beta_j(x) - g(x)$. Individual i wants to maximize $B_i(x) + \Sigma_{j \neq i} \beta_j(x) - g(x)$ and the center is going to choose x to maximize $\phi(x) = \beta_i(x) + \Sigma_{j \neq i} \beta_j(x) - g(x)$. This means that i can 'force' the center to maximize his utility by reporting $\beta_i = B_i$. And this is true regardless of the reports β_j submitted by the other individuals j. Therefore, truthful revelation is a dominant strategy. In plain words, given the rules of the Groves–Clarke mechanism, it is in an individual's interest to report truthfully. This means that x^*, the Pareto optimal level of x, will actually be produced. Therefore, the outcome of the Groves–Clarke mechanism will be Pareto optimal if and only if $\Sigma_{i=1}^{n} y_i = \Sigma_{i=1}^{n} \Omega_i - g(x^*)$, where y_i is i's consumption of the private good. And this equality will hold if and only if the government budget is balanced. Unfortunately, there will be a surplus.

Let's determine the size of the government budget surplus.

$$T_i = c_i(x^*) + \Sigma_{j \neq i}[B_j(x^i) - c_j(x^i)] - \Sigma_{j \neq i}[B_j(x^*) - c_j(x^*)].$$

(We know that each person will report his true benefit function.) Therefore,

$$\Sigma_{i=1}^{n} T_i = \Sigma_{i=1}^{n} c_i(x^*) + P = g(x^*) + P, \qquad \text{where}$$
$$P = \Sigma_{i=1}^{n}\{\Sigma_{j \neq i}[B_j(x^i) - c_j(x^i)] - \Sigma_{j \neq i}[B_j(x^*) - c_j(x^*)]\}.$$

P must be positive because for each i we have defined x^i as the value of x that maximizes $\Sigma_{j \neq i}[B_j(x) - c_j(x)]$. This means that

$$\Sigma_{j \neq i}[B_j(x^i) - c_j(x^i)] \geq \Sigma_{j \neq i}[B_j(x^*) - c_j(x^*)]$$

holds for each i. Then $\Sigma_{i=1}^{n} T_i$ equals $g(x^*)$ plus a positive number, and therefore there is a surplus.

Suggestions for further reading: Feldman (1980, chapter 6).

Exercises

1   Show that the Groves–Clarke mechanism defined in section 6 is actually a special case of the mechanism defined in this section. In other words, prove that when there are only two options the surcharge formula of this section agrees with that of section 6.

2   Prove that when x^* units of the public good are produced the final allocation will be Pareto optimal if and only if the government budget is balanced.

3   At the end of this section we proved that the budget surplus is zero or positive. We did not actually prove that it is always strictly positive. What can you say about the likelihood of a positive surplus?

4   Assume that individuals pay equal shares of the cost of funding public projects (apart from any supplementary tax employed to get them to reveal their true preferences). For the case $B_i(x) = \alpha_i x$ ($i = 1, \ldots, n$) with $\alpha_i > 0$ and $g(x) = (1/2)x^2$, show that the Groves–Clarke mechanism induces individual 1 to report his true α_1.

5   Assume that individuals pay equal shares of the cost of funding public projects (apart from any supplementary tax employed to get them to reveal their true preferences). For the case $n = 3$, $g(x) = 2x$, $B_1(x) = 4\sqrt{x}$, $B_2(x) = 8\sqrt{x}$, $B_3(x) = 16\sqrt{x}$, and $\Omega_i = 168$ for all i determine the outcome generated by the Groves–Clarke mechanism. Specify the level of output of the public good, the share of the cost of financing that public good that is borne by each individual, and the surcharge paid by each person. Compute the utility of each person at the Groves–Clarke equilibrium and compare it with the utility that each enjoys when no public goods are produced and each person simply consumes his endowment. What does this comparison reveal about the properties of the Groves–Clarke mechanism?

6   Assume that an individual's share of the cost of funding public projects (apart from any supplementary tax employed to get them to reveal their true preferences) is proportional to the person's income, Ω_i. For the case $n = 3$, $g(x) = 2x$, $B_1(x) = 4\sqrt{x}$, $B_2(x) = 8\sqrt{x}$, $B_3(x) = 16\sqrt{x}$ and $\Omega_1 = 40$, $\Omega_2 = 100$, and $\Omega_3 = 60$ determine the outcome generated by the Groves–Clarke mechanism. Specify the level of output of the public good, the cost of financing that public good that is borne by each individual, and the surcharge paid by each person. Compute the utility of each person at the Groves–Clarke equilibrium and compare it with the utility that each enjoys when no public goods are produced and each person simply consumes his endowment. Compare the final utility with that of the solution to the previous exercise. What conclusions can you draw from these comparisons?

7   Assume that individuals pay equal shares of the cost of funding public projects (apart from any supplementary tax employed to get them to reveal their true preferences). For $n = 3$, $g(x) = x$, $B_1(x) = 2\alpha\sqrt{x}$, $B_2(x) = 2\delta\sqrt{x}$, $B_3(x) = 2\lambda\sqrt{x}$, and arbitrary Ω_i, show that person 2's Groves–Clarke surcharge is zero if $\alpha + \lambda = 1/3$. What is the underlying intuition?

8   Rework the problem of allocating a single indivisible object to a group of n individuals by using the framework and notation of this section. Now, show that the allocation rule and surcharge rule defined by the second-price sealed-bid auction coincide with the respective formulas of the Groves–Clarke mechanism.

9   Consider the following modification of the Groves–Clarke mechanism: Use the same rule for determining the level of output of the public good but change the tax formula by dropping the term R_i from the expression for the

surcharge levied on arbitrary individual i. Prove that truthful revelation is still a dominant strategy. Assume that there is some value of x for which the expression $\sum_{i=1}^{n} \beta_i(x) - g(x) > 0$. Now prove that the government budget is always in deficit as a result of the modified tax formula.

10 An impossibility theorem

The defects of the Groves–Clarke mechanism that were uncovered in the two-option case also show up in the continuum case. Now we consider whether there exists *any* mechanism that induces truthful revelation and yields Pareto optimal outcomes without sometimes leaving some individuals with less utility than if the mechanism had not been used at all. We prove that there is no such mechanism. This result was first discovered and proved by Leonid Hurwicz.[3] As in Hurwicz (1972) and Roberts (1979), our proof only calls on the type of individual preferences that are commonplace in economic models. This contrasts with the proof of the Gibbard–Satterthwaite theorem (Chapter 7), which assumes that *any* logically possible preference scheme is a possible individual preference ordering.

The second part of the hypothesis of the impossibility theorem is the *participation constraint*. This requires $u_i(x') = B_i(x') + \Omega_i - c_i(x') \geq \Omega_i$ to hold for each individual i if x' is the amount of the public good specified by the mechanism when each i reports the benefit function $B_i(x)$. In words, the individual must receive assurance that participation in the mechanism will never leave her worse off. We assume that the production of x units of X requires x^2 units of Y as input. In symbols, $g(x) = x^2$. Therefore, efficiency requires that $\sum_{i=1}^{n} c_i(x) = x^2$ holds. Further, we limit the benefit functions $B_i(x)$ to the family of functions of the form $\beta_i \ln(x + 1)$, where β_i can be any positive constant. We begin by characterizing the Pareto optimal allocations.[4]

We proved in section 3 that for the case of public goods and quasi-linear preferences an interior allocation is Pareto optimal only if it maximizes $\sum_{i=1}^{n}[B_i(x) + y_i]$ subject to the requirement that $\sum_{i=1}^{n} y_i$ equals $\sum_{i=1}^{n} \Omega_i$ less the amount of the private good required to produce x units of the public good. (An interior allocation is one for which y_i is strictly greater than zero for all i.) Under the production assumption that we have just introduced we must have $\sum_{i=1}^{n} y_i = \sum_{i=1}^{n} \Omega_i - x^2$, and subject to this constraint we wish to maximize $\sum_{i=1}^{n}[\beta_i \ln(x + 1) + y_i]$. It will be easier to follow the argument if we set $n = 2$. That is $N = \{1, 2\}$. Therefore, we want to maximize

$$\beta_1 \ln(x + 1) + \beta_2 \ln(x + 1) - x^2 + \Omega_1 + \Omega_2$$

which is equivalent to maximizing

$$\beta_1 \ln(x + 1) + \beta_2 \ln(x + 1) - x^2. \tag{1}$$

The first derivative of this function is

$$\beta_1/(x + 1) + \beta_2/(x + 1) - 2x \qquad [2]$$

and the second derivative is therefore equal to

$$-\beta_1/(x + 1)^2 - \beta_2/(x + 1)^2 - 2$$

which is negative for all values of x. Therefore, setting [2] equal to zero will lead to a unique maximum of [1]. We have $\beta_1/(x + 1) + \beta_2/(x + 1) - 2x = 0$ and thus $2x^2 + 2x - \beta_1 - \beta_2 = 0$, which yields $x = -\frac{1}{2} + \frac{1}{2}[1 + 2\beta_1 + 2\beta_2]^{1/2}$. (There is a second root for which $x < 0$, but it is of no interest in this case.) Therefore, an interior Pareto optimal allocation must satisfy $x = -\frac{1}{2} + \frac{1}{2}[1 + 2\beta_1 + 2\beta_2]^{1/2}$ and $\sum_{i=1}^{n} y_i = \sum_{i=1}^{n} \Omega_i - x^2$. Because any such allocation maximizes total utility in the community subject to the production constraint it must be Pareto optimal. Therefore, an interior allocation is Pareto optimal *if and only if* $x = -\frac{1}{2} + \frac{1}{2}[1 + 2\beta_1 + 2\beta_2]^{1/2}$ and $\sum_{i=1}^{n} y_i = \sum_{i=1}^{n} \Omega_i - x^2$. Let x^* denote $-\frac{1}{2} + \frac{1}{2}[1 + 2\beta_1 + 2\beta_2]^{1/2}$. Note that *any* Pareto optimal allocation (not just an interior one) must satisfy $x \leq x^*$. If $x > x^*$ then $\beta_1 \ln(x + 1) + \beta_2 \ln(x + 1) - x^2$ is strictly less than $\beta_1 \ln(x^* + 1) + \beta_2 \ln(x^* + 1) - x^2$ because that function has a unique maximum at x^*. Because we can increase total utility by reducing the production of x and distributing the quantity of the private good that is thereby released to the two consumers in proportion to their marginal benefit we can simultaneously increase the utility of both consumers. (Recall the argument of section 3. We cannot rule out $x < x^*$ in general because the production of additional X, although it will increase total utility $\beta_1 \ln(x + 1) + \beta_2 \ln(x + 1) + \sum_{i=1}^{n} \Omega_i - x^2$, may not lead to an increase in 1's utility unless 2 contributes some of his private good consumption to the production of more X, but we may already have $y_2 = 0$. That possibility is precisely what is ruled out by the supposition that the allocation is interior.)

Now that we have described the basic model and have characterized the set of interior Pareto optimal allocations we turn to the problem of designing a satisfactory mechanism. We want a mechanism that will induce truthful revelation of individual preferences and so identify a Pareto optimal allocation. This means, of course, that the outcome will be sensitive to the information provided by households. Therefore, individual cost shares c_i will also be sensitive to reported information, and thus households may be able to transmit misleading information in order to induce an outcome that they prefer (according to their true preferences) to the one that emerges when they reveal their private preference information truthfully. We want a mechanism that is not vulnerable to this sort of strategic play, one that gives individuals the incentive to report truthfully and yields Pareto optimal outcomes when they do so. We also want a mechanism that does not cause any individual's utility to fall as a consequence of her participation. At this point it is necessary to be more specific about what is meant by a mechanism. A resource allocation mechanism first of all specifies a set M_a of strategies or messages for each agent a. Each consumer a is required to transmit a message m_a in M_a that reflects his preferences according to the rules of the mechanism, and each firm a is required to transmit a message m_a in M_a that reflects its technology (or production function) according to the rules of the mechanism. For each configuration e of individual endowments, individual preferences, and production technologies the mechanism specifies an equilibrium profile $s(e)$ of strategies or messages. We refer to e as an environment; it gives the fundamental data for the economy in a particular situation or application. A strategy profile s identifies a strategy or message m_a in M_a for each agent a. Finally, the mechanism identifies an allocation $\theta(s)$ for each equilibrium strategy profile s. Therefore, the mechanism ultimately is a mapping $\theta[s(e)]$ from environments into allocations, or outcomes. In the case of the public goods model under discussion, e would specify β_1, Ω_1, β_2, Ω_2, and the amount of the private good required as input for each level of output of the public good. Depending on the mechanism, s_a could be a voting pattern, or an announcement of the preference parameter β_a, or the marginal benefit schedule, etc. The allocation $\theta[s(e)]$ must specify the amount x of the public good to be produced and the amount y_i of the private good delivered to each household i. We say that household i can *manipulate* the mechanism at environment e if there is another environment e' that is identical to e except with respect to the specification of i's preference scheme *and* i prefers the allocation $\theta[s(e')]$ to the allocation $\theta[s(e)]$ according to the preferences of i described by e. To motivate this definition think of e as the specification of the true preferences and technology for the agents. Environment e' is identical except with respect to agent i, and e' specifies a different preference scheme for individual i than does e. Environment e' is the one that actually determines the equilibrium (although e is the true environment) because i misrepresents his preference scheme by playing the game as though his preference scheme were the one described for i by e'. This results in an equilibrium outcome $\theta[s(e')]$. If i is able to manipulate the mechanism at e then i prefers $\theta[s(e')]$ *according to his true preferences* to the outcome $\theta[s(e)]$ that emerges when i represents his preference scheme truthfully and behaves the way the rules of the mechanism require an individual with that preference scheme to behave. We want our mechanism to satisfy the participation constraint in addition to being invulnerable to manipulation. For our simple family of preferences, a mechanism satisfies the participation constraint if for any specification β_1 and β_2 of the individual preference parameters we have $\beta_1 \ln(x + 1) + y_1 \geq \Omega_1$ and $\beta_2 \ln(x + 1) + y_2 \geq \Omega_2$, where x, y_1, and y_2 are the equilibrium quantities.

Theorem *Suppose a resource allocation mechanism satisfies the participation constraint and always yields Pareto optimal equilibrium allocations over the* *family of environments specifying a utility function* $\beta_i \ln(x + 1) + y_i$ *for* i = 1, 2, *constant endowments* $\Omega_1 = \Omega_2 = 5/2$, *and the production technology requires* x^2 *units of the private good as input in order to produce* x *units of the public good. Then the mechanism can be manipulated.*

Proof Specify the environment e by setting $\beta_1 = \beta_2 = 2$. Then x^* is equal to $-\frac{1}{2} + \frac{1}{2}[1 + 4 + 4]^{1/2} = 1$. Suppose that the allocation (x, y_1, y_2) is Pareto optimal for e. Then we must have $x \leq 1$. (See the end of the third paragraph of this section.) Suppose in addition that $y_i = 0$. Then i's utility cannot be greater than

$$2\ln(1 + 1) < 1.4 < 2.5 = \Omega_i.$$

Therefore, the participation constraint implies that the allocation is interior, and in that case Pareto optimality implies $x = x^* = 1$. This requires 1 unit of the private good as input so we must have $y_1 + y_2 = 5/2 + 5/2 - 1 = 4$. Therefore, either $y_1 \leq 2$ or $y_2 \leq 2$. Without loss of generality, assume that $y_1 \leq 2$.

Let e' be the environment with $\beta_1 = 2/9$ and $\beta_2 = 2$. For any interior Pareto optimal allocation (x', y_1', y_2') for e' we must have $x' = -\frac{1}{2} + \frac{1}{2}[1 + 2\beta_1 + 2\beta_2]^{1/2} = -\frac{1}{2} + \frac{1}{2}[1 + 2(2/9) + 2(2)]^{1/2} = 2/3$. Let (x', y_1', y_2') be the equilibrium allocation associated with e'. Pareto optimality implies $x' \leq 2/3$. The participation constraint implies

$$(2/9)\ln(2/3 + 1) + y_1' \geq (2/9)\ln(x' + 1) + y_1' \geq 5/2,$$

and this in turn implies

$$y_1' \geq 5/2 - (2/9)\ln(5/3) > 0.$$

But $y_1' > 0$ implies $x' = 2/3$. (Because $\beta_2 = 2$ for e' we have already established $y_2' > 0$.) Finally, $x' = 2/3$ and $y_1' \geq 5/2 - (2/9)\ln(5/3)$ implies

$$2\ln(x' + 1) + y_1' \geq 5/2 - (2/9)\ln(5/3) + 2\ln(5/3) > 3.40.$$

Because $y_1 \leq 2$ we have

$$2\ln(x + 1) + y_1 \leq 2\ln 2 + 2 < 3.39.$$

Therefore, person 1 can manipulate at e.

Exercises

1   Design a resource allocation mechanism (for the model of this section) that satisfies the participation constraint and is invulnerable to manipulation by any individual. (Of course, it won't be the case that the equilibria are always Pareto optimal.)

2   Design a resource allocation mechanism (for the model of this section) that satisfies the participation constraint and always yields equilibria that are Pareto optimal. (Of course, it has to be the case that at least one individual can manipulate the mechanism in some situations.)

3   Design a resource allocation mechanism (for the model of this section) that
         is invulnerable to manipulation by any individual and such that the equilib-
         rium outcome is always Pareto optimal. (Of course, there will be situations
         in which one or more individuals are worse off than if they had not partici-
         pated in the mechanism.)

7

The Gibbard–Satterthwaite theorem

This chapter deals with a wide family of hidden characteristic problems by means of a single, simple model. In each case the hidden characteristics are the preferences of the individuals that make up the society, which could be almost any group: the student body in a particular college; the members of a firm's board of directors, citizens of a town or a country; a team of experimental physicists, etc. In each case there is a well defined group of individuals and a well defined set of feasible outcomes. Any outcome is to be valued in terms of the preferences of the group members. We don't necessarily use the efficiency criterion to evaluate outcomes as a function of individual preferences. The society may want to sacrifice some efficiency if that enables other goals to be realized. The theorem proved here applies to decision schemes that do not pass the efficiency test as well as those that do. But individual preferences always matter to some extent, so the decision scheme has to elicit those preferences, and we are looking for schemes that always give each individual an incentive to report his *true* preferences. Because the outcome has to be sensitive to the preferences of individuals, the outcome will typically change when an individual (say Max) changes his reported preference. But individuals care about the outcome, and when Max announces a preference scheme that is not his true preference, the outcome that results may be one that he prefers *according to his true preferences* to the outcome that would emerge if he were to announce his true preference scheme. In that case we say that Max can *manipulate* the decision scheme. The theorem is this: If there are more than two eligible outcomes then the only decision schemes that are invulnerable to manipulation are those that give exclusive control to a single individual! This result was independently discovered by Gibbard (1973) and Satterthwaite (1975). *If* Max had exclusive control, then by definition he could ensure that his most-preferred outcome were selected; hence Max would have every incentive to announce his true preferences. No one else's preferences matter, so no one else has an incentive to misrepresent his preferences. In short, no one has anything to gain by deviating from truthful revelation. But why is that the *only* decision scheme that is invulnerable to manipulation?

The Vickrey (or second-price, sealed-bid) auction is not dictatorial and it induces truthful revelation of reservation prices, as we saw in section 1 of Chapter 3. Within that framework an individual's preference scheme is completely charac-terized by her reservation value. Why, then, does this not disprove the Gibbard–Satterthwaite (G–S) claim? Because the proof of the G–S theorem assumes that any logically possible ranking of the feasible outcomes is a conceivable prefer-ence scheme for any individual. In other words, the G–S theorem applies only to decision schemes that are versatile enough to precipitate a decision (or outcome) for every conceivable specification of individual preferences. Chapter 3 estab-lished that truthful revelation of one's reservation price is a dominant strategy, but the argument applied only to very special individual preferences – only to prefer-ences schemes that can be completely characterized by means of a reservation value. Section 9 of the next chapter investigates this claim more fully.

Here is an interpretation of our model in which it is plausible that any ranking of the feasible options is a conceivable preference scheme for any individual: The society is a community – perhaps even a nation – that has to determine collec-tively how to spend an amount of money that has already been collected. (Think of a town dividing the money between an independence day parade or fireworks, or a nation dividing the money between national defence and medical research. An outcome is a number between zero and one, the fraction to be spent on the first option.) The individuals disagree about the way to rank the different outcomes; but whatever the outcome, each individual will benefit from it to some degree. There is no natural way to disqualify a particular ranking of the outcomes as an ordering that could never be representative of the preferences of some individual. This is quite different from the auction story. We reject as a possible preference scheme for Samantha any that ranks the outcome "Max obtains Picasso's 'Self-Portrait' for a price of \$100" above the outcome "Samantha obtains Picasso's 'Self-Portrait' for a price of \$50" (assuming that Samantha's reservation value is above \$50). Now we introduce the formal representation of our model.

1 Introduction

A voting scheme selects a single alternative for each configuration of reported individual preferences. A particular configuration is called a *profile* and is de-noted by the Greek letter ψ. If $T = \{1, 2, 3, \ldots, n\}$ is the finite set of n voters then profile ψ specifies a preference scheme $\psi(t)$ for each t in T. A set X of available alternatives is specified in advance. A voting scheme g selects an outcome $g(\psi)$ in

X for each profile ψ. The selected alternative is the winner of the election represented by the voting scheme. Consider a classic example, the Borda scheme.

1.1 Borda's voting scheme

There are m alternatives. Alternative x receives $V(R, x)$ votes from individual t if there are exactly $m - V(R, x)$ alternatives ranking above x in t's reported preference scheme R. If ψ is the profile of *reported* preferences then alternative x's score is $\Sigma_{t \in T} V(\psi(t), x)$ and the winner is the alternative with the highest score. (Ties are broken in some nonrandom fashion.)

True preferences			Reported preferences		
1	2	3	1	2	3
w	z	y	w	z	x
x	w	x	x	w	y
y	x	w	y	x	z
z	y	z	z	y	w

To illustrate, suppose that all preferences are *linear*. This means that alternative x can be indifferent to y in some individual preference scheme if and only if $x = y$. If alternative x is t's most-preferred alternative then x will receive m votes from t. The second-most-preferred alternative will receive $m - 1$ votes from t, and so on. Suppose there are four alternatives w, x, y, z, and three individuals 1, 2, 3. The true and reported preferences are given by the table above. (Alternatives are listed under a person's name in decreasing order of preference: Person 1 prefers w to x, x to y, and y to z according to her true preferences. The other columns are interpreted similarly.) If everyone reports – i.e., votes according to – her true preferences the winner will be w with nine votes: that is, 4 votes from person 1, 3 votes from 2, and 2 votes from 3. (Alternative x receives 8 votes, with 7 for y and 6 for z.) However, it is not in everyone's interest to report truthfully in every situation. For example, if 1 and 2 report truthfully then 3 can profit by reporting the preference scheme assigned to her in the last column, with x top ranked. With these reported preferences alternative x will win with 9 votes (8 for w, 7 for z, and 6 for y). Person 3 prefers x to w *according to her true preferences* and has profited from the misrepresentation. Alan Gibbard (1973) and Mark Satterthwaite (1975) independently proved that *every* voting scheme is vulnerable to this sort of manipulation except dictatorial ones or cases where there are fewer than three eligible alternatives. Before proving this we need some new definitions and notation. (Chapter 6 of Kelly, 1978, gives a brief history of the theory of manipulation. Chapters 10 and 11 of Kelly, 1988, provide substantial motivation for the treatment of strategic voting.)

1.2 Manipulation

We will assume that an individual is never indifferent between two distinct alternatives. Such preferences are referred to as *linear*. (Extending the proof of the Gibbard–Satterthwaite theorem to the more general case is relatively easy. Exercise 2 at the end of section 2 suggests a method. The complete argument can be found in chapter 5 of Campbell (1992). Our *domain,* then, is the family D of all profiles of linear preference orderings. A linear preference ordering on X is a binary relation R that is *antisymmetric, complete,* and *transitive.* Before defining these terms it is necessary to define a binary relation on a set X. If R is a binary relation on X then xRy signifies that alternative x in X ranks at least as high as y according to the preference scheme that is represented by R. In other words, xRy signifies that x is preferred or indifferent to y. If xRy holds but yRx does not then we say that x is strictly preferred to y, and if both xRy and yRx hold we say that x is indifferent to y. Now, the formal definitions:

> The relation R is *antisymmetric* if xRy and yRx can both hold only if $x = y$.
> The relation R is *complete* if for any x and y, either xRy or yRx holds.
> The relation R is *transitive* if xRy and yRz imply xRz.

Then D is the set of all profiles ψ such that for each individual t the binary relation $\psi(t)$ is linear (antisymmetric, complete, and transitive).

Formally, a voting scheme is a function g mapping D into X. The outcome function g selects an alternative $g(\psi)$ in X for each profile ψ in D. We *assume* that every member of X is selected as the outcome in at least one situation. Formally, $X = \{g(\psi) \mid \psi \in D\}$, the *image* of g. (Is it possible that the presence of dummy variables – that is, variables that appear on the ballot but can never be selected – will allow the construction of a nondictatorial voting scheme that induces truthful revelation? Exercise 7 at the end of section 2 asks you to show that the answer is "no.")

We say that a voting scheme can be manipulated if in some situation, some individual can by misrepresenting her preferences precipitate an outcome that she prefers *according to her true preference ordering* to the one that emerges when she announces her true preference ordering. For the Borda example of 1.1, individual 3 can advantageously misrepresent her preferences. Formally, the voting scheme $g : D \to X$ can be *manipulated* by individual t at profile ψ via the relation R' if $R = \psi(t)$ and $g(\psi')$ is strictly preferred to $g(\psi)$ by person t under preference R, for ψ' defined by $\psi'(t) = R'$ and $\psi'(i) = \psi(i)$ for all $i \neq t$. Accordingly, the voting scheme is nonmanipulable if for all $\psi \in D$ and $t \in T$ we have $g(\psi)Rg(\psi')$ for all $R = \psi(t)$ and $\psi' \in D$ such that $\psi'(i) = \psi(i)$ for all $i \neq t$. In this definition $\psi'(t)$ plays the role of t's reported preference scheme and $\psi(t)$ is interpreted as t's true preference relation. The alternative $g(\psi)$ represents the socially best outcome when the individual preferences are as specified by ψ. It is not obvious how g should be defined to incorporate the notion of a socially best outcome, but even if that problem has been solved we can ask if the definition can be subverted by individuals misrepresenting their preference relations. As we will see, that answer is "yes," excepting two trivial cases.

Exercises

1   Let X be a finite set and let R be a linear order on X. Prove that R can be represented by a finite list that designates a first-place alternative, a second-place alternative, and so on.

2   Let Y be a finite subset of X and let R be a linear order on X. Prove that there is one and only one alternative x in Y with the property xRy for all y in Y.

2 Proof of the theorem

We can prove that every nondictatorial voting scheme is vulnerable to manipulation even in the case of a two-person society. We prove this by showing that if it is *not* manipulable then it must be dictatorial (if there are more than two eligible alternatives). Therefore, we will assume that the society consists of two individuals, called persons 1 and 2. We can let R represent the preference order reported by 1 and we let S represent the preference scheme reported by 2. Then $g(R, S)$ is the outcome determined by the voting scheme g when 1 reports preference relation R and 2 reports S. If we need to consider alternative announcements by person 1 we can use the symbol R' to make a distinction between one preference scheme and another scheme R. Similarly, S' and S represent alternative announcements by person 2. For convenience, let's restrict attention to the alternatives that are eligible for election. That is, we assume that each member of X is actually selected as the outcome in at least one situation. (*Situation* is another word for profile – i.e., a pair of announcements, one by each individual.)

One more definition is required – the *option correspondence* O_1 of individual 1 associated with voting system g. For each preference relation S of person 2 let $O_1(S)$ denote the set of outcomes $g(R, S)$ that are generated as R varies over the set of possible preference schemes that 1 could report, with person 2's announcement fixed at S. Formally,

$$O_1(S) = \{g(R, S) \mid R \text{ is an admissible announcement for person 1}\},$$

the set of alternatives that 1 can precipitate when 2 announces preference relation S. To illustrate, suppose that g always selects the most-preferred alternative according to the preference relation R reported by person 1. Then $O_1(S) = X$ for all S. To ensure that x is selected person 1 just has to report an R that has x top-ranked. If, on the other hand, g always selects the most-preferred alternative according to the preference relation S reported by person 2 then $O_1(S) = $ {the top-ranked member of S}, because 1's report has no effect on the outcome. Now, suppose that $X = \{x, y\}$ has exactly two members and there is an odd number of voters. Suppose that g is simple majority rule. In this case we can let S represent the result of a simple majority rule election in which every vote *except* person 1's is counted. Set $S = 1$ if x wins, $S = 0$ if there is a tie, and $S = -1$ if y wins. Then $O_1(1) = \{x\}$ because x will win by at least two votes if it wins with an even number of individuals voting. Similarly, $O_1(-1) = \{y\}$. But $O_1(0) = \{x, y\}$ because person 1 casts the deciding vote.

Six preliminary lemmas are required. The proof is due to Barberà (1983). The first lemma proves that $g(R, S)$ has to be person 1's most-preferred member of the set $O_1(S)$ if g is nonmanipulable. That is, for any pair (R, S) there is no alternative in $O_1(S)$ that is strictly preferred to $g(R, S)$ according to the preference ordering R. Of course, $g(R, S)$ belongs to $O_1(S)$ by definition.

Lemma 1 *Suppose that* g *is a nonmanipulable voting scheme. Then for any choice of* R *and* S, *the alternative* g(R, S) *belongs to* $O_1(S)$ *and no other member of* $O_1(S)$ *ranks above* g(R, S) *in the preference ordering* R.

Proof Let $g(R, S) = x$. Let's use the symbol y to denote the top-ranked member of $O_1(S)$ according to the linear order R. (We may have $y = x$, but we can't take that for granted; it will have to be proved.) By definition of 1's option correspondence, because y belongs to $O_1(S)$ there is some R' available to 1 such that $g(R', S) = y$. Suppose that y ranks above x in the order R. (This implies that $x \neq y$, of course.) But then 1 can manipulate g at (R, S) via R'. (By reporting R' instead of R when 1's true preference relation is R, person 1 could precipitate outcome y which 1 prefers according to his true preference scheme R.) This contradicts the claim that g can't be manipulated. Therefore we have to drop the supposition that there is some y in $O_1(S)$ that 1 prefers to the alternative $g(R, S)$. □

We have just shown that the outcome will always be the one that ranks higher in person 1's reported ordering than any other alternative in his option set. This does not imply that 1 is a dictator, because 1 may not have many options. (Verify Lemma 1 for the three examples of the second paragraph of this section.) Now we prove that the alternative in X that is most-preferred according to S, the *other person's* reported preference scheme, belongs to 1's option correspondence.

Lemma 2 *Suppose that* g *is a nonmanipulable voting scheme. Then for any specification* S *of person 2's preference relation, the alternative that ranks at the top of* S *actually belongs to* $O_1(S)$.

Proof Suppose that x is the top-ranked alternative in X according to S. There is some profile (R^*, S^*) such that $g(R^*, S^*) = x$. (*Remember:* The set X is the set of alternatives that are generated as outcomes in at least one situation.) If $g(R^*, S) = y$ and $x \neq y$ then S ranks y below x, because we have just said that x ranks at the top of S. That is, x is strictly preferred to y according to S. But this means that 2 can manipulate g at (R^*, S) via S^*. This, of course, contradicts the supposition that g cannot be manipulated. Therefore, we must have $g(R^*, S) = x$. Then x belongs to $O_1(S)$ by definition. $\qquad\square$

To summarize, Lemma 1 says that 1 can get his most preferred alternative in $O_1(S)$ by truthful revelation: If x is the member of $O_1(S)$ that is ranked highest by R, and R is 1's true preference relation, then x will be the outcome when 1 reports R. In symbols, $g(R, S) = x$. And Lemma 2 says that if S is person 2's true preference relation, there is a strategy available to 1 that will guarantee that the outcome is the alternative in X that 2 most prefers. That could be because 2 is a dictator and 2 will get his first choice no matter what 1 does, or it could be because 1 is a dictator and 1 can guarantee the election of any outcome, whether it is 2's first choice or not. But we are a long way from proving that someone is a dictator. We need four more lemmas. The third one won't come as a surprise. It proves that if g can't be manipulated then person 1 gets his most-preferred alternative if 2 has the same most-preferred alternative.

Lemma 3 *Suppose that* g *is a nonmanipulable voting scheme. Then for all pairs* R *and* S *with the same top-ranked alternative, the outcome* g(R, S) *is the alternative that ranks highest in* R *and* S.

Proof Let x represent the alternative in X that is ranked highest by R. We don't assume anything about R and S except that x also ranks at the top of S. Then x belongs to $O_1(S)$ by Lemma 2. This implies that $g(R, S) = x$ by Lemma 1. $\square$

Now we prove that 1's options are identical in two situations if the most-preferred alternative of person 2 is the same in these two situations, whether or not persons 1 and 2 have the same top-ranked alternative in either case. Notice that we still don't have to assume that X has more than two members.

Lemma 4 *Suppose* g *is nonmanipulable. Then* $O_1(S)$ *is identical to* $O_1(S')$ *for all* S *and* S' *having the same top-ranked alternative.* Here is another way of stating this claim: Let x be any member of X. Choose any two orderings S and S' for person 2. If x ranks at the top of both S and S' then $O_1(S) = O_1(S')$.

Proof Suppose that x ranks at the top of both S and S'. Suppose y belongs to $O_1(S)$ but not to $O_1(S')$. By Lemma 2, x belongs to both $O_1(S)$ and $O_1(S')$. This means that x and y are different outcomes because x belongs to $O_1(S')$ but y does not. Now, choose R so that y ranks at the top of R and x is ranked second by R. Then

$g(R, S) = y$ by Lemma 1, because y belongs to $O_1(S)$ and hence is top-ranked in $O_1(S)$ according to R. But $g(R, S') = x$ by Lemma 1, because y does not belong to $O_1(S')$ by assumption, and hence x is the highest ranking member of $O_1(S')$ according to R. We have $g(R, S) = y$ and $g(R, S') = x$. But then 2 can manipulate g at (R, S) via S', contradicting the assertion that g cannot be manipulated. Therefore, we must abandon the supposition that $O_1(S)$ and $O_1(S')$ can be different.   □

The proof of Lemma 4 depends on our being able to find a preference R for person 1 with y ranking at the top and x ranking second. If x and y are allocations of private goods and x assigns more of every good to person 1 than y does, we will not be able to find the necessary R within the family of classical economic preferences. Similarly, if x and y are allocations of public goods and x provides more of every public good than y then we will not be able to find R within the family of classical economic preferences. It is clear that the assumption that any ranking of X is an admissible preference scheme for an individual is critical to our proof. (But it is not critical to the theorem. The proof gets a lot harder without it, though.) The next lemma proves that in any situation either individual 1 cannot influence the outcome at all, or else individual 1 can precipitate the selection of *any* outcome by an appropriate strategy choice.

Lemma 5 *Assume that* g *is a nonmanipulable voting scheme. For all* S, *either* $O_1(S)$ *is a singleton or else* $O_1(S) = X$. (In other words, for arbitrary S, either 1's option set contains only one alternative, in which case 1's reported preference has no effect on the outcome when 2 announces S, or else 1's option set is the entire set of outcomes, in which case person 1 can have whatever outcome she wants when 2 announces S.)

Proof If X has exactly two members then any nonempty subset of X will have either one or two members. Therefore, the lemma is established in this case. Suppose, then, that X has three or more members. We will provide a proof by contradiction for this case. Suppose, contrary to the claim of Lemma 5, that we can find a report S for which $O_1(S)$ contains more than one alternative but not all of X. Let's say that x and y belong to $O_1(S)$, with x distinct from y, but z does not belong to $O_1(S)$. Then by Lemma 2, outcome z cannot rank at the top of S. Let w denote the alternative that does rank at the top of the ordering S. (We might have $w = x$, or $w = y$, but w might be different from either of these two alternatives; at this point we just know that w is not equal to z.) Choose any relation S' for which w is top-ranked by S' *and* z is ranked second by S'. Then $O_1(S') = O_1(S)$ by Lemma 4 because S and S' have the same top-ranked alternative, w. Therefore, z does not belong to $O_1(S')$ but w belongs to $O_1(S')$ by Lemma 2. Suppose that w is distinct from y. (That is, $w \neq y$.) We know that $z \neq y$ because y belongs to $O_1(S)$

while z does not. Then S' ranks w above z and z above y. Now, choose any R that places z at the top and y second. Then $g(R, S') = y$ by Lemma 1, because y is the top-ranked member of $O_1(S')$ according to R. Remember, our supposition is that z does not belong to $O_1(S)$ and hence does not belong to $O_1(S')$ by Lemma 4. What happens when 1 and 2 both report the preference scheme R? We have $g(R, R) = z$ by Lemma 3. This means that 2 can manipulate g at (R, S') via R: Suppose that S' is person 2's true preference relation and that person 1 announces R. By playing R instead of S', while 1 continues to announce R, 2 can precipitate the outcome z which he prefers to y according to his true preference ordering S', and y is what 2 gets when he reports truthfully. This contradicts the fact that g cannot be manipulated, so we have to drop the supposition that w is distinct from y. Then $w = y$, which implies that $w \neq x$.

Now, we suppose that $w \neq x$. And we know that $z \neq x$ because x belongs to $O_1(S)$ while z does not. Then S' ranks w above z and z above x. Now, choose any R' that ranks z at the top and ranks x second. Then $g(R', S') = x$ by Lemma 1, because x is the top-ranked member of $O_1(S')$ according to R'. (Our supposition is that z does not belong to $O_1(S)$ and hence does not belong to $O_1(S')$ by Lemma 4.)

What happens when 1 and 2 both report the preference scheme R'? We have $g(R', R') = z$ by Lemma 3. This means that 2 can manipulate g at (R', S') via R' because $g(R', R')$ ranks above $g(R', S')$ in the preference ordering S'. The fact that g is nonmanipulable is contradicted whether we assume $w = y$ or not. This contradiction establishes the lemma: If z belongs to X but not to $O_1(S)$ then $O_1(S)$ cannot contain two distinct alternatives. $\square$

The last lemma extends the previous one by showing that $O_1(S) = X$ for every report S of person 2, unless $O_1(S)$ is a singleton for some preference ordering S, in which case $O_1(S)$ will be a singleton for *every* choice of S.

Lemma 6 *Assume that* g *is nonmanipulable and* X *has at least three members. Either* $O_1(S)$ *is a singleton for all* S *or else we have* $O_1(S) = X$ *for all* S.

Proof Suppose that $O_1(S) = X$ for some S and $O_1(S') = \{x\}$ for some preference order S' and some alternative x belonging to X. Choose S'' as follows: Set $S'' = S$ if x ranks at the top of S. If some alternative other than x, say y, ranks at the top of S then let S'' be any preference scheme that places y at the top and x second. Then S and S'' have the same top-ranked alternative, so $O_1(S'') = O_1(S)$ by Lemma 4. This means that $O_1(S'') = X$. Because X has at least three members we can choose some z in X distinct from x and y. Because $O_1(S'') = X$, the alternative z belongs to $O_1(S'')$ and this means that there is some R such that $g(R, S'') = z$. Remember, $x \neq z$ and $y \neq z$ and therefore S'' has x ranking above z. Because $O_1(S') = \{x\}$ the outcome will be x whenever person 2 announces S'. To say that x is the only member of 1's option set when 2 announces S' is to say that, as long as 2 announces S', the outcome will be x whatever person 1 reports. Therefore, $g(R, S')$ = x. Consider: $g(R, S') = x$, $g(R, S'') = z$, and x ranks higher than z according to the preference scheme S''. This means that person 2 can manipulate g at (R, S'') via S'. When 2's true preference ordering is S'' she does better by announcing S' than by truthfully revealing that her ordering is S''. Because g is nonmanipulable, we are forced to abandon the supposition that $O_1(S) = X$ for some choice S of preference relation for person 2 while $O_1(S')$ is a singleton for some other relation S'. As a consequence of Lemma 5 only one possibility remains: Either $O_1(S)$ is a singleton for all S or else we have $O_1(S) = X$ for all S.   □

The Gibbard–Satterthwaite theorem *Assume that* g *is nonmanipulable. Then* g *is dictatorial if* X *has at least three members.*

Proof Suppose that $O_1(S)$ is a singleton for every linear order S. Lemma 2 proved that for any S, the alternative in X that is ranked highest by S always belongs to $O_1(S)$. Therefore, if $O_1(S)$ only contains one alternative, it must be 2's most-preferred outcome according to S. And if $O_1(S)$ is a singleton, say $O_1(S) = \{x\}$, we have $g(R, S) = x$ for every R, by definition of the option correspondence O_1. This means that for every choice of R and S, $g(R, S)$ is the alternative in X that is ranked highest by S. In plain words, person 2 is a dictator.

If there is even one S for which $O_1(S)$ contains more than one alternative we have $O_1(S) = X$ for *all* S by Lemma 6. But then person 1 is a dictator by Lemma 1, which says that for any R the outcome $g(R, S)$ is the alternative in $O_1(S)$ that is ranked highest by R. When $O_1(S) = X$ it must be the case that $g(R, S)$ is the alternative in X that is ranked highest by R. This makes person 1 a dictator. Our proof is complete.   □

Exercises

1   Let $X = \{x, y, z\}$ and $n = 3$. Prove the Gibbard–Satterthwaite theorem for this case. *Hint:* Given a profile ψ let R denote $\psi(1)$, let S denote $\psi(2)$, and let Q denote $\psi(3)$. Given the voting scheme g define a voting scheme g^1 for the society $\{1, 2\}$ by setting $g^1(R, S) = g(R, S, S)$. And define a voting scheme g^2 for the society $\{2, 3\}$ by setting $g^2(S, Q) = g(Q, S, Q)$. Finally, define a voting scheme g^3 for the society $\{3, 1\}$ by setting $g^3(R, Q) = g(R, R, Q)$.

2   Let $X = \{x, y, z\}$ and $n = 2$. Prove the Gibbard–Satterthwaite theorem for the domain D^* of all profiles of complete and transitive binary relations on X. This means that we are admitting individual indifference: an individual preference ordering need not be linear. (*Hint*: Let g^* be a nonmanipulable voting scheme for the domain D^* such that each member of X is selected by g^* for at least one profile. Then g^* induces a voting scheme g on D by

setting $g(\psi) = g^*(\psi)$ for all ψ in D. As above, D is the family of all profiles of linear orderings, a subset of D^*. Obviously, g is nonmanipulable because g^* is. Then section 2 proves that g is dictatorial *if* every member of X is selected by g. Let t denote the dictator. Now prove that t is a dictator for g^*.

3   Consider the following voting scheme defined for two individuals, 1 and 2, and three alternatives x, y, z: The individuals report a preference ordering of the three alternatives and if there is one alternative that is ranked at the top of both reported preference orderings then that alternative is the winner, and otherwise person 1's top-ranked alternative is the winner. The voting scheme is defined over the family of individual preferences such that two distinct alternatives are not indifferent to each other in any individual's preference scheme. Prove that truthful revelation is a dominant strategy for this voting scheme. Does this contradict the Gibbard–Satterthwaite theorem? Explain.

4   Consider the following voting scheme defined for two individuals, 1 and 2, and three alternatives x, y, z: The individuals report a preference ordering of the three alternatives and if there is a unique alternative that is ranked at the top of both reported preference orderings then that alternative is the winner, and otherwise person 1's top-ranked alternative is the winner if there is a single alternative that is top-ranked by person 1. If there are two or more alternatives that are tied for top rank in person 1's reported preference scheme then the winner is person 2's most preferred alternative (according to 2's reported preference scheme) *in the set of top-ranked alternatives in the preference ordering reported by person 1*. If there are two or more alternatives that are top ranked in 1's reported preference scheme and within that set there is not a unique outcome that is highest ranked in 2's reported scheme then the outcome is x. Prove that truthful revelation is not a dominant strategy for this voting scheme. Modify g so that it is non-manipulable.

5   a Describe person 1's option correspondence for the following two voting schemes. In each case there are three alternatives, $x, y,$ and z.
    i Person 2 is a dictator.
    ii If there is a common alternative at the top of both reported preference orderings then that alternative is the outcome, but if the top-ranked alternatives are different then the outcome is x.
    b Is the voting scheme of part (ii) manipulable? If so, demonstrate that fact with an example. If it is not manipulable, explain why.

6   Let $X = \{x, y\}$, a two element set. Assume that there are two individuals. Define g by setting $g(R, S) = y$ if y is ranked at the top of both R and S. Otherwise $g(R, S) = x$. (This is simple majority rule with a tie always

broken in favor of x.) Define O_1 and show that it satisfies the conclusion of Lemmas 1–5 but *not* Lemma 6.

7   Prove that it is not possible to add dummy variables, variables that appear on the ballot but can never be selected, to construct a nondictatorial voting scheme that induces truthful revelation as a dominant strategy. Here is a suggested method of attack: Suppose that truthful revelation is a dominant strategy for g, with the reported preferences ordering the alternatives in set X. We know from our proof in section 2 that X cannot be equal to $\{g(\psi) \mid \psi \in D\}$, the image of g. Let Y, a proper subset of X, represent the image of g. Let Z denote the alternatives in X that do not belong to Y. Let Q^* be a fixed linear order of Z. Now define a voting scheme g^* on Y. For each profile ψ of preferences on Y let ψ' be the profile on X derived from ψ by attaching Q^* to the bottom of $\psi(t)$ for each individual t. Now set $g^*(\psi) = g(\psi')$. Prove that truthful revelation is a dominant strategy for g^*.

3 Examples

We now highlight the definition of manipulability and the role of the assumptions in proving the theorem by means of some examples of voting schemes.

3.1 Inverse dictatorship

Define g by setting $g(\psi)$ equal to the alternative that is *lowest* ranked in X according to $\psi(1)$.

Clearly, person 1 controls the outcome, but only by reporting the inverse of her true preference relation can she control the outcome to her greatest advantage. Even though 1 has complete control, the mechanism is manipulable according to our definition.

3.2 Limited dictatorship

$X = \{x_1, x_2, x_3, \ldots, x_{99}, x_{100}\}$. For each ψ let $g(\psi)$ be person 1's most-preferred alternative in the set $X_g = \{x_1, x_2, x_3\}$ for the preference scheme R of person 1 specified by ψ.

Obviously, $g(\psi)$ is not person 1's most-preferred alternative in X for most profiles ψ. The Gibbard–Satterthwaite theorem is false if dictatorship is taken to mean that $g(\psi)$ is the dictator's most-preferred alternative in X for all ψ. To disqualify schemes such as example 3.2 that are essentially dictatorial we have broadened the definition of dictatorship: A voting scheme is dictatorial if 1 always gets her most-preferred alternative in the subset of X comprising the set of outcomes that are eligible to be selected by the mechanism.

3.3 Majority rule

$T = \{1, 2, \ldots, n\}$, n is odd, and $X = \{x, y\}$. Let $g(\psi)$ be the alternative that ranks first in the majority of preferences. Then g is nonmanipulable and nondictatorial.

Majority rule is obviously not dictatorial. It is also nonmanipulable if there are only two available alternatives. If $g(\psi) = x$ then person t can change the outcome only if x is most-preferred according to $\psi(t)$. But t wouldn't want to change the outcome if $\psi(t)$ is her true preference scheme. Therefore, majority rule is nonmanipulable if there are only two alternatives. The assumption that there are more than two eligible alternatives is crucial to the impossibility theorem, as is the assumption that the domain contains *all* the linear orders on X. To illustrate the last point, suppose that X has more than two alternatives but D is restricted so that there is always a single majority winner. That is, for each $\psi \in D$ there is some x in X that defeats each other y in X by a simple majority. (Refer to section 3.1 of Chapter 3.) Then the voting scheme that selects the majority winner is nonmanipulable. If $g(\psi) = x \neq y = g(\psi')$ and $\psi'(i) = \psi(i)$ for all $i \neq t$ then x is the majority winner when t reports $\psi(t)$ and y is the majority winner when t reports $\psi'(t)$ and all other individual preference announcements are unchanged. If y defeats x when t reports $\psi'(t)$ but x defeats y when t reports $\psi(t)$ truthfully then t must cast a vote for x over y under truthful revelation: t truly prefers x to y.

Suppose, however, that $T = \{1, 2, 3\}$, $X = \{x, y, z\}$, and if there is no clear majority winner then $g(\psi) = z$, which we take to be the status quo. If there is a clear majority winner w then we set $g(\psi) = w$. Let the domain SP be defined by taking $\{R^1, R^2, R^3, R^4\}$ from the following list as the admissible family of linear orders. (See also section 3.1 of Chapter 3.)

R^1	R^2	R^3	R^4	R^5	R^6
z	x	y	y	z	x
y	y	x	z	x	z
x	z	z	x	y	y

Then there is a clear majority winner for each $\psi \in D$. As we have just argued this restricted majority rule scheme is nondictatorial and nonmanipulable (according to the definition of section 1.2). Define $\psi \in D$ by setting $\psi(1) = R^1$, $\psi(2) = R^2$, and $\psi(3) = R^4$. Then $g(\psi) = y$. Although R^5 does not belong to any profile in the domain SP, if 1 announces R^5 the outcome will be z as long as 2 and 3 continue to announce R^2 and R^4, respectively, and 1 prefers z to y according to her true preference scheme R^1. Suppose that each individual's true preference ordering is always in SP but the authorities cannot be sure of that. Therefore, when 1 announces R^5 there is no way of determining that she is misrepresenting her preference ordering and thus majority rule, even on the restricted domain, is manipulable in this extended sense. (See Blin and Satterthwaite, 1976.)

4 The revelation principle

One purpose of a voting scheme is to elicit information about individual preferences so that the outcome of the voting process will reflect these preferences in the appropriate way. If individuals have an incentive to misrepresent their preference the purpose of the scheme is defeated. Is there any voting procedure that is not vulnerable to this kind of manipulation? In order to increase the chance of an affirmative answer let us broaden the definition of a voting scheme to include *mechanisms*.

There are three or more alternatives. A mechanism requires individual t to announce some message m_t. This message could be a complete description of t's preference scheme; it could be the name of some alternative; it could be both; it could be a list of numbers. Nothing is ruled out, but each particular mechanism will be based on a particular kind of message. In addition, the mechanism specifies which message is to be reported by t for each possible preference scheme. Let $\sigma_t(R)$ denote the message that t is required to send when t's true preference ordering is R. Finally, the mechanism specifies the outcome, or winner, for each possible configuration of messages transmitted by the voters. Let μ be the outcome function. The function μ specifies an outcome $\mu(m)$ in X for each profile $m = (m_1, m_2, \ldots m_n)$ of individual messages. To summarize, a mechanism specifies the type of message, the behavioral rules σ_t, and the outcome function μ to identify the winner. The referee observes t's message m_t but cannot tell whether m_t equals $\sigma_t(R)$ when R is t's true preference scheme. That is because R cannot be observed. If it were verifiable by an outside observer there would be no need for a mechanism in the first place. The only way to ensure that individual t sets $m_t = \sigma_t(R)$ is to design the mechanism so that t always has an incentive to do so. We want this to be a *dominant strategy*. That is, for every possible preference scheme R that t might have and whatever messages the others report there is no message m_t that t could send that would result in an outcome that ranks higher in the ordering R than the outcome that results when t reports $\sigma_t(R)$, given the messages of the others. A mechanism with this property (for each individual t) is said to be *strategy-proof*.

Suppose that we have a strategy-proof mechanism. Then we can define a nonmanipulable voting scheme g by setting $g(\psi) = \mu(m)$ where $m_t = \sigma_t(\psi(t))$ for each t. (This observation is known as the revelation principle.) And g is nondictatorial if the mechanism is. Therefore, the impossibility theorem of section 2 extends to mechanisms.

Exercise

1   Prove the claim of the last paragraph of section 4, that g is nonmanipulable if the underlying mechanism is nonmanipulable, and that g is nondictatorial if the mechanism is nondictatorial.

8

Incentives, efficiency, and social cost

The welfare of the individual members of an institution depends on coordination of individual actions, and coordination hinges on the effectiveness of incentives and information transmission. The first six chapters evaluate the effectiveness of a variety of real-world institutions by means of the efficiency criterion. This chapter investigates the efficiency–incentive nexus from a different angle. We now suppose that the community is not committed to any particular institution, or mechanism. It is our job to design a mechanism that will elicit truthful revelation of individual preferences, leading to the production of an efficient outcome. We will *prove* that this requires the use of prices; moreover, price must equal social cost. We abstract from uncertainty in this chapter, so we are not forced to make trade-offs between risk-spreading and incentives.[1] Before defining social cost and proving our claim we consider a number of examples (sections 1–6). The derivation of social cost pricing is contained in sections 7 and 8, which can be read independently of the first six sections.

1 Resource allocation

Consider a private ownership market economy. At equilibrium, each consumer chooses a consumption plan at which the marginal rate of substitution between goods X and Y is equal to the ratio P_X/P_Y of the respective prices. This holds for any two goods X and Y that are consumed. The opportunity cost incurred by Max when he orders a unit of X is P_X/P_Y: It costs P_X dollars to buy a unit of X; each dollar will buy $1/P_Y$ units of Y, so P_X dollars spent on X could have been used to purchase P_X/P_Y units of commodity Y. Max takes his opportunity cost P_X/P_Y of X into consideration in determining his utility maximizing consumption plan. Because P_X/P_Y also equals Liz's marginal rate of substitution (MRS_L), Max is being forced to take the preferences of Liz into consideration when Max formulates his consumption plan. Every unit of X consumed by Max is worth MRS_L to Liz, in

314

the sense that $\mathrm{MRS}_L = P_X/P_Y$ is the minimum amount of Y that would compensate her for the loss of a unit of X. We can say that MRS_L is the cost to society of Max's taking a unit of good X for himself. In other words, P_X/P_Y is the cost that one imposes on society by consuming a unit of good X.

P_X/P_Y is also the amount of Y that could have been produced, given available technology, with the resources required to provide one more unit of X to consumers. A special case of this is presented in section 5 of Chapter 1, where X is labor/leisure and Y is the good that is produced with labor as input. P_X is the wage rate and at equilibrium P_X/P_Y is the marginal product of labor – i.e., output of Y per unit of labor at the margin. Therefore, the consumption of an additional unit of leisure deprives the economy of P_X/P_Y units of commodity Y. This is another sense in which P_X/P_Y can be viewed as the cost an individual imposes on society by ordering a unit of commodity X for his own use.

2 Constrained optimization

Mathematical programming gives us another example of social cost pricing. The goal is to characterize the solution to the problem

$$\text{maximize } f(x, y) \qquad \text{subject to } g(x, y) \leq a \quad \text{and}$$
$$h(x, y) \leq b.$$

(We can have f depend on more than just the two variables x and y, and we can have more than two constraints g and h, but this simple example is all we need.) The function f represents the goal or objective, and we want to pick the values of x and y that maximize f. But there are constraints g and h, and they restrict the values of x and y that we can select. If f refers to the value to society[2] of the plan (x, y) then g and h reflect resource utilization by the plan of two inputs A and B – labor and capital, say – with a and b denoting the total amount available of A and B, respectively. The plan (x, y) uses $g(x, y)$ units of labor, and that cannot exceed the total amount of labor, a, in the economy. Similarly, the plan (x, y) uses $h(x, y)$ units of capital, and the economy has only b units of capital. The solution can be characterized by means of two *Lagrangian* (or *Kuhn–Tucker*) variables α and β associated with the respective constraints g and h. If $x°$ and $y°$ constitute a solution to the problem then there exist $\alpha > 0$ and $\beta > 0$ such that

$$\frac{\partial f(x°, y°)}{\partial x} - \alpha \frac{\partial g(x°, y°)}{\partial x} - \beta \frac{\partial h(x°, y°)}{\partial x} = 0 \qquad \text{and} \qquad [1]$$

$$\frac{\partial f(x°, y°)}{\partial y} - \alpha \frac{\partial g(x°, y°)}{\partial y} - \beta \frac{\partial h(x°, y°)}{\partial y} = 0 \qquad\qquad [2]$$

The variable α is a price in the sense that it is the value of the resource A underlying constraint g: If additional units of A can be obtained then α is the rate at which f will increase per unit of A added. And

$$\frac{\partial g(x^\circ, y^\circ)}{\partial x}$$

is the rate at which A is consumed at the margin. B and β are interpreted similarly. Therefore, α and β truly are social cost prices. Notice that we arrive at the same optimal plan (x°, y°) if we maximize

$$f(x, y) - \alpha g(x, y) - \beta h(x, y)$$

treating α and β as given prices of A and B, respectively. Note that $\alpha g(x, y)$ is the price of A multiplied by the amount of A consumed by the plan (x, y). And $\beta h(x, y)$ is the price of B times the amount of B consumed. If we take partial derivatives and equate to zero we get the first order conditions [1] and [2]. We haven't proved that there exist α and β such that [1] and [2] have to hold if (x°, y°) is a solution to our original problem. You may be inspired to look into the proof to see why it is that prices can be used to characterize the solution to a problem that at the outset may have nothing to do with prices, or at least is articulated without any reference to prices.[3] If you want to make a smaller investment of time consider the following numerical example.

2.1 A simple example

All functions are linear. Suppose that the problem is

maximize $4x + 7y$ subject to $x + 3y \le 34$ and
$$2x + y \le 18.$$

The diagram (Figure 1) shows that the solution will occur at the plan (x°, y°) where the lines $x + 3y = 34$ and $2x + y = 18$ meet. Solving these two equations yields $x^\circ = 4$ and $y^\circ = 10$, yielding $4x^\circ + 7y^\circ = 86$. The solution is the plan $(4, 10)$ where the lines $x + 3y = 34$ and $2x + y = 18$ intersect because the slope of the line $4x + 7y = 86$ is in between the slopes of the lines $x + 3y = 34$ and $2x + y = 18$. (The absolute values of the slopes of $g, f,$ and h are, respectively, $\frac{1}{3} < 4/7 < 2$.) This means that 1 and 2 will hold at $x^\circ = 4$ and $y^\circ = 10$. Then we can solve 1 and 2 for α and β:

$$4 = \alpha + 2\beta \quad \text{and} \quad 7 = 3\alpha + \beta.$$

This yields $\alpha = 2$ and $\beta = 1$. Our claim is that if we obtain one more unit of resource A, and replace the constraint $x + 3y \le 34$ with $x + 3y \le 35$ then the solution value of the objective function will increase by $\alpha = 2$. Let's confirm this. The solution this time is the plan $x = 3.8$ and $y = 10.4$ where the lines $x + 3y =$

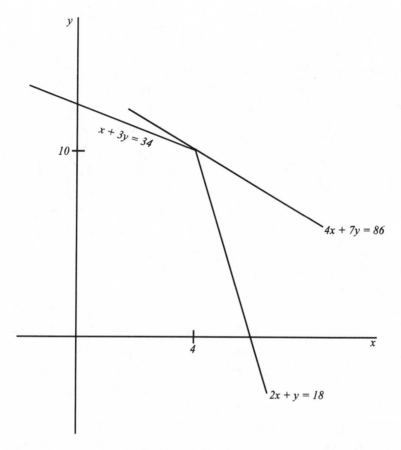

Figure 1

35 and $2x + y = 18$ meet. The value of the objective function is $4 \times 3.8 + 7 \times 10.4 = 88$, an increase of 2 over the value of f when $a = 35 - 1$ and $b = 18$. Now let's have b increase by 1. We will see that the maximum value of the objective function will increase by $\beta = 1$. The solution to the constrained optimization problem this time is $x = 4.6$ and $y = 9.8$ at the intersection of the lines $x + 3y = 34$ and $2x + y = 19$. This time, the value of the objective function is $4 \times 4.6 + 7 \times 9.8 = 87$, an increase of 1.

2.2 A geometric treatment

Consider the simple linear equation $5x + 2y = 0$. It is represented in Figure 2a, where we see that the vector of coefficients $(5, 2)$ makes a ninety degree angle with the line generated by those coefficients. We begin by showing that this always holds: The victor (p, q) makes a ninety degree angle with the line $px + qy = 0$. Let's look at the specific case $5x + 2y = 0$ first. If $x = 2$ then we must have $y = -5$ if the point (x, y) is to be on the line. (Just solve $5 \times 2 + 2y = 0$ for y.) Then we have a triangle with the three vertices $(5, 2)$, $(2, -5)$, and $(0, 0)$ with sides a, b, and c as depicted in Figure 2b. We want to show that angle θ is a right angle, so we need to prove that $a^2 + b^2 = c^2$, the Pythagorean equality. (Section 2.3 shows why θ is a right angle *if* the Pythagorean equality holds.)

$$a^2 = (5 - 0)^2 + (2 - 0)^2 = 25 + 4 = 29.$$
$$b^2 = (2 - 0)^2 + (-5 - 0)^2 = 4 + 25 = 29.$$
$$c^2 = (2 - 5)^2 + (-5 - 2)^2 = 9 + 49 = 58.$$

Therefore, $a^2 + b^2 = c^2$ and hence θ is a right angle. In general, the point $(q, -p)$ is on the line $px + qy = 0$ so we have a triangle with the three vertices (p, q), $(q, -p)$, and $(0, 0)$. Consult Figure 2a again.

$$a^2 = (p - 0)^2 + (q - 0)^2 = p^2 + q^2.$$
$$b^2 = (q - 0)^2 + (-p - 0)^2 = q^2 + p^2.$$
$$c^2 = (q - p)^2 + (-p - q)^2 = q^2 - 2qp + p^2 + p^2 + 2pq + q^2$$
$$= 2(p^2 + q^2).$$

Therefore, $a^2 + b^2 = c^2$ and hence θ is a right angle.

Because (p, q) makes a right angle with the line $px + qy = 0$, if we start at a point (x, y) on the line $px + qy = \Omega$ and move in the direction (p, q) then we are increasing the value of $px + qy$ at the fastest rate, as illustrated by Figure 3. The directions A_1 and A_2 do not make right angles with the line (ℓ_0) and they get us onto the respective level curves ℓ_1 and ℓ_2, which are below the level curve ℓ_{pq} associated with the direction (p, q). (We have normalized the arrows so that they have the same length, say unit length.)

Return to the generic constrained optimization problem for linear functions.

$$\text{maximize } f_1x + f_2y \quad \text{subject to } g_1x + g_2y \le a \quad \text{and}$$
$$h_1x + h_2y \le b.$$

f_1, f_2, g_1, g_2, h_1, and h_2 are given constants. We deal with the family of problems for which the solution occurs at the plan (x°, y°) where the lines $g_1x + g_2y = a$ and $h_1x + h_2y = b$ meet (Figure 4a). The vector (f_1, f_2) must lie between (g_1, g_2) and (h_1, h_2). Otherwise (x°, y°) would not be the solution (see Figure 4b). But this means that (f_1, f_2) can be expressed as a linear combination of (g_1, g_2) and (h_1, h_2) *and* that the weights α and β will be positive (or at least nonnegative). For the example of Figure 4a we have $(f_1, f_2) = 2(g_1, g_2) + 1(h_1, h_2)$. That is

$$f_1 = 2g_1 + h_1 \quad \text{and} \quad f_2 = 2g_2 + h_2$$
$$(4 = 2 \times 1 + 1 \times 2 \quad \text{and} \quad 7 = 2 \times 3 + 1 \times 1)$$

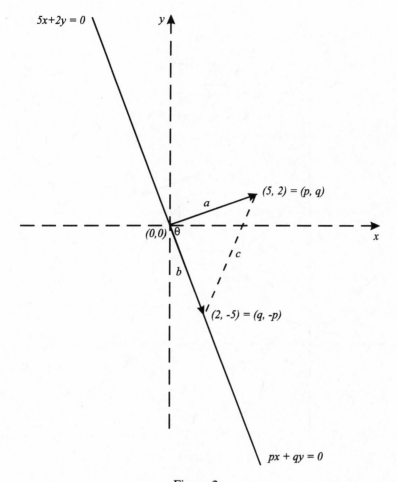

$5x + 2y = 0$

y

a

$(5, 2) = (p, q)$

$(0,0)$ θ

x

c

b

$(2, -5) = (q, -p)$

$px + qy = 0$

Figure 2a

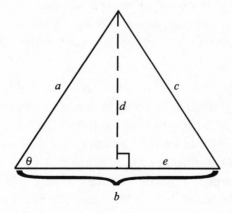

a

c

d

θ

e

b

Figure 2b

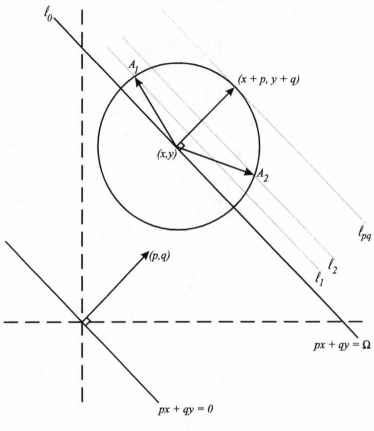

Figure 3

To give meaning to all of this consider two special cases. (1) The lines $f_1x + f_2y = v$ and $g_1x + g_2y = a$ coincide, where v is the optimal value of the objective function. Then the arrows (f_1, f_2) and (g_1, g_2) point in the same direction and we must have

$$f_1 = \alpha g_1 + 0h_1 \quad \text{and} \quad f_2 = \alpha g_2 + 0h_2$$

for $\alpha > 0$. What does this tell us? Consult Figure 5. An increase in the B resource, shifting the boundary of the h constraint out from ℓ_b to ℓ_{b+1}, will not lead to any increase in the value of the objective function f. The diagram shows that there is no production plan in the expanded feasible region that puts us on a higher level curve. Clearly, the marginal value of resource B is zero: additional amounts of it are not beneficial. This is why $\beta = 0$. Now, case (2): The lines $f_1x + f_2y = v$ and $h_1x + h_2y = b$ coincide, so (f_1, f_2) and (h_1, h_2) are colinear. Hence

$$f_1 = 0g_1 + \beta h_1 \quad \text{and} \quad f_2 = 0g_2 + \beta h_2$$

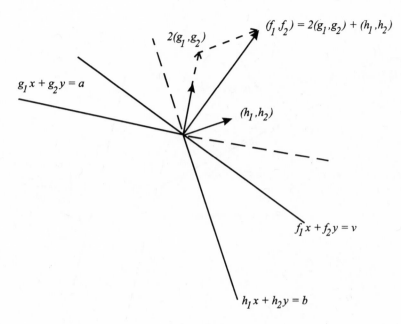

Figure 4a

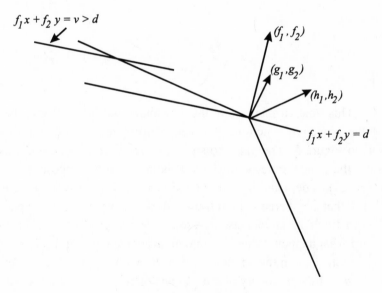

Figure 4b

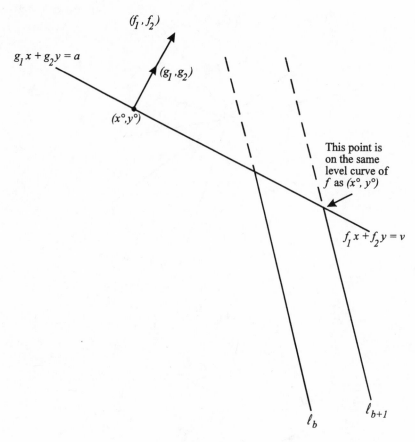

Figure 5

for $\beta > 0$. This time an increase in the A resource will not increase the optimal value of the objective function. You can confirm this by drawing a diagram analogous to Figure 5. The value to society of resource A is zero in this case.

Consider the typical case, with α and β both positive. Suppose that (f_1, f_2) is close to (g_1, g_2) as depicted in Figure 6a. Then α will be large relative to β, and this tells us that an increase in resource A will have a bigger impact on the objective function than an increase in resource B. We demonstrate this by considering in turn what happens when the amount available of input A increases from a to $a + 1$, and then when the amount of input B increases to $b + 1$. When input A increases to $a + 1$ the boundary of the "A constraint" shifts up from ℓ_a to ℓ_{a+1}, as Figure 6a shows. The other boundary line is unchanged, because b has not changed. We can move to a higher level curve, reflecting an increase in the optimal value of f. The optimal plan moves from S° to S^{a+1}. Figure 6b shows what happens when the amount available of input B increases to $b + 1$. The boundary of the "B constraint" shifts out, from ℓ_b to ℓ_{b+1}, and ℓ_a is unchanged.

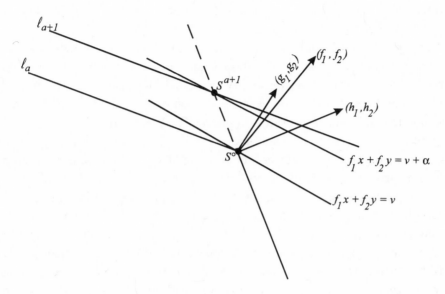

Figure 6a

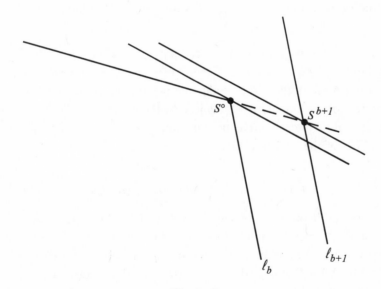

Figure 6b

We again move to a higher level curve (from plan S° to S^{b+1}), but the move is not nearly as great as when we get an additional unit of resource A. Therefore, resource A is substantially more valuable than resource B: there is a much bigger increase in the optimal value of f when we get an extra unit of A. That is why α is much bigger than β. To convince yourself that α is *precisely* the rate at which the optimal value of f increases per additional unit of resource A – and analogously for B – go back to the calculation of 2.1.

The Lagrangian (or Kuhn–Tucker) variables α and β are prices in the sense that they equal the value to society of additional units of the respective resources. The variable α is the cost imposed on society by a firm using a unit of A. This unit of A could be employed elsewhere to generate an additional α units of "social welfare" – assuming that is what f measures. Imposing a cost on the firm of α per unit of A employed by the firm promotes efficiency in that it forces the firm to provide at least α units of social welfare per unit of α employed. Otherwise it would take a loss. Similarly, for β with respect to B. How we get the firm to maximize profit is the next question. (Refer to Chapter 2.) We haven't discussed incentives in this section, but we have seen that prices can be used to guide an economy, or a firm within an economy, to an efficient outcome. We didn't begin with the determination to employ prices. The prices were forced on us by the mathematics.

If the functions f, g, and h are nonlinear, then the above argument goes through if we interpret f_1 as the partial derivative of f with respect to x, evaluated at the optimal plan, with f_2 representing the partial of f with respect to y, also evaluated at the optimal plan, and similarly for g_1, g_2, h_1, and h_2. Confirm that [1] and [2] are the first order conditions associated with the maximization of

$$\mathcal{L} \equiv f(x, y) - \alpha g(x, y) - \beta h(x, y).$$

Recall that $g(x, y)$ is the amount of A used up by the plan (x, y). Then if the price α is the cost to society of employing one unit of A, $\alpha g(x, y)$ is the cost to society of the amount of A required by the production plan (x, y). Similarly, $\beta h(x, y)$ is the cost to society of the amount of B required by the plan (x, y). Therefore, maximization of $\mathcal{L}$ can be interpreted as the maximization of the value to society of the plan (x, y) net of the cost to society of the resources consumed by that plan.

2.3 The converse of the Pythagorean theorem

The Pythagorean theorem proves that $a^2 + b^2 = c^2$ if θ is a right angle. To prove that θ is a right angle if $a^2 + b^2 = c^2$, drop a line from the vertex at the intersection of sides a and c, so that the line meets side b at a right angle. (See Figure 2b.) Call this line d, and let e represent the third side of the right triangle that has as its other sides d and c. (We let the same letters represent the *length* of the sides.) By the Pythagorean theorem, $c^2 = d^2 + e^2$. By definition of cosine, $\cos\theta = (b - e)/a$, and so $(b - e)^2 = a^2\cos^2\theta$. By the Pythagorean theorem $a^2 = d^2 + a^2\cos^2\theta$, and hence $d^2 = a^2 - a^2\cos^2\theta$. And because $\cos\theta = (b - e)/a$, we have $e^2 = [b - a\cos\theta]^2$. Therefore,

$$c^2 = a^2 - a^2\cos^2\theta + [b - a\cos\theta]^2 = a^2 + b^2 - 2ab\cos\theta.$$

But if $c^2 = a^2 + b^2$ then $\cos\theta = 0$ and hence θ is ninety degrees.

Exercises

1   Use an algebraic argument to show that if we take a step of unit length in any direction from the point (x, y) then we will obtain the greatest increase in the value of $f_1 x + f_2 y$ if we move in the direction (f_1, f_2).

2   a $(f_1, f_2) = (0, 1)$, $(g_1, g_2) = (2, 2)$, and $(h_1, h_2) = (1, 0)$. Draw a diagram to show that (f_1, f_2) does not lie between (g_1, g_2) and (h_1, h_2). Now use algebra to show that we cannot have $(f_1, f_2) = \alpha(g_1, g_2) + \beta(h_1, h_2)$ for nonnegative α and β.

      b   Repeat (a) with $(f_1, f_2) = (4, 1)$, $(g_1, g_2) = (1, 2)$, and $(h_1, h_2) = (2, 1)$.

      c $(f_1, f_2) = (2, 2)$, $(g_1, g_2) = (0, 1)$, and $(h_1, h_2) = (1, 0)$. Draw a diagram to show that (f_1, f_2) lies between (g_1, g_2) and (h_1, h_2) and then find $\alpha > 0$ and $\beta > 0$ such that $(f_1, f_2) = \alpha(g_1, g_2) + \beta(h_1, h_2)$.

      d   Repeat (c) with $(f_1, f_2) = (2, 1)$, $(g_1, g_2) = (1, 2)$, and $(h_1, h_2) = (4, 1)$.

3   See question 4 at the end of section 9, Chapter 1.

3 A computer network

Suppose that the society that we are studying is actually a network of computers. Each computer is capable of carrying out a variety of tasks, but some agent must assign tasks to the individual computers. Computer scientist C. A. Waldspurger and colleagues at the Palo Alto Research Center (owned by Xerox) have programmed another computer to assign the tasks.[4] One *could* program the central computer to gather data on the computational burden that each computer is currently carrying and then do the complex job of computing the optimal assignment of new jobs. Instead, the Xerox technicians have the central computer auction computer time. An individual computer can bid for time on other computers – each computer is given a "budget." Computational capacity is transferred from computers that 'have time on their hands' to computers that currently do not have enough capacity to complete their assigned tasks. The price at which the transaction takes place is adjusted by the center in response to demand and supply. (There are also artificial intelligence models that use marketlike evaluation to direct the transition of a computer from one state to another. See, for example, Waldrup, 1992, pages 181–189.)

4 Tort law

A *tort* is an instance of unintentional harm to person A as a result of the action of person B. If the injury occurred because B did not exercise reasonable care then B can be held liable for the damages to A according to U.S. law and the law of many other countries. Frequently, the potential harm to *B* can be prevented by means of a contract between *A* and *B*. In such cases government intervention is not required, except to enforce the contract. For example, the contract signed by a professional athlete and his employer can specify penalties in the event the athlete fails to show up for a game, or even a practice. But in many cases, it would be too costly to strike all the contracts necessary for efficiency. I can't enter into a contract with every motorist who could possibly injure me as I walk down the sidewalk. By allowing me to collect for damages in civil court, tort liability implicitly imposes costs on anyone who unintentionally injures another. The closer the tort liability is to the amount of harm inflicted the greater the incentive an individual has to take decisions that incorporate the potential harm to others as a result of personal negligence. (See chapter 8 in Cooter and Ullen, 1994. Also Ullen, 1994.)

5 The Groves–Clarke mechanism

The Groves–Clarke mechanism discussed in Chapter 6 (sections 6–9) induces truthful revelation of the benefit that an individual derives from a public project. It does so by imposing a tax surcharge on voter *A* that is equal to the loss in utility suffered by everyone else as a result of *A*'s participation. If *A*'s participation has no effect on the outcome then there is no loss suffered by others and hence no surcharge paid by *A*. But if the outcome would have been *F* without *A*'s participation and, as a result of *A*'s submitting his benefit function, the outcome actually is *G* then *A*'s tax surcharge is the difference between the total utility that everyone but *A* would have derived from *F* and the total utility that everyone but *A* will derive from *G*. This makes the tax surcharge equal to the cost that *A*'s action (participation) imposes on the rest of society.

6 Shareholders and managers

What payment schedule should the owners of a firm offer to the firm's manager in order to maximize their income? Before addressing this question (which is treated at length in section 7 of Chapter 2) we simplify by assuming that any deviation by the manager from a policy that maximizes the firm's profit takes the form of leisure consumption by the manager – leisure consumption reduces the effort put into management. Assume away uncertainty as well, for the moment. If the manager makes a fixed payment of *V* dollars to the owners and keeps any residual profit realized by the firm, then the cost to the owners of leisure consumption by the manager is equal to the cost to the manager of her own leisure consumption. Why would shirking by the manager impose any cost at all on the owners when the owners receive a fixed payment and the manager gets the residual profit? Shirking diminishes the firm's overall profit, and hence lowers the payment V that the owners can exact. Because the manager keeps all of the firm's revenue net of V and the costs of production, any diminution of profit as a result of shirking comes directly out of the manager's pocket. That is why the cost imposed on the owners by the manager's leisure consumption is equal to the cost borne by the manager of her own leisure consumption. Because the manager will strive to maximize profit under this contractual arrangement – obviously – we have another example of social cost pricing fostering appropriate incentives. (As we discover in Chapter 2, the payment V will be just large enough to leave the manager with more utility than she can obtain elsewhere.) If uncertainty introduces a random component to profit, then social cost pricing still maximizes the return to the owners of the firm as long as the manager is risk neutral. But if the manager is risk averse then social cost pricing will not be optimal for the firm's owners. (See section 7 of Chapter 3.)

7 The Vickrey auction

A painting is to be given to one member of a group. The individuals have different *reservation values*, V_t. V_t is the maximum that individual t would be prepared to pay for the object. Recall that submitting a bid equal to one's true reservation value is a dominant strategy for the auction devised by Vickrey (1961). This auction is also called the second-price, sealed-bid auction. (See section 2 of Chapter 3.) With this auction, the individuals submit sealed bids and the object goes to the highest bidder, who actually pays an amount of money equal to the second highest bid. It is in a person's interest to enter a bid equal to his true reservation value. Consider a simple example: There are a number of bidders, including Sam, whose reservation value is 50. What should Sam bid? If Sam bids 75 and the next highest bid is 70 then Sam is awarded the object at a price of 70. She would pay \$70 for something worth only \$50 to her. So, submitting a bid above one's reservation value can be very unprofitable. Can it ever be beneficial? If Sam is awarded the object and pays less than \$50 for it, then she benefits, and her gain is 50 less the purchase price P. If P is below 50 then all bids other than Sam's were below 50. This means that a bid of 50, exactly equal to her reservation value, would also have been highest, and she would have obtained the object at same purchase price P equal to the second highest bid. Sam gets the object at a price of P whether she bids her reservation value or something more. Therefore, submitting a bid above one's reservation value can never help; it can only hurt.

Now, suppose Sam enters a bid of 30 and the high bid is 40. The object goes to the person who bid 40. Sam could have obtained the object with a bid of 50. The price would be 40 in that case because 40 is the next highest bid. The change in Sam's utility is $50 - 40 = 10$ when her bid equals her reservation value and the next highest bid is 40. Sam will miss out on a \$10 profit if she bids well below her reservation value. Submitting a bid below one's reservation value can never help; it can only hurt. (Why will it never be profitable?) In short, no matter what the others bid, one can't improve on the strategy of entering a bid equal to one's reservation value. We say that entering a bid equal to one's reservation value is a *dominant strategy*: Given the strategies chosen by others, it is the utility maximizing strategy for any specification of the strategies selected by others.

Let H denote the individual with the highest bid. This bid will equal individual H's reservation value, so V_H is the high bid. Let J denote the individual submitting the second highest bid. This means that V_J is the second highest bid, and hence the price that will be paid by H who receives the object. By claiming the object for himself, person H is taking utility away from the rest of society. How much utility? Only one person can benefit from the object, and the largest amount of utility that can be generated by giving the object to someone other than person H is V_J, the reservation value of the person with the next highest reservation value. In other words, V_J is the opportunity cost to society of giving the object to H. The object can go to only one person, so the cost to society of its going to H is the maximum utility that can be generated by an alternative assignment. For example, if Max has a reservation value of 100, Sam has a reservation value of 70, and everyone else's reservation value is below 40 then the cost to society of giving the painting to Max is 70, and the cost to society of giving the painting to Sam is 100. But if Sam's reservation value is only 45 then the cost to society of giving the painting to Max is 45.

Exercise

1   Explain why the second-price, sealed-bid auction mechanism is not dictatorial.

8 A derivation of social cost pricing

The price systems above merely show that social cost pricing is *one* instrument that can be used to achieve efficiency. Now we show that social cost pricing is *implied* by efficiency and incentive compatibility. We employ the simple model of the previous section: A single indivisible object is to be assigned to one of n persons. The object provides utility only to the individual in possession of it, and the object has a different value to each of the individuals. This value, individual t's *reservation value,* is the maximum sum of money that t would be willing to pay for the object, which we denote by V_t. With the second-price, sealed-bid auction, the person receiving the object pays a price equal to the cost she imposes on society when she acquires it. We have seen that this price system gives the individual incentive to reveal her preferences truthfully. We are about to see that it is the *only* system of transmitting information that

1 induces *truthful revelation,*
2 satisfies *provisional efficiency,* and
3 satisfies the *participation constraint.*

That is, charging a price equal to the cost an individual's participation imposes on society is necessary and sufficient for truthful revelation of preferences if provisional efficiency and the participation constraint are satisfied. Sufficiency was proved in section 2 of Chapter 3 (and informally in the previous section). Now we prove necessity, but before doing so we explain criteria 2 and 3.

We actually have a two-commodity model. Commodity X is the indivisible object – a private good – that is to be awarded to one of the n members of society. Commodity Y is a divisible private good that we can refer to as money. We have implicitly assumed quasi-linear utility functions. Individual t's utility function is

$$U_t(x_t, y_t) = B_t(x_t) + y_t.$$

Here, y_t is the amount of 'money' available to t, and we set $x_t = 1$ if t receives the object, and $x_t = 0$ otherwise. Recall (section 11 of Chapter 2) that efficiency in this setting implies the maximization of the sum of individual utilities. $\Sigma U_t(x_t, y_t) = \Sigma B_t(x_t) + \Sigma y_t$, where summation is over all individuals t. In the present context, nothing is being produced: an object is changing hands, and possibly money is changing hands. Therefore, the efficient outcomes have Σy_t equal to the original sum. Thus efficiency implies maximization of $\Sigma B_t(x_t)$. But x_t is 0 or 1, with $x_t = 1$ for exactly one person. Therefore, maximization of $\Sigma B_t(x_t)$ is equivalent to giving the object to the individual with the highest $B_t(1)$. But $B_t(1)$ is just the reservation value of individual t. Let's confirm this. We can set $B_t(0) = 0$. Individual t has Ω_t units of Y to begin with. If t received the object and paid a price $P < B_t(1)$ for it then t's utility would be $B_t(1) + \Omega - P$ which is greater than Ω_t. But t's original utility level is $B_t(0) + \Omega_t = \Omega_t$. Therefore, if t pays less than $B_t(1)$ for the object his utility will increase. In other words, he will willingly pay any price less than $B_t(1)$ for the object. Would he pay more? If t received the object and paid $P > B_t(1)$ for it his utility would be $B_t(1) + \Omega_t - P$ which is less than Ω_t, his original utility level, when $P > B_t(1)$. Therefore, t would not willingly pay any price higher than $B_t(1)$ for the object. Therefore, $B_t(1)$ is the maximum that he would be willing to pay for the object – his true reservation value. Therefore, awarding the object to the individual with the highest reservation value maximizes $\Sigma B_t(x_t)$. Maximization of $\Sigma B_t(x_t)$ is necessary for efficiency.[5] (It is not sufficient because some of good Y may be wasted.) Therefore, we have *provisional* efficiency if $\Sigma B_t(x_t)$ is maximized. The participation constraint simply requires that individuals who don't get the object don't make any payments. This ensures that they will not be harmed by participating in economic activity.

Now, let's prove that 1–3 imply the Vickrey payment schedule. We don't *assume* any particular pricing schedule (or mechanism). We will *derive* one from our determination to satisfy criteria 1–3 of the previous paragraph. Efficiency demands that the object be given to the individual with the highest reservation value.

S_1 denotes the reported reservation value[6] (strategy) of individual 1, S_2 is the reported reservation value of individual 2, and so on. The object is given to the individual t with the highest S_t. There are n persons in all, so S_1, S_2, ..., S_n is the list of bids, or reported reservation values. Let $P(S_1, S_2, ..., S_n)$ be the price paid by the person to whom the object is awarded. Of course, $P(S_1, S_2, ..., S_n)$ is a function, yet to be determined, of the actual bids submitted. Therefore, if individual 1's bid is highest she is awarded the object and is charged $P(S_1, S_2, ..., S_n)$. The other individuals receive nothing, and make no payment, positive or negative. Therefore, an individual who does not receive the object gets a utility of zero. Her utility does not change, because her consumption does not change. If 1 gets the object then her utility is $V_1 - P(S_1, S_2, ..., S_n)$. Now we consider the incentive to report truthfully.

For convenience, we assume that the individuals have been labelled so that $S_2 \geq S_t$ for all $t \geq 2$. In words, person 2's bid is the highest bid, with the possible exception of individual 1's. Suppose that $V_1 > S_2$, which means that person 1's bid would be highest *if* she were to report truthfully. If she chooses some $S_1 < S_2$ she will not get the object and her utility would be zero. Therefore, incentive compatibility requires that person 1's utility is not less than zero when she bids $V_1 > S_2$ and is awarded the object. A basic incentive compatibility condition, then, is

$$V_1 - P(V_1, S_2, ..., S_n) \geq 0 \qquad \text{whenever } V_1 > S_2.$$

If we substitute the variable S_1 for V_1 this can be written as follows:

$$S_1 - P(S_1, S_2, ..., S_n) \geq 0 \qquad \text{whenever } S_1 > S_2. \qquad [1]$$

Suppose that we actually have $P(S_1, S_2, ..., S_n) > S_2$ for $S_1 > S_2$, with $S_1 = V_1$. Then person 1 will get the object and pay $P(S_1, S_2, ..., S_n)$ for it. Intuitively, we see that it would be possible for 1 to lower her bid and still be the high bidder. She will get the object, but at a lower price than when she reports truthfully, contradicting incentive compatibility. Therefore, incentive compatibility would seem to imply that $P(S_1, S_2, ..., S_n) \leq S_2$ when $S_1 > S_2 \geq , ..., \geq S_n$. Let's see then if we can actually prove that $P(S_1, S_2, ..., S_n) \leq S_2$ must hold whenever $S_1 > S_2 \geq , ..., \geq S_n$.

If $P(S_1, S_2, ..., S_n) > S_2$ let T_1 be the average of $P(S_1, S_2, ..., S_n)$ and S_2. That is, $T_1 = \frac{1}{2}P(S_1, S_2, ..., S_n) + \frac{1}{2}S_2$. This means that T_1 will be less than $P(S_1, S_2, ..., S_n)$ but more than S_2. We have

$$P(S_1, S_2, ..., S_n) > T_1 > S_2. \qquad [2]$$

Therefore, [1] implies $P(S_1, S_2, ..., S_n) > T_1 \geq P(T_1, S_2, ..., S_n)$. Therefore

$$P(S_1, S_2, ..., S_n) > P(T_1, S_2, ..., S_n).$$

But we also have $T_1 > S_2$ by [2]. Therefore, the strategy T_1 results in 1 getting the object, but at a lower price than when she bids $S_1 = V_1$. This results in more utility for 1 than when she reports truthfully by bidding $S_1 = V_1$. Truthful revelation therefore requires

$$P(S_1, S_2, ..., S_n) \leq S_2 \qquad \text{whenever } S_1 > S_2.$$

Suppose that we actually have $P(S_1, S_2, ..., S_n) < S_2$ and $S_1 > S_2$. Set $V_1 = \frac{1}{2}P(S_1, S_2, ..., S_n) + \frac{1}{2}S_2$. That is, suppose that 1's true reservation value is halfway between $P(S_1, S_2, ..., S_n)$ and S_2. We have $P(S_1, S_2, ..., S_n) < V_1 < S_2$. When person 1 (untruthfully) reports S_1 she gets the object, and her utility is $V_1 - P(S_1, S_2, ..., S_n) > 0$, which is greater than the utility she gets (zero) by reporting V_1 truthfully: When $V_1 < S_2$ she does not get the object if her bid is V_1. Therefore, truthful revelation rules out $P(S_1, S_2, ..., S_n) < S_2$ when $S_1 > S_2$. There is only one possibility left: We have to have $P(S_1, S_2, ..., S_n) = S_2$ whenever $S_1 > S_2 \geq , ..., \geq S_n$, confirming our intuition. But we know that this scheme induces truthful revelation, so we must have $S_2 = V_2$ and $P(V_1, V_2, ..., V_n) = V_2$ which is the cost to society of giving the object to person 1.[7] In general, if V_H is the highest reservation value and V_J is second highest, then we must have $P(V_1, V_2, ..., V_n) = V_J$ with the object going to H. In words, the person who gets the object must pay a price equal to the cost she imposes on society by making the object unavailable for consumption by anyone else. Moreover, this social cost pricing scheme has been *derived from* considerations of efficiency and incentive compatibility. Makowski and Ostroy (1987) reach the same destination by a different route. (See also Roberts, 1979, and Makowski and Ostroy, 1991 & 1993.)

We could modify the pricing rule so that individuals who don't receive the object still have to pay a fee. But that would violate the *participation constraint*. We could have payments made to individuals who do not receive the object. But who would make the payment? It can't be the person who is awarded the object because that would increase the price that she would have to pay. But any higher price than the second-highest bid would spoil the incentive to report truthfully, as we have seen. The payment can't come from one of the losers if the participation constraint is to be respected. Therefore, charging the losers precisely nothing and having the winner pay a price equal to the second highest bid – and hence equal to the cost imposed on society by the winner's participation – is the only pricing scheme that precipitates a provisionally efficient outcome and satisfies both the truthful revelation and participation constraints. But do we really have efficiency? Who *gets* the payment made by the winner? It can't be one of the bidders. Otherwise, one of them would have an incentive to submit a high bid, just under the winner's reservation value, to increase the fee paid by the winner and hence the amount of money going to those who don't get the object. The problem with that is that individuals no longer have an incentive to submit bids equal to their respective reservation values. Therefore, the payment by the winner can't go to anyone. This represents waste and destroys the efficiency of the system.[8] In this setting, efficiency is equivalent to the maximization of $\sum_{t=1}^{n} U_t$ subject to

$$x_t = 1 \quad \text{for one and only one individual } t,$$
$$y_t \geq 0 \quad \text{for all } t, \quad \text{and} \quad \sum_{t=1}^{n} y_t = \sum_{t=1}^{n} \Omega_t.$$

However, if the one who gets the object makes a payment that doesn't go to anyone else in the society, then we have $\sum_{t=1}^{n} y_t < \sum_{t=1}^{n} \Omega_t$ and hence an inefficient outcome. (Hurwicz and Walker, 1990, prove that some inefficiency is almost inevitable. Their argument applies to a wide variety of models of resource allocation.)

Why don't we give the payment to the person who owned the object initially? There are two objections to this. If we want to *derive* the efficient and incentive compatible pricing schedule, private ownership should emerge as part of the solution; it shouldn't be assumed at the outset. Moreover, as soon as we put an original owner on stage, and have the winner's payment go to him we again spoil the incentive for truthful revelation. Consider: Let agent 0 be the seller, whose reservation value is V_0. Suppose that the seller's bid S_0 is used when determining the second highest bid and hence the price to charge the winner. If the winner's payment goes to the seller then the seller has an incentive to overstate his reservation value, to increase the payment that he will receive. On the other hand, suppose that S_0 is not taken into consideration when determining the price that the winner of the object will pay. We just use S_0 to determine if the seller should keep the object. Efficiency still demands that the object go to the agent with the highest reservation value. If S_0 is higher than every other reservation value, efficiency requires that agent zero keep the object. If $S_t > S_0$ then the object goes to whichever $t \neq 0$ has the highest S_t. But suppose that $S_1 > V_0 > S_2$. The object will go to agent 1 at a price of S_2. But the seller has to part with the object and receives less than its worth to him. In this case the seller would have an incentive to misrepresent his reservation value, and report $S_0 > S_1$. If there is an initial owner of the object we cannot "close the system" so that the winner's payment goes to the seller without destroying the incentive for truthful revelation. If, however, we have a large number of agents then there will be a very low probability that one and only one person has a reservation value above or close to that of a seller. The probability that there is a significant efficiency loss will be very low when social cost pricing is employed and the commodity in question does not have substantial externalities. Rob (1982) proves this claim for a model in which the output of a pure *public* good is determined by the Groves–Clarke mechanism, which employs social cost pricing.

Exercises

1   This question pertains to the second-price, sealed-bid auction (or Vickrey auction) when the object to be auctioned is owned by one of the participants, individual 0, whose true reservation value is V_0. Answer the following two questions by means of specific numerical examples, one for (a) and one for (b).

a   Show that if the owner's bid S_0 is used when determining the second highest bid (and hence the price to charge the winner) then the incentive for truthful revelation is spoiled if the buyer's payment goes to the individual 0.

b   Now, suppose that S_0 is not taken into consideration when determining the price that the winner of the object will pay. We just use S_0 to determine if the agent 0 gets to keep the object. Show that efficiency may be sacrificed.

2   Prove that an outcome is efficient *if and only if* it maximizes the sum of individual utilities when $U_t(x_t, y_t) = B_t(x_t) + y_t$ for each t. Here, y_t is the amount of 'money' available to individual t, and we set $x_t = 1$ if t receives the object, and $x_t = 0$ otherwise, with $B_t(0) = 0$. Individual t has Ω_t units of Y to begin with. Of course we have to respect the constraints $y_t \geq 0$ for each t, and $\sum_{t=1}^n y_t \leq \sum_{t=1}^n \Omega_t$.

9 Relation to the Gibbard–Satterthwaite theorem

Chapter 7 proves the Gibbard–Satterthwaite theorem: There does not exist a nondictatorial incentive scheme for inducing truthful revelation when there are more than two possible outcomes. The pricing scheme of the previous section is certainly not dictatorial: We don't have one individual getting all the money and the object as well. And there are more than two possible outcomes. For a start, there is an infinite number of possible prices that could be charged for the object. Nevertheless, truthful revelation is a dominant strategy for the second-price, sealed-bid auction. Do we have a contradiction? No, because the previous section assumes a restricted family of individual preferences. Let's look at the auction from the standpoint of a mechanism as defined in Chapter 7, and then see why the proof of the Gibbard–Satterthwaite theorem does not go through with the limited preference domain of this chapter.

An outcome specifies an assignment x, with $x_t = 1$ if the object goes to individual t and $x_t = 0$ otherwise, and an amount of money y_t available to each t. An outcome is feasible if $y_t \geq 0$ for each t and $\sum_{t=1}^n y_t \leq \sum_{t=1}^n \Omega_t$. (Recall that $\sum_{t=1}^n \Omega_t$ is society's total stock of Y.) Not all of these feasible outcomes can be selected by the auction for some specification $S_1, S_2, \ldots, S_n$ of the individual strategies. Our first task is to identify the outcomes that could emerge. To do this we need only two variables: the name of the person to whom the object is assigned and the price paid by that individual. Therefore, an outcome of the auction is a pair $\alpha = (t, P)$ where t is the identity of the individual receiving the object and P is the price that he pays. An outcome α is feasible if t is the name of one of the members of society and $P \geq 0$. (The second highest bid *could* be zero, so any nonnegative price is a possibility.) To deal with ties, we arbitrarily decide that if there are two or more individuals submitting the high bid then the object will go to whichever of the high bidders has the lowest 'name' t. For example, if there are two individuals in all ($n = 2$) then a tie goes to person 1. The family of preferences, or the preference *domain*, is described as follows:

Individual t gets utility of zero from (i, P) if $t \neq i$.
Individual t gets utility of $V_t - P$ from (t, P).

To specify the individual utility function, it suffices to specify $V_t = B_t(1)$. Assume that $n = 2$, so that we can compare the auction mechanism with the statements in Chapter 7. Consider Lemma 5 of Chapter 7. According to Lemma 5, for any reported preference S_2 by person 2, either 1's option set contains only one alternative, in which case 1's reported preference has no effect on the outcome when 2 announces S_2, or else 1's option set is the entire set of eligible outcomes, in which case person 1 can have whatever outcome he wants when 2 announces S_2. Is this true of the auction mechanism? What is 1's option set when 2 reports S_2. If 1 reports $S_1 > S_2$ then 1 will get the object at a price of S_2, so one option is the outcome $(1, S_2)$. If person 1 announces $S_1 < S_2$ then 2 will get the object at a price of S_1. Therefore, any outcome $(2, P)$ for $P < S_2$ is an option for person 1. Therefore, person 1's option set contains more than one alternative; for $S_2 > 0$, there are an infinite number of possibilities consistent with $P < S_2$. But there are many outcomes that 1 cannot precipitate when 2 reports S_2. In particular, $(1, P)$ is not possible for any $P < S_2$. Therefore, in the case of the auction mechanism, for $S_2 > 0$ the option set of person 1 contains more than one outcome but it does not contain all outcomes. Lemma 5 is false for the limited preference domain of the previous two sections, and hence the proof of the theorem breaks down. Two questions remain: First, where does the *proof* of Lemma 5 break down with the limited preference domain, and second, what does the Gibbard–Satterthwaite theorem tell us about the auction mechanism on that limited domain?

The proof of Lemma 5 begins with the supposition that 1's option set contains more than one alternative but not every alternative. Then it reaches a contradiction. We are asked to select any two distinct outcomes in 1's set, say $\alpha = (1, S_2)$ and $\beta = (2, \frac{1}{2}S_2)$. Then we are asked to select any δ not belonging to 1's option set. Well, $\delta = (1, 0)$ does not belong when $S_2 > 0$. The next step in the proof consists of selecting a possible preference scheme U_2 for person 2 such that δ is preferred by 2 to every other outcome but one. But that is impossible, given the family of preferences that we have assumed. The proof breaks down at this point. Why is it impossible? If $V_2 > 0$ then person 2 will prefer *any* outcome $(2, P)$ with $P < V_2$ to the outcome $\delta = (1, 0)$, which gives 2 a utility of zero. If $V_2 = 0$ then there is *no* outcome preferred by 2 to $\delta = (1, 0)$. We can't find an admissible preference for person 2 that has $\delta = (1, 0)$ ranking below exactly one alternative.

What does the Gibbard–Satterthwaite theorem tell us about the auction mechanism on the limited preference domain? The auction mechanism is clearly nondictatorial. And there are obviously more than two eligible outcomes. Therefore, truthful revelation is *not* a dominant strategy when the family of admissible preferences is widened to include the preferences that are assumed in the proofs of the six lemmas. But the family of preferences that we employed in section 8 (and in section 2 of Chapter 3) is quite plausible on the one hand; but on the other hand, it is restrictive enough to permit the design of a mechanism that elicits truthful revelation as a dominant strategy.

Exercises

1 Determine person 1's option set $O_1(S_2)$ for the second-price, sealed-bid auction mechanism. (See Chapter 7 for a definition of the option set in general.)

2 Take each of the six lemmas in the proof of the Gibbard–Satterthwaite theorem (Chapter 7) and determine whether the statement of the lemma is true in the case of the second-price, sealed-bid auction mechanism and the restricted family of preferences of sections 7 and 8 of this chapter.

3   Why do the outcomes $\alpha = (1, S_2)$ and $\beta = (2, \frac{1}{2}S_2)$ of section 9 belong to person 1's option set when person 2 employs the strategy $S_2 > 0$? (See chapter 7 for a definition of the option set.)

4   Why does outcome $\delta = (1, 0)$ of section 9 not belong to person 1's option set when person 2 employs the strategy $S_2 > 0$? (See Chapter 7 for a definition of the option set.)

5   Prove that truthful revelation is *not* a dominant strategy for the second-price, sealed-bid auction mechanism when the family of admissible preferences is widened to include all utility functions on the set of feasible outcomes.

6   This question pertains to the second-price, sealed-bid auction (or Vickrey auction). Bring private ownership into the picture. (Excuse the pun.) Al owns the object initially, and his true reservation value is V_0. Answer the following questions by means of specific numerical examples.

   a Show that if Al's bid S_0 is used when determining the second highest bid (and hence the price to charge the winner) then the incentive for truthful revelation is spoiled if the buyer's payment goes to the seller, Al.

   b Now, suppose that S_0 is not taken into consideration when determining the price that the winner of the object will pay. We just use S_0 to determine if the seller should keep the object. Show that efficiency may be sacrificed.

Notes

1 Introduction

1 The economies of India and the former Soviet Union give us real-world examples. Baumol (1993) contains many examples of entrepreneurial responses to incentives, some of which reach back to ancient Greece and Rome.

2 Legal costs can be very high. See chapter 4 of Baumol (1993) for examples.

3 See Stiglitz (1993) for a good discussion of the limits of prices in transmitting information.

4 See Kandel and Lazear (1992) for a discussion of the role of peer pressure in motivating partners.

5 Arrow (1985) uses the term "hidden information" for what we are calling "hidden characteristics."

6 And legal defense insurance would cause legal fees to soar. Why? Why have physicians' incomes soared over the last few decades in all countries that provide national health insurance, even if it's only to those over sixty-five?

7 Private legal defense insurance is available in the U.S. – mostly in group form – but it does not provide significant coverage for criminal cases.

8 The U.S. already has three lawyers for every one thousand residents.

9 By looking only at the garage *owner's* incentive we are glossing over two important issues that will receive much attention in later chapters: Mechanics have different levels of ability. How does a customer or employer distinguish a highly skilled mechanic from one with less skill? And given the skill level, can the mechanic's employer be sure that the mechanic is motivated to put a lot of effort into the job?

10 Because our scheme leads to truthful repair estimates, it promotes consumer welfare. Why, then, did not this arrangement arise as a result of market forces? Consumers would have no incentive to do comparison shopping without an independent institution like the state bankrolling the difference between the high and low payments.

11 However, see Grossman and Stiglitz (1980) on the pitfalls of assuming that I don't have to bear the cost of monitoring a supplier because others will do that for me. Are the others making the same assumption?

12 If there is no central authority that collects information from the producing and consuming units and transmits information and instructions back to those agents, then we say that the system is *decentralized*, as in the case of a private ownership market economy. In this case the planner is fictitious and is intended to represent the interests of society – i.e., consumers in general.

13 Sections 1 and 7 of Chapter 2 consider the problem of giving a firm's manager the incentive to follow the planner's instructions.

14 *For this utility function,* MB_h is actually equal to the marginal rate of substitution. In general, the marginal rate of substitution is the ratio of marginal utilities: the marginal utility of X divided by the marginal utility of Y. The marginal utility of X is what we are calling MB_h here, and if $u_h = B_h(x_h) + y_h$ then the marginal utility of Y is constant and equal to 1.

337

15 This necessary condition for efficiency gets a little more complicated in more general models. We won't actually define efficiency until section 5, but you can see why a system is unsatisfactory if it fails to take advantage of an opportunity to make some people better off without harming anyone.

16 This example is due to Ryngaert (1988).

17 If they both hold out and there is no takeover then their shares are worth only $10 each. We still have a prisoner's dilemma game.

18 A condition of sale at the $20 price is that Doncam will be merged with a company Max already owns, once Max has 50% of the shares, and the outstanding Doncam shares will be purchased for $10 each.

19 We can make the same point by discounting the stream of payoffs.

20 Of course, $V'(x)$ is the symbol for the first derivative of V evaluated at x.

21 For this discussion it is vital that you pay attention to the difference between $a < x$ and $a \le x$, and to the distinction between $x < b$ and $x \le b$.

22 The MRS at a point $(x°, y°)$ is the absolute value of the slope of the indifference curve through $(x°, y°)$. Let C be that indifference curve. C is defined by $U(x, y) = c°$, where $c°$ is the constant $U(x°, y°)$, and it implicitly gives us y as a function of x. According to the implicit function theorem, the derivative dy/dx of that implicit function is the negative of the ratio of the partial derivatives of U.

23 Strictly speaking, this is not true unless we restrict the set of admissible outcomes to those that not only are feasible but leave everyone with a positive consumption of Y. See Campbell and Truchon (1988).

24 See Katzner (1970), p. 152, for the more general result, which covers preferences that are not quasi-linear.

2 Hidden action

1 There are firms whose owners are *not* diversified, and hence are not risk neutral.

2 Restructuring of the firm following a merger sometimes eliminates projects with negative net present value. See Jensen (1988).

3 This form of shirking was said to be a common practice of managers in the USSR.

4 See Kanter (1989) for examples of devices for motivating workers.

5 Quoted in a November 17, 1990, *Washington Post* story.

6 McMillan (1992).

7 We might expect to see a reduction in research and development spending by newly acquired U.S. firms. The evidence is mixed: See Hall (1988).

8 Bernstein (1992).

9 The profitability of a randomly selected firm may not increase by anything close to 10% as a result of an investigation of management practices. But firms that are suspected of being poorly managed may well be capable of yielding 10% more profit.

10 See Harrison (1993).

11 A long run project is arbitrarily defined as one that is not expected to turn a profit for five years. See Solomon (1993).

12 See Jarrell et al. (1988) for an introduction to the various forms of takeover.

13 This process can also correct deviations from profit maximization caused by management error, as opposed to management shirking.

14 A bank is insolvent if the market value of its assets falls well below the dollar value of its liabilities. Although they were not the first to highlight the critical role of gambling for resurrection, Romer and Weingast (1991) take the analysis further than others, in tracing the problem back to Congress. Part of this section is based on their paper.

15 This is not to say that deposit insurance is antisocial. Its chief value is in averting bank runs.

16 Between 1890 and 1966 only twelve Canadian chartered banks failed, and in only six of those failures did depositors lose any money. The stability can be traced to portfolio diver-

sification of Canadian branch banks, as well as to the monitoring incentive. (See Carr, Matthewson, and Quigley, 1994.) Nationwide branch banking is severely limited by regulation in the U.S.

17 The selling of naked call options on bonds is a good example of a wildcat scheme. When A sells a naked call option to buyer B, B has the right to buy bonds from A at any time in the future, at a fixed price determined when the call option is sold. It is a naked call option if A doesn't actually own any bonds! This was the only "asset" of an S & L that failed after only a year in business. (See Milgrom and Roberts, 1992, p. 174.)

18 For example, see Mishkin (1992, p. 260) on the scandal surrounding Charles H. Keating, Jr., and Lincoln Savings & Loan.

19 The boss must monitor occasionally, for the threat of bond forfeiture to have force. But the existence of the threat substantially reduces monitoring costs.

20 Different consumers would have different functions B, and hence different efficient levels of X.

21 The wage is income *per year*.

22 See Hsiao et al. (1988) for reference to this and other studies on the incidence of unnecessary treatments. Cutler (1994) also discusses this issue in the context of proposed reforms of the U.S. health care system.

23 However, low income Canadians are much healthier on the whole than low income Americans.

24 In 1992 Quebec introduced a $1.60 charge per prescription for residents over sixty-five. This group had been receiving free medicine. The fee was expected to save the province $16 million a year, but the annual savings have been closer to $40 million. A resident who had been customarily getting refills "just in case" would now wait until it was clear that the medication was needed – and so on. (Low income patients do not pay the nominal charge.) See Zeckhauser (1970) for an important early contribution to the study of deductibles and similar devices.

25 Lazear (1992) contains a number of examples.

26 Cuba spends almost the same fraction of its GDP on health care as the U.S. and has a slightly higher life expectancy. The Cuban system offers little in the way of sophisticated equipment or treatment but is skewed toward preventive care.

27 Note that if M is the size of the claim cheque and R is the cost per dollar of available claim, then $M = c + pc$, and hence $R = pc/M = p/(p + 1)$. In other words, our policy is couched in terms of M and R. The cost of insurance will still be a linear function of the quantity of insurance.

28 We are assuming away the hidden characteristic problem, which is the subject of section 10 of the next chapter. If there is no hidden characteristic – i.e., if everyone has the same probability of an accident – then the insurance company will allow the individual to select the amount of coverage c in response to the announced price p.

29 That is $\partial V/\partial c$ is the derivative of V with respect to c when we treat e as a constant. (Suppose that e is already at the level appropriate for the maximization of V.) Similarly, $\partial V/\partial e$ is the derivative of V with respect to e when we treat c as a constant, supposing that c is already at the appropriate level.

30 Investment banking has largely converted from partnerships to the standard corporate owner–employee form. See Milgrom and Roberts (1992), pp. 522–523.

31 In each of these maximization problems there is an implicit lower bound of 0 on x, and an upper bound of Ω that is reached when $y = 0$. But $u = 0$ if $x = 0$ or $y = 0$, and thus the first derivative of the objective function (of x) has to be zero at the maximum. See section 9 of Chapter 1.

32 We assume that $u(\Omega - e^\beta, y^\beta)$ is at least as high as the individual reservation utility which is the utility available in the best alternative.

33 Do you tend to study in teams of two or three persons or in larger groups?

34 This was inspired by Olson (1993).

35 Cook (1990) quoted in Milgrom and Roberts (1992), page 14.

36 Given a realization of the random variable the manager's utility is U. The lowercase u refers to expected utility, before the realization of uncertainty.

37 I have taken this example from McMillan (1992), pp. 205–208.

3 Hidden characteristics

1 See Mann and Wissink (1988, 1990a, & 1990b) for a more thorough discussion.

2 The federal agency that was established in 1934 to guarantee deposits in the S & L industry was abolished in 1989. The Resolution Trust Corporation was created to oversee the liquidation of assets from failed thrifts.

3 Demsetz (1968) suggested that the government auction the right to be the sole supplier of a particular good in the case of a natural monopoly. Laffont and Tirole (1987) extend this to the auctioning of the right to complete a government project.

4 In the language of auction theory, we are assuming *private values*. At the other extreme is the *common values* case in which the asset has a specific value – its equilibrium market price – and every bidder accepts this, but they have different estimates of that market value. By assuming private values, we are simplifying our task. The Sternberg (1991) paper analyses the sale of thrift assets under each assumption. See McMillan (1994) for a related discussion.

5 And no matter how one arranges x, y, and z along the horizontal axis, there will always be at least one double-peaked preference ordering in Table 1.

6 There is an implicit assumption on which this claim depends: The Pareto optimal allocation gives each individual a positive amount of the private good. See Campbell and Truchon (1988) for the full treatment.

7 Why not produce 56 more units of X, to bring output up to the efficient level? That would in fact yield the maximum increase in utility. But to show that the market equilibrium is inefficient, it suffices to show that there is *something* that we could do to increase everyone's utility.

8 The identity of H is known *after* the individual choices are made, but if H knows in advance that this disclosure will be used to modify the outcome then H will behave differently in the first place.

9 After a probationary period of six or seven years, the employee is either given permanent employment or released. But why up or out? If a worker is found to be of low quality, why not offer him a lower wage? Why terminate employment? In general, the up-or-out policy gets around the problem of the *employer* giving the worker a false low rating in order to cut labor costs. If other firms could observe the worker's quality, this wouldn't work. But when information is hidden it is a serious possibility. This function of the up-or-out contract was pointed out by Kahn and Huberman (1988).

10 We refer to the payment to the worker as a wage, but it is in fact the present value of the expected earnings over the lifetime of the job.

11 The gap between the average earnings of high school and college graduates almost doubled between 1979 and 1991 (Mishel and Bernstein, 1992). Much of this increase in the rate of return to education is attributable to training in the use of computers. Krueger (1993) finds that the proliferation of computers accounts for at least one-third, and perhaps as much as one-half, of the increase in the rate of return to education.

12 The same argument will not work for H-types. If they form their own firm they will face the same problem as existing employers: L-types will attempt to masquerade as high productivity workers. In that case, a wage that would be viable if the firm were staffed by H-types alone would not be viable if L-types joined the firm and received the same wage.

13 The bargaining example of this section is based on Samuelson (1984 & 1985). See also Farrell (1987) and Maskin (1994).

14 I do the correcting at intersections; I never actually read while the car is in motion. "What never?" Well . . . hardly ever.

15 The event "Dorrit has an accident" is statistically independent of the event "Shmuel has an accident." We are assuming that individuals are identical, except for the value of π, for analytical convenience. Don't jump to the conclusion that they have accidents simultaneously.

16 Remember, we're talking about the case where H and L obtain the same policy and hence have the same consumption baskets.

4 Reputation

1 A similar story could be told for the field of medicine.
2 In spite of the difficulties that we've pointed to, construction companies are not heedless of their reputation. Nevertheless, housing construction is typically regulated by the government as well as by the market. Because the cost of mistakes or fraud can be enormous, there is a case for government regulation even if the defects could be eventually attributed to the producer. It is no coincidence that regulation is more stringent in Florida and California, where hurricanes and earthquakes are a constant worry.
3 In some areas of the former East Germany 90% of children suffer respiratory disease. Pollution-related cancers and infant mortality soared in Czechoslovakia during the 1970s and 1980s. Ninety-five percent of Polish rivers are polluted and the leukemia rate is soaring (*Business Week,* March 19, 1990, pp. 114 and 115).
4 These scientists often, though not always, compete for recognition and for positions in better equipped and better staffed laboratories.
5 Gross output per U.S. worker doubled over the first fifty years of this century – see Solow (1957).
6 Enhanced training may reduce injuries. But force equals mass times acceleration, so there may not be any net social gain in injury reduction when everyone adds muscle bulk.
7 Some readers are skeptical that the win–loss record plays a big role in decision making. I haven't done any research on this issue; my aim is to provoke discussion.
8 See Roth (1984 & 1990) and Roth and Sotomayor (1990).
9 Some students visit colleges before making their selection. And many physicians visit two or three hospitals before submitting their rankings. A candidate will make an on site inspection if the private benefit exceeds the private cost. There is no reason to believe that this contributes to inefficiency.
10 If you set $e_1 = e_2$ before taking the derivative to maximize person 1's utility you ascribe to person 1 the ability to control 2's effort supply.
11 Consider the infinite sum $a + a\delta + a\delta^2 + \ldots a\delta^t + \ldots$ where $0 < \delta < 1$. Let θ_{t+1} denote the sum of the first $t + 1$ terms. Then $\delta\theta_{t+1} = a\delta + a\delta^2 + \ldots a\delta^t + a\delta^{t+1} = \theta_{t+1} - a + a\delta^{t+1}$. Solving $\delta\theta_{t+1} = \theta_{t+1} - a + a\delta^{t+1}$ for θ_{t+1} yields $\theta_{t+1} = (a - a\delta^{t+1})/(1 - \delta)$. Now, $a\delta^{t+1}$ gets arbitrarily close to zero as t gets arbitrarily large, so it is easy to show that θ_t gets arbitrarily close to $a/(1 - \delta)$ as t gets arbitrarily large. Therefore, we say that the infinite sum $a + a\delta + a\delta^2 + \ldots a\delta^t + \ldots$ equals $a/(1 - \delta)$.
12 This is Friedman's theorem (Friedman, 1971), which is stated and proved in section 6.
13 This section is based on Gibbons (1992), p. 225.
14 Kreps et al. (1982) actually prove that given π, if there is a large number of periods then the players will cooperate in every period until they are close to the terminal period. See Calvert (1986, pp. 47–54) for related treatments of reputation in economics and politics.

5 Resource allocation: private goods

1 Basic references are Arrow (1951) and Debreu (1959).
2 See Stiglitz (1993) for more on this theme.
3 As we have said, the complete market assumption rules out externalities. See Campbell (1987), pp. 56–60.
4 Production functions also have to have a negative (or at least nonpositive) second derivative, but we only look at exchange in the section.
5 We can also derive this property by maximizing ab subject to $p_1a + p_2b = m$. Then $b = m/p_2 - p_1a/p_2$ from the budget constraint, so we want to maximize $a[m/p_2 - p_1a/p_2] \equiv V(a)$. $V'(a) = 0$ is required. (Why?) Hence, we have $0 = V'(a) = m/p_2 - 2p_1a/p_2$ and thus

$a = m/2p_1$. Then $b = m/p_2 - p_1[m/2p_1]p_2 = m/2p_2$. Confirm that $b/a = p_1/p_2$. (See section 3.3 as well.)

6 The firm's production function is the hidden characteristic that is misrepresented in this case.

7 Let $t(x)$ be any real-valued function. Then the average, $t(x)/x$, is itself a function of x, which we name $a(x)$. Take the derivative of $a(x)$:

$$a'(x) = x^{-1}t'(x) - t(x)x^{-2} = [t'(x) - t(x)/x]/x = [t'(x) - a(x)]/x.$$

Then the average is falling – i.e., a' is negative – if and only if $t'(x) < a(x)$. But t' is the marginal. Therefore, the average is falling if and only if the marginal is less than the average. This is quite intuitive. If the grade that you get in your next course is higher than your GPA then your GPA will rise; but if your grade in the next course is lower than your GPA then your GPA will fall.

8 However, see section 1 of Chapter 2 for some countervailing arguments. See Ostrom (1990) for counterexamples.

6 Resource allocation: public goods

1 The proof of this claim in section 11.1 of Chapter 1 is incomplete, although quite insightful. That argument claims to show that efficiency is equivalent to maximization of the sum of individual utilities in *any* model in which each individual has a quasi-linear utility function. But it does not ensure that $y_i \geq 0$ holds for each i.

2 Assume that the fireworks are for an annual holiday celebration.

3 Hurwicz (1972). The Hurwicz theorem and proof apply to an exchange economy with private goods only. This section employs the proof given by Roberts (1979) for the standard public goods model.

4 We obtain a *stronger* theorem if the mechanism is required to operate successfully over a narrower range of cases.

8 Incentives, efficiency, and social cost

1 The basic references on mechanism design under uncertainty are Arrow (1979) and d'Aspremont and Gerard-Varet (1979).

2 The society could be the shareholders of a particular firm, with $f(x, y)$ denoting the profit from the production of x units of commodity X and y units of commodity Y. The constraints represent limitations such as warehouse and transportation capacity, etc. The point is that the example has a wide range of interpretations.

3 A good introductory treatment can be found in chapter 12 of Weintraub (1982). Chapters 5 and 6 of Novshek (1993) provide a more thorough account.

4 See Waldspurger et al. (1990).

5 A lot of people are tempted to say at this point, "It doesn't matter. If Liz has a reservation value of 1000, Sam has a reservation value of 600, and if Sam gets the painting then they can strike a mutually profitable trade." In general, it would not be easy for an individual to locate another with a higher reservation value. How would Sam know that Liz's reservation value is 1000? We are back to the original hidden characteristic problem.

6 We have slipped in the revelation principle. See section 4 of Chapter 7.

7 See Green and Laffont (1979) for the analogous treatment of the pure public goods case. A more general result is presented in Walker (1978). Holmström (1979b) treats private goods.

8 This also happens with public goods. We saw that the Groves–Clarke scheme (Chapter 6) induced truthful revelation but requires a surplus to be collected, and this surplus can't be returned to the community without destroying the incentive to report truthfully the benefit derived from the public good.

References

Akerlof, G. A. (1970). The market for 'lemons': Qualitative uncertainty and the market mechanism. *Quarterly Journal of Economics* 84: 488–500.

Alchian, A. and H. D. Demsetz. (1972). Production, information costs, and economic organization. *American Economic Review* 62: 777–795.

Arrow, K. J. (1951). An extension of the basic theorems of classical welfare economics. Pp. 507–532 in J. Neyman, ed., *Proceedings of the Second Berkeley Symposium on Mathematical Statistics and Probability*. Berkeley: University of California Press.

Arrow, K. J. (1963). Uncertainty and the welfare economics of medical care. *American Economic Review* 53: 941–973.

Arrow, K. J. (1971). *Essays in the Theory of Risk-Bearing*. Chicago: Markham.

Arrow, K. J. (1979). The property rights doctrine and demand revelation under incomplete information. Pp. 23–39 in M. Boskin, ed., *Economics and Human Welfare*. New York: Academic Press.

Arrow, K. J. (1985). The economics of agency. Pp. 37–51 in J. Pratt and R. Zeckhauser, eds., *Principals and Agents: The Structure of Business*. Boston: Harvard Business School Press.

Ashenfelter, O. (1989). How auctions work for wine and art. *Journal of Economic Perspectives* 3: 23–36.

Axelrod, R. (1984). *The Evolution of Cooperation*. New York: Basic Books.

Baker, S. and C. Elliott. *Readings in Public Sector Economics*. Lexington, MA: D. C. Heath.

Barberà, S. (1983). Strategy proofness and pivotal voters: A direct proof of the Gibbard–Satterthwaite theorem. *International Economic Review* 24: 413–418.

Bardhan, P. K. and J. E. Roemer. (1993). *Market Socialism: The Current Debate*. New York: Oxford University Press.

Baumol, W. J. (1993). *Entrepreneurship, Management, and the Structure of Payoffs*. Cambridge, MA: M.I.T. Press.

Bernstein, P. (1992). *Capital Ideas*. New York: The Free Press.

Binmore, K. (1992). *Fun and Games*. Lexington, MA: D. C. Heath.

Binmore, K. and L. Samuelson. (1992). Evolutionary stability in repeated games played by finite automata. *Journal of Economic Theory* 57: 278–305.

Blin, J.-M. and M. A. Satterthwaite. (1976). Strategy-proofness and single-peakedness. *Public Choice* 26: 51–58.

Brickley, J. A., J. L. Coles, and R. L. Terry. (1994). Outside directors and the adoption of poison pills. William E. Simon Graduate School of Business Working Paper, University of Rochester.

Calvert, R. L. (1986). *Models of Imperfect Information in Politics*. Chur, Switzerland: Harwood Academic Publishers.

Campbell, D. E. (1987). *Resource Allocation Mechanisms*. New York: Cambridge University Press.

Campbell, D. E. (1992). *Equity, Efficiency, and Social Choice*. Oxford: The Clarendon Press.

Campbell, D. E. and M. Truchon. (1988). Boundary optima in the theory of public goods supply. *Journal of Public Economics* 35: 241–249.

Carmichael, H. L. (1988). Incentives in academics: Why is there tenure? *Journal of Political Economy* 96: 453–472.

Carmichael, H. L. (1989). Self-enforcing contracts, shirking, and life-cycle incentives. *Journal of Economic Perspectives* 3: 65–83.

Carr, J. L., G. F. Mathewson, and N. C. Quigley. (1994). Stability in the absence of deposit insurance: The Canadian banking system 1890–1966. University of Toronto Department of Economics and Institute for Policy Analysis working paper no. 9408.

Clarke, E. H. (1971). Multipart pricing of public goods. *Public Choice* 8: 19–73.

Cook, C. (1990). A survey of perestroika. *The Economist* April.

Cooter, R. D. and T. S. Ullen. (1994). *Law and Economics,* 2nd edition. Glenview, IL: Scott, Foresman.

Cutler, D. M. (1994). A guide to health care reform. *Journal of Economic Perspectives* 8: 13–29.

d'Aspremont, C. and L.-A. Gerard-Varet. (1979). Incentives and incomplete information. *Journal of Public Economics* 11: 25–45.

Debreu, G. (1959). *Theory of Value*. New York: Wiley.

Demsetz, H. (1968). Why regulate utilities. *Journal of Law and Economics* 11: 55–65.

Diamond, Peter. (1992). Organizing the health insurance market. *Econometrica* 60: 1233–1254.

Downs, A. (1957). *An Economic Theory of Democracy*. New York: Harper & Row.

Drèze, J. and A. K. Sen. (1989). *Hunger and Public Action*. Oxford: Oxford University Press.

Easterbrook, F. (1985). Insider trading as an agency problem. In J. Pratt and R. Zeckhauser, eds., *Principals and Agents: The Structure of Business*. Boston: Harvard Business School Press.

Farrell, J. (1987). Information and the Coase theorem. *Journal of Public Economics* 1: 113–129.

Feldman, A. (1980). *Welfare Economics and Social Choice Theory*. Boston: Martinus Nijhoff.

Feldman, A. (1988). Manipulating voting procedures. Pp. 316–330 in S. Baker and C. Elliott, eds., *Readings in Public Sector Economics*. Lexington, MA: D. C. Heath.

Friedman, J. (1971). A non-cooperative equilibrium for supergames. *Review of Economic Studies* 38: 1–12.

Gale, D. and L. S. Shapley. (1962). College admissions and the stability of marriage. *American Mathematical Monthly* 69: 9–15.

Gibbard, A. (1973). Manipulation of voting schemes: A general result. *Econometrica* 40: 587–602.

Gibbons, R. (1992). *Game Theory for Applied Economists*. Princeton, NJ: Princeton University Press.

Green, J. and J.-J. Laffont. (1979). *Incentives in Public Decision Making*. Amsterdam: North-Holland.

Grossman, S. J. and O. Hart. (1980). Take-over bids, the free-rider problem, and the theory of the corporation. *Bell Journal of Economics* 11: 42–64.

Grossman, S. J. and J. E. Stiglitz. (1980). On the impossibility of informationally efficient markets. *American Economic Review* 70: 393–408.

Groves, T. (1973). Incentives in teams. *Econometrica* 41: 617–631.

Hall, B. H. (1988). The effect of takeover activity on corporate research and development. Pp. 69–96 in A. J. Auerbach, ed., *Corporate Takeovers: Causes and Consequences*. Chicago: University of Chicago Press.

Harrison, B. (1993). Taking the high road to growth. *Technology Review* October: 68.

Hicks, J. R. (1939). *Value and Capital*. London: The Clarendon Press.

Hirshleifer, J. and J. G. Riley. (1992). *The Analytics of Uncertainty and Information*. Cambridge: Cambridge University Press.

Holmström, B. (1979a). Moral hazard and observability. *Bell Journal of Economics* 10: 74–91.

Holmström, B. (1979b). Groves' schemes on restricted domains. *Econometrica* 47: 1137–1144.

Hsiao, W. C. et al. (1988). Resource-based relative values: An overview. *Journal of the American Medical Association* 260 (16): 2418–2424.

Hurwicz, L. (1972). On informationally decentralized systems. Pp. 297–336 in C. B. McGuire and R. Radner, eds., *Decision and Organization*. Amsterdam: North-Holland.

Hurwicz, L. and D. Schmeidler. (1978). Construction of outcome functions guaranteeing existence and Pareto optimality of Nash equilibria. *Econometrica* 46: 1447–1474.

Hurwicz, L. and M. Walker. (1990). On the generic nonoptimality of dominant-strategy allocation mechanisms: A general theorem that includes pure exchange economies. *Econometrica* 58: 683–704.

Jarrell, G. A., J. A. Brickley, and J. M. Netter. (1988). The market for corporate control: The empirical evidence since 1980. *Journal of Economic Perspectives* 2: 49–68.

Jensen, M. C. (1988). Takeovers: Their causes and consequences. *Journal of Economic Perspectives* 2: 1–48.

Jensen, M. C. and W. H. Meckling. (1976). Theory of the firm: Managerial behavior, agency costs, and ownership structure. *Journal of Financial Economics* 3: 305–360.

Jensen, M. C. and K. J. Murphy. (1990). Performance pay and top-management incentives. *Journal of Political Economy* 98: 225–264.

Kahn, C. and G. Huberman. (1988). Two-sided uncertainty and "up-or-out" contracts. *Journal of Labor Economics* 6: 423–445.

Kandel, E. and E. P. Lazear. (1992). Peer pressure and partnerships. *Journal of Political Economy* 100: 801–817.

Kanter, R. M. (1989). *When Giants Learn to Dance*. New York: Simon & Schuster.

Katzner, D. W. (1970). *Static Demand Theory*. New York: Macmillan.

Kelly, J. S. (1978). *Arrow Impossibility Theorems*. New York: Academic Press.

Kelly, J. S. (1988). *Social Choice Theory*. Berlin: Springer-Verlag.

Koopmans, T. C. (1957). *Three Essays on the State of Economic Science*. New York: McGraw-Hill.

Kotowitz, Y. (1989). Moral Hazard. Pp. 207–213 in J. Eatwell, M. Milgate, and
  P. Newman, eds., *Allocation, Information, and Markets*. New York: Norton.

Krauss, L. M. (1993). *The Fear of Physics*. New York: Basic Books.

Kreps, D. M. (1990). *Game Theory and Economic Modelling*. Oxford: Oxford University Press.

Kreps, D. M., P. Milgrom, J. Roberts, and R. Wilson. (1982). Rational cooperation in
  the finitely repeated prisoners' dilemma. *Journal of Economic Theory* 27:
  245–252.

Krueger, A. B. (1993). How computers have changed the wage structure: Evidence
  from microdata, 1984–1989. *Quarterly Journal of Economics* 107: 33–60.

Laffont, J.-J. (1994). The new economics of regulation ten years after. *Econometrica*
  62: 507–537.

Laffont, J.-J. and J. Tirol. (1987). Auctioning incentive contracts. *Journal of Political
  Economy* 95: 921–937.

Lazear, E. P. (1979). Why is there mandatory retirement? *Journal of Political Economy* 87: 1261–1284.

Lazear, E. P. (1992). Compensation, productivity, and the new economics of person-
  nel. Pp. 341–380 in D. Lewin, O. Mitchell, and P. Sherer, eds., *Research Fron-
  tiers in Industrial Relations*. Madison, WI: Industrial Relations Research
  Association.

Leland, H. E. (1992). Insider trading: Should it be prohibited? *Journal of Political
  Economy* 100: 859–887.

Leontief, W. W. (1936). Composite commodities and the problem of index numbers.
  Econometrica 4: 39–59.

Lichtenberg, F. R. (1992). *Corporate Takeovers and Productivity*. Cambridge, MA:
  M.I.T. Press.

Litan, R. E. (1991). Comment on T. Romer and B. R. Weingast's article, 'Political
  foundations of the thrift debacle.' In Alberto Alesina, ed., *Politics and Economics
  in the 1980's*. Chicago: University of Chicago Press.

Makowski, L. and J. M. Ostroy. (1987). Vickrey–Clarke–Groves Mechanisms and
  Perfect Competition. *Journal of Economic Theory* 42: 244–261.

Makowski, L. and J. M. Ostroy. (1991). The margin of appropriation and an extension
  of the first theorem of welfare economics. Los Angeles: Department of Economics, U.C.L.A. working paper.

Makowski, L. and J. M. Ostroy. (1993). General equilibrium and market socialism:
  Clarifying the logic of competitive markets. Pp. 69–88 in P. K. Bardhan and
  J. E. Roemer, eds., *Market Socialism: The Current Debate*. New York: Oxford
  University Press.

Malatesta, P. and R. Walking. (1988). Poison pill securities: Stockholder wealth, profitability, and ownership structure. *Journal of Financial Economics* 20: 347–376.

Malkiel, B. G. (1981). *A Random Walk down Wall Street*, 4th edition. New York: Norton.

Mann, D. P. and J. P. Wissink. (1988). Money-back contracts with double moral hazard. *Rand Journal of Economics* 19: 285–292.

Mann, D. P. and J. P. Wissink. (1990a). Hidden actions and hidden characteristics in
  warranty markets. *International Journal of Industrial Organization* 8: 53–71.

Mann, D. P. and J. P. Wissink. (1990b). Money-back warranties vs replacement warranties: A simple comparison. *American Economic Review* 80: 432–436.

Manne, H. G. (1965). Mergers and the market for corporate control. *Journal of Political Economy* 73: 110–120.

Manne, H. G. (1966). *Insider Trading and the Stock Market*. New York: The Free Press.

Maskin, E. S. (1977). Nash equilibrium and welfare optimality. Unpublished mimeographed material, Massachusetts Institute of Technology.

Maskin, E. S. (1994). The invisible hand and externalities. Cambridge, MA: Harvard Institute for Economic Research, Discussion Paper No. 15.

McAfee, R. P. and John McMillan. (1988). *Incentives in Government Contracting*. Toronto: University of Toronto Press.

McConnell, J. J. and C. J. Muscarella. (1986). Corporate capital expenditure decisions and the market value of the firm. *Journal of Financial Economics* 14: 399–422.

McKelvey, R. D. and T. R. Palfrey. (1992). An experimental study of the centipede game. *Econometrica* 60: 803–836.

McMillan, John. (1992). *Games, Strategies, and Managers*. Oxford: Oxford University Press.

McMillan, John. (1994). Selling spectrum rights. *Journal of Economic Perspectives* 8: 13–29.

McPhee, J. (1966). *Oranges*. New York: Farrar, Straus, and Giroux.

Milgrom, P. R. (1987). Auction Theory. In T. Bewley, ed., *Advances in Economic Theory: Fifth World Congress*. Cambridge: Cambridge University Press.

Milgrom, P. R. (1989). Auctions and bidding: A primer. *Journal of Economic Perspectives* 3: 3–32.

Milgrom, P. R. and J. Roberts. (1992). *Economics, Organization, and Management*. Englewood Cliffs, NJ: Prentice Hall.

Mirlees, J. (1974). Notes on welfare economics, information, and uncertainty. Pp. 243–258 in M. Balch, D. McFadden, and S. Wu, eds., *Essays in Economic Behavior Under Uncertainty*. Amsterdam: North Holland.

Mishel, L. and J. Bernstein. (1992). Declining wages for high school and college graduates. Washington, DC: Economic Policy Institute Working Paper.

Mishkin, F. S. (1992). *Money, Banking, and Financial Markets*. New York: Harper Collins.

Modigliani, F. and M. H. Miller. (1958). The cost of capital, corporation finance, and the theory of investment. *American Economic Review* 48: 655–669.

Moore, J. and R. Repullo. (1988). Subgame perfect implementation. *Econometrica* 56: 1191–1220.

Novshek, W. (1993). *Mathematics for Economists*. San Diego: Academic Press.

Olson, Mancur. (1993). Why is economic performance even worse after communism is abandoned? Unpublished mimeographed material. Fairfax, VA: George Mason University, Center for the Study of Public Choice.

Ostrom, E. (1990). *Governing the Commons: The Evolution of Institutions for Collective Action*. Cambridge: Cambridge University Press.

Phlips, Louis. (1981). *The Economics of Price Discrimination*. New York: Cambridge University Press.

Poundstone, W. (1992). *Prisoner's Dilemma*. New York: Doubleday.

Radner, R. (1991). Dynamic games in organization theory. *Journal of Economic Behavior and Organization* 16: 217–260.

Rapoport, A. (1989). Prisoner's dilemma. Pp. 199–204 in J. Eatwell, M. Milgate, and P. Newman, eds., *Game Theory*. New York: Norton.

Riley, J. (1989). Signalling. Pp. 287–294 in J. Eatwell, M. Milgate, and P. Newman, eds., *Allocation, Information, and Markets*. New York: Norton.

Rob, R. (1982). Asymptotic efficiency of the demand revealing mechanism. *Journal of Economic Theory* 28: 207–220.

Roberts, D. J. (1979). Incentives in planning procedures for the provision of public goods. *Review of Economic Studies* 46: 283–292.

Roberts, J. and A. Postlewaite. (1976). The incentive for price-taking behavior in large exchange economies. *Econometrica* 44: 115–127.

Roberts, K. (1979). The characterization of implementable choice rules. Pp. 321–348 in J.-J. Laffont, ed., *Aggregation and Revelation of Preferences*. Amsterdam: North-Holland.

Romer, T. and B. R. Weingast. (1991). Political foundations of the thrift debacle. Pp. 175–209 in Alberto Alesina, ed., *Politics and Economics in the 1980's*. Chicago: University of Chicago Press.

Ross, S. (1973). The economic theory of agency: the principal's problem. *American Economic Review.* 63: 134–139.

Roth, A. E. (1984). The evolution of the labor market for medical interns and residents: A case study in game theory. *Journal of Political Economy* 92: 991–1026.

Roth, A. E. (1990). New physicians: A natural experiment in market organization. *Science* December 14: 1524–1528.

Roth, A. E. and M. A. O. Sotomayor. (1990). *Two Sided Matching: A Study in Game-Theoretic Modeling and Analysis*. Cambridge: Cambridge University Press.

Rothschild, M. and J. E. Stiglitz. (1976). Equilibrium in competitive insurance markets: An essay on the economics of imperfect information. *Quarterly Journal of Economics* 80: 629–649.

Rubinstein, A. (1986). Finite automata play the repeated prisoners' dilemma. *Journal of Economic Theory* 39: 83–96.

Ryngaert, M. (1988). The effect of poison pill securities on shareholder wealth. *Journal of Financial Economics* 20: 377–417.

Saari, D. G. (1994). *Geometry of Voting*. Berlin: Springer-Verlag.

Samuelson, W. (1984). Bargaining under asymmetric information. *Econometrica* 52: 995–1005.

Samuelson, W. (1985). A comment on the Coase conjecture. In A. Roth, ed., *Game-Theoretic Models of Bargaining*. Cambridge: Cambridge University Press.

Sappington, D. E. M. (1991). Incentives in principal-agent relationships. *Journal of Economic Perspectives* 5: 45–66.

Sappington, D. E. M. (1993). Designing incentive regulation. University of Florida, College of Business Administration working paper no. 93-94-10.

Satterthwaite, M. (1975). Strategy-proofness and Arrow's conditions: Existence and correspondence theorems for voting procedures and social welfare functions. *Journal of Economic Theory* 10: 187–217.

Scherer, F. M. (1988). Corporate takeovers: The efficiency arguments. *Journal of Economic Perspectives* 2: 69–82.

Scully, G. W. (1989). *The Business of Major League Baseball*. Chicago: The University of Chicago Press.

Sen, A. K. (1981). *Poverty and Famines: An Essay on Entitlement and Deprivation*. Oxford: Oxford University Press.

Sen, A. K. (1993). The economics of life and death. *Scientific American* May: 40–47.

Sheffrin, S. M. (1993). *Markets and Majorities*. New York: The Free Press.

Shleifer, A. and R. W. Vishny. (1988). Value maximization and the acquisition process. *Journal of Economic Perspectives* 2: 7–20.

Shoven, J. B., S. B. Smart, and J. Waldfogel. (1992). Real interest rates and the savings and loan crisis: The moral hazard premium. *Journal of Economic Perspectives* 6: 155–167.

Solomon, S. D. (1993). Things the tortoise taught us. *Technology Review* May/June: 20–27.

Solow, R. M. (1957). Technical change and the aggregate production function. *Review of Economics and Statistics* 39: 312–320.

Sonnenschein H. F. (1983). The economics of incentives: An introductory account. Nancy L. Schwartz Memorial Lecture. J. L. Kellog Graduate School of Management, Evanston, IL: Northwestern University.

Spence, A. M. (1973). *Market Signalling: Information Transfer in Hiring and Related Processes*. Cambridge, MA: Harvard University Press.

Stern, S. and P. Todd. (1992). A test of Lazear's mandatory retirement model. Discussion Paper 236. Charlottesville: University of Virginia, The Thomas Jefferson Center for Political Economy.

Sternberg, T. (1991). FDIC auctions of failed banks: One way to measure the acquiror's surplus. Berkeley: University of California, Haas School of Business.

Stiglitz, J. E. (1974). Incentives and risk sharing in sharecropping. *Review of Economic Studies* 41: 219–255.

Stiglitz, J. E. (1993). Market socialism and neoclassical economics. Pp. 21–41 in P. K. Bardhan and J. E. Roemer, eds., *Market Socialism: The Current Debate*. New York: Oxford University Press.

Thelin, J. R. and L. R. Wiseman. (1989). *The Old College Try: Balancing Athletics and Academics in Higher Education*. Report Number 4. Washington, DC: The George Washington University, School of Education and Human Development.

Tideman, T. N. and G. Tullock. (1976). A new and superior principle for collective choice. *Journal of Political Economy* 84: 1145–1159.

Tirole, J. (1988). *The Theory of Industrial Organization*. Cambridge, MA: M.I.T. Press.

Ullen, T. S. (1994). Rational victims–rational injurers: Cognition and the economic analysis of tort law. Unpublished mimeographed material, Department of Economics, University of Illinois at Urbana-Champaign.

Vickrey, W. (1961). Counterspeculation, auctions, and competitive sealed tenders. *Journal of Finance* 16: 8–37.

Waldrup, M. M. (1992). *Complexity.* New York: Simon and Schuster.

Waldspurger, C. A., T. Hogg, B. A. Huberman, J. O. Kephart, and S. Stornetta. (1990). Spawn: A distributed computational economy. Palo Alto, CA: Systems Sciences Laboratory, Xerox Palo Alto Research Center.

Walker, M. (1978). On the existence of a dominant strategy mechanism for making optimal public decisions. *Econometrica* 46: 147–152.

Weintraub, E. R. (1982). *Mathematics for Economists*. Cambridge: Cambridge University Press.

Zeckhauser, R. (1970). Medical insurance: A case study of the tradeoff between risk spreading and appropriate incentives. *Journal of Economic Theory* 2: 10–26.

Index